SEEING THROUGH TEXTS

theology for a culture
- Phen. conception authorship
- Thomas

from a culture back to ours
- Song
- Clooney

"read well together" p266

use Clooney Tiruvaymoli & John p267-269.

Song - use 1 or 2 examples

Thomas - use K of God?

reading one helps us understand the other.

SUNY Series, Toward a Comparative Philosophy of Religions
Paul J. Griffiths and Laurie L. Patton, Editors

SEEING THROUGH TEXTS

Doing Theology among the Śrīvaiṣṇavas of South India

Francis X. Clooney, S.J.

State University of New York Press

Chapter 5 contains material reprinted from *Prayer* by Hans Urs von Balthasar, by permission of Ignatius Press, © 1986.

Chapter 5 also contains material reprinted from *The Journey of the Mind to God* by Bonaventure, translated by Philotheus Boehner, edited by Stephen F. Brown, by permission of Hackett Publishing Company, Inc., © 1993.

Published by
State University of New York Press, Albany

Printed in the United States of America

For information, address State University of New York Press, State University Plaza, Albany, N.Y. 12246

Production by M. R. Mulholland
Marketing by Theresa A. Swierzowski

Library of Congress Cataloging-in-Publication Data

Clooney, Francis Xavier, 1950–
Seeing through texts : doing theology among the Śrīvaiṣṇavas of South India / Francis X. Clooney.
p. cm. — (SUNY series, toward a comparative philosophy of religions)
Includes bibliographical references and index.
ISBN 0-7914-2995-4 (hardcover : alk. paper). — ISBN 0-7914-2996-2 (pbk. : alk. paper)
1. Nammāḻvār, Tiruvāymoḻi. 2. Nammāḻvār—Religion. 3. Śrī Vaishṇava (Sect)—Doctrines. I. Title. II. Series.
PL.4758.9.N3155T53296 1996
294.5'95—dc20 95-35858
CIP

10 9 8 7 6 5 4 3 2 1

Dedicated to

Ignatius Hirudayam, S.J. (1910–1995)
A.K. Ramanujan (1929–1993)

Rise, come near them, pay your respects!
Holy verses on their tongues,
they never leave the pure path of knowledge
rich with flowers, incense, lamps, sandal scent, pure water,
devoted,
the Lord's people,
they approach and reverence the one who never fails:
our world is full
because of such people.

Tiruvāymoḻi V.2.9

Contents

Chapter One:
Taking a First Look

Chapter Two: Getting Inside *Tiruvāymoḻi*

Chapter Three: *Tiruvāymoli* as Meditation, Narrative and Drama: Reading with the *Ācāryas*

Chapter Four: Five Ways to Think about *Tiruvāymoḻi*: Following the *Ācāryas'* Practical Response

Chapter Five:
Seeing through Texts: Some Marginal Insights, Presented in Reflections

Foreword

Paul J. Griffiths
Laurie L. Patton

Francis X. Clooney's book, *Seeing through Texts,* begins with a ninth-century poem about a young woman who has just returned from the South Indian temple town of Tolaivillimaṅkalam, where she has become newly captivated by "what everyone else had long known and come to take for granted." Like this young woman's experience, *Seeing through Texts* is a book in which something very old—the Śrīvaiṣṇava tradition—is continued and enriched by the incorporation of something new—placement in a comparative context. Clooney's work is a highly engaging account of captures and counter-captures between two theological imaginations—Vaiṣṇavite and Catholic Christian—whereby the preferred method of seizure is not surprise, but slow, deliberate apprehension.

Such a method is painstaking and yet rewarding. The reader of this book must work slowly through several stages: the experience of the young woman who is captured by her god, Viṣṇu; the verse of the ninth-century Tamil poet Śaṭakōpan̲, who captures hers and others' experience of Viṣṇu in his work, *Tiruvāymoḻi,* the writing of medieval commentators, who capture the meaning of Śaṭakōpan̲'s poetry and create a Vaiṣṇavite theological tradition; and the ruminations of a twentieth-century comparativist, who has been captured by his encounter with medieval Vaiṣṇavite theology. If readers do not previously know Śaṭakōpan̲'s *Tiruvāymoḻi,* they may through this book also become captured by it, and to see it, as Clooney intends, as a lover might. If this does happen, and if they already have other religious loves, they will be forced to ask just the theological questions that Clooney raises: what does it mean, theologically, to learn a new religious language, apprehended by a love that is significantly and interestingly different from the loves they already have?

The implications of such a capture—linguistic, ethical, intellectual, cultural, and stylistic—are profound, and have only begun to be explored in the comparative philosophy of religions. John Keenan's *The Meaning of Christ: A Mahāyāna Theology* (Orbis, 1989) and in his Buddhist commentary on the Gospel of Mark (forthcoming from the same publisher), are two intriguing recent examples of this new kind of theological writing. In *Seeing through Texts,* Clooney develops this new perspective with characteristic patience, care, and depth. The answer to this question was begun in his earlier work in this series, *Theology After Vedānta,* and is fully developed in these pages: readers can only find out what new loves might mean, theologically, for their relationship to the old ones, by immersing themselves in the minutiae of the new ones. Readers must learn to avoid, as he puts it, seeing *around* their new loves to some theory of what they might mean, and instead working *through* their details attentively.

This approach requires, among other things, an attitude toward the acts of reading and interpretation significantly different from that of most contemporary readers. As Clooney puts it, one must eschew sheer novelty and bold progress, and "allow smaller and more enduring changes to take place from the inside out." Chapters 2 through 4 are examples of the ways in which such enduring changes can take place. They provide accounts of a text opening opportunities for and placing demands upon its Vaiṣṇavite community of readers and listeners—the devotees who listened to and sang the poems, and the *ācārya*s who commented upon them.

These middle chapters also raise important issues about commentary that are developed from a comparative perspective in fifth and final chapter. Being a skilled reader, according to Clooney, is in the end almost indistinguishable from being a user of commentary; and this requires him in the final chapter of this book to explore what it might mean to juxtapose and read together—to "see through" texts from two different traditions conjointly. Clooney juxtaposes the *Tiruvāmoḻi* and its commentarial traditions with the *Song of Songs,* the *Gospel of John,* Bonaventure's *Journey of the Mind to God;* Ignatius' *Spiritual Exercises;* and Von Balthasar's *Prayer.* He offers suggestive insights in this chapter on the nature of commentary; the practice of using commentaries and of reading though them; and the epistemology and piety implied by such reading.

Clooney's work here connects with recent work by Indologists on the nature of commentary (Norman Cutler, "Interpreting the Tirukkūral: The Role of Commentary in the Creation of a Text," [Journal of the American Oriental Society 192. 1992: 549–566]; Jeffrey Timm, *Texts in Context: Traditional Hermeneutics in South Asia* [Albany: State University of New York Press, 1992]; and Laurie Patton, *Myth as Argument: The Bṛhaddevatā as Canonical Commentary [Berlin: DeGruyter Mouton, 1996]).* And yet Clooney's thinking does not stop at the Indological. As he puts it, his aim is more than to provide simply *something* to think about, but *somewhere* to think about it. In this he builds the foundations of an intellectual place where comparative theologians can do their work.

In this final chapter Clooney thus fulfills a desire found throughout the pages of his book: to do Christian theology through a richly detailed reading of a body of texts that are emphatically not Christian. His results will delight those who are interested in the theory and practice of reading comparatively; in theology done in the comparative modes; and in the technicalities and religious meaning of Śrīvaiṣṇava devotion. As editors we can assure such readers that they will find themselves very much like the young woman just returned from Tolaivillimaṅkalam: newly captivated by what others had thought they had long known, and had come to take for granted.

SEPTEMBER, 1995

Preface

Seeing through Texts: Doing Theology among the Śrīvaiṣṇavas of South India is about the Tamil language songs of Śaṭakōpaṉ in the 9th century, about the commentaries on those songs by the *ācāryas*—learned teachers—of the Śrīvaiṣṇava Hindu tradition in the 12th–14th centuries, and about how to do theology there, among poets and teachers, at the end of the 20th century.

The beginnings of this book go back almost fifteen years, when I first studied Tamil and started to read the songs of the Tamil Vaiṣṇava saints, the *āḻvārs*. Other projects intervened, and this project itself divided into smaller tasks: reading and translating the 1102 verses of *Tiruvāymoḻi*; learning to follow the subtle and rich style and thought patterns of Śrīvaiṣṇava commentary in its several, intermingled languages; visiting Madras for extended stays in 1982–3 and 1992–3; finding my way, as much as possible, into the Śrīvaiṣṇava community, listening, watching and learning, making friends, finding some boundaries that could not be crossed; discerning my theme, purpose and audience in the process of writing and rewriting; learning how to teach and do theology at home. Taking all this time has, I hope, worked out for the better: "to see through"—to pay attention, to clear a way, to become a skeptic but then to learn to take another look; to see by way of what people say and do and write—this is not a simple process, it ought to take time.

Seeing through Texts is in some ways a sequel to *Theology after Vedānta* (SUNY, 1993), even though it need not be read in conjunction with that book. Like that earlier work, *Seeing through Texts* seeks to balance Indological, comparative and theological commitments, trying to make them flourish together instead of just compete for attention. The goal has been to read some ancient devotional hymns and the commentaries on them in a way that opens into the wider set of concerns that occupy us today when we do comparative study and think about things religious. It seeks to be substantive, concerned about what is real and true, while yet remaining aware of the vagaries of language, and the many ways we go about finding the meaning of what has been said before, in addition to saying what we mean now. To clarify these issues in the midst of cross-cultural study—there, among those I study, and not entirely from a distance—*Seeing through Texts* devotes a great deal of attention to tradition and how its works: for example, how does our present ability to see things depend on how well we remember? It is comparative, not in the sense of lining things up and measuring them by yet another standard, but by following the pathways back and forth between the traditions we begin in and those we visit, once and many times. This seeks also to be a theological work, not simply in the sense of professing the beliefs of one particular religious community, but as a way of trying to understand everything: by probing the importance of religious roots, deep beliefs, intense love, and the ways in which we make these evident, and by examining, as if in a mirror, how we bring what we most deeply care about into our scholarly work and let this change how we read and how we write. What happens when an American, Roman Catholic priest studies Śrīvaiṣṇava texts? It has become evident to me that the issues of reading and writing involved in this particular example have been very particular, but have also had to open out into concern for the basic desires, commitments, loyalties and loves that form and direct even our scholarly attention. The songs of Śaṭakōpaṉ's *Tiruvāymoḻi,* to which this work is committed, are all about passionate love and anguish at the loss of love, about nourishing the memories of other people in times of absence, about how we speak about what we see, with words that hide and slip away. These songs are appealing and very engaging, but they do not welcome spectators; they ask us to stay, to listen again, to get involved, as with melodies that stay with us long after a performance is done. These songs were passed down in the Śrīvaiṣṇava tradition, remembered, used, and taught in just certain ways by great teachers, *ācāryas.* Yet, the *ācāryas* are a complicating factor, requiring careful attention. In the end it has been better to read with these ancient and contemporary teachers, to learn from them even as we must go our own way.

If readers finish this book and want to start over—to go to the original texts and see for themselves—then its several purposes will have been met quite satisfactorily: it should not stand in the way of the intensely beautiful things of which it speaks. Some Śrīvaiṣṇava readers of this book may be puzzled by aspects of my presentations, ready to welcome some, correct others—though I am sure that by their customary kindness they will bear with the all too small insights of this beginner, a now-and-then visitor to the Tamil country. But I hope too that they will recognize that one of the basic goals of this book is to present their tradition coherently, integrally, in an intellectually and spiritually sensitive fashion, over here, in this other part of the world, and thus for a wider audience than it has had up to this time.

Many translations are included in this book, and three brief notes are in order. First, since a complete and adequate translation of *Tiruvāymoḻi* is not yet available (those that are adequate are not complete, while those that are complete are not adequate), I have rather amply included verses throughout. Since almost nothing has yet been translated from the commentaries, excepting some texts of the first *ācārya,* Piḷḷāṉ, I have included many excerpts from the commentaries, some rather long, to give a feel for how they write and what they say. Second, regarding both the songs and the commentaries, I labored to be as faithful to the originals as possible, but in the end I have also wanted them to be translations which can be enjoyed too, and so have smoothed them out, made them flow; experts will surely check the original texts, anyway. Third, though all translations from the songs and commentaries are my own, for the former I am happily in debt to my colleagues. Some verses of *Tiruvāymoḻi* were beautifully translated by A.K. Ramanujan in his *Hymns for the Drowning* (1983). Vasudha Narayanan has translated more of them in her several books, including some complete songs, and I have read all of these in preparing my own translations. Currently I am collaborating with Narayanan and John Carman on a complete translation of *Tiruvāymoḻi.* All three of us are greatly indebted to Ramanujan, who until his untimely death had been our collaborator and inspiration.

There are many people who have helped me along the way in this project, although I can name just a few. The American Institute of Indian Studies made my research visit to India during 1992–3 possible, the Kuppuswami Sastri Research Institute in Madras once again offered me its official hospitality, and Boston College graciously afforded me sabbatical leave. I owe continuing gratitude to my first Tamil professors at the University of Chicago, James Lindholm and Norman Cutler; Norman has been helpful too with insightful comments into an earlier version of this book. Patricia Mumme, currently a professor at Capital University in Ohio, provided me with expert advice, and kept me honest on the details. Paul Griffiths of the University of Chicago and Laurie Patton of Bard College offered good advice and great encouragement in the last stages of this project. I am grateful once again to my friends at the Jesuit Interreligious Dialogue Center and Ashram in Madras, Aikiya Alayam, where Fathers R. Dhanaraj, S.J., Director and Maria Jeyaraj, S.J., Sister Margaret Mary Bastin, and Mr. V.A. Ponniah made my visit easier and happier in many ways. My fellow Jesuits at Boston College, especially at Barat House, continue to make my life more liveable and my work more fruitful. Of my guides in India, a few come to the fore: Professor A. Thiruvengadathan, with whom I read commentaries for the first time in the summer and fall of 1983; Professor M.A. Venkatakrishnan, who helped me obtain necessary texts and with whom I read during 1992–3; Professor Anand Amaladass, S.J., who graciously invited me to give the De Nobili Lectures at the Institute for Culture and Philosophy in Thiruvanmiyur, Madras in December, 1992, thus prompting me to put into writing some ideas central to this book; Mr. M.V. Mohana Rangan, a friend who graciously assisted me in many ways during my research in Madras, advising me on where to go, whom to meet, which books to buy; in Mylapore, K. Ramadurai Bhattacharya of the Matava Perumal temple in Mylapore, and Sri Satakopanacarya of the Kesava Perumal temple, who welcomed me into daily life and great festivals at those temples; Sri Anaviar Srinivasan, a friend and guide to all things Vaiṣṇava, who invited me to Āḻvārtirunagari in January, 1993 and welcomed me into his home, so that I could share the winter festival in celebration of *Tiruvāymoḻi* and, for once, seem to stand almost inside the tradition I was studying; Sri Kumaravati Ramanujacharya, who graciously allowed me to join his weekly circle of students in studying the commentaries on *Tiruvāymoḻi,* and who helped me to understand both the meanings of the texts and what it means to live a life infused with their vitality; and most especially, Professor T.E. Sampath Kumaran, retired professor of philosophy from Vivekananda College, who generously shared with me endless amounts of his time, his insight, and his love of the songs—day after day—helping me to see the brilliance and depth and passion of Naṃpiḷḷai's *Īṭu,* as well as what it is like to sit with a true *ācārya.*

Seeing through Texts is dedicated to two persons who in different ways taught me how to read wisely and deeply. It was A.K. Ramanujan who first advised me to study Tamil, told me of the *āḻvārs* and how it was that I would become deeply interested in them, helped me to appreciate both the songs of Śaṭakōpaṉ and the readings of the *ācāryas* and, in general, was for me the very ideal of the careful, sensitive reader. Father Ignatius Hirudayam, S.J., the founder and for many years director of Aikiya Alayam, was for me a living embodiment of the truth that one can remain rooted in one's own tradition and enter very deeply into another, keeping mind and heart and spirit alive and together in the process. Two sons of south India, different in many ways, they illumined the path on which I have managed finally to see this project through to completion. Raman showed me the wholeness of the scholar, and Ignatius, the wholeness of the Jesuit scholar.

Chapter **1**

Taking a First Look

Let us begin in the middle of things:

She worships lofty Tirutolaivillimaṅkalam with its great houses,
flawless jewels,
so leave her alone, women, have no hopes regarding her;
she cries, "the bright, radiant conch and discus," she cries, "the
wide lotus eyes,"
she keeps standing there, tears welling in her radiant kuvaḷai
flower eyes, she bursts. (1)

She has entered Tirutolaivillimaṅkalam noisy with the deep din
of festivals,
so have no hopes regarding her, this girl with her sweet nectar
words;
transformed, she stands speechless, crying, "lord, God of gods,"
her mouth twisting this way and that, her eyes welling tears,
she bends, she breaks, she comes apart. (2)

This girl with her sweet poetic words has entered
Tirutolaivillimaṅkalam with its cool paṇai trees and green
groves on river banks,
so have no hopes regarding her;
tears flowing from her slender eyes, she raves about how
he lay upon the waves of the sea,
measured the whole earth, herded the cows. (3)

After seeing Tirutolaivillimaṅkalam where people prosperous in
the abiding four Vedas dwell,
she's lost all self-control, see, she's beyond you, women;

she cries, "Lord Kaṇṇaṉ, dark as the sea, is everything that can be learned,"
she has no modesty left, she keeps rejoicing, delighted within, she melts away. (4)

The poor thing, she melts, her face shines, for after entering Tirutolaivillimaṅkalam
you showed her the lord with the red lotus eyes, the splendid light;
starting then, her eyes have rained like clouds, she is amazed, women,
her mind has gone inside there,
she keeps on looking in that direction, worshipping. (5)

Everywhere you see sugar cane, tall ripening paddy, and luxuriant red lotuses
at rich Tirutolaivillimaṅkalam on the north bank of the cool Porunal;
after seeing this she looks nowhere but that direction, all day, every day,
and the only word in her mouth is the name of the jewel colored one, women. (6)

Women, this great lovely peahen, this little doe, has escaped our hands,
whatever you say she hears nothing but "Tolaivillimaṅkalam;"
is this the outcome of things she did before
or the magic of the cloud colored lord?
all she wants is to learn his signs, his names. (7)

She worshipped Tirutolaivillimaṅkalam on the northern bank of the Porunal
where the perfect Vedas and sacrifices and great women mingle together;
from that first day until this day, that girl with eyes dark and wide
keeps crying, "Lotus eyed one!" she weeps, she fades. (8)

She grieves all day long, her face alarmed, tears splashing,
crying, "Jewel colored one!" so even the trees pity her;
ever since she learned the name of that city
all she does is join her hands in worship and say,

"Tirutolaivillimaṅkalam, home of the one who split the horse's mouth!" (9)

Is she Piṉṉai born here? or Nīlā? or the Lady?
what marvel is this? she stands calling, "My tall lord!"
To hear the name of that town, to bow before Tirutolaivillimaṅkalam
where he who came before stands, sits, dwells—that is her only thought. (10)

In thought, word, and deed Śaṭakōpaṉ of splendid Kurukūr
reached the point of calling the lord of the gods his mother and father;
whoever masters these ten pure Tamil verses about Tirutolaivillimaṅkalam from his venerable thousand verses
will serve Tirumāl. (11)[1]

This song is about a young woman who went to visit a temple; it is also about the other women from the village, her neighbors, who had evidently prompted her to pay this temple a visit. It tells us what happened to her, and what did not happen to them, as a consequence of that visit.

Though the young woman's words are quoted, it is actually a friend of hers who does the talking. First (1–5) the friend valiantly tries to explain to the neighbors how the young woman is preoccupied with God, and how it is futile on their part to try to get her to return to normal. Indeed, she claims, her plight is all their fault, for it was they who had taken the young woman to the temple town of Tirutolaivillimaṅkalam at festival time. They had walked through the lovely temple precincts (environs which are still lovely today), they had entered the temple with her, and with her viewed the lotus-eyed lord enshrined there. For them it was a quick, pious look, a paying of respects, after which they could return to their homes, to normal life, quickly settling back into their ordinary activities. But the young woman could not forget what she had seen, she could not simply observe and then move on. Her ordinary life came to an abrupt halt. The women, it seems, had very much underestimated the impact a temple visit could have on someone; they wrongly assumed that the young woman was more like themselves.

In the next verses (6–9), the friend focuses on the young woman's current state, how since then she has lived entirely and only for God, her world occupied by a divine presence—filled with sacred memory—and yet torn apart because she wants more than she now has. Her memory is not enough, the temple image is not enough, she wants an enduring presence and immediacy; she has seen too little to be satisfied, too much to settle for less. She looks only toward the temple (6), crying out the names she heard and the divine emblems she saw there (7). She is slowly reduced to crying just one name (8), to the simplest act of worship (9).

The tenth verse of the song forms a brief third section. Here the friend, who had been trying to manage the situation, stops short, astonished as are the women. Her words stumble, reduced to questions; amazed at the extent of the young woman's preoccupation with God, the friend begins to wonder whether the young woman is one of the lord's three divine consorts: this unusual obsession with God is perhaps a manifestation of divinity.

The 11th verse of the song shifts to yet another level of discourse; it is a statement about the first ten verses, about the young woman and her neighbors, and about the friend who speaks of them:

> *In thought, word, and deed Śaṭakōpaṉ of splendid Kurukūr*
> *reached the point of calling the lord of the gods his mother and father;*
> *whoever masters these ten pure Tamil verses about*
> *Tirutolaivillimaṅkalam from his venerable thousand verses*
> *will serve Tirumāl.*

This verse invites listeners to become part of the story they have listened to, to become intimate with the lord like the author Śaṭakōpaṉ; to master his verses—to memorize them, recite them, understand them—and on that basis become able to enter into service of the lord, Tirumāl.

I. Some Opening Questions

Thus goes VI.5, the 5th song of the Sixth book in a very large Tamil work known as *Tiruvāymoḻi*, "the holy (*tiru*) word (*moḻi*) of mouth (*vāy*)," composed by a south Indian Hindu named Śaṭakōpaṉ in the 9th century. He was the most important of the twelve saints from that time period, known as the *āḻvārs* (i.e., "those immersed" in God) who composed songs in praise of the God Viṣṇu.

This song by Śaṭakōpaṉ is not meant to stand alone, it has connections. In its place among 100 songs composed by Śaṭakōpaṉ of Kurukūr as his *Tiruvāymoḻi* (and thereby also in relation to the larger set of devotional songs of the *āḻvārs* known as the "Divine Text," the *Divya Prabandham*), this song about Tirutolaivillimaṅkalam has been remembered, recited, used ritually, meditated on, taught, and written about by the Śrīvaiṣṇava Hindu community of south India, over the past 1000 years, as it still is today. For a thousand years the *ācāryas*—revered teachers—of the Śrīvaiṣṇava tradition doted over each word of this song (as they did with the other 99), reverently, lovingly, passionately uncovering the deep meanings they found within it. For a thousand years devotees have listened to their *ācāryas* and taken the song to heart, seeking, if not to be divinely radiant like the young woman, at least (for now) to find their way to service of lord Viṣṇu, Tirumāl.

Let us listen-in on what they have to say. Tirukkurukaippirāṉ-piḷḷāṉ (henceforth, and more easily, Piḷḷāṉ), the 12th century *ācārya* whose commentary is the earliest to come down to us, had this to say in introducing the song:

> In the preceding songs the *āḻvār* has meditated on how the Lord dwells in various holy cities, Tiruviṇṇakar, etc., His divine descents, His divine deeds, all His auspicious qualities, His beauty, etc. Now he expresses his delight—but also the sheer depression which comes about because he cannot achieve external union with that Lord. He expresses his feelings in the voice of the young woman. Because she desires to see the Lord in Tirutolaivillimaṅkalam, but is unable to get to do that, she is exceedingly depressed, and

so she cries out, talking about His good qualities—His beauty, etc.—His symbols and deeds, and about Tirutolaimaṅkalam. When her mother and relatives see this, they are afraid—"We have lost her!"—so they decide, "We must stop her from loving Him!" and entreat her friend to help out. But the friend looks at them and speaks in this song.[2]

Nañcīyar, a generation later, adds:

The friend understands what the young woman is thinking, and says: "After seeing Tirutolaivillimaṅkalam, from that time on she abandons everything inside and outside, excepting the glance of her Lord, Aravinda. He is her everything: her mind, her speech, her body are very much inclined toward Him." She makes them aware of how her nature has matured and says, "After showing her Tirutolaivillimaṅkalam as the place to enter, are you now thinking of 'saving' her? is that possible now? End your hopes in regard to her!"

In a much ampler comment which builds on the earlier ones, Nañcīyar's disciple Naṃpiḷḷai[3] observes that here the āḻvār is speaking about his own true nature and not just about the lord; he is vividly explaining the hardest thing of all, the essence of the human self. Periyavāccāṇpiḷḷai, a contemporary of Vaṭakkutiruvītippiḷḷai and another disciple of Naṃpiḷḷai, recollects on earlier understandings of the song:

Earlier ācāryas had this to say: "In previous songs the āḻvār experienced Kṛṣṇa; unable to contain that joy inside him, a desire for external union was born. But when he could not get that union, he experiences total dependence on the Lord. He expresses this in the words of the young woman."

But Bhaṭṭar had a different view: "Previously the āḻvār had already experienced flawless joy, so the previous interpretation cannot explain the link of those songs with this song. Rather it is like this: just as when someone is drinking water and begins to choke, and his experience of the sweet taste is disturbed and he is afflicted, so the āḻvār is describing here how his experience of delight has been disturbed and he has become dependent on this other."

Or, perhaps: from the first verse of *Tiruviruttam*[4] to this point he had never had a full experience of the Lord—but now he has one. He describes that abundant inclination toward the Lord that has arisen within him. Up to this point he had spoken about the Lord of all, whereas in this song he is speaking about himself.

Śatakōpan̲, they find, is himself the young woman who has lost the ability to exist separately from the lord. As they read each verse, the *ācāryas* elaborate such connections and meanings, always with an eye toward what all of this means for the audience of simple believers listening to their teachings. At the end of the 11th verse of VI.5 Naṃpiḷḷai emphasizes the song's power; it equals that of the lord's ancient descents (*avatāra*) into the world, just as it equals the ancient Sanskrit *Veda*, rendering it in the clear Tamil vernacular: "Just as the lord of all descended here in like form to other beings, here the *Veda* itself descends in their midst in Tamil form . . . For Tamil expresses the *Veda's* meaning most clearly."

Even as the song is identified as a local, Tamil work, it seems also more broadly universal. The reality of the song is meant to become the reality of the attentive listener: those who are skilled in repeating these verses will surely get to be servants of the lord, the husband of the Goddess Śrī. The song intends wider audiences, replicating and expanding its presence through a series of new ears, new voices. Recitation widens the audience, and in the audience there are those who will also come to recite and perhaps explicate the song again, adding their voices to the conversation around the young woman's unforgetting preoccupation with her lord. Whoever can hear and speak, that is the audience for the song, and there too are those who can learn to see as she saw, by way of the song.

It is possible too, as we trace the widening conversation encircling the young woman's cry, that the song—by itself, with the 99 other songs, with the *ācāryas'* explications of it—has something to say to the real newcomer, the true outside reader, who encounters the song in a foreign place, foreign tongue, for some reason or another: curiosity, reading, keeping busy, becoming a scholar, seeking truth, seeking God. This listener, casual or engaged, hears and possibly has something to say regarding the song. But with what practical import can such really new readers meaningfully can engage the religious worldview inscribed in the song? Indeed, can readers from outside the Śrīvaiṣṇava tradition become at least able to understand what it would mean to worship the lord who "lay upon the waves of the sea, measured the whole earth, herded the cows"? Or are the intellectual, cultural, religious distances from the song to the modern reader so great as to bar any such engaged, affective encounter?

Such questions are clearly not simple ones to answer, and even estimates of their significance must vary. Insofar as they are taken as straightforward and highly particular questions posed to individuals who must decide how to respond personally to potentially spiritual opportunities, they are not answerable here; they must be left to those individuals in their own social and (non)religious settings. It is possible, though, to ask how we read and how we handle what we have read, about what we do with what is truly new to us, and about the power of texts, religious texts in particular. We can examine how a text like *Tiruvāymoḻi* comes laden with possibilities, how it invites the casual reader to become deeply involved in the world which opens from within the song. From looking at this song and then at the others that accompany it, the reader may in the end be invited into a kind of seeing-through-texts, wherein these words—unusual, obscure, translated, hampered—become the vehicle of substantive religious encounters.

Such possibilities must be located according to who is seeking them, and we shall have to move consciously back and forth, in and out of religious environs as we proceed, noticing how religious and academic perspectives variably overlap, diverge, conflict, totally miss one another. Still, a common starting point is the attentiveness to the value of language that most of us share today. The Śrīvaiṣṇavas of south India, like many Christians and members of other religious communities, think that no one in this life can simply and directly see—have an unmediated experience of—God. The religious person ends up talking boldly of things he or she does not know, drawing blindly, in the dark. Yet, at the same time, such words mark both one's distance from some higher goal—God, whatever—and the path by which that distance can be overcome. Words make proximate what they obscure; understanding them, (re)voicing them, one begins to see through them: they are limited, and they are windows.

But there is a long way to travel before we are ready to say more on the possiblity of such verbal insights. We must first become familiar with the words themselves. We shall first have to examine *Tiruvāymoḻi* as carefully as possible, as the context where songs like VI.5 belong, in order to see the opportunities this text has opened and the demands it has placed on its readers. This we shall do by attention to *Tiruvāymoḻi* itself (chapter 2), and by attention to the particular, exemplary fashion in which it has been used by the Śrīvaiṣṇava community (chapters 3 and 4). Only then, with the spectrum of possibilities of both text and tradition before us, can we attempt to locate ourselves, experimentally rephrasing what we know, what we have read, with whom, who we are, in relation to these songs (chapter 5).

In the remainder of this chapter there are some exploratory inquiries to be carried out as we assess the problems before us and the resources available to us when we read *Tiruvāymoḻi* and posit that there can be religious significance in doing so. In section two, we review first the text and its contexts—when have we read enough? In sections three and four, we look for the author in his text and listen-in on the community which read and passed the songs down—with whom are we to read? In section five, we uncover some of the resources and expectations we ourselves bring to our reading—who are we, most of us outsiders to that community who yet venture to read these songs, to converse with these *ācāryas*, to see through these songs? Let us take up these points consecutively.

II. Getting Inside Tiruvāymoḻi

Let us first pay closer attention to what it means to understand a song, such as the one with which we started, about the young woman who visited Tirutolaivillimaṅkalam. This is a song that presents itself well; it has a story to tell and a point to make. One can get quite far by reading the song and following out the implications of what it says—and even further if one listens-in on what the *ācāryas* had to say about it.

Yet as we have noted, this song is not meant to be read separately. It is only one among a hundred songs in *Tiruvāymoḻi,* a large text in the Tamil language, dedicated to lord Viṣṇu, and composed by a person named Śaṭakōpaṉ (or Māṟaṉ), known more familiarly as Nammāḻvār—our saint, our *āḻvār*—in the Śrīvaiṣṇava tradition. His songs offer many different perspectives on Viṣṇu—as manifest in transcendent glory, as creating, controlling and destroying the universe, as present in various descents (*avatāras*, especially as Kṛṣṇa, Rāma and Vāmana the dwarf), at holy places such as Tiruveṅkaṭam (more commonly referred to as Tirupati), Kurukūr (the present day Āḻvārtirunagari), Śrīviḷḷiputtūr and Śrīraṅgam, and as dwelling within every person. The songs also represent different personae in relation to Viṣṇu: the humble devotee, the lover from the beginning intermingled with the lord, the young woman in love with her absent lover, the visionary seeing devotees on their way to heaven, the thinker who wonders whether even "Viṣṇu" is a good word to indicate the transcendent Viṣṇu. In some songs it is this lord who is addressed, in others the community of devotees, in others the unheeding people of the world; in some, the poet appears as if speaking largely to himself (yet so as to be overheard in his soliloquy). Almost none among the 100 songs can be said to be entirely simple and straightforward: themes are combined and intertwined, played off against one another over and over; even at verse one, we are always already in the midst of a religious discourse that is part remembered, part expected, part happening even as one hears of it. Yet *Tiruvāymoḻi* is also narrowly fixed in its form, almost entirely predictable. It is comprised of 1102 verses divided into 100 songs of 11 verses each,[5] and the 11th verse of each song is always a kind of secondary reflection on the first ten.

Tiruvāymoḻi is also woven together and in a circle, by means of what is known as *antāti* ("the end-to-beginning" style): the last word of each verse is always the first of the next, the last in X.10.11 being the first in I.1.1. When the Śrīvaiṣṇavas build an entire world within the boundaries established by the songs, they have been invited to do so by *Tiruvāymoḻi,* ever turning-in upon itself, recollecting everything within its circle of songs. As far as possible, we too will seek to contain our analysis within that circle, testing where we can reach within those confines.

Of course, a decision to work within the confines of the text is itself a kind of fiction, one which stands at odds with legitimate concerns about context, history, distance, etc. At the beginning of this book we must account for choosing a limited focus, what we think we gain and lose in paying little direct attention to the broader context of *Tiruvāymoḻi* in history, culture, and literature. It is certainly not true that *Tiruvāymoḻi* lacks context or does not need any. It was composed against the background of a rich religious and cultural tradition in the Tamil area, which was also already open to northern, Sanskrit influence. It was composed when other Vaiṣṇava and Śaiva texts—dedicated respectively to Viṣṇu and Śiva—were being composed, and one can find without too much difficulty other songs by other authors about the same temples and myths and religious values of which Śaṭakōpaṉ sings.[6]

There are obvious candidates which provide directly relevant context for *Tiruvāymoḻi*—beginning with the three other works attributed to Śaṭakōpaṉ, *Tiruviruttam, Tiruvāciriyam, Periyatiruvantāti;* and then the other works of the *Divya Prabandham.* Some of these works are likely to have been composed earlier than *Tiruvāymoḻi* and therefore might conceivably be influences on it, while others at least suggest illuminating comparisons. Parallel Śaiva devotional songs have many of the same literary and devotional motifs. Older Tamil works survive from the four or five centuries before *Tiruvāymoḻi,* ranging from the love (*akam*) and war (*puṟam*) poetry of the *caṅkam* period to *Paripāṭal* as well as certain songs in *Cilappatikāram.* Nor can one ignore Sanskrit works, such as the *Mahābhārata,* the *Viṣṇu Purāṇa* and *Rāmāyaṇa,* in which the myths and narratives to which Śaṭakōpaṉ refers are elaborated. These aid us in specifying the meaning of *Tiruvāymoḻi,* and may have aided Śaṭakōpaṉ as well. To know about these varied works will surely help us to understand *Tiruvāymoḻi* better, so that we can assess more surely the choices Śaṭakōpaṉ had before him in deciding what to use, and how, in composing *Tiruvāymoḻi*. Not to know the wider context surely threatens to distort our reading.[7]

Even as we acknowledge the importance of paying attention to all the relevant details of context, we must assess carefully what we can and cannot do at the present stage of scholarly inquiry. For one thing, there are considerable difficulties to be faced in understanding these other older and contemporary works before reference to them will aid us in understanding *Tiruvāymoḻi*. They are often large and complex, and many of them, particularly in Tamil, have not yet been studied carefully by modern scholars. Most of them are in fact less well understood than *Tiruvāymoḻi*, which has profited from the fact of the large commentarial tradition around it and from a variety of modern studies.[8] Moreover, when one does try to specify relevant connections, it is striking that contextual studies often remain inconclusive or insufficient to establish definite historical connections or literary influences such as would pin down the inherited and original features of Śaṭakōpaṉ's achievement. Beyond the kind of generalities I have already hinted at—"older and contemporary works are important"—there is very little in the way of direct evidence which indicates that Śaṭakōpaṉ, strikingly original in his re-use of available resources, actually borrowed from any actual source, or actually knew of any of the other works one might think he should have known about. Given this situation, much remains tentative, and many questions are left open for later resolution.

But a final, basic point is that *Seeing through Texts* is an impatient book. Though informed by a concern for the wider context, it represents a theological project which does not wait upon the completion of the relevant research by other scholars. Although very much open to improvement and correction, its premise is that we can get quite far by learning to think, imagine, and desire within the world bounded by the songs of *Tiruvāymoḻi*. Just as it would be unfortunate to jump to conclusions, it would be unfortunate to postpone serious consideration of the text as a literary whole until that future date when the context is exactly understood. This study takes the swifter path, engaging *Tiruvāymoḻi* as an integral literary document possessed of its own dynamics as a work of literature, with its own style of interaction with its readers. None of which features can be ignored merely in favor of understanding its components in relation to components of other earlier and contemporary texts.

Awareness of the broader context provides a note of caution to accompany this study. We will try not to discover uniqueness where it is not actually to be found, nor to make too much of features that may turn out, in fact, to be rather common. Conversely, we will highlight what seems unusual and rare, and also what is missing, such as what one might have expected to find in a work like *Tiruvāymoḻi* but does not. Still, our major concern is to be something like an *āḻvār*, immersed in the songs; we shall suggest the manner and implications of this gradual immersion in chapter 2.[9]

III. Pondering the Author: Sifting the Multiple Contexts

The opportunities and risks of a focus on the text as given to us rather than on the resources exterior to it which enable us to dissect it become all the more clear when we consider the text in relation to the most important contextual factor, its author, Śaṭakōpaṉ. How ought we to take into account his intentions in composing the songs? Who was Śaṭakōpaṉ, what ought we know about him, when is the narrative "I" truly the voice of the author? If we focus our attention on Śaṭakōpaṉ, are we better able to understand *Tiruvāymoḻi*? If we resist the appealing but vague category of experience, how are we to read what is before us and yet find the author in that reading?

The problems related to an understanding of the author are of course complex, and many of them have to do with literature in general: problems regarding authors in general, authorial intention in any kind of writing, the inscription of self in writing, the existence of authors behind texts, etc. Such larger concerns cannot be resolved here, but we must at least keep in mind the caution against naiveté to which they exhort us. Let us review what we know about the author Śaṭakōpan̲ from his songs and from the Śrīvaiṣṇava tradition; I will show how these resources together confirm our instinct to interpret the text as an integral whole.

1. Locating Śaṭakōpan̲ Historically

Insofar as research can make a contextual, historical contribution, we must concede that the materials available for this research are minimal, insufficient for the construction of a reliable and comprehensive biography of Śaṭakōpan̲. However, some minimal specifications are possible. The basic historical sketch has been given numerous times, most recently and competently by G. Damodaran (1978) and F. Hardy (1979); I will borrow from their accounts in rehearsing the main lines of the story of Śatakōpan̲.[10]

Śaṭakōpan̲ probably lived in the 9th century CE, though some scholars have placed him as much as two centuries earlier,[11] in Kurukūr deep in south India, in Tamil Nadu. His real name was probably Mār̲an̲—perhaps his grandfather's name, perhaps a name given in honor of the king in whose court his father may have served. It was probably only later he was given the honorific name "Śaṭakōpan̲," which is explained variously in relation to his power to destroy ignorance.[12] Damodaran suggests that the relative inaccessibility of some of the hill temples of which Śaṭakōpan̲ sings may indicate that he was from the hill country of modern Kerala, to the west of Tamil Nadu. The elegance and sophistication of his compositions and the inclusion in them of a significant number of Sanskrit words suggest that Śaṭakōpan̲ was a well-educated person. There is not much else to add to this scant account that is of direct importance to how we read the songs.

2. Finding Śaṭakōpan̲ in his Songs

As we delve more attentively into the songs themselves, other kinds of useful information come to the fore, particularly regarding the construction of Śaṭakōpaṉ as a spiritual figure. To begin with, the 11th verses which conclude each song—perhaps Śaṭakōpaṉ's own verses, a kind of reflection on his own songs, perhaps the work of a very early redactor[13]—are vivid and ample in the spiritual characterization of Śaṭakōpaṉ they offer; they set the tone for how he was to be remembered in later generations. According to these verses, for example, Śaṭakōpaṉ is the one:

"who lives by the grace of Māl, astonished and crying repeatedly, 'Māl, wondrous lord, great wondrous one!'" (I.5.11);

who spoke "about how he desired the lord Kaṇṇaṉ, God of gods, who stands the very highest," (I.9.11);

who possessed "an insatiable love for the Cause of all things without exception, the light," (II.1.11);

"who knows that there is no other way to rise than Kaṇṇaṉ's bright lotus feet, (IV.3.11);

"who thought only about reaching the holy feet of Nārāyaṇa, Keśava, the highest light," (IV.9.11);

"who daily has only one thought, 'Our refuge is the feet of the lord on the snake,'" (V.10.11);

"who has reached the point of calling the lord of the gods his mother and father, by thought, word, and deed," (VI.5.11);

"who was the sort to see that nothing here nor there can exist without holy Māl," (VII.9.11);

"whose mind is purely for the pure one, who thinks, 'there is no other refuge after knowing the pure one,'" (VII.10.11);

"who grieved about parting from him of whom the lovely, decorated cowherd women cry out in the evening unable to live apart from him," (IX.9.11);

> *"who is crowned with the grace of the tall one,"* (X.5.11);
>
> *"who has destroyed desire and gained release, who calls on Aran̲ and Ayan̲ and Ari who encompasses and fulfils desire,"* (X.10.11).[14]

His songs are

> *"composed in awe,"* (VII.7.11),
>
> *"uttered from knowledge,"* (VII.8.11),
>
> *"a work of humble service,"* (IV.1.11, X.1.11, V.6.11, etc.)

And so on. Such characterizations contribute to a spiritual biography—Śaṭakōpan̲ as the paradigm of full, perfect devotion—not a historical one. Yet they are important, primary responses to the energy and passion of the songs, and they suggest how the tradition will think of him, how he functions in relation to his songs.

It is reasonable to move beyond the eleventh verses to the body of the songs themselves, to fill out this literary and spiritual portrayal of Śaṭakōpan̲, extrapolating from the verses to their author. The tradition has done this fairly liberally; the *ācāryas* work with the hypothesis that everything in the songs marks some moment in the *āl̲vār's* inner journey. This verse, in the young woman's voice,

> *"My rice for eating, my water for drinking, my betel for chewing, my lord Kaṇṇan̲!"*
> *she keeps crying, tears flooding her eyes;*
> *when she searches for his city, abundant in his excellence, in all the earth,*
> *Kōḷūr is surely the place my young doe will enter.* (VI.7.1)

was taken by Nañcīyar to indicate that the *āl̲vār* neither ate nor drank, but depended on the lord alone: "His nature was such that he could not for a moment endure separation from the lord, he who from his birth had the lord as his sustenance, etc."[15] In introducing I.10.8,

When I hear someone say, "Nārāyaṇa our Treasure,"
tears flood my eyes, I search for him;
how amazing, day and night he never stops favoring me,
my master, young master, he never leaves me. (I.10.8)

Naṃpiḷḷai offers this fascinating anecdote, one of just several which tell us something about Śaṭakōpaṉ "outside" his songs:

> The *āḻvār* thought, "Up to now we have erred in thinking and speaking; now we must put all this aside and go to a place where His qualities are not celebrated." So he lay down near a ruined wall, covering his head. But just then a man came along carrying a heavy bundle; as he put it down he sighed, 'Śrīmāṉ Nārāyaṇa!' When the *āḻvār* heard these words he was astonished that his senses were so inclined toward what he heard. (I.10.8)

Apart from such individual verses read autobiographically—as verses in the Psalms have been read to indicate events in the life of King David—there are some entire songs which seem particularly to invite autobiographical interpretation. Several seem prompted by visits to particular temples which Śaṭakōpaṉ appears to have known in detail,

Flocks of herons daily feeding in the flowering marshes,
when you see the lord with the berry-red lips and discus in his hand,
the lord who lives in Tiruvaṇvaṇṭūr where fine rice ripens tall—
worship him, tell him of this sinner's love. (VI.1.1)

Some seem to presume his encounters with devotees,

This alone suits my eye:
the people of Vaikuṇṭa's lord are established everywhere in this world by their marvels, but they do one thing only;

have no doubt, there is no escape, even if you are born demons or ungodly folk:

they will kill you, sirs, overturning this age. (V.2.5)

or his encounters with worldly types,

Skilled singers of such fine songs,
why do you put aside the lord of our heaven-dwellers
who shows the path to travel from age to age, many ages without end,
just to sing of others hardly worth thinking of? (III.9.3)

or his sudden realization of some aspect of God's grace,

In that time when I did not know you, you made me love your service,
in the midst of my unknowing confusion, you made me your servant;
disguised as a dwarf, you asked, "Three steps of earth, great Bali,"
you tricked him unawares,
and now you've mingled inside my self. (II.3.3)

or his vision of the faithful on their way to Heaven,

The people of the heavenly worlds worship, they pour out incense and a fine rain of flowers
before the people who belong to him who once measured the earth;
silent sages along both sides cheer them on, "Come higher!"
they step forward saying, "This is the road to Vaikuṇṭa!" (X.9.3)

These verses are lovely and memorable; yet the difference between the "I" in the songs and the "I" of the author cannot be overlooked; the effect is not so much to establish the identity or history of the author as to infuse the songs with the values of first-person recollection: the depiction of "I" is one more tool at the composer's disposal.

Four songs (III.9, IV.5, VII.9, X.7) gain particular prominence because they appear to express Śaṭakōpaṉ's self-identity directly, as the speaker turns explicitly to a consideration of his own craft and articulates his self-understanding of his art.[16] III.9, already cited, portrays what one bard has to say to other bards. In each verse, in one way or another, the speaker insists that he sings only of the lord and that those who do otherwise are to be criticized: "These lords think of themselves as something special; they esteem their riches as true wealth—why should I sing of them?" (2); "others hardly worth thinking of" (3); "frail men" (4); "You'll get no rewards to keep, by wearing out your mouths praising the glories of wealth: it's like digging around in a dung heap!" (5); "there are no real benefactors in this world. But even if you praise your own favorite god with sweet songs, you still reach holy Māl with the bright, radiant hair" (6); "So what words can I mouth about foolish people?" (8); "I am not one to mouth the praise of men" (9). We have here a strong public voice; in some loose sense at least, Śaṭakōpaṉ seems to be a member of a "poets' guild." He has peers to argue with, he is not alone.

IV.5, VII.9 and X.7 reflect on the experience of inspiration, and the involvement of the lord in the composition of these songs in his honor. IV.5 reiterates, in a kind of refrain, the speaker's amazement that he has been allowed to undertake the precious task of offering songs to the lord, by the lord's grace. His words, the garland he offers to the lord, are totally satisfying to himself, and amazingly marked by the kind of intimate union he seeks. These verses are indicative of the song's direction:

The unfalling one who dwells within the bounds of undying joy,
excellence undying, flower eyes, lord of heaven-dwellers,
I praise him with garlands of songs undying through time,
I come near him, I dwell within the bounds of undying joy.

To those who come near him in worship, the lord comes near,
and makes their deeds go away;
his the lovely feathered eagle, his the war discus,
my tongue praises him with garlands of song and I come near
him;
but I cannot understand how he's made my self his self.

The lord shows us the right way, the lofty lord of the immortals,
the one who spreads out all things, my lord;
I praise him, weaving a garland of words, I have reached the
state of rejoicing every day,
my deeds and diseases become ashes before the wind. (IV.5.3–5)

Subsequent verses similarly weave together praise and self-reflection: ". . . I praise him with garlands of songs with proper words, I get inside him: from now on can there ever be anything difficult for me?" (6); ". . . it's my destiny to weave garlands of fine words about him: what then could I lack?" (7); ". . . is anyone in the wide heavens equal to me who can compose such garlands of words?" (8); ". . . I have threaded this radiant Tamil about him, cloud of joy for his servants." (10) These testimonies naturally encourage us to look on *Tiruvāymoḻi* from the perspective of its author; though in the middle of this garland woven beginning to end, they succeed in getting us to look again at the whole, in terms of what it might have meant to Śaṭakōpaṉ.

We hear most clearly of the divine origins of Śaṭakōpaṉ's intensely personal songs in VII.9, which announces the unity of divine and human voices, as the poet meditates on how his words are, at the same time, really divine words:

He has uplifted me for all time, day after day he has already
made me himself;
Now he sings himself through me in sweet Tamil,
my lord, my First One, the abiding light: what can I say about
him?

What can I say about him?
Become one with my sweet life, he sings in me these sweet songs
which I sing in my own words,
he now praises himself in his own words, my marvellous one,
the First One who in three forms sings ahead of me.

He does not sing his song about himself by the sweet songs of
the best singers
but now joyfully he becomes one with me and through me
sings fine songs about himself: Vaikuṇṭa's lord. (VII.9.1, 2, 6)

Operative here are both a sense of divine intervention—every word is God's—and the speaker's conscious assent to this process—his words are all the richer because they are not merely his and because he knows this. The lord speaks, the text is invested with authority, the status of the author is enhanced, even while remaining dependent on the lord.

X.7 confirms the same theme, weaving it together with praise of the lord at Tirumāliruṅcōlai:

> *To punish the demons who would not come to him,*
> *to make the good immortals radiant,*
> *to make the silent sages who think what can't be thought*
> *reach the heights of joy,*
> *become me himself, he himself sang these sweet melodious*
> *songs,*
> *my lord, the lord of Tirumāliruṅcōlai.* (X.7.5)

All four of these songs seem evidently self-expressive; they serve to establish how Śaṭakōpaṉ thinks of his compositions, and of their value as testimony about himself and his lord. We seem to be given glimpses of his understanding of his own art, his relation to divine creativity, and the nature of *Tiruvāymoḻi*. These songs—forty verses which seem to overflow and infuse all eleven hundred verses with their perspective—seem consciously invested with the power of a divine-human authorship. The poet's self-awareness extends to the discovery of God's power in his own words.

This is certainly a remarkable kind of contextualization: the entirety of *Tiruvāymoḻi* is subsumed into the personality and religious experience of its author, and the author into God. But we must still refrain from too autobiographical a reading of these four songs, even if we inevitably favor them because of their first-person tone. For they too have to be read in the context of the whole, where the author has taken up many styles and perspectives. There is nothing in *Tiruvāymoḻi* which draws special attention to them, no indications which signal these songs as illuminative of the whole or indicative of the author's mind in a decidedly privileged fashion. They are neither first nor last among the songs, nor are they even placed together, and no other song or refrain points to them specially. From the perspective of the whole, even what appears to be insight into the author's mind and heart must be taken as just one way to understand what is going on in *Tiruvāymoḻi*. While it may satisfy our desire to catch sight of the author's "I" to give these songs particular prominence, we must resist the identification of the "I" in the text with the "I" of the author.

It is preferable, more interesting, and more fruitful, to understand that *Tiruvāymoḻi* encompasses an entire religious world in part by including everything in the midst of everything else. This means that it includes, among other things, even the author's apparent testimony about himself, the useful datum of first-person discourse. These confessional expressions by the poet constitute just one among the many strategies of expression adopted by Śaṭakōpaṉ in *Tiruvāymoḻi*. There is no perfect self-expression of the author lying beneath or behind the complexities of *Tiruvāymoḻi*; no Text within the text, no "most important songs"—at least until readers choose to confer such importance, due to interest in one theme or another, or interest in the author, or interest in historical reconstruction, etc. While such choices are inevitable, they must constantly be tested by reference to the whole, which alone remains the object of inquiry; for *Tiruvāymoḻi* as a whole is what Śaṭakōpaṉ intended to tell us.

This, of course, is the point of VII.9 and X.7: every word is the fruit of Śaṭakōpaṉ's encounter with God, every word is God's word, the whole is much greater than its author. So we must master the *whole* of *Tiruvāymoḻi* if we are to know Śaṭakōpaṉ. This commitment to the whole subordinates every point of focus to the dynamics of the whole, in lieu of a dispersal of that commitment into questions of context or into a selective entrée which privileges the genius of the author as glimpsed in certain songs or verses.

3. Śaṭakōpaṉ Under the Tamarind Tree: Learning from Hagiography

A commitment to the whole is supported in an unexpected fashion by the Śrīvaiṣṇava hagiographies of Śaṭakōpaṉ; secondary accounts which might seem to be of little interest in determining the significance of either *Tiruvāymoḻi* or its author. Yet these accounts turn out to be wisely supportive of the project of working closely within, inside the text. Let us see, briefly, what they have to say about Śaṭakōpaṉ and his work. I draw here on the earliest account we have, the Sanskrit *Divyasūricaritam* ("The Acts of the Divine Sages") attributed to the 12th century theologian Garuḍavāhana,[17] and the somewhat more expansive Tamil *Guruparaṃparāprabhāvam* ("The Splendor of the Lineage of Teachers") of Piṉpaḻakiya Perumāḷ Jīyar (late 13th–14th century).[18]

The story at the core of these accounts is simple and vivid. Because of lord Nārāyaṇa's limitless compassion for the world, the boy Māṟaṉ (Śaṭakōpaṉ) was born at an auspicious moment in the southern town of Kurukūr. He was marked from birth by the fact that he did not behave like a normal child: he refused to eat or drink or even look around. When efforts to make him normal led nowhere, his parents finally placed him under a tamarind tree near the temple, trusting that God would care for the unusual boy. He was to sit there for 16 years in what was later revealed to have been a prolonged period of intense meditation. During that time he was visited by the divine Viṣvaksena, who had been sent by the lord from the heavenly Vaikuṇṭa to teach Śaṭakōpaṉ all that he needed to know about everything divine and human.

Placing the boy in isolated meditation in this way makes it clear that the songs occurs first of all *within* Śaṭakōpaṉ. *Tiruvāymoḻi* takes shape by an internal process and internal instruction, without input from the world around him. The *Divyasūricaritam* emphasizes this point when describing how the actual text came forth:

> When sixteen years had come to an end, his overwhelming happiness burst forth from within him like water from a full lake, appearing in the form of his poems. When he had composed various songs which were lovely by virtue of the Lord's qualities which they described, he immersed himself in the ocean of His bliss, swooned and then recovered.[19]

By that same *Divyasūricaritam* account, there was an external instigation for this eruption. Maturakavi, a man native to nearby Tirukkōḷūr but who had been travelling in far-off north

India, saw a light in the south, and travelled homeward in search of its source. He was eventually led all the way to Kurukūr where he found Śaṭakōpaṉ still meditating under the tamarind tree. Śaṭakōpaṉ took him as his disciple, and taught him the songs of *Tiruvāymoḻi* which came forth from within him all at once.[20]

The account in the *Guruparaṃparāprabhāvam* is distinctive in the details it adds to this account. As for the origins of the *āḻvār's* works, the lord Nārāyaṇa himself directly revealed to Śaṭakōpaṉ the lord's own proper self, his forms, qualities, glorious manifestations and saving deeds, and made him able to experience them to a fullness that would eventually burst forth from him. This is why the *āḻvār* begins *Tiruvāymoḻi* with the words, "Who possesses the highest, unsurpassable good? that One." (I.1.1) The *Guruparaṃparāprabhāvam* also notes another, significant divine visitation (presumably before rather than after the composition of the songs, though it is not clear): Śaṭakōpaṉ was visited by the tutelary deities of the temples he sang about; this was necessary assistance, since he never moved about, never actually visited the temples of which he sang. Even geography came from within.

Though of course we need to study such hagiographical accounts critically and soberly if we are to understand their function—without confusing it with history—still we can appreciate the perceptiveness of their three underlying claims regarding the source and composition of *Tiruvāymoḻi*. The first claim is that Śaṭakōpaṉ did not assemble materials for *Tiruvāymoḻi* from the world about him, from nature or temples or the community or texts of any sort; rather it all came from inside him, the fruit of his dialogue with God and assisting deities. Second, despite its perfection, *Tiruvāymoḻi* was not the product of a series of compositions gradually composed, refined, perfected; rather, it was fully experienced and perfectly composed within the mind and, it seems, *in silence*, only thereafter to come forth as a complete work, expressing his full experience of God. Third, *Tiruvāymoḻi* has its original, proper context and referent point neither in time nor in space: it is a text from within, spoken out into a wider world that is ordered by time and space. The hagiographies are (correctly) pointing us back into the world of the text itself; indirectly, at least, they support this present project of seeking an understanding from within of all that goes in the songs. The whole is as it were simultaneous to itself, though linearly extended; to know the part is to know the whole. To understand *Tiruvāymoḻi,* one must ultimately understand it all at once.

As we commit ourselves to getting inside *Tiruvāymoḻi,* to look around there, to see through it to where it comes from and what it means, we must attend to one more key element in this intertextual engagement: the profile of the reader who reads and interprets *Tiruvāymoḻi.* If this book is marked by its intention to stay with the whole of the text, it must also be distinguished by refining as much as possible a sense of the kinds of commitments readers have made (IV) and can make (V) in response to *Tiruvāymoḻi.*

IV. Joining the Conversation: Tiruvāymoḻi *and its* Ācāryas

Though each reader must in some way be solitary when faced with the text—each under his or her own tamarind tree, as it were—reading is not a solitary activity, any more than speaking is a private affair. We write from what we have read, we write to be read, and both are intertwined with our speaking and hearing. Reading is learned; a matter of habits, acquired tastes, and imitation. I teach as I have been taught, I read as I have seen my teachers read.

This book is premised in part on the idea that it is better to read with those who have read very well, to learn to hear *Tiruvāymoḻi* with the earliest readers of *Tiruvāymoḻi* by allowing them to reshape our habits and expectations, even if in the end we shall make up our own minds about what all this means. What they have to say shall preoccupy us in chapter 3 (where we examine how they understand *Śaṭakōpaṉ* in relation to *Tiruvāymoḻi*) and chapter 4 (where we examine what they expect from the Śrīvaiṣṇava community in response to *Tiruvāymoḻi*), but here let us simply introduce these wise readers, the *ācāryas* who trace themselves back to Śaṭakōpaṉ.

1. Introducing the Ācāryas and What They Thought

When I speak of the *ācāryas* of the Śrīvaiṣṇava tradition, I have in mind some early teachers whose teachings have come down to us in written form. All of them look back with the greatest reverence to Rāmānuja (1017–1137), the great Vedānta theologian whose writings provide the theoretical basis for Śrīvaiṣṇava theology, and whose life, remembered in the community, provides its inspirational measure. The *ācāryas* we shall be reading with are the following:

Tirukkurukaippirāṉ Piḷḷāṉ (12th century), a disciple of Rāmānuja, wrote the "6,000 unit commentary;"[21]

Nañcīyar (1182–1287), a disciple of Parāśara Bhaṭṭar (himself the son of Kurattāḻvār, a disciple of Rāmānuja), wrote the "9,000 unit commentary;"

Naṃpiḷḷai (beginning of the 13th century) lost the text of Nañcīyar's exposition in a river, tradition holds, but then wrote it down again in a style which Nañcīyar admired as an improvement on his own; Naṃpiḷḷai did not write a commentary but inspired the following three *ācāryas* to do so;

Vaṭakkutiruvītippiḷḷai (1217–1312) is said to have faithfully recorded Naṃpiḷḷai's discourses in the great *Īṭu*; the "36,000 unit commentary;"[22]

Periyavāccāṉpiḷḷai (b. 1228) crafted Naṃpiḷḷai's discourses into a formal commentary, the "24,000 unit commentary"—into a refined version of the "36,000;

Vātikesari Aḻakiya Maṇavāḷa Cīyar (1242–1350), another disciple of Naṃpiḷḷai, recapitulated and distilled Naṃpiḷḷai's teaching into a freestanding and original commentary, the "12,000 unit commentary."

I will also have occasion to refer to the observations of Āttāṉcīyar, whose *Aruṃpatam* is a commentary on the *Īṭu* and also, in the course of recollections recorded in the *Īṭu*, to the influential interpretations of Parāśara Bhaṭṭar, a disciple of Empār who was a disciple of Rāmānuja. Neither Parāśara Bhaṭṭar nor Empār wrote commentaries or had them recorded.

Let us first note the theological commitments that underlie their work at every stage, commitments that can be indicated by pointing to their identity as proponents of Vedānta. "Vedānta" generally refers to a body of concepts and a number of schools of thought which claim as their primary referent and authority the Sanskrit-language *Upaniṣads,* a group of texts from the middle and late Vedic period (after 800 BCE). In the *Upaniṣads,* speculation about the orthodox rituals of ancient India was increasingly accompanied by speculation on the nature of the world in which ritual is efficacious, on human nature, and on the nature of the "higher" or *post-mortem* reality which renders human experience ultimately significant. Inquiries into, and discourses about, the vital breath (*prāṇa*), the self (*ātman*), and the corresponding spiritual and cosmic principle (*brahman*) are prominent in the *Upaniṣads.* These upaniṣadic explorations proceed by experiment, by question and answer, by exposition and summation. In their rough texture they replicate earlier oral debates and inquiries. The most ancient *Upaniṣads* are only partially homogenized collections of still more ancient debates and teachings; they are not presented as single works by single authors, and are far from complete systematizations. Consequently, *Vedānta's* theological appropriations of the *Upaniṣads* are marked from the start as systematic projects of interpretation which had necessarily to go beyond the texts in bringing order to them. Bādarāyaṇa's *Uttara Mīmāṃsā Sūtras* (perhaps 4th or 5th century C.E.) is a set of 555 brief, terse aphorisms (*sūtras*) which ambition just such a (re)organization of upaniṣadic speculations into a system of thought focused on *brahman,* the absolute and transcendent, cosmic and microcosmic principle of life. As interior, *brahman* is occasionally equated with that Self/self known as the *ātman.* Recalling and revising the views of various earlier and probably contemporary *Vedānta* teachers, Bādarāyaṇa attempts a descriptive systematization of the *Upaniṣads,* a regularization of their meaning and identification of their main tenets.

Vedānta discourse is modelled on the paradigm of the older exegetical system known as the *Mīmāṃsā*, which was dedicated to the exegesis and rationalization of the Vedic rituals and the texts generative of them. Though claiming to move beyond *Mīmāṃsā, Vedānta* for the most part remains in continuity with *Mīmāṃsā* as its designated predecessor. If it introduces some concepts and practices incompatible with *Mīmāṃsā* and claims also to supersede it, even these claims are made according to the norms of *Mīmāṃsā* thinking. Vedāntins will argue at length that knowledge ought not to be thought of as an action, and that "to know" cannot be necessarily consequent upon "to do;" nevertheless, in its emphasis on the path to knowledge through meditation on texts, in its modes of exegesis, in its recognition that knowledge is gained gradually through engagement in the texts which are the subject of exegesis, and even in its treatment of the final realization of *brahman* as an actual event, it shares the *Mīmāṃsā* attunement to performance. Though *Vedānta* may appear more philosophical than *Mīmāṃsā*, its articulation of theory and doctrine resides within the confines of *Mīmāṃsā's* practical emphasis. It too roots all theoretical and doctrinal pronouncements in textual knowledge, and so persistently orients the seeker back into the practice of interpretation. Enlarging the canon of scripture to include the *Upaniṣads* (and, later, the *Bhagavad Gītā* and other texts), it nevertheless extends *Mīmāṃsā* modes of exegesis to the *Upaniṣads*. When we say that the Śrīvaiṣṇava *ācāryas* are commentators on *Tiruvāymoḻi* who are also indebted to the *Vedānta*, we are emphasizing that even their philosophical heritage is a heritage of reading and interpretation within which praxis is very central. The Śrīvaiṣṇava *ācāryas* are Vedāntins, and the Vedāntins are Mīmāṃsakas.

As direct disciples of Rāmānuja, the Śrīvaiṣṇava *ācāryas* accept his version of *Vedānta*, which preserves the distinction of *ātman* and *brahman* even in their ultimate state of oneness.[23] The *ācāryas* extend and specify and, to some extent, reprioritize his theology in light of the Tamil tradition. They fashion a *maṇipravāḷa*—an adornment of jewel and coral together—in bringing the languages together, and in reforming each way of thinking to enhance the other. Less elegantly, one might say they simply applied the Sanskritic ideas of Rāmānuja (who wrote nothing in Tamil) to Tamil materials; yet we need also to take seriously the claim of the Śrīvaiṣṇavas that Rāmānuja himself was deeply immersed in the Tamil tradition, and that his *Vedānta* is already deeply influenced by *Tiruvāymoḻi*.[24] Though this book is not the place to trace the mutual influences of Tamil devotion and *Vedānta* on one another, we shall see in chapter 3 how the theological problematic of vision as proposed by Rāmānuja is key to the *ācāryas'* formulation of what *Tiruvāymoḻi* is about, and how there may well be roots in *Tiruvāymoḻi* for Rāmānuja's thinking about the nature of meditation.

The key *Vedānta*/Śrīvaiṣṇava doctrines operative in the commentaries can be briefly summarized: Viṣṇu, Nārāyaṇa, is the one and only one supreme lord, beyond all other gods; he is eternally accompanied by his consort Śrī Lakṣmī; he is the only source of the world which is comprised of all things insentient and sentient; at opportune moments he descends (by *avatāra*) into the world with any of myriad animal and human forms, most famously as Rāma and Kṛṣṇa; he alone is the source of human happiness and the effector of human liberation from the mass of sufferings and pleasures which make up this world; he is to be approached with humble devotion and love; he is most pleased by the service devotees perform for one another; he is described accurately and efficaciously in the *Upaniṣads*, *Bhagavad Gītā*, the epics and *Purāṇas*, and can be known through meditation on those texts. The project of the *ācāryas* in their commentaries is the exposition of *Tiruvāymoḻi* as the theoretical and practical embodiment of these doctrines, the most articulate and beautiful presentation of the religious and moral life, the most direct way to know God in this life. Though these beliefs offer valuable points of entrance into the Śrīvaiṣṇava worldview and though one could approach the tradition thematically, tracing *Vedānta* themes to the commentaries and commentarial themes to the songs, even highlighting correlations with other theological traditions, the primary factor for our purposes is the lineage of teachers in whom even the textual tradition has subsisted, where the doctrines have their living place.

2. The Commentarial Conversation

The *ācāryas'* ongoing conversation is both expert and open to all. A high priority is placed on the expertise of *ācāryas* who have studied with revered senior teachers and learned how to read properly; it is also open, since the *ācāryas* also took great pains to make this treasured expertise accessible to the wider and less learned audience. Much of chapters 3 and 4 is devoted to an account of the theological, narrative and practical strategies by which they opened the text, highlighting its accessibility to listeners whose only necessary characteristic is the desire to see God, to serve God. On both counts, expertise and accessibility, finding one's place near this lineage of *ācāryas* and their disciples is the highest priority.

Śaṭakōpaṉ himself was quite aware of the importance of a community of devotees:

> *Keśava's people they have become,*
> *my people in seven generations before and after,*
> *gaining this great good fortune, our prosperity increases,*
> *due to the lord, our dark jewel, my lovely red Kāṇṇaṉ,*
> *lord of the heaven-dwellers, my lord, my ruler,*
> *Nārāyaṇa.* (II.7.1)

And,

> *Highest ruler, Kaṇṇaṉ, Himself the lord with the discus,*
> *my pure jewel-colored one with the marvellous four shoulders:*
> *see, those who worship him, joining hands to feet*
> *are the lords who rule me in all my births, for all days.* (III.7.2)
>
> *The lord, father, who ate the world once measured by his feet,*
> *who rested on the tree's leaf, the incomparable child:*
> *his servants' servants' servants' servants' servants' servants'*
> *servants*
> *are my masters.* (III.7.10)

Śaṭakōpaṉ, perhaps as author, perhaps as narrative voice in the text, may still appear to be acutely alone in certain songs:

I am not there, I am not here,
fallen into desire to see you, I am nowhere, lord, destroyer of
Laṅkā;
you live among the lofty buildings of Cirīvaramaṅkalanakar
with their jewels fit for the moon,
holder of conch and discus:
but I am alone, be gracious to me. (V.7.2)

But that loneliness is expressed and accentuated within a community, and to be with the community of believers matters all the more when one is alone:

I am alone, but those servants are our kings,
the servants of the servants of the servants of the eternal servants
of my lord in whose hand is the golden discus who has four arms,
a body like great kāyā flowers:
to get to be their family is my enduring glory. (VIII.10.10)

Obviously, Śaṭakōpaṉ is always striving to communicate to his contemporary audience—an audience which also turns out to be the community constituted around his songs. For more than a thousand years *Tiruvāymoḻi* has been heard and enjoyed by an attentive audience, cherished and handed down by the Śrīvaiṣṇavas of south India, orally and in writing, for use in meditation, ritual and study. Moreover, he set a tone that has been preserved as well: Śrīvaiṣṇavas situate themselves by their lineage, head to foot, sitting near their teachers, tracing their learning back to the great *ācāryas* at whose feet they wish to sit, and who themselves were at the feet of their teachers.

As we have seen, Maturakavi is considered by the tradition to be the one who discovered Śaṭakōpaṉ. His own verses deserves notice here, since these verses emphasize the deep bond between himself and Śaṭakōpaṉ, his *ācārya*, thereby setting the paradigm for future such relationships. In honor of Śaṭakōpaṉ Maturakavi composed eleven verses, the *Kaṇṇi nuṇ ciṟutāmpu* ("The knotted, slender cord"). These verses form the first extant statement about Śaṭakōpaṉ from outside *Tiruvāymoḻi*, an extraordinary indication of the reverence with which both text and author were to be treated in the Śrīvaiṣṇava tradition. Verses

1–6 introduce Maturakavi, the first person singer, and Śaṭakōpaṉ, "the lord of Kurukūr," and indicate the intense commitment of the former to the latter:

In place of my Father, the great marvellous one
who had himself tied with the knotted, slender cord,
I now draw near and speak of the lord of southern Kurukūr,
and it flows as ambrosia, my tongue's delight. (1)

I have gained the pleasure of praising him with my tongue;
I enjoy his golden feet,
truly, I know no other gods;
I wander, singing the sweet melodious songs of the lord of
Kurukūr. (2)

From now on and for seven births more
my abiding lord has graciously granted that I praise him;
see, the lord of Kurukūr with its mountainous houses never
scorns me. (6)

By his extraordinary reverence, Maturakavi places Śaṭakōpaṉ in the stead even of the lord whom Śaṭakōpaṉ was praising; obedient, loving recognition of one's *ācārya* is the surest approach to the lord.

Verses 7–9 emphasize the correspondence between Śaṭakōpaṉ's works and the Sanskrit *Vedas,* and assert the status of the 1,000 verses as Śaṭakōpaṉ's great gift to the world. This claim, common later in the tradition but not explicit in *Tiruvāymoḻi* itself, appears here first:

Lord Kārimāṟaṉ has seen me,
he has graciously destroyed my old, strong deeds;
I praise Śaṭakōpaṉ's gracious, splendid Tamil, all eight directions
know it. (7)

That devotees who praise his grace might gain pleasure,
he has graciously given the meaning of the difficult Vedas,
singing in sweet Tamil these gracious thousand verses;
see, his grace abounds in this world. (8)

The 11th verse self-consciously extends the tradition by investing Maturakavi's own words with religious power; each *ācārya* embodies the tradition:

Those who put their trust in this word spoken by Maturakavi
who is in love of the lord of southern Kurukūr town
who loves all those who reach Love himself:
see, their place is Vaikuṇṭa. (11)

A few generations later, after the songs were retrieved from oblivion by the sage Nātamuni, in the 10th century Āḷavantār (Yāmuna) gives us the first Sanskrit words in praise of Śaṭakōpaṉ. In his *Stotraratna,* he first praises his immediate teachers, Nātamuni and Parāśara (1–3, 4), and then lauds Śaṭakōpaṉ, "the lord of our family," in words that echo Maturakavi's confession:

I reverently bow down my head to the blessed feet of the first
lord of our family,
pleasing with vakula flowers, alone eternally mother, father,
women, sons and wealth
to every one of my relatives. (5)[25]

The rest of the *Stotraratna* is devoted to the lord alone.

For Āḷavantār, Śaṭakōpaṉ is first in the line of teachers after the lord himself, he is the link between the lord and all subsequent teachers. Śaṭakōpaṉ transmits the sacred teaching by speaking from his vantage point at the lord's feet, and thus makes the basic value clear: to be at the feet of one's teacher—prostrate, but also sitting there as a student, truly docile, ready to be taught—puts one in touch with the lord, so that thereafter one's own words too become the occasion of proximity for those who come later. It is the task of the *ācāryas* who follow Maturakavi and Āḷavantār to embody the wisdom of the songs for each generation of the community, a succession of learners and teachers.

We do not have much further information on *Tiruvāymoḻi*'s reception before the time of Rāmānuja, excepting some anecdotes preserved in later commentaries, about how Rāmānuja and others learned *Tiruvāymoḻi.* In the period after Rāmānuja, however, the evidence is abundant; the connected, serial commentaries of the *ācāryas*—Piḷḷāṉ, Nañcīyar, Naṃpiḷḷai, Vaṭakkutiruvītippiḷḷai, Periyavāccāṉpiḷḷai and Vātikesari Aḻakiya Maṇavāḷa Cīyar—document both the fact and substance of traditional learning.

The style and development of the increasingly larger commentaries indicate an irenic and progressive development. This development may be put schematically as follows, as far as the written texts are concerned:

- Piḷḷāṉ offers a prose summary of the verse of *Tiruvāymoḻi*, drawing heavily on Rāmānuja's Sanskrit terminology;
- Nañcīyar offers a brief opening comment on the verse, and then a series of specific comments elucidating particularly difficult or interesting words in the text;
- Periyavāccāṉppiḷḷai incorporates almost everything found in Nañcīyar's commentary, but amplifies it with comments on more of the individual words and with more elaborate and philosophical expositions of the ideas in the songs;
- Vaṭakkutiruvītippiḷḷai, recording Naṃpiḷḷai faithfully, says more in every way. It is tempting to say that Vaṭakkutiruvītippiḷḷai's commentary is a fuller version of Periyavāccāṉpiḷḷai's but, if we respect the tradition that both are reports of Naṃpiḷḷai's teachings, it is more accurate to see Periyavāccāṉpiḷḷai's as a "condensation" of Naṃpiḷḷai's teaching which was recorded more expansively in Vaṭakkutiruvītippiḷḷai's *Īṭu*.

Even if one finds original elements in each of the commentaries, the repetition is enormous: most of Nañcīyar's commentary recurs in Periyavāccāṉpiḷḷai's, and most of his in the *Īṭu*. This repetition is indulged and enjoyed, as is indicated by the persistence of reverence for all these commentaries (plus later ones too) over many generations, and it is a key indicator of the sensitivities of the Śrīvaiṣṇava *ācāryas*. Within certain limits—particularly in expectation of what we will learn through further "archaeological" studies in the history of the commentaries—we can entertain the idea that there is really just one "Śrīvaiṣṇava explication" of *Tiruvāymoḻi*. The Śrīvaiṣṇava commentaries comprise a single complex conversation among like-minded devotees; it is proper to think of each of these early commentaries as the incorporation and amplification of earlier commentaries, in an atmosphere largely devoid of interpretive and doctrinal differences. To read the commentaries entails tracing the various contractions and expansions of this single discourse, learning its language and style, habits and shorthand; it is a matter of becoming familiar, in a way, a part of the family.[26]

I have stressed these conversational and communal aspects of the Śrīvaiṣṇava tradition in order to indicate our point of entrance into the traditional understanding of *Tiruvāymoḻi*, a task which will preoccupy us in chapters 3 and 4 and, implicitly, color the interpretation of the "songs themselves" in chapter 2. To read with the *ācāryas* is a valuable aid to our understanding of *Tiruvāymoḻi*, and a wise undertaking, even if at some point we must make our own independent judgments. We profit from moving back and forth between the commentaries and the songs, seeking to understand the subtle comments and the larger patterns of interpretation. The tone of this book is therefore irenic; we read with the *ācāryas*, even if we have our own words to contribute.

A great opportunity becomes available to us when we decide to read with the commentators rather in a merely utilitarian fashion, whereby we borrow their explanations without respecting their interpretations. With their help we are drawn, in a certain way, into each song's worldview, and into the deeper moral and spiritual commitments it entails. In particular, to read with Naṃpiḷḷai—i.e., Naṃpiḷḷai as recorded by Vaṭakkutiruvītippiḷḷai—is to begin to share the memories of the early Śrīvaiṣṇava community, and gradually to come into contact with the surrounding environs of the tradition, from a starting point in its inside. The *Iṭu* is a peculiarly formative text, one which educates us on these various levels at once. By the time we consider certain texts from the Biblical and Christian traditions in chapter 5, our expectation is that we shall be looking into those texts newly, with eyes opened in the course of sharing the Śrīvaiṣṇava conversation.

V. Being a Reader of Tiruvāymoḻi, *Now*

We have thus far introduced *Tiruvāymoḻi,* Śaṭakōpaṉ, and the *ācāryas,* introducing the issues which will generally occupy us in chapters 2, 3 and 4, respectively. Thus far it has sufficed to emphasize how it is possible, within clear but viable limitations, to read *Tiruvāymoḻi* from within, as a carefully formed text which invites readers to certain kinds of reading, thinking, imagination. This has been done for centuries, it can be done now. Of course, as readers are engaging attentively in the songs themselves, they also find their way back to issues of author and authority, doctrine and theme, context and traditions, the range of issues which are properly subsequent and not prior to engagement in the songs themselves. A great deal can be accomplished, I suggest, just by taking the texts—the available, published, translated texts—seriously.

However, the more available these resources, the more skilled and judicious the reading of them must be for the venture to be a worthwhile one. A great deal depends on becoming a skillful reader who can read the songs and the commentaries carefully, with sensitivity.

Since we are concerned with whether this engagement might add up to something worthwhile—whether it might lead the reader beyond observation and study and toward positive commitments, we must also specify the identity of the vulnerable, open reader from outside the Śrīvaiṣṇava tradition: the reader who maintains his or her own religious commitments, if any, and yet also takes seriously the claims and invitations posed by another religious tradition. What does the reader need to take into account from his or her own background? What matters—not only in regard to how one reads, but also in regard to the commitments one has already made, when one becomes a reader of *Tiruvāymoḻi* and its commentaries? And how specific must one get, personally or by making oneself an example—to be described, critiqued—in the course of one's project? How does it matter (for this book, for instance) that I am a Roman Catholic born in the United States, reading and writing at the end of the 20th century? How do I deal with the demands of *Tiruvāymoḻi*—and how might this differ from the way other readers would manage this? To answer such questions, I must now say something about theological commitments (1), the opportunities created by this particular theological comparison (2), and the functional (given and reconstructed) identity of this author in this project (3). Introduced here, all three concerns will recur in an ampler form in chapter 5.

1. Comparative, Theological Commitments

In an earlier study, *Theology after Vedānta,* I presented a number of preliminary ideas on comparative theology as a theology that remains rooted in one tradition while seriously engaging another tradition and allowing that engagement to affect one's original commitments. As theological, it hearkens back in some way or another to the basic features and requirements of theology as "faith seeking understanding," as an inquiry which seeks knowledge of God as a meaningful and possible goal. As comparative, it locates both the possibilities and the obstacles in a context composed of more than one religious tradition.

In the context of initiating a relatively new kind of study of the Non-Dualist (*Advaita*) tradition of *Vedānta*—as a primarily exegetical and commentarial school of theological discourse—*Theology after Vedānta* emphasized the importance of an engaged and patient commitment to the project of understanding the tradition one is encountering, while yet neither neutralizing nor merely bracketing one's own prior commitments in the process of taking that other tradition seriously. In defining the vehicle of this simultaneous openness and commitment, I proposed that we focus our attention on the process of reading, and in particular on what happens when we read the texts of traditions other than our own. Though one could also proceed with a focus on images, rites, etc., reading is in fact the primary vehicle of study for most of us. As trained readers we are accustomed to balance attentiveness to what is new with a sophisticated (re)use of what we already know. Whatever our academic and theological loyalties may be, we nevertheless can and do read texts which we neither fully understand nor, as we come to understand them, fully agree with. Whatever our commitments, the things we read will have some effect on what we read next and how we read it. In this process of learning, the goal is not neutrality, but a critical awareness of the influences which affect what one is doing at any given point in a comparison. Analogously, but also by the simple fact that most theology, comparative and otherwise, is "book learning" at some crucial stage, I suggested that comparative theology is best understood as an experiment in careful reading, accompanied by all the balancing acts that reading entails.[27]

Though comparative and theological at its roots, the present study differs in certain respects, due to the difference between *Tiruvāymoḻi* and the *Vedānta* texts. It is one thing to do a comparative study based on the *Upaniṣads* and the *Vedānta* systematization of the *Upaniṣads,* and quite another to study *Tiruvāymoḻi.* These texts are quite different in content, style and intent; they provoke different responses—in their traditions and in today's readers—and thus raise different Indological and theological issues. Even in Rāmānuja's school, as a Sanskrit tradition, *Vedānta* did not dwell on concrete particulars in their perceptible accessibility and locality with the same intensity as does Śaṭakōpaṉ and the Śrīvaiṣṇava *ācāryas;* the problem of the young woman at Tirutolaivillimaṅkalam cannot, on the face of it, be appreciated as a problem Vedāntins would worry about.

When we turn to *Tiruvāymoḻi* in its Śrīvaiṣṇava milieu, we are faced with passionate and particular commitments mediated through textual knowledge. Instead of an (aural) realization that comes after (hearing) texts, we have the possibility of traversing the spatiality of the work to a kind of insight, or a seeing through it. We thus push comparative study to a certain extreme, where its scholarly and speculative nature is deliberately endangered by the prospects of affective absorption, a falling in love that is not simply synonymous with Vedāntic realization. Accordingly, this comparison must proceed differently than did the comparison undertaken in *Theology after*

Vedānta. When we turn to *Tiruvāymoḻi*, we are dealing with a text which engages us in its particularity, where the import of the particular is central, where the disposition of the particular things one receives is the basic point: when does one fall in love? To whom does one give oneself? Like the young woman in the song, the reader here may possibly be drawn into a particular religious moment, attracted to one song in particular, but inevitably too to the hundred songs in *Tiruvāymoḻi*, which itself finds its place among the large collection known as the *Divya Prabandham*, in the context of older Tamil literature, etc. One may find oneself attracted to this particular temple at Tolaivillimaṅkalam, to the sacred image in the center of the temple, or to the God who is present(ed), and spoken about in these words. The reader may also be drawn into the community of those who listen to the song—with or without taking the further step of becoming a member of that community (which itself may or may not welcome such interest).

2. This Particular Venture: Seeing Christianity and Śrīvaiṣṇavism Together

Of course, not all reading and not all theologies are the same. This inquiry begins with a certain kind of theological interest that perhaps only an author with strong classicist tendencies and Roman Catholic "scholastic" instincts (of an old-fashioned sort) would entertain. It would certainly be wrong to suggest that what follows is the only way into the Śrīvaiṣṇava tradition, even in its commentarial form. Nevertheless, I suggest that this approach will prove to be a very productive one. There is much in favor of this particular comparative encounter between the Śrīvaiṣṇava tradition and the (Roman Catholic) Christian tradition as I understand it. There are many particular theological, exegetical, liturgical similarities which generate a favorable atmosphere.

Some general points of consonance can be stated briefly: both traditions are theistic and, in regard to soteriological concerns, in fact monotheistic too; the reality of the world and the real distinction between humans and God is defended; human activity is valued, while grace is given primacy; reason is valued, scripture given a central role, and tradition taken very seriously; moral values are kept closely aligned with religious ones, as are the intellectual and the spiritual. Five features deserve special notice.

First, Śrīvaiṣṇavas hold that the experience of God is real but mediated through human realities; this experience is natural and constructed, visual and verbal, present and distant and remembered, private and communal, observed and participatory. This view is familiar to the Jewish and Christian traditions. Even when the Hebrew Bible resists making images of God, this is not to deny that God can be immediately present or possibly experienced, but rather to insist that experience does not occur by way of spectacle, objectifying and controlling; one meets God in God's great deeds, and one responds through a corresponding hearing and doing of the word of God; the delay of vision is interconnected with the commitment to service. Nevertheless, the Christian tradition, somewhat cautiously at first, managed to balance a commitment to sight with an enduring emphasis on word. Even the Incarnation—which, from the Christian perspective, is the direct appearing of God in the person of Jesus—is balanced with the enduring invisibility of the Father, even as Jesus is understood as the Word of God. The Word remains simultaneously a direct and indirect means of encountering God, one sees God through this Word, if one can see what is being said. Even the Christian mystical tradition—if again we may generalize very broadly!—is on the one hand oriented to direct experience and cognizant that words must be transcended, while on the other it is quite evidently committed to the value of words in creating situations in which verbal knowledge has a limited but real propaedeutic purpose.[28] The problematics related to experience, its delay and enablement by mediation(s), and the need to undertake some deliberate strategies to find one's way through the resources of one's traditions in order to reach God: these are problematics common to both the Śrīvaiṣṇava tradition and the Christian tradition.

Second, to compare these traditions is to take up the project of universalization shared by both traditions. Both traditions seek to place their "others," their "outsiders" properly and vis à vis themselves. Comparison is an inevitable need of each tradition, even before one goes about comparing them one to the other.

Third, both traditions balance commitments to truth and an unlimited desire for God with sober, realistic apprehensions of what is perceived possible in a given situation. However such points are made theologically, both traditions understand the value of nature and the need for grace, the finitude of the human condition and virtually unlimited possibilities before any given person. Desire is not denied, though it is focused and infused through other, intermediate aspects of what one does.

Fourth, stressing community, the Christian tradition, like the Śrīvaiṣṇava, ultimately expects the individual to stand freely in face of the basic issues of sin, truth, salvation, encounter with God. However extensive and formally complete theology becomes, the individual must work through the specific implications of what is known in general: Christians and Śrīvaiṣṇavas agree that one must practice one's faith, freely enacting it.

Fifth, like *Tiruvāymoḻi*, the classics of the Christian exegetical, spiritual and theological traditions encourage attitudes and practices which will lead toward (a kind of) direct experience of God. In neither tradition is reading just reading. Texts are not simply there, passive and available to the curious; rather, they make great demands on us. Neither tradition welcomes merely casual observation or unengaged readings. When we view the two traditions together and read their texts at the same time, the various formal considerations of the theory and practice of comparison, though indispensable, stand merely as parts of a longer process where issues of understanding merge into issues of self-identity, encounter and response. The problems of comparison recede into the background in deference to more immediate and urgent concerns. Like the Śrīvaiṣṇava tradition, the Christian tradition presents and expects complete ways of looking at the world: religious texts have to do with personal and communal experience, they are to be taken along with ritual practices, they expect moral implementation and they enable whole ways of life; the emotional, instinctive and spiritual are imbued with reason, and invite the most strenuous exercise of the human mind; reason does not remain cool and detached, the project is no longer one to be completed satisfactorily, on time.

The particular venture undertaken in this volume asks how an attempted engagement in Śrīvaiṣṇava materials leads to a certain kind of retrieval of the Christian tradition, a second look at it, a re-reading of it. Like other practices, this depends in important ways on the particular practitioner, so the preceding general indications must be supplemental to more personal ones.

3. This Theologian

It is a delicate issue whether an author should say anything about himself or herself in setting up the prospects and boundaries of a book, and there are good reasons for maintaining the virtues of scholarly objectivity and distance. Yet today most of us are also comfortable with the idea that not only do subjective elements intrude in every research project, but also that it is wise to take these intrusions into account positively, tracing how they help to shape and deform the scholarly agenda, rather than merely engaging in the endless quest to eradicate such influences. In theology, where commitments are explicitly at issue, it is just as well to pay attention from the start to the particular ways in which one's interests and narrowed concerns affect one's work. We saw earlier how Śaṭakōpaṉ seems to be using his own self as one more resource in the array of resources available to him in his reconfiguration of the religious universe. In chapter 4 we shall see how the *ācāryas* themselves become resources in their project of making *Tiruvāymoḻi* practically accessible to their audience: see what has happened to us, let it happen to you. If the intentions, skills and fate of the comparative theologian are at issue in this study, it is appropriate to say something about where this author, by way of example, stands at the beginning of the particular venture.

When I arrived at the University of Chicago for Ph.D. studies in 1979, after a number of years of theological study, I met

A.K. Rāmānujan, who was at that time Chair of the Department of South Asian Languages and Civilizations, as well as Professor of Tamil. Just about the first thing he said to me was that I would do well to study Tamil and that, given my interests, I should quickly move on to a study of the *ālvārs* and the Śrīvaiṣṇava commentaries on them. He was, in his own soft-spoken but right-to-the-heart-of-things fashion, giving me a sense of where my studies were to go, beyond the plans I had already made for studies in the Sanskrit tradition. Though not a theologian, he knew what would intrigue the theologian and merit attention from theological as well as Indological perspectives. It was a while before I could begin to read the texts he mentioned—I had to learn Tamil first, under the able supervision of James Lindholm and Norman Cutler—but when I was ready, Rāmānujan was there, willing to read both songs and commentaries with me. We began our reading with these verses, rich in vivid detail and yet ripe for a Vedāntic reading:

Lustrous eyes, full ripe red lips, white bright teeth within,
crocodile earrings, shaking and shining,
four arms, bent bow, bright conch, club, discus, sword:
that peerless one is inside me at his feet.

Inside me at his feet, inside my body, inside the cosmic egg,
inside what's outside it:
you may say "He is like this," but he isn't;
higher than the highest, his is that great unceasing joy which by
nature destroys joys and sorrows:
honey with pervasive fragrance, the peerless one, beyond thought.

Beyond thought, the peerless one, by his grace
in my thought I have placed him, to hold him, and that too is his
sweet grace.
All mind, all breath, all body, the infinite are mere waste,
so he makes me think,
in the end, he ended up as me himself. (VIII.8.1–3)[29]

At this point, I was hooked; my study of the *ālvārs* was to be more than a casual glance, a long inquiry had begun.

By the time I went to Madras for dissertation research in *Pūrva Mīmāṃsā* in 1982, I was also somewhat familiar with

Tamil, and able to find my way about in Śaṭakōpaṉ's songs and the commentaries on them. Though most of that first stay in Madras was devoted to the reading of Sanskrit texts, I was able, in the summer and fall of 1983, to read the First Introduction (*Mutal Śriyaḥpaṭi*) to the *Īṭu* with Professor A. Thiruvengadathan, at that time professor at the Vaiṣṇava College in Madras. With the help of Professor Thiruvengadathan and of Professor M.A. Venkatakrishnan at the University of Madras, I also acquired the primary texts needed for study of the *āḻvārs*.

Back in America, after taking up my current teaching position at Boston College in 1984, I undertook the longterm project of doing a complete English translation of *Tiruvāymoḻi* for use in class. As the basis for work in the commentaries, I wanted to resist the temptation to become too immersed in the commentaries without first having become knowledgeable of the songs themselves. By 1992 I had completed my translation and, by a fortunate turn of events, was collaborating with Rāmānujan, Vasudha Narayanan and John Carman, in the production of a new and definitive translation of *Tiruvāymoḻi* for publication.

During 1992–3 I used my sabbatical in Madras to embark on a prolonged effort to become more deeply involved in the world of the *ācāryas*. Though not hoping to achieve anything approaching mastery of the text, I was interested in becoming as open to it as possible, both the songs and the commentaries. By an effective but (for me) unusual route—by meeting devotees and asking around at the Keśava Perumāḷ temple in Mylapore, Madras—I came in contact with two learned teachers who would be of inestimable help to me during the 10 months I was to spend in Madras. The first was Kumaravati Ramanujacharya, a learned teacher and the editor of *Tirumāl*, a monthly Vaiṣṇava publication. He allowed me to sit in on his home classes on the *Iṭu*, at first once a week but then increased to twice a week in the latter part of the year. The second was T.E. Sampath Kumaran, Professor of Philosophy at Vivekananda College and proud descendent of the family of the great 15th century *ācārya* Śrī Maṇavāḷamāmuni. He generously gave me two or more hours of his time each day in reading extended sections of the *Iṭu* and answering my questions on whatever other sections I was examining on my own. For part of the year I was also to read with Professor Venkatakrishnan at the university.

In order to understand the milieu of the text and commentaries, I also undertook a series of related practices for the year. I acquired tapes of the whole of *Tiruvāymoḻi* and began listening to one or more songs each day, a practice I continued back here in Boston until the completion of this book. I also made it a habit to visit a temple every day, a practice which allowed for great variety in Madras, a city with many small and large temples. These visits not only gave me a feel for the daily worship of Hindus and of Vaiṣṇavas in particular, but also introduced me to a number of friendly Vaiṣṇavas who were only too ready to help me in my project. The priests at the Lakṣmī temple in Besant Nagar were notably friendly, and K. Ramadurai Bhattacharya, the priest at the Mātava Perumāḷ temple in the Mylapore section of Madras, was very friendly and helpful, always concerned that I know the temple schedule and feel welcome at the various *pūjās* and festivals. Sri Satakopanacharya, the *adhyāpaka* (reciter and teacher of the *Tiruvāymoḻi* and the other works in the *Divya Prabandham*) at another Śrīvaiṣṇava temple, the Keśava Perumāl, was always ready to give me advice, and to make sure that I knew about upcoming festivals, particularly those at which *Tiruvāymoḻi* was to be recited. By the end of my stay, I had been present for large parts of three complete recitations of *Tiruvāymoḻi*.

Trips outside Madras enabled me to visit a number of the temples praised by Śaṭakōpaṉ in *Tiruvāymoḻi*, particularly Tiruveṅkaṭam (at Tirupati), Tirukuṭantai (in Kumbakonam), Tirukkaṇṇapuram, Śrīraṅgam, Tirumāliruṅcōlai and most importantly for my purposes, Tirukkurukūr (Āḻvārtirunagari), the temple town where Śaṭakōpaṉ is said to have meditated and composed *Tiruvāymoḻi*. Due to the gracious hospitality of Śri Anaviar Srinivasan, I was able to spend a week at Tirukkurukūr during the great festival in the month of December–January, and thus observe closely the celebration of the *āḻvār* and his *Tiruvāymoḻi*.

In all of these situations, both in study and in travel, I remained an exotic, marginal figure. I certainly did not blend in by appearance, my spoken Tamil has remained earnest but "in need of practice;" I was always quite open about the fact that while I came with a determination to be more than a mere spectator and was seeking earnestly to step back from my presuppositions about what I was hearing and seeing, I nevertheless remained always a Jesuit, a Roman Catholic priest who was also helping out on Sunday mornings in a large urban parish, etc. I was interested in entering a new conversation, while keeping old commitments; it was as if, like the Śrīvaiṣṇavas themselves, I was fashioning my own *maṇi-pravāḷa* discourse. Half-jokingly, people suggested to me that I had been a Śrīvaiṣṇava in seven previous births, or that I was a latter-day Maturakavi, come from afar to see this glorious, south Indian light. Still, I neither looked nor sounded the part.

Sometimes I would encounter "Hindu only" signs which, though sometimes serving only to exclude casual tourists, but often intended also to exclude even devout foreigners—such as members of ISKCON—who lived as believing Hindus, often at great personal sacrifice. I remember vividly the debate which occurred among the staff at one temple in Madras regarding the kind of statement I would have to sign in order to be allowed in; when it turned out that it would have been a testimony that I actually was a Hindu (and not just a Śrīvaiṣṇava!)—"fully believing everything in the Hindu religion"—I had to decline the offer. At Śrīraṅgam, the contrast of openness and closedness was most remarkable. Though I could not enter very far into that famous and grand temple, I was amply and generously provided with every possible text in praise of the temple. Though I could not approach the place where the *ācāryas* revelled in the beauty of Viṣṇu as Lord Raṅganātha, where they thrilled him with their recitation and exposition of *Tiruvāymoḻi*, I could read the songs of *Tiruvāymoḻi* that so pleased Lord Raṅganātha, plus the intimate accounts of how they themselves were caught up in the songs. Though I could not visit the pavillion inside the temple where Rāmānuja had taught the highest forms of devotion to one and all, there was no problem in purchasing and reading his hymns in praise of the lord's accessibility. The temple doors were, at a certain point, closed, and temple vision forbidden; but by contrast, the texts were very accessible, very open, very available. Whatever I was going to see, I would see through texts. I had been given the secondary means and denied the primary; or was it the other way around?

The whole experience had a great deal to do with facing my own limits—race and family, culture and religions, skills and levels of ineptitude—and facing the limits imposed on me by others. I was very interested, involved and, by the standard of foreign visitors, knowledgeable about *Tiruvāymoḻi* and the commentaries. But I was not a member of the Śrīvaiṣṇava community, and there were remarkable deficiencies in what I knew. I and my Śrīvaiṣṇava friends had to learn how to respond to one another, sorting out levels of knowledge, ways of conversing and arguing, commitments, traditions, attitudes toward novelty. I had come to talk with them, but they had to decide whether they wanted to talk with me.

This book is deeply imbued with the questions that arose during that time, and the effort to discover the limits and possibilities of textual knowledge is rooted in that year—and the preceding, preparatory years—of reading Śrīvaiṣṇava texts and (re)doing my theology among the Śrīvaiṣṇavas. Chapters 2, 3, and 4 can be taken as written accounts—in which this author is for the most part concealed—of what I learned through *Tiruvāymoḻi* and the ācāryas' readings of it, while chapter 5 can be understood as a certain kind of literary and theological representation—a kind of biblio/biography—of what I came to see through these texts. As I suggest in chapter 5, this book is biographical and bibliographical at the same time and, after a manner of speaking, even biological. It is about how one is alive, or enlivened, by reading and seeing.

VI. Where All of This Leads

In the preceding pages we have considered text and context, author, and the community of *Tiruvāymoḻi* readers and theologians, ancient and modern. If changes of mind and heart are possible, then the stakes in an inquiry across religious boundaries turn out to be very high indeed. It matters very much how one or another particular reader goes about saying what is gained through this reading. At issue is the "more" promised by comparative study, whether an openness to what one studies can be defended as coherent with commitments already made, whether it is worthwhile, and by what standards one can assess what is achieved in this process. Yet this "more" must be small, quiet, and modest enough that it invites rather than demands attention. On the whole, the goal is more a reappropriation of the old than a discovery of the novel.

There is an interesting account in the commentaries, at song II.7, which captures the ambivalence traditions have regarding novelty: it must happen, but preferably some other time. The discussion is occasioned by the problem of the connection between the fourth and fifth verses of the song. The fourth verse mentions Kōvalaṉ and his great deeds:

> *"Kōvintaṉ, Pot-dancer, Kōvalaṉ," I repeat again and again,*
> *bowing low, singing of his divinity, his nature, as I dance;*
> *he takes hold of me, destroying, discarding my sin,*
> *he makes my people for seven generations each way desire him,*
> *my lord is mighty, my Viṣṇu* (II.7.4),

while verse 5 is a meditation on the appearance of Viṣṇu:

> *Viṣṇu, radiant light; lotuses: his feet hands eyes,*
> *pervading, radiant dark shining mountain: his body,*
> *pervading, radiant moon: his conch, his discus: the sun,*
> *pervading, radiant hair,*
> *my lord, Matusūtaṉa—it's all for him.* (II.7.5)

The question which bothers the *ācāryas* is this: why does verse five follow verse four? They presume that there must be reasons for the sequence in the text itself, ready to be uncovered by attentive readers. Naṃpiḷḷai recalls a conversation between Rāmānuja and his teacher Āṇṭāṉ on just this point, and whether one should finally limit one's curiosity and be content with reasons already given. Āṇṭāṉ seems to have held Āḷavantar's view regarding the rationale for the sequence of II.7.4 and 5: verse 4 tells us what the lord does, while verse 5 simply tells us who the lord, the divine agent, is. He is satisfied with that interpretation, and is therefore upset when Rāmānuja asks for more:

> So one day Āṇṭāṉ said [regarding verses 4 and 5], "Surely you need not to do a Viśvāmitra creation here!"[30] But Rāmānuja responded, "In this verse, the *āḻvār* means, 'It is by the beauty of His members that He has made me His own.'"

Rāmānuja does not dispute the older, accepted viewpoint, but he is dedicated to the equally traditional expectation that there are sufficient and satisfying reasons everywhere in the songs. So he suggests a reading that strengthens the connection between the verses: the lord is able to aid his devotees (in verse 4), *because* of his radiance (in verse 5). Without criticizing either viewpoint, Naṃpiḷḷai then recalls a third reading, given a generation later by Parāśara Bhaṭṭar, who sees the verse as telling us how the lord is changed in the course of his experience of the *āḻvār*: "This fifth verse speaks of the brilliance that is born in the lord's sacred body when he has made the *āḻvār* and the *āḻvār's* companions his own:" i.e., the lord becomes radiant *because of* his interaction with his devotees.[31]

It seems clear that there is nothing terribly novel or disruptive at stake in these three interpretations of the sequence of verses, at least insofar as the measure is orthodoxy and reverence for the songs and for the tradition of teachers. Āṇṭāṉ, Rāmānuja and Bhaṭṭar share the same commitments, the same theological positions, and the same confidence in commentary. They agree that exegesis is possible and worthwhile, and they remain in substantial agreement on everything involved. Yet Rāmānuja and Bhaṭṭar offer interpretations which go beyond what their predecessors said. In this case at least Āṇṭāṉ represents the tendency of the community to rest content with older viewpoints and to fail to see the value of fresh ideas; yet the songs overflow these boundaries.

Though by definition this book is a venture that crosses traditional boundaries, it is best seen as offering something new only in the most selective of ways, as reopening the old: one peers into the other, one sees oneself differently, and the violation of tradition is also a rediscovery. Once a conversation across religious boundaries is under way—in this case by reading texts and their commentaries—it becomes necessary to balance a dual commitment to one's own tradition and to finding out what is in the texts and how it matters to those who live by them. The goal is to participate in a wider conversation, to hear and see more, yet in a way that remains recognizable to one's conversation partners, old and new, without merely doing something novel: for example, to change from within, as Rāmānuja and Bhaṭṭar find Viṣṇu to be changing, growing newly radiant. To achieve this, sheer novelty and bold progress must be eschewed, giving way to smaller and more enduring changes that take place from the inside out, until everything is irreversibly transformed and splendid. This seems to have been the point at Tolaivillimaṅkalam, where the young woman was captivated not by a startling new revelation, but by what everyone else had long known and taken for granted. There was no revelation, only a fresh apprehension of what had always been there, seen a thousand times before. She unsettled her friends by taking seriously what they had seen a thousand times.

If we are to move forward slowly, incrementally, to see where we end up when we begin to get involved in these songs, then we have to work through them, step by step, to see where this leads us. We cannot see around them, we have to see through them. Such is the task of the next three chapters. In the short-run, progress toward answers to the larger questions of comparison will seem minimal, for we shall be concerned mainly with details—as much as possible staying on the surface of things, describing what is said, in relation to what else. We need to learn to be observant, to see what is evident, patiently and without haste, enjoying what we notice, and being content with this kind of religious observance, so to speak. The goal of the following chapters then is both to describe something of what I have found in reading *Tiruvāymoḻi* and the traditional interpretation of it, and by this differentiated account, to make it possible for the interested reader of this book to begin to imagine and think within the same boundaries of text and commentary, or to do more than a comparison of theologies: to do theology among the Śrīvaiṣṇavas.

In chapter 2, I offer a comprehensive characterization of *Tiruvāymoḻi* in order to recognize and appreciate the varied possibilities opened up by the dazzling array of songs. I also say something about the way the text both in its parts and as a whole interacts with readers' expectations, and (even more hypothetically) about what it means to begin to live within the worldview sketched by Śaṭakōpaṉ in his 100 songs.

In chapters 3 and 4 I describe the reading that was undertaken by the Śrīvaiṣṇava *ācāryas,* with an eye toward making their reading available as one we can share, provisionally, in a way, to some extent. In chapter 3, I describe their construction of an integral reading of the text, as they combine literary insights with prior theological understandings in order to achieve, finally, a richly filled-out narrative and dramatic rendering of *Tiruvāymoḻi.* In chapter 4 I turn to their practical interpretation of the songs as implemented in five specific strategies, as they persuade and enable readers to become participants in the text they hear, recite, and study.

These considerations open the way for chapter 5, where we return to the concerns raised in this chapter, and describe, still in an introductory way, what happens to the committed reader who begins to see, again, through *Tiruvāymoḻi,* albeit from outside the tradition that has flourished around the songs. There I widen the context for our reflection by introducing a series of texts from the Biblical and Christian traditions, arranging them by memory, as it were, around *Tiruvāymoḻi,* which remains the center of our attention. Yet even at its conclusion, this book will remain in a way speechless, bereft of a fully systematic presentation of the ideas behind the heard and the seen: it will remain a project to be completed by the reader at another time. There is all the more reason, then, to insist that the last chapter cannot make sense on its own: it follows from chapters 2, 3 and 4, it is a response, not a summation; the answers are not given at the back of the book.

Somewhat imaginatively, then, but with serious intent, we are seeking to write this volume from within the crisis that occurs in VI.5, near the temple, near the young woman. We want to see where paying attention gets one, where the limits of detached scholarship lie, where one can stand, sympathetic, scholarly, committed and yet open, and where one crosses boundaries too far and gets lost:

The poor thing, she melts, her face shines, for after entering
Tirutolaivillimaṅkalam
you showed her the lord with the red lotus eyes, the splendid
light;
starting then, her eyes have rained like clouds, she is amazed,
women,
her mind has gone inside there,
she keeps on looking in that direction, worshipping. (VI.5.5)

Chapter 2

Getting Inside *Tiruvāymoli*

"He became the cowherd, he became the fish and boar;"
as soon as you say this, he's become a million more. (I.8.8)

Our lord is hard to know when they say, "He is of this nature;"
our lord is easy to know when they say, "He is of this nature;"
our lord has a thousand names and many forms;
"no, he hasn't any name and form;" "no, he's not lacking them:"
that's the dispute. (I.3.4)

Singers of fine words, look after yourselves, serve him:
that marvellous deceiver and thief from Tirumāliruñcōlai
has come as a great poet and mixed inside my heart
in a way people don't notice
he has eaten my heart and mind and become me himself
filling me completely. (X.7.1)

I. Listening to the Songs

1. A Dubious Beginning

What is *Tiruvāymoli* like and what is one to do with it? Is it possible, how would it be possible, to act properly—or listen properly, so as to awaken one's imagination adequately, to make credible comparisons, to write theology in response to this text—if one is not already a Śrīvaiṣṇava within the cultural and theological tradition of this south Indian Hindu community? Such questions can of course be posed as personal ones: given his or her particular background and commitments, what ought the reader do in response to *Tiruvāymoḻi*? Or they can be turned into general ones: what does it mean to take seriously a primary text from a religious tradition other than one's own? at what point can one say that one has done this credibly, in sufficient depth so as to make one's reading an integral engagement with the text one reads, and not just a selective borrowing from it?

This chapter sets the stage for a response to such questions, by estimating the kind of text that *Tiruvāymoḻi* is, and by beginning on the basis of that estimate to predict the kinds of responses available to readers within the tradition (as we shall see primarily in chapters 3 and 4) and outside it (as we shall see primarily in chapter 5).

We began with one particular song, VI.5, and reflected on the intense attraction of the local and the specific, as portrayed within the song with reference to the temple, but also as represented by the song itself in its particularity. But we also recognized that no song in *Tiruvāymoḻi* stands alone, that every verse singled out will at some point need to be returned to its place in the whole "garland" of verses. To listen to just one verse well makes us more likely to listen more closely to every other one, in the end, as each one leads us to the next.

In chapter I, I already sketched some of the general features of *Tiruvāymoḻi*: 1102 verses divided into one hundred songs of 10+1 verses each, each set of ten verses having its own consistency, either in setting or imagery or theme or form, each concluded by a verse in praise of the author, the song, and the lord praised throughout. The songs as wholes, as well as the individual verses within them, are linked end-to-beginning (in *antāti*: *anta*-to-*āti*), set in one particular order; yet this order is not determinative of meaning in any evident way, since the songs and verses are not serial in their contribution to the meaning of the whole.[1] *Tiruvāymoḻi* is firmly rooted within Vaiṣṇava theology: Viṣṇu is the one lord of the universe, accompanied eternally by the goddess Śrī Lakṣmi, and all reality belongs to him and finds happiness in him. Such points are clear enough, whether one agrees with them or not, and they have been amply defended throughout Śrīvaiṣṇava history. But the songs are richly varied in their genres and ways of getting at the meanings of these broad and basic religious viewpoints, and they are endlessly inviting and alluring and provocative. It is these local, varied strategies that interest us most in the following pages, as ways into the world of *Tiruvāymoḻi,* since the theology by itself is both more evident and less likely to engage the outsider profoundly.

The basic problem facing us in this chapter is how to begin this appropriation of *Tiruvāymoḻi* from the inside as it were. How we can begin to say something about the songs in what is a rather difficult and complex situation: for example, although I shall be referring to very many parts of the text, its entirety has not been reproduced here, neither in Tamil nor in translation; neither I nor (almost) any member of the presumed audience has memorized the songs; insofar as *Tiruvāymoḻi* is in some ways distilled and reproduced here, we shall still be engaged in reading and not in the more original, fundamental practice of hearing the songs; further, the songs are poetry, and poetry in any case eludes fixed explanations, it spoils easily in prose summation; also, *Tiruvāymoḻi* exhibits an especially dazzling mastery of language, how words say things, hide things, and indirectly say more than they are capable of saying; and there is the rich and vivid vocabulary of the Tamil language and the particular syntactical structures of Tamil so skillfully used by Śaṭakōpaṉ; lastly, this is an ancient text, composed for an audience which in part "remembered" and in part "forgot" some images and myths and places about which we know little at all (while modern readers, especially those from outside the tradition, know a great deal about other things which make the study of *Tiruvāymoḻi* our own project, for our own times). These factors do not add up to a promising starting point from which to engage the songs, and the more scrupulous among us may be inclined to postpone an engagement of the literary and religious significance of *Tiruvāymoḻi.* But let us do the best we can to chart the course for just such an encounter, by the first view which makes up this chapter.

2. On (Not) Knowing Tamil

Though it is not possible here to delve too deeply into the structures of the Tamil language and the effect of *Tiruvāymoḻi* as a work of Tamil literature, I wish to make a few observations on some of the features that might affect the way we think about reading the songs.[2] For the modern reader from outside the Tamil and Indian traditions and of course from outside traditions of oral poetry, *Tiruvāymoḻi* is a marvel to behold, to hear, to read. Immense in its 1102 verses, it bears a variety of complex and varied meters woven together with an elegant diversity of vocabulary and style; although elements recur constantly, and almost nothing is ever repeated verbatim.

For example, one particularly striking and attractive feature of the songs that is captured only with difficulty in translation and gets quickly lost as we think about the songs is the feature of initial rhyme or repetition. Often enough, the very same word or syllable begins each line of a verse, as the following examples suggest; I cite the Tamil as well as the English, in hopes that something of the flavor of the verses might reach the reader, even aside from the translations:[3]

aṟiyā kkālattuḷḷē aṭimaikkaṉpu ceyvittu
aṟiyā mā māyattu aṭiyēṉai vaittāyāl
aṟiyāmai kkuṟaḷāy nilam māvali mūvaṭi eṉṟu
aṟiyāmai vañcittāy eṉatāviyuḷ kalantē (II.3.3)

When I did not know you, you made me love your service,
when I was unknowing, greatly confused, you made me your servant;
when no one knew you, as the dwarf you asked, "Three steps of earth, great Bali,"
when he did not know, you tricked him, and now you've mingled inside my self.

Or,

viṭṭu ilaṅku ceñ jōti ttāmarai pātam kaikaḷ kaṇṇkaḷ
viṭṭu ilaṅku karuñ cuṭar malaiyē tiruvuṭampu
viṭṭu ilaṅku matiy aṃ cīr caṅku cakkaram pariti
viṭṭu ilaṅku muṭiyammāṉ matucūtaṉaṉ taṉakkē (II.7.5)

Viṣṇu,[4] *radiant light; lotuses: his feet hands eyes,*
pervading, radiant dark shining mountain: his body,
pervading, radiant moon: his conch, his discus: the sun,
pervading, radiant hair,
my lord, Matusūtaṉa—it's all for him.

In some cases, such as the following, the emphatic repetition has a meaning that is not entirely lost in translation:

vayiṟṟil koṇṭu niṉṟu oḻintārum yavarum
vayiṟṟil koṇṭu niṉṟu oru mūvulakum tam
vayiṟṟil koṇṭu niṉṟa vaṇṇam niṉṟa mālai
vayiṟṟil koṇṭu maṉṉa vaittēṉ matiyālē

In his stomach he holds all three worlds which hold
in their stomachs everyone who holds anything
in his stomach and this dark lord who is the sort to stay
in my stomach when I've placed him there with his
consent. (VIII.7.9)

And,

cūḻntu akaṉṟa āḻntu uyarntu muṭiyil perum pāḻēyō
cūḻntu ataṉil periya parantaṉ malar ccōtīyō
cūḻntu ataṉil periya cuṭarñāṉaviṉpamēyō
cūḻntu ataṉil periya eṉṉavā aṟa ccūḻntāyē

Surrounding, inside, filling, uplifting every thing, unlimited
great Matter;
surrounding that, and greater still, the highest blossoming flame;
surrounding that, and greater still, the fiery knowledge and bliss;
surrounding that, and greater still, my desire for you, but that
too you finish, you surround me. (X.10.10)

Alliteration occurs occasionally at the end of a line, as in the striking example of III.4, where the word *eṉkō* occurs at the end of almost every line of the first, fifth and the seventh verses; thus, in the first (though transposing the repeated element to the beginning of the verse),

pukaḻu nal oruvaṉ eṉkō poruvil cīr ppūmi yeṉkō
tikaḻum taṇ paravai eṉkō tī eṉkō vāyu eṉkō
nikaḻum ākācam eṉkō nīḷ cūṭar iraṇṭum eṉkō
ikaḻvili vvaṉaittum eṉkō kaṇṇaṉai kkūvam āṟē

If I say, "Unique one whose deeds are praiseworthy," if I say,
"Earth with incomparable excellence,"
if I say, "Cool radiant ocean," if I say, "Fire," if I say, "Wind,"
if I say, "Splendid ether," if I say, "Twin lofty lights," if I say,
"All that is blameless,"
are those the ways to say something about Kaṇṇaṉ? (III.4.1)

Such linguistic adornments invite the reader to become a listener, to enjoy this "sweet Tamil." The songs keep offering more, to their more refined readers. They lure us into learning Tamil.

It is undeniable then that a very fine way to approach *Tiruvāymoḻi* would be to memorize it in its entirety. By memorization one would become able to recite the text and sing it, thus enabling others to hear it too. By memorization the whole would become available all at once, operative in a kind of immediacy that includes, but passes beyond, every individual strategy for putting the text in manageable order in one way or another. The memorized text, present all at once, becomes the place where the thematic elements are able to play off against one another in an endless series of possible combinations, according to patterns of similarity and difference that are bound only by the literary features of the text and then by the reach of one's imaginative powers.[5]

If we do not memorize *Tiruvāymoḻi* before studying it—if we do not hear the songs before we read them—at least we must continually remind ourselves of the price we pay for this omission, and for our remedial efforts to find other ways to appropriate the songs. Still, in the rest of this chapter we shall try as best we can to give a sense of *Tiruvāymoḻi,* how it marshals its resources, how it goes about asserting its own meaning in its own way, placing some options before us, foreclosing others, leaving us on our own at certain key moments. We must seek to describe in a careful and productive way some of the forms and textures, continuities and novelties that comprise *Tiruvāymoḻi* as it invites various responses, including those put forward by the *ācāryas* (as we shall see in chapters 3 and 4) and those that a reader from whatever background, inside or outside the Śrīvaiṣṇava tradition, with or without a theological interest, might propose today (as we shall see mainly in chapter 5). In all of this, we must chart the way in which we come to be familiar with *Tiruvāymoḻi*—a basis on which to begin to plan further theological and comparative moves in response to the songs.

To do this, I first introduce some key elements and factors that make *Tiruvāymoḻi* the text it is. I identify a series of thematic elements which constitute most of what is said in the songs (II), some recurrent formal elements which give the parts and the whole their structure, which interact with the themes and give them their place (III), the patterns by which we read around the text and so construct meanings for it (IV), and the pervasive self-transcendence, or ecstasy, of the songs, which constitutes them as "a text of desire," (V). Lastly, we will ask what is available to listeners and readers who seek to organize these elements, both helped and hindered by these songs which invite our attention but do not readily let us see through them (VI).

II. Thematic Resources

1. Some Major Themes

Tiruvāymoḻi is rich in resources available in Śaṭakōpaṉ's time and place. The perspective of his Vaiṣṇava worldview frames and informs each song, but *Tiruvāymoḻi* is distinguished rather more importantly by his reuse of the details of this perspective in unanticipated and pleasing combinations. I introduce here eight of the major thematic elements which Śaṭakōpaṉ draws into play repeatedly: a. the perfection and transcendence of God; b. the gracious acts of divine nearness; c. holy places where God chooses to dwell; d. the beauty of God; e. moral and religious appeals; f. love songs in an ancient genre; g. the self-understanding of the poet; and h. ways of expanding and exceeding the religiously described world.

A. The Transcendent Perfection of God. As the very first verses of *Tiruvāymoḻi* declare, God is perfect, powerful, and beyond understanding:

Who possesses the highest, unsurpassable good? that one;
who graciously gives the good of mind which removes
confusion? that one;

who is the chieftain of the unforgetting immortals? that one:
so bow down at those radiant feet that destroy affliction
and then rise up, my mind.

He is not within the scope of the understanding of minds which blossom and rise when impurity is banished,
he is not within the understanding of the senses;
this one is the entire good of understanding,
there is no one like him past, present or future;
he is my good life, there is no one greater than him. (I.1.1–2)

Such claims are buttressed by bold assertions of his uncontested supremacy:

When there was nothing, gods, worlds, life, nor anything else at all,
he made the four-faced god and with him the gods, and the world and life,
this first lord who dwells in tall Kurukūr, its jeweled terraces like mountains:
apart from him, do you seek another deity?

Pervading divinity and many worlds he created, and then
all at once he swallowed, concealed, vomited, crossed, dug them:
you see all this but you don't understand it;
except for being part of that highest one in Kurukūr
where the immortals bow their heads in worship
there is no divinity, people of the varied worlds:
so say it! (IV.10.1,3)

But at issue too is the mystery of language, which communicates best when admitting its failure to communicate properly:

He is hard to know if you think, "He lacks that," "He has this;"
he bears all forms in earth and heaven, but has no form;
with the senses, yet not of the senses; unlimited, all pervading,
the incomparable one who has the good:
to him we draw near. (I.1.3)

So too,

Even for me who meditates on this one abiding thing,
it is not understood,
nor at all by those who say that that it is this or that;

always higher than the highest, no thing, unfading,
hard to know as good or evil, even beyond right
knowledge. (VIII.8.5)

This grand, all-encompassing understanding and mystery is presupposed in all that follows; it is the basis for the varied and imaginative reformulations of what "God" and faith mean.

B. The Gracious Acts of Divine Nearness. Though transcendent, God is graciously and intimately involved in his devotees' lives; he is recognized and named now because his great deeds of the past are still remembered and recognized; thus, the fact of his descents (*avatāra*) is mentioned frequently enough:

"He became the cowherd,
He became the fish and boar;"
as soon as you say this,
he's become a million more. (I.8.8)

For all things beginning with birth and its ceaseless afflictions,
unique, unflagging source, protector of the three worlds,
he became the horse, the tortoise, the fish, the man,
lord, first God of the gods,
the one who makes me pure. (II.8.5)

Certain descents receive repeated attention: the boar (*varāha*) who dug the earth, the Man-lion (*narasiṃha*) who killed Hiraṇya, the Dwarf (*vāmana*) whose small stature tricked King Bali into giving away his kingdom, Rāma the warrior and spouse, Kaṇṇaṉ—in Sanskrit, Kṛṣṇa—the child and cowherd; thus,

Having lain, sat, stood, he measured it,
as the boar he entered beneath it and dug through it, hid it
in himself, vomited it, embraced it with his broad,
great arms—
the Earth:
who can see the marvels performed by Māl for Lady
Earth? (II.8.7)

Furious at his son who said, "Kaṇṇaṉ is everywhere,"
Hiraṇya shouted, "Well, he isn't here," and struck the pillar;
then, there, to his astonishment, my lion lord appeared:

is there anyone excellent enough to understand his greatness? (II.8.9)

In that time when I did not know you, you made me love your service,
in the midst of my unfathomable confusion you made me your servant;
disguised as a dwarf, you asked, "Three steps of earth, great Bali," and you tricked him unawares,
and now you've mingled inside my self. (II.3.3)

If people do not learn of lord Rāma
who uplifted everything which lived in Ayodhyā, the moving and unmoving, starting with the expanse of grass and the tiny ants, without any doing of theirs
—will they learn about anything else, in this land of the four-faced one? (VII.5.1)

It is a rare song that focuses on just one descent, as VI.4 focuses on Kaṇṇaṉ:[6]

"He wove his dance with the cowherd women, he lifted that incomparable mountain,
he burned up the serpent in the potent pond, he did many other things too!"
Night and day I never cease shouting the marvellous deeds of the lord on the snake bed: so what then do I lack?

"He played sweets songs on the flute, grazed the herd,
he joined with the shoulders of Piṉṉai, her bright eyes like keṇṭai fish, her hair fragrant, flowered, he did many other things too!"
I think on these and many other deeds of my marvelous, lovely lord;
my mind melts, time passes in love: what world is equal to me?

"To extinguish the great burden of the earth, he waged the great, unique Bhārata war
doing marvels he schemed to destroy their armies,
then he entered his dwelling beyond the sky!"
I have come near, I have gotten to worship the feet of this highest light—who else could be my leader? (VI.4.1–2, 10)

Such songs are powerfully evocative for those who know the stories behind them: to remember these great deeds stirs great emotion in the listener who sees the present through the lens of the past, and comes to live in a mythically revisioned world where similar divine interventions remain possible—or absent in a puzzling, tantalizing fashion.

Two points must be stressed. First, *Tiruvāymoḻi* never merely informs its audience. It never tells a myth completely, but is always reminding the audience of what it already knows; it is a text of memory. It speaks old words in a new time and place, leading the audience to see again the old and familiar in light of a present, new situation. Even VI.4 does not say enough about Kaṇṇaṉ that someone might reconstruct from it the basic purāṇic version of his life; only a person already familiar with the whole Kaṇṇaṉ story could reconstruct it from *Tiruvāymoḻi*. The other myths are even less fully recounted.[7] These songs are primarily for those who already know the stories, and listeners must reconstruct for themselves what is only partially recollected here. But this means too that those newcomers who look to the songs simply for information—on Hindu mythology, for instance—are likely to be frustrated and to pay more attention to informative footnotes than to what the verses themselves allude to, or remember partially. The new reader, the outsider, stands at a loss, and must seek to fill in the background, working from the given details to the implied backgrounds; likely too is the phenomenon that this reader will supply other memories, appropriate or not, which fill out the meaning of "divine activity in the world," however that might be interpreted. Thus, a Christian reader may unconsciously recall the Christian doctrine of the incarnation to fill in the background for the partially-sketched doctrine of descent found in the songs, etc.

Second, the myriad fragmentary allusions to the stories make them, and all their parts, contemporary to one another in a single tableau where all the divine deeds are viewed together in the present moment of the listener's awakened memory. None of the stories stands alone as normative, and even Kaṇṇaṉ is one among many. It is rather the memory of all these *avatāras* together that matters, each as a part of a single larger narrative of divine intervention. All the thematic elements we are identifying here are subjected to this relativization; they enhance and relativize one another in the confines of their shared context, where none is allowed to stand first or alone or complete.

C. Holy Places Where God Chooses to Dwell. The memory of God's ancient deeds is supported and extended spatially by means of reference to the divine presence in temples (most of which temples are still in use today). Here too certain elements are routine: such holy places are beautiful, immensely attractive even to celestial beings. They are places where devotees can find God easily; God and humans share mutual enjoyment in them.

If we exclude the mandatory reference to Kurukūr in each eleventh verse, Tiruveṅkaṭam is the most often praised of these holy places:

> *Ever the eye for earth-dwellers and heaven-dwellers,*
> *cool Veṅkaṭam, the hill of the heaven-dwellers, is his.* (I.8.3)

> *It is our desire to abide for time without end and offer perfect service*
> *to our father, our fathers' father,*
> *the beautiful light at Veṅkaṭam of the roaring cascades.* (III.3.1)

> *They sing, they babble the many names of our father in northern holy Veṅkaṭam with its lovely cool cascades and pools, and everyone calls them crazy;*
> *they enter the many towns or perhaps they don't;*
> *the world laughs at them, but they keep on dancing,*
> *they worship with great devotion*
> *and the gods worship them.* (III.5.8)

> *"When will we ever see the twin lotus feet that once paced the world?"*
> *asks the host of unwinking immortals as they praise you each day,*
> *O lord of holy Veṅkaṭam,*
> *standing, waiting, serving you with body, tongue, mind:*
> *when is the day when this servant will reach the truth, touch your feet?* (VI.10.6)[8]

But the following verses spoken by the anguished young woman in praise of Tiruvallavāḻ—we shall return to her plight below—are among the most lavish and poignant:

Good, doe-eyed women, day by day this sinner wastes away:
when will this servant reach the feet of the king who dwells in
Tiruvallavāḻ amidst honey-filled gardens
where lovely kamuku trees fill the heavens and honey-rich
mallikai trees send forth such a fragrance?

Friends, why are you afflicting me?
when will we servants wear the dust of the feet of the lord who
dwells in the town of Tiruvallavāḻ
where the south wind carries the scent of shimmering gold
puṉṉai trees, mahir trees and fresh mātavi flowers?

Women, the flowers in your hair are lovely, but tell me,
will I ever be able to look steadfastly on the feet of the lord who
has long dwelled in cool Tiruvallavāḻ
where the smoke of oblations wafts aloft in every direction,
where the chanting of the good Veda resounds like the sea,
as my grief-stricken self wastes away?

Why are you constantly bothering me, friends?
the Lord who lies on the bed of a poisonous snake in cool
Tiruvallavāḻ
where slender green kamuku, pala, coconut and mango trees rise
above terraced houses—
he alone is our good.

Good women, will my eyes ever get to see that radiant light
which holds my good, that cane sugar, fruit, sweet amṛta
itself?
He dwells in cool Tiruvallavāḻ
where the smoke of the sacrifices of good brahmins conceals the
dark, lofty sky.

Gentle women, your mouths are like ripe fruit;
will this sinner ever get to see the lotus flower feet of the lovely
lord, the beautiful dwarf in Tiruvallavāḻ
where fresh breezes carry the songs of bees everywhere
amidst the luxuriant seashore groves, flourishing trees, lofty
branches? (V.9.1–6)

D. The Beauty of God. Although the yearnings of the *āḻvār* to see his lord seem often unrequited, Nārāyaṇa's lovely face, hair, lips, chest, shoulders, weapons, etc., are vividly described throughout *Tiruvāymoḻi*, as if they had indeed been seen. The listener is encouraged, it seems, to be enflamed with the same desire to see and enjoy God:

> *Viṣṇu, radiant light; lotuses: his feet hands eyes,*
> *pervading, radiant dark shining mountain: his body,*
> *pervading, radiant moon: his conch, his discus: the sun,*
> *pervading, radiant hair,*
> *my lord, Matusūtaṉa—it's all for him.* (II.7.5)

> *Women, how can you be angry at me?*
> *after I saw our master who lives in lovely Tirukuṟuṅkuṭi,*
> *my heart has united with his conch, his discus, his lotus-eyes, his incomparable red fruit mouth. (V.5.1)*

> *Lustrous eyes, full ripe red lips, white bright teeth within, crocodile earrings, shaking and shining,*
> *four arms, bent bow, bright conch, club, discus, sword:*
> *that peerless one is inside me at his feet.* (VIII.8.1)

Occasionally, too, the other senses are engaged:

> *Many, many are his ornaments, many, many are his names,*
> *many, many his forms of light, if you reckon up his traits;*
> *many, many are the delights you see, eat, hear, taste, smell;*
> *many, many are the things we know about him*
> *who lies on the snake bed.* (II.5.6)

> *There is the joy experienced by the five senses, seen, heard, touched, smelled, tasted, and*
> *there is that hard to know, unlimited, small joy:*
> *but when I see you and the lady with shining bracelets, abiding as both,*
> *then I've seen the visible radiance, I've reached your feet.* (IV.9.10)

E. Moral and Religious Appeals. More often than not the songs seek to instruct and inspire the listener, promoting transformation of life and arousing love, even when direct experience does not seem readily available. Several songs instruct the listener on the danger of the senses, the need to renounce the world, the error of attachment to lesser goods, the need to seek and worship the Lord alone.[9] The emphasis is moral, though always verging on a more specifically religious appeal.

For example, the second song in *Tiruvāymoḻi* gets right to the point:

> *Surrender everything, and after surrendering that,*
> *surrender to the One who holds your life, at your surrender.*
> *Say, "It's like lightning, this body where the spirit dwells is*
> *unstable,"*
> *then think on the lord.* (I.2.1–2)

Some songs target specific groups:

> *These lords think of themselves as something special;*
> *they esteem their riches as true wealth:*
> *should I sing of these men instead of the lord of my fathers,*
> *my father who truly dwells in Kuruṅkuṭi among the fields and*
> *pools?*
>
> *Skilled singers of such fine songs,*
> *why do you put aside the lord of our heaven-dwellers*
> *who shows the path to travel from age to age, many ages with-*
> *out end,*
> *just to sing of others hardly worth thinking of?* (III.9.2–3)

And,

> *They ruled the world as a whole, all one kingdom,*
> *but now black dogs nip at their heels, they carry cracked pots,*
> *everybody watches them, in this life they are beggars:*
> *so meditate on the feet of Tiru's Nārāyaṇa, be uplifted,*
> *seize the moment.*
>
> *Once they said, "Give us tribute if you want to live," these rulers*
> *of the world,*
> *but now their sweet wives have left them for others' embraces;*
> *gone to wild places, these men wither in the glaring hot sun:*
> *so come in haste to the feet of the lord of Tiru*
> *whose hair is bright and radiant.* (IV.1.1–2)

Even at the end of *Tiruvāymoḻi* the same appeals are still being made, as the balance of moral and devotional commitments is still being worked through, though with a shift to the latter:

If you plan to approach the feet of Kaṇṇaṉ,
the holy name worth reckoning is surely "Nārāyaṇa"!

He will rule, reclined on the deep ocean, on the bed, the
powerful-jawed snake:
put flowers at his feet, seek them all day long.

Seek him all day long, with unfading flowers:
sing his names, be free.

If you keep chanting "Mātava" over and over,
no evil will stick to you, no suffering will touch you.

Clustered strong dark deeds will be frightened and flee,
so place good lotus flowers near him, think on the tall
one. (X.5.1,4,5,7,10)

Though these directly moral and religious appeals occupy only a rather small part of *Tiruvāymoḻi,* they give *Tiruvāymoḻi* a practical and moral tone, establishing it as a text oriented to practice: to understand the songs means to act in a certain way. We shall trace the development of this emphasis by the *ācāryas* in chapter 4.

F. Love Songs in an Ancient Genre. Among the most striking and distinctive of the songs in *Tiruvāymoḻi* are the 27 songs in which the classical genre known as *akam*—pertaining to interiority—predominates. These songs are about a young woman in love with an often absent lover, and about the intense, shifting moods in which she approaches him: love, fear, doubt, anger, confusion. In the songs of *Tiruvāymoḻi* and in other *āḻvār* works, this *akam* model is used to speak of the paradigmatic devotee and her divine lord. In some songs the young woman herself speaks, often in deep desire or anguish. We have already seen some of the young woman's verses in praise of Tiruvallavāḻ; here are some other examples, each sensuous, passionate, and evocative, in its own way:

Release from the circle of births in the body, life and everything
else,
he made appear the orb of the ocean,
he sleeps on it, the lord of the war club:

if you see him, tell him what I've said,
deep, gentle heart,
don't stop until this doer of deeds is one with him. (I.4.10)

The city sleeps, all the world is intense blackness,
all the waters calmed, one long night stretches out.
our lord who ate the whole earth, who lies on the snake bed,
does not come.
Alas, who will protect the life of this stubborn sinner
now? (V.4.1)

I have set out to get him, what more is there to give?
I've lost my lovely bracelets, my heart and everything else,
long ago I lost my honor among those women with their many
bracelets,
but he is mighty and victorious in war with his discus, raising
high his dancing eagle, pot-dancer living in the rich district
of southern Kuḷantai, surrounded with creeper-covered
walls and houses:
I desire him. (VIII.2.4)

The south wind fragrant with the mallikai scent cuts through
me, alas;
the sound of the splendid kuriñji pierces me, alas;
the evening where light departs confuses me, alas;
the fine clouds in the red sky ruin me, alas;
my lord, his eyes like lovely, tender lotuses,
my lord, great bull among the cowherds, great lion, my dark
one,
had clasped my shoulders and breasts,
but I don't know where to enter, now I am alone. (IX.9.1)

As we saw in VI.5, sometimes it is her friend who speaks; here is another example of the friend's words:

What can I tell you about her, neighbors?
Except for the names of the one
whose bed is the hooded snake in cool Tiruppuliyūr which
conceals the land of the immortals in the firm skies with the
wafting clouds of smoke of the ghee fires, the sacrifices of
those who possess great wealth and the northern-language
Veda,
she has nothing to say.

Night and day she speaks of nothing but the fame of
Tiruppuliyūr
amidst the ordered fields where tanks of lotuses bloom like lamps everywhere, where the tank is full of crocodiles, where the din of the learned brahmins with their metered Vedas echoes like the sea where cool-water-color Kaṇṇaṉ dwells.
What else could be the reason for her emitting this lovely cool tulasi scent?
She has met the holy grace of the marvelous lord
who dwells in Tiruppuliyūr in Kuṭṭanāṭu, a vermillion dot on the south country where rows of lovely houses flourish, with palaces like great jewels on hills. (VIII.9.8–10)

Sometimes it is the young woman's mother who speaks:

"My rice for eating, my water for drinking, my betel for chewing, my lord Kaṇṇaṉ!"
she keeps crying, tears flooding her eyes;
when she searches for his city, abundant in his excellence, in all the earth,
Kōḷūr is surely the place my young doe will enter.

Without helping me, my young doe has left me and gone off to Kōḷūr,
the ornament of the south country;
after seeing her Tirumāl's eyes and red mouth she fades, little by little,
her slender eyes flooding with cold tears. (VI.7.1, 6)

Two ideas about God are implied in these songs, undergirding their dramatic tension: God is known to be faithful and gracious, but God is often found to be absent, even when needed. This clash of recognitions lends a power to the songs even beyond that evoked by the various myths remembered by the *āḻvār*.

So too, the dramatic form of these songs—the young woman, her absent lover, her friend, her mother, the uncomprehending women of the town—invites the reader to imagine this to be the dramatic context for Śaṭakōpaṉ's own desire, frustration and approach to union. By analogy, the reader is encouraged to read the songs as presenting a company of players with different perspectives and reactions to the activities and absences of the divine player, Viṣṇu. Ultimately, too, the reader is soon enough invited to play a part in this company. By a further extension, the multiplicity of players in the drama of these songs provides a model for a reading of the text as speaking on several levels of discourse, from the most direct, to complex layers of indirect discourse in which one speaks about what another says about a third or even a fourth speaker: *Tiruvāymoḻi* becomes a recollected conversation.

G. The Self-Understanding of the Poet. *Tiruvāymoḻi* is a text of echoes, a text which speaks of itself. In chapter 1 we reviewed four songs (III.9, IV.5, VII.9, X.7) in which Śaṭakōpaṉ speaks in a particularly explicit fashion of his understanding of himself as a poet and of the role of his lord in the composition of his poetry. This theme is most strikingly captured in VII.9 where the two voices are both recognized and marked as one; verses 1–3 were cited in chapter 1, and here are three more:

> *Can I ever forget my father?*
> *become me, he himself faultlessly sings himself in these songs,*
> *he uplifts me, keeps on purifying this doer of unequalled evil:*
> *I have seen his excellence.*
>
> *Even after I saw his excellence and was purified*
> *I still lacked the excellence to sing proper sweet songs,*
> *but even so he made lowly me himself, the highest one,*
> *and by me sings sweet songs which the earth praises.*
>
> *By the sweet songs of the best singers*
> *he himself does not sing himself in his song,*
> *but now come near, he makes me one with him*
> *by me he sings mighty songs of himself, Vaikuṇṭa's*
> *lord.* (VII.9.4–6)

Though particularly fascinating in today's self-conscious world, such verses are *not* privileged vis à vis the whole of *Tiruvāymoḻi* in any evident way. Rather, they lie in the middle of the great text, in just one song among many; indeed, they make the fact of authorial voice itself just one more theme in the text. They certainly ought not be taken as "the real Śaṭakōpan̲," as if in the course of more discreet, indirect communication he suddenly turned to the audience to explain things as they really are.

Still, though, for the audience these verses inevitably serve as important guides by which to understand the process of reading; they inscribe both the author and his lord within *Tiruvāymoḻi* itself, thus confirming the preceding themes while yet asserting that every word in every verse is somehow reflective of the relationship between the *āḻvār* and Viṣṇu, expressive of human and divine interiority. Nevertheless, they do make us think about the songs, their origins and authority, while we are engaged in enjoying and imagining them. Authorial candor and distance become resources utilized in this religious world.

The eleventh verses too have a role in affording a self-conscious tone to the songs, as each directs the reader's attention to the efficacy and authority of the set of ten verses preceding it. They give the reader a sense of how the songs are to be pragmatically viewed and used in expectation of what rewards will follow. These range from the mundane to the ending of deeds and births, to the heavenly Vaikuṇṭa or to liberation, or to finding a place at the lord's feet or, as in VI.10.11, at the feet of other devotees.[10]

Forty-five of the one hundred eleventh verses remind us that the audience must be comprised of people who are capable, skilled (*vallār*). Though generally the word *vallār* is used without further specification, occasionally it is further marked: skill in music (I.5.11), in singing (II.3.11, VII.1.11), in chanting (I.6.11), in proclaiming (II.5.11), in declaring (V.9.11). So too, they tell us, one ought to have a disposition for these verses (IX.3.11) and be devoted to them (X.5.11); a premium is placed on teaching (III.10.11), learning (I.10.11), understanding (V.5.11) and knowing (X.10.11), and we are invited into a kind of intelligent study that is likely to be fruitful.

Though intelligent mastery of the songs remains the key to the promised rewards, some of the eleventh verses give an active power to the songs themselves. For instance,

This ten . . . breaks and banishes all diseases, (I.7.11);
This ten . . . in the end will bring you near to the feet of the gracious one, (II.10. 11);
This ten . . . will destroy that birth, which rises on this earth with the roaring waters, (III.1.11);
This ten . . . will bring you to the holy feet and make you one with them, (IV.9.11);
This ten . . . destroys all impurities in the mind, (V.2.11);
By this ten . . . devotees will be without flaw, (VI.4.11);
This ten . . . will give victory to those who learn it well, (VII.4.11);
This ten . . . is your life, servants, (VIII.1.11);
This ten . . . will graciously lift you above the heavens and end the great wondrous dance of births, (VIII.4.11);
This ten . . . looks with lustrous eyes, and births wear out, cease, (VIII.7.11);
By this ten . . . the lord . . . has graciously placed us at his feet, (VIII.8.11);
For this nine plus one . . . the three worlds melt, (IX.5.11);
This ten is the great 'I' and great source . . . , (X.7.11)

The songs are hypostatized as agents, imbued with their own power. The whole bears a cumulative, full power rooted in all its parts; the audience is invited to participate, and so to begin to share Śaṭakōpaṉ's articulation of his world—and thus too of the divine viewpoint on such things.

H. Expanding and Exceeding the Described Religious World. We have seen how the songs have much to say about Viṣṇu, his consort, his descents, his temples, his devotees. Such commitments and claims need to be taken seriously as argumentative and doctrinal—as truth claims—within the limits of their poetic expression. Claims about Viṣṇu are often strengthened by claims about other gods, as in IV.10.1 (cited above), and as these verses indicate:

In form the radiant flame of knowledge devoid of all sorrow, the lord garlanded with tulasi,
possessed of all the forms he needs to perform his many marvellous transformations,

he can swallow and hold inside himself Śiva and Brahmā and everyone else and everything:
when I have him, I am not weak at all. (III.10.9)

By the perfect sound of the finely etched conch which made fire burn within his enemies, he ended the earth's grief that day;
he is worshipped by Śiva who is hard to know and Brahmā and the king of the immortals, his praise is wide:
so if he is not captivated by my garment, it has no use. (IV.8.8)

"Even though I've done no penance in order to see your feet, I cannot wait to see them,"
say the subtle blue-throated one, the perfect four-faced one[11] *and Indra,*
O lord of holy Veṅkaṭam, where they and their women whose eyes sparkle delight:
Māl, dark and entrancing, come to me, your servant, as you did before. (VI.10.8)

Nor does Śaṭakōpaṉ hesitate to lash out at alien religious systems and practices, or at the devotees of Śiva and his *liṅgam*, and Buddhists (*śākyas*):

You people with your liṅga texts, you ascetics and śākyas, you all get excited, you argue;
but he abides as all of you and all your gods,
he is the lord who prospers in Kurukūr where the abundant ripe grain waves like yak tails:
it's no lie at all,
look at him, praise him, (IV.10.5)[12]

Sometimes there is unexpected heat, against what seems to be simply unacceptable:

Women, take note: whatever you have done with this witch's word,
don't strew about meat and wine;
if you would but worship the feet of the marvellous lord in whose hair rests honeyed tulasi,
that alone would be the rare cure for her disease.

Following the advice of that queer deceptive priestess
you have mixed black and red rice there in the sanctuary—
but for what result?

if you would only say the name of the great God who swallowed
and spit out the seven worlds all at once,
then you would get her back. (IV.6.3–4)

Certain deities—or is it only village goddesses?—seem to have no place at all in Śaṭakōpaṉ's Vaiṣṇava world; his inclusivism does not extend that far.

Though the faith of the Vaiṣṇava community is emphasized within *Tiruvāymoḻi,* we need also to notice a series of elusive statements about the "one God" and the "three gods," which subtly unsettle the worldview wherein Viṣṇu stands as a positively familiar, central deity. Occasionally, Śaṭakōpaṉ simply identifies Viṣṇu with the other gods—particularly Śiva and Brahmā (Ayaṉ), as in these dramatic evocations:

You have become water, earth, fire, wind, the vast ether
and that excellent fiery pair, Śiva and Ayaṉ:
bearing your sharp discus and bright conch, come to cruel me,
so that each day those in earth and heaven will rejoice. (VI.9.1)

Silent sage! four-faced Brahmā! three-eyed Śiva! flawless jewel!
lips like fruit, eyes like lotuses, my thief,
full self for me who am alone:
you have come upon my head
and now I will not let you go,
don't tantalize me anymore. (X.10.1)

But there are also verses which can be read as achieving a certain distance from a sectarian commitment to Viṣṇu, as if "Viṣṇu" might be only one of God's names. Consider these verses which link Viṣṇu (Ari, Hari) with Ayaṉ (Brahmā, the Four-Faced One) and Araṉ (Śiva):

Thinking, thinking, but even if you keep thinking about this
state below, within, above, beyond form, it is still hard to
know the lord's state, people;
so keep thinking, keep speaking of the one who is called "Ari,
Ayaṉ, Araṉ,"
keep thinking, propounding, and then worship:
what you are thinking of is One.

Abiding in forms such that it is hard to know whether he is one
or many, he is called good, lovely Nārāyaṇa, the four-faced
one, and Araṉ;

> *place in your mind the one, reflecting, destroy your two-fold bond:*
> *such is good, today is the day to do what is right before him.* (I.3.6–7)

And so too the very last verse of *Tiruvāymoḻi*:

> *Those who know this ten in the desirous antāti style which completes the thousand in desirous antāti style*
> *sung by Śaṭakōpaṉ of Kurukūr who has destroyed desire and gained release,*
> *who calls on Ayaṉ, Araṉ and Ari surrounding, finishing desire—*
> *they are born above.* (X.10.11)

The translation "who calls on Ayaṉ, Araṉ and Ari surrounding, finishing desire" rather weakly reproduces an ambiguity in the Tamil: *avāvaṟa ccūḻ ariyai ayaṉai araṉai alaṟṟi,* where the prefixed clause "surrounding, finishing desire" (*avāvaṟa ccūḻ*) *could* modify all three deities (*ariyai ayaṉai araṉai*)—each of which satisfies desire—or just the first of the three, Ari (Hari, Kṛṣṇa). Though it is reasonable to choose the latter alternative, it is nevertheless striking that the possibility of the other interpretation seems deliberately present in the very last verse of *Tiruvāymoḻi.* Śaṭakōpaṉ does not support smug religious sectarianism.

This modulation of theological priorities in context is itself theologically interesting, as a tradition is both constantly reaffirmed and subtly unsettled. Though such ironic verses cannot be privileged in any decisive way over against the many more verses which stress that Viṣṇu is the One from whom Brahmā, Śiva and other gods come forth, neither can we ignore the implication of such verses which take the received mytheme of the "three"—among whom Viṣṇu is only one—and place "God" above all three. This particular combination of bold assertion with attention to alternatives leads to a questioning of too sure understandings of monotheism. It seems an admission of the limitations of religious language, even in *Tiruvāymoḻi* itself. Any unthinking repetition of what the songs say is discouraged, therefore, as if the words themselves certify the reality of which they speak.

But here we face again the yet broader theme of the author's reflection on his own use of language, particularly the "uncertainty principle" enunciated in the beginning:

He is hard to know if you think, "He lacks that," "He has this;"
he bears all forms in earth and heaven, but has no form;
with the senses, yet not of the senses; unlimited, all pervading,
the incomparable one who has the good:
to him we draw near.

"He sat, he stood, he lay down, he moved about;"
"He didn't sit, he didn't stand, he didn't lie down, he didn't move about:"
he is hard to know, if you think he has one nature:
thus always is his nature, my steadfast one.

If you say "He is," he is, and his form is all these forms;
If you say "He is not," his non-form is all these non-forms;
"He is," "He is not:" if he has these qualities, he exists with both natures,
without limit he pervades everything. (I.1.3, 6, 9)

Our lord is hard to know when they say, "He is of this nature;"
our lord is easy to know when they say, "He is of this nature;"
our lord has a thousand names and many forms;
"No, he hasn't any name and form;" "No, he's not lacking them:"
that's the dispute. (I.3.4)

There are many such verses in *Tiruvāymoḻi*, and it would be a mistake to undervalue their influence as guides to how one is to read the rest of *Tiruvāymoḻi*. Being Vaiṣṇava must include the effort to avoid settling into a merely complete and comfortable naming of the lord. Nothing one can say is final, a certain holy irony forecloses overconfidence in things spiritual. To speak religiously is to speak simply, and with irony.

It is also the case that we should not make too much of the thematic summation I have just completed. We must be skeptical of the assumption that we have understood the text by making an adequate thematic tabulation or, worse, by reducing the text to the sum total of the "realia" to which it refers. As noted above in regard to the incompletely told and juxtaposed recountings of the myths, the themes accumulate near one another, and none concedes the ordered space in which an isolated consideration of another might occur. None of these eight themes occurs in isolation, and although it has been useful to identify them, our main task is to make it possible to think about them together. The creative contribution of Śaṭakōpaṉ lies rather in his (re)use of these traditional resources, their resignification in the new context of *Tiruvāymoḻi*, near one another, capable of urging listeners toward a grasp of new possibilities.

III. Some Formal Components of Tiruvāymoḻi

If the themes are significant only in their arrangement together, then it is all the more important then to notice the structured space in which these themes occur, how they are framed, the margins in which we ought to examine them. Let us consider some of the formal features of *Tiruvāymoḻi* as one integral text, 1102 ordered verses, one hundred songs, woven together, end to beginning.

1. How the Themes are Located

A. The Litany Effect. A first way to appreciate the role of form is simply to notice what might be termed the "litany effect," the sheer accumulation of images and vocatives that grows as one reads, rereads, remembers. For example, let us consider VI.10, where very many vocatives come together in what amounts to a grand litany of praise. Since we shall have numerous occasions to refer to this important song in subsequent chapters, it is worth citing in full:

Great-mouthed fellow who ate the world, lord of incomparable fame,
form of light surrounded by everlasting radiance,
tall one, your servant's life breath,
O lord of holy Veṅkaṭam, sacred mark on the brow of the world:
summon me, that this servant, descendant of an old clan, may reach your feet.

You hold the sacred wheel of raging fire that breaks down, razes to the ground, burns to ash entire clans of wicked demons, king of the gods,
O lord of holy Veṅkaṭam where lotuses red as flames grow in muddy pools:
show me your grace, that this servant who loves you without end
may reach your feet.

Your color is the color of a lovely cloud, so dark,
lord of miracles, ambrosia that seeps sweetness into my mind, commander of the gods,
O lord of holy Veṅkaṭam where clear waterfalls crash spilling gems, gold and pearls:
great one, just say, "Ah, there he is!" and bring this servant to your feet.

Demons who won't say "Ah, ah!" torment this world,
but your bow rains arrows of fire on their lives, husband of the great goddess Tiru, God,
O lord of holy Veṅkaṭam which gods and sages love:
unite with this sinner that I may deserve your feet covered with flowers.

You are mighty with the bow that pierced the compact row of seven trees that day,
you crawled between two giant trees twined together, first one,
O lord of holy Veṅkaṭam where elephants herd like dense clouds,
lord of the strong cārṅka bow,
when is the day when this servant will reach your feet?

"When will we ever see the twin lotus feet that once paced the world?"
ask the host of unwinking immortals as they praise you each day,
O lord of holy Veṅkaṭam, standing, waiting, serving you with body, tongue, mind:
when is the day when this servant will reach the truth, touch your feet?

Ambrosia that this servant loves so well, God of the unwinking gods

with the fierce bird on your banner, lips luscious like fruit, lord,
O lord of holy Veṅkaṭam, antidote to sins that multiply like weeds:
I cannot wait a second to see your feet, though I've done no penance.

"Even though I've done no penance in order to see your feet, I cannot wait to see them,"
say the subtle blue-throated one, the perfect four-faced one and Indra,
O lord of holy Veṅkaṭam, where they and their women whose eyes sparkle delight:
Māl, dark and entrancing, come to me, your servant, as you came before.

You don't come as you came, as you didn't come, you come;
eyes like red lotuses, lips like red fruit, four-shouldered one, ambrosia, my life,
O lord of holy Veṅkaṭam where glowing gems make night into day:
alas, this servant cannot be away from your feet even for a moment.

"I cannot be away even for a moment," says the maiden on the flower who dwells on your chest;
you are unmatched in fame, owner of the three worlds, my ruler,
O lord of holy Veṅkaṭam where peerless immortals and crowds of sages delight:
with no place to enter, this servant has entered right beneath your feet.

"Come, enter right beneath my feet and live, servants," the lord without any equal keeps saying, offering them his grace;
about him Śaṭakōpan̲ of Kurukūr where paddy fields are plentiful
has perfected these thousand verses—
whoever holds on to anyone who holds on to these ten about holy Veṅkaṭam will be enthroned in the high heavens.

Part of its recitation is its sheer doxological value, its expression of praise; from it we can select more than forty vocatives:

"Great-mouthed fellow who ate the world!"
"lord of incomparable fame!!"

"form of light surrounded by everlasting radiance!"
"tall one!"
"your servant's life breath!"
"lord of Tiruveṅkaṭam!" (in each verse) (1)

"you who hold the sacred wheel of raging fire!"
"king of the gods!"
"this servant who loves you without end!" (2)

"Your color is the color of a lovely cloud!"
"lord of miracles!"
"ambrosia that seeps sweetness into my mind!"
"commander of the gods!"
"great one!" (3)

"your bow rains arrows of fire on their lives!"
"husband of the great goddess Tiru!"
"God!" (4)

"mighty with the bow that pierced the compact row of seven trees that day!"
"you crawled between two giant trees twined together!"
"first one!"
"lord of the strong Cārṅka bow!" (5)

you whose "feet once paced the world!"
you whom "the host of unwinking immortals praise each day!" (6)

"ambrosia that this servant loves so well!"
"God of the unwinking gods!"
"with the fierce bird on your banner!"
"lips luscious like fruit!"
"lord!"
"antidote to sins that multiply like weeds!" (7)

"Māl, dark and entrancing!" (8)

"you who don't come as you did, as you didn't come, you come!"
"eyes like red lotuses!"
"lips like red fruit!"
"four-shouldered one!"
"ambrosia!"
"my life!" (9)

"the lady on the flower dwells on your chest!"
"you are unmatched in fame!"
"owner of the three worlds!"
"my ruler!" (10)

"lord without any equal! (11)

The presence of so many vocatives in a single song produces an overall effect that operates noticeably even apart from what the song ostensibly is about. Each appellation and image gives us something more to think about, to see and possibly to voice. A Śrīvaiṣṇava can sing VI.10 in praise of holy Veṅkaṭam, or with the desire to take refuge at the lord's feet, as does the *āḻvār*—or, more simply, to enjoy the many names of the lord invoked in the song. As our imaginations are stimulated to recognize and enjoy this litany, one begins also to enunciate an inscribed text for worship and the beginnings of an understanding of the God who is thus conceived. The pious and imaginative combinations thus made possible are endless, and they are also pedagogically effective, for the listener who hears the text frequently enough to internalize it has his or her mind filled with the vocatives, their possible combinations, and all that this internalization entails.

We also notice a tendency that is opposite to the preceding, i.e., a dispersal that marks the 100 songs. There are no simple litanies that are neatly thematic; there are no songs which are only about the lord's transcendence, no section of *Tiruvāymoḻi* devoted solely to the praise of holy places, no preamble in which the author introduces the paradox of divine-human authorship, no special chapter on love or on reununciation, etc. Rather, the themes are distributed everywhere, mingled, overlapping, encompassing and marginalizing each other. The meaning of *Tiruvāymoḻi* is intrinsically linked with this formal dispersal of meanings throughout the whole, disconnecting thematic continuities and establishing in their place ones that depend on linguistic regularities. Of course, it is these formal structures, continuities and dispersals which the earnest comparativist in search of the meaning of the songs is inclined to overlook or to overcome; yet it is they that are the key to the work's larger meanings. We need then to specify key formal features of the text, the linguistic and literary setting within which the themes are inscribed, repeated, and dispersed.

B. Form as Frame. Some features are clear, beginning with the simple but impressive fact that *Tiruvāymoḻi* is so regular in form. Excepting four songs which have only two lines in each verse, each verse has four lines; excepting song II.7 with its 12+1 verses in honor of 12 names of Viṣṇu, every song has 10+1 verses, the last verse being, if not an addition, at least a second-order composition which stands in evident relation with the previous ten. The text is thus uniform in appearance, one hundred songs lined up in a row; whatever theme is taken up, it is always treated at exactly the same length as any other, in ten verses. Whatever novelties and surprises there may be, they always occur within this uniform, conventionally-defined space. Every theme and every issue receives the same treatment.

Though, as admitted at the beginning of this chapter, this is not the place for a more detailed linguistic analysis of *Tiruvāymoḻi* as a work of Tamil literature, in the following section I give special notice to two formal features: the technique of *antāti,* and the formal role of the eleventh verses.

2. *Antāti*

By the practice of *antāti* we mean that the last words or word or syllable of each verse is the first of the next. Thus, to draw on the same examples we used at the beginning of this chapter, we have this connection between II.3.3 and II.3.4, in Tamil,

> . . . eṉatāviyuḷ kalantē (II.3.3d)
>
> eṉatāviyuḷ kalanta peru nallutavi kkaimāṟu . . . (II.3.4a)

or, in English,

> *. . . and now you've mingled inside my self* (II.3.3d)
>
> *You've mingled inside my self, for this great help what return shall I make?* (II.3.4a)

We have this link between VIII.7.9 and VIII.7.10,

> . . . vayiṟṟil koṇṭu maṉṉa vaittēṉ matiyālē (VIII.7.9d)
>
> vaittēṉ matiyālē eṉathuḷḷattakattē (VIII.7.10a)

i.e.,

> . . . *in my stomach when I've placed him there with his consent.* (VIII.7.9d)
>
> *With his consent I've placed him inside me . . .* (VIII.7.10a)

Antāti connects verses to verses, song to song, and the last word of X.10.11 to the first word of I.1.1, "above" (*uyarntu*):

> . . . piṟantār uyarntē (X.10.11d)
>
> uyarvaṟa vuyar nalam . . . (I.1.1a)
>
> . . . *they are born above.* (X.10.10d)
>
> *The good with nothing above it . . .* (I.1.1a)

Antāti, without meaning anything in particular, tightly binds the whole of *Tiruvāymoḻi* together. *Antāti* places a fixed border around the verses, instructing us to think about them serially; we are guided to expect a serially presented unity for the whole. The *antāti* thus puts before us the whole text in its sequence; regardless of what it says, every verse is formally, firmly located where it belongs in the ordering of the whole, and the whole is strung together so that nothing can drop out or be added. It serves to insure that each song is discovered just where it is in the whole, precisely between just two others, liable to intentional thematic dispersal and potentially creative shifts from mood to mood. When the *antāti* fixes the sequence among the verses within any individual song, we must take them in the order in which we find them, though there is often no convincing thematic reasons for the given order as opposed to some other that might have been given. Of course, this tightness of form encourages us to find a thematic progression which renders the sequence significant. We are led to expect that the succession of one song after another means something, and it is not surprising when a reader finds meaning in the sequence, reasons for the order and (posited) progress of the songs as we find them, one after the other. Psychologically prepared by reading the verses in one order, the reader can easily confer and then defend narrative continuity by deciding what is primary in each song, and by stating how the other songs reflect, or build on, or contrast with, such primary points.

It is not difficult to confirm this expectation if one wants to, since the openings between verses and songs invite completion as the reader chooses. Thus, if one begins with "*uyarvaṟa uyar nalam uṭaiyavaṉ yavaṉ avaṉ* . . ." and moves through the songs to "*avāvaṟa ccūḻ ariyai ayaṉai araṉai alaṟṟi*""—to cite I.1.1 and X.10.11 by their first words in Tamil—it is obviously possible to invest these two songs with great significance based on their being first and last. I.1.1 then becomes a good beginning,

> *Who possesses the highest, unsurpassable good? that one;*
> *who graciously gives the good of mind which removes confusion? that one;*
> *who is the chieftain of the unforgetting immortals? that one:*
> *so bow down at those radiant feet that destroy affliction*
> *and then rise up, my mind* (I.1.1),

and X.10.10–11 a good ending:

> *Surrounding, inside, filling, uplifting every thing, unlimited great Matter;*
> *surrounding that, and greater still, the highest blossoming flame;*
> *surrounding that, and greater still, the fiery knowledge and bliss;*
> *surrounding that, and greater still, my desire for you, but that you finish too, you surround me.*
>
> *Those who know this ten in the desirous antāti style which completes the thousand in desirous antāti style sung by Śaṭakōpaṉ of Kurukūr*
> *who has destroyed desire and gained release, who calls on Ayaṉ, Araṉ and Ari surrounding, finishing desire—*
> *they are born above.* (X.10.10–11)

Or, since we find at the end of the text a vision of the journey to Vaikuṇṭa (X.9) and after that, a song (X.10) that ends with a climactic image of envelopment and can easily be taken as conclusive, we *can* legitimately treat these last two songs as a dramatic conclusion, though we also note that X.9 is not a first-person narrative (it is the *āḻvār*'s vision of other people's heavenly journey, not his own), and though we ought not forget how Śaṭakōpaṉ does not seem to expect this kind of otherworldly conclusion (for what he wants is "God-here," not that he himself go "there"). Still, one is often left with the sense that had the songs been arranged differently, we would find that arrangement quite appropriate too.

Of course, *antāti* means that we are never finished reading *Tiruvāymoḻi*, can never fix an end to our encounter with it. At its end, always it begins again, the *antāti* leads us on. As we have seen, the last word of X.10.11—*uyarntu*—immediately shifts one's attention back to I.1.1, which begins with *uyar*. The *antāti* is instructing us that this is not a text to be finished with—every ending is a beginning, every beginning flourishes on the basis of the ending which precedes it. The *antāti* defeats the notion that there is any single beginning or ending to the text: it does not allow it to proceed simply toward a climax, for it is always revolving back on itself, beginning anew. One never really begins it, nor finishes it, neither the recitation nor interpretation is ever finished.

Śaṭakōpaṉ himself provides a useful image in IV.5, where he refers to his songs as a garland:

> . . . *"Hail!" I say, I worship fully, hands joined, offering this garland of words . . .*
>
> . . . *I praise him with this garland of songs in fine words,*
> *I get inside him . . .*
>
> . . . *I praise him with garlands of songs undying through time,*
> *I come near him, I dwell within the bounds of undying joy.*
>
> . . . *my tongue praises him with garlands of song and I come near him;*
> *but I cannot understand how he's made my self his self.* (IV.5.1–4)

The notion that there is a beginning to *Tiruvāymoḻi*, or an end, is arbitrary, valuable for various good reasons, ranging from the needs of the beginner (who reads it like a book, for whom the whole has not been internalized by memorization) to the decision of the *ācāryas* (which we shall examine in chapter 3) that *Tiruvāymoḻi* has a plot, a beginning and end coincident with the *āḻvār's* spiritual progress; yet the *antāti* unsettles this narrative, making every conclusion another beginning.[13]

3. The Formal Contribution of the Eleventh Verses

I mentioned in chapter 1 that the eleventh verses are secondary, at least in the sense that they are rarely thematically connected with the ten verses they follow. Rather, they speak formulaically of the lord, of Śaṭakōpaṉ of Kurukūr, and of the results that accrue to the skillful recipient of the text.

Their function is clear and does not vary much from song to song, regardless of what any given song might be about. In form and style, they stand in a closer relationship to one another than to the intervening sets of ten verses which separate them. Here are a few of these eleventh verses, just to remind us of their familiar structure:

> *This ten from the artfully-composed thousand sung by*
> *Śaṭakōpaṉ of Kurukūr*
> *at the feet of that highest one who abides as wide sky, fire, wind,*
> *water, earth, as fine sound, vigor, strength, cool affection,*
> *patience—*
> *this ten is your freedom.* (I.1.11)

> *This ten belongs among the thousand excellently woven together*
> *by Śaṭakōpaṉ of lovely Kurukūr with its abundant*
> *ponds.* (I.2.11)

> *Those skilled in this ten from among the thousand in good taste,*
> *Śaṭakōpaṉ's humble service amidst the fertile gardens of*
> *Kurukūr*
> *about the maker of the turbulent sea where the immortals could*
> *rise and worship him*
> *—they rise on high with the immortals, and destroy their*
> *tangled bonds of birth.* (I.3.11)

> *The rich recitation of these ten from the thousand verses in*
> *surpassing antāti,*
> *excellently uttered by Śaṭakōpaṉ of lovely Kurukūr surrounded*
> *by rich paddy,*

about Kaṇṇaṉ, the lord of the peoples of the seven surpassing worlds—
that will get you great riches, abundant even to the heavens. (I.4.11)

Those skilled in this ten from among the thousand
played by masters of Tamil like mother's milk, musicians, and devotees,
songs of Śaṭakōpaṉ of Kurukūr who lives by the grace of God
astonished and crying repeatedly, "Māl, wondrous lord, great wondrous one!" —
they will never be afflicted. (I.5.11)

Eleventh verses tell us about Śaṭakōpaṉ of Kurukūr; they emphasize the artistic value of the songs; they impress upon us certain features of the whole and its composition: e.g., the verses are artfully, faultlessly composed and sung, in lovely pure Tamil, woven together as a garland in this *antāti*, transforming understanding and giving salvific knowledge.[14] On rare occasion, they do refer more definitely to what the preceding ten verses are about. In some, there is a connection with the preceding verses, as in this striking verse which comes at the end of the young woman's evening lament about the absent Kṛṣṇa:

With this ten from the thousand uttered about the one who ate and disgorged the earth
lord Śaṭakōpaṉ of lovely Kurukūr grieved about parting from him of whom the lovely, ornamented cowherd women cry out in the evening, unable to live apart from him—
with this ten, cry out in this world, survive, live, come near to this garland of words, worship! (IX.9.11)

More often, though, this connection is likely to be the construction of the expectant reader.[15]

We emphasize that these verses are crucial in extending the *antāti* to the whole, for it is only through them that the songs are fixed in the order in which we now find them. Without them, the one hundred more unified sets of ten verses each would stand together more as a collection, an anthology which could be easily rearranged. Even if there are other structural and thematic regularities throughout *Tiruvāymoḻi*, such regularities do not suffice to establish a sequence among the songs. Only these verses, which do not rely on theme, connect the one hundred songs to one another in this particular sequence. A unity is put in place without a definite meaning being fixed upon it.

The formalities we have been considering here—regularity of length, *antāti*, secondary eleventh verses, and so also the initial rhyme considered at the beginning of this chapter—are not unique to *Tiruvāymoḻi*. They can be explained on a variety of grounds related to literary traditions and the demands of oral poetry, and it would be a mistake to attribute their creation to the originality of Śaṭakōpaṉ. Nevertheless, they are intrinsic to *Tiruvāymoḻi* as we have it, they constitute the frame of *Tiruvāymoḻi* within which whatever else is said in the songs has its full meaning. Clearly in Tamil, implicitly in translation, they serve to direct our expectations as we seek to discover the meaning(s) of *Tiruvāymoḻi*.

IV. Understanding Tiruvāymoḻi

1. The Direction of the Text

In the course of describing important thematic and formal features of *Tiruvāymoḻi* we have postponed introducing a third key element which we must now consider: the direction of the text, its movement and energy which bind the themes and formal structures into a whole capable of informing, exciting and challenging its audience. Most simply, this is the issue of deciding the "point" of any given song, and its expected direction given the resources that are at work within it.

Within limits, it is not difficult to determine what most of the songs are about, in general. Image, dramatic appeal, repetition, sequence and other strategies contribute to the meaning of the individual songs in *Tiruvāymoḻi*. VI.5, the song with which we began this book, is a song about a temple. Like many other songs, it is about the young woman and her friend. But unlike any other song, it is single-minded in its exploration of the implications of what it means to "see God"—receive *darśan*—in a temple. It is about how a life can be entirely changed by what others persist in taking for granted. If it seems to climax with the friend's questions in verse 10: "Is she Piṉṉai born here? or Nīlā? or the Lady? what marvel is this?" the point seems to be that the fullness of vision is also the revealing of divinization.

Some songs are clearly marked by direction-setting elements. Thus, every verse of V.5 has as its concluding words, "after I saw the Lord. . . ." VI.10, cited in full earlier in this chapter, is in general clearly about holy Veṅkaṭam, which is mentioned in every verse; it is also about the *āḻvār's* quest for a permanent place at the lord's feet, which are also mentioned in every verse. The sending of messengers gives unity to some songs, (I.4, II.1, VI.1, IX.7), the recurrent evocation of the *tulasi* plant to one (IV.2), the drama of a heavenly journey to another (X.9).

Sometimes the patterning is particularly striking: in I.9, for example, the reader is led on a journey up through the body:

> *he is in everything that surrounds me* (1);
> *he is in what is near to me* (2);
> *he is with me* (3);
> *he is on my hip* (4);
> *he is within my heart* (5);
> *he is in my arms* (6);
> *he is on my tongue* (7);
> *he is in my eye* (8);
> *he is right here within my brow* (9);
> *he is within the crown of my head* (10);
> *his long feet will rest on their heads too* (11).

Though myths are recollected in many songs, and the value of true knowledge is analyzed frequently, no song is so intricately interconnected as VII.5 in its analysis of the epistemology of religious knowledge, through a reflective layering of kinds of knowledge according to the *antāti*, as this pattern shows:

hearing (2),
  hearing and knowing (3),
    knowing and meditating (4),

meditating and hearing and thinking (5),
hearing and thinking and seeing (6),
seeing and thinking (7),
thinking and knowing (8, 9),
knowing and understanding (9–10)

Thus, for instance,

> *Will the people born in this land serve anyone but Nārāyaṇa who was born in this land, who suffered for humankind what had not been suffered before, who searched out and destroyed the kings who afflicted the land, who sought ways to protect it, to uplift it*
> *—after they've heard all the things He did?*
>
> *Will the people who have heard all this listen to anything but the fame of Keśava whose feet even Śiṣupāla reached, though his hostility had long ripened and though he so basely abused Keśava that it burnt the ears of listeners*
> *—after they come to know this from those who truly know?*
>
> *Will the people who truly know all this serve anyone but the one who made the good waters, made the four-faced one, mixed within himself all the old things, and made every thing appear anew after that long period when every thing of every sort had perished*
> *—after they have meditated on these skillful exploits?*
>
> *Will the people who have meditated on these skillful exploits embrace the feet of anyone but the marvellous one who took the form of the boar when the earth was drowning in the great deep waters and he held it on His horn so that it wouldn't sink*
> *—after they have heard and thought about all this?* (VII.5.2–5)

And so forth.[16] Although this layering of connections is carefully composed, there is no evident, necessary sequence involved, as to why "hearing," "knowing," "meditating," "hearing and thinking," must succeed one another. But once the terms are found in this order, one can begin to chart the path from one to another, finding reasons for the order.

Given these occasional directive elements, it is all the more striking that in regard to the whole of *Tiruvāymoli̱* there is no clearly repeated element or regular feature which guides the whole. Apart from the formal elements mentioned earlier, the text does not seem to have any clear structure. It cannot be simply outlined (hence the lack of an outline in this chapter!), and efforts to describe it, such as are undertaken in this chapter, become elaborate constructions. In chapter 3 we shall examine the most influential of these constructions, whereby the *ācāryas* read *Tiruvāymoli̱* as the narrative of the *āl̠vār's* spiritual journey, but for now let us simply examine a few aspects of this process of constructive reading.

2. Understanding Tiruvāymoli̱*: Reading Across the Text*

The identification of themes, forms and directions is of course not equivalent to mastering *Tiruvāymoli̱*. In some way or another one must still become skilled in each set of ten verses, all one hundred songs, 1102 verses in all. One must appropriate and internalize the whole to become truly skilled (*vallar*) in it. If we do not memorize the whole, we must observe carefully how we do go about learning to comprehend *Tiruvāymoli̱*, in some incremental and gradual fashion, as it is picked up, put down, and browsed—one song after another taken as small chapters in a book or poems in an anthology.

We must begin of course with an awareness of our own presuppositions about poetry, literature, books, about how they begin, progress, develop characters and plots, come to climax and conclusion, mean one thing or another, and presume other things which they do not say themselves. If for example we think *Tiruvāymoli̱* is like the Biblical psalms, we will read its songs as if they were psalms; if we think of it as poetry, we read it as poetry, like the *Song of Songs* in the Bible or contemporary lyric poetry. If we find it rich in philosophical insight, we will privilege its philosophical viewpoints. If we think it free of the elaborate interpretations commentators have imposed on it, we will seek lighter, freer ways to approach it. If we are studying the text in translation, or are not native speakers of Tamil when we pick up the Tamil text, we will read it—hear it, in a sense—according to the rhythms that survive in translation or come rather from our own language background. And so on.

It is important to think of the project of careful reading as a process comprised of numerous smaller activities, ending with mastery of the text; strategies by which we begin to sort out the parts of the whole. Our mastery will have to do with a deepening and complicating of our understanding of each particular part of the whole, a process of familiarization, as we reach toward the achievement of a richer sense of what matters in the context and judgments which highlight our choices, all according to a gradually composed set of realizations and responsible operations by which the component resources of the text interplay within the space of the whole as we apprehend it.[17]

When we read any particular song or verse in *Tiruvāymoḻi*, we encounter both a series of elements often quite familiar from elsewhere in the text, and also a fresh ordering of those elements. By attention to context, we sharpen our familiarity with each element in this location and elsewhere—so as to appreciate what is being done in each particular instance. We scrutinize the part, while remembering the whole, as the young woman in the temple might focus on her Lord's eyes while yet being filled with innumerable other memories about him.

It is important then to appreciate what we are doing when we begin to construct the meaning of a text like *Tiruvāymoḻi*. Let us begin by examining how we determine the meaning of a particular word, and then how we interpret several larger units of the text.

A. Finding a Context: "Tall One." The vocative "tall one" (*neṭiyāy*), which we hear at VI.10.1, is a relatively obscure title for the lord:

> *Great-mouthed fellow who ate the world, lord of incomparable fame,*
> *form of light surrounded by everlasting radiance, tall one, your servant's life breath . . .*

Readers who do not already understand what "tall one" means are given no help here. Does "tall one" simply mean that the lord is tall? grown tall? powerful? reaching the heavens? high in the sky like the stars? And, whatever it means, why *this* vocative *here*? Is the reference pointed, a hint at some particular activity of the lord? Or is the reason for this vocative simply metrical?

If we seek help elsewhere in *Tiruvāymoḻi* to fill in the meaning of "tall one," we find 27 other references. Most are similarly simple references, also without any helpful explanatory qualifications.[18] A few carry some limited clarification: e.g., in VII.10.6 it is the shoulders of the lord that are "tall"—"the one whose lovely tall shoulders are always joined with the woman Uruppiṇi"—while in VIII.2.10, the lord is a "a fine tall incomparably lovely blue hill." Five verses identify this "tall one" as Kaṇṇaṉ,[19] and he in turn is strikingly described as the one who (in the *Mahābhārata*) was gracious to the five Pāṇḍava brothers—"the tall one who once was gracious to the Five and eradicated the hundred" (III.7.11)—and who was the agile "tall potdancer" (IV.10.10). Several verses identify the "tall one" with "the one who grew large and possessed the earth:"

> *He is sharp and cruel, the tall lord, his feet holding the earth,*
> *his marvellous body hard to comprehend.* (V.3.5)

> *The tall one whose banner bears the bird with lovely highly*
> *praised wings, whose feet measured the earth without*
> *skipping a step . . .* (IX.4.10)

> *. . . snatching the doll from our hands is no thing for you to do,*
> *pure one who ate sea and earth, tall one . . .* (VI.2.7).

These references to tallness make more sense, for we can understand tallness to mean "the one who *grew* tall," who became very large, cosmic in size, in his descent as the dwarf (*vāmana*), in the course of his conquest of the demon king Bali.

Several verses seem to echo the connection made in VI.10.1—"*tall one,* your servant's life breath . . ."—linking the Lord as "tall" with the Lord as "life:"

The tall one with the far-shining discus, who gave ambrosia to the immortals . . . (I.6.6)

My ambrosia, I can never get enough of you, in love for you my body softens, melts, flows like water, tall lord who melts me . . . (V.8.1)

Be gracious to me who does not know, life of those who do; fragrant form of light, this servant's tall lord . . . (VI.9.8)

The "tall one," then, seems to be one who is beautiful, powerful, distant, towering and overwhelming, comprehending the earth. As one reads, one accumulates a set of parallel cases and resonances. The initially odd term gains a history, an interest and power, and all kinds of echoes and resonances. "Tall one" does not mean anything we want it to mean; it evokes some words and some memories, and echoes throughout *Tiruvāymoḻi* in a particular way that invites the more attentive and learned reader to a heightened appreciation.

Still, it is not possible to pin down exactly what "tall one" means in general, nor to specify its meaning perfectly in any given instance. Part of its meaning is perhaps irretrievably concealed in the oral tradition behind *Tiruvāymoḻi,* and lies outside the text; part is located in the wealth of possibilities nurtured in a poetic text. Here at least, attention to context is an educational activity which surely excludes wrong ideas, but never finally fixes the right meaning: the reader learns a great deal, but is never finished learning, and ultimately has to add his or her own judgment, deciding how to use the image of the "tall one."

Were we to go back to the verse and repeat this reading process with other terms—"great-mouthed one," "one who ate the world," "form of light," etc.—the effect would be the same: in many cases, nothing is decisive, but there is nevertheless a helpful accumulation of resonances. Even a term as important, and clear as "your feet," or "your feet covered with flowers," may still bear with it a local south Indian significance that only repeated readings and acts of interiorization can appreciate. Eventually, though, the process teaches one to be open, to stand positioned to appreciate what is uncertain, and to respond to it better: every repeated word is new when I hear it, this time.

B. Finding a Context: "With No Place to Enter, I Have Entered Right Beneath Your Feet." One can undertake the same kind of analysis across the text for lines and verses too. For example, let us consider the words "with no place to enter, I have entered right beneath your feet," (VI.10.10d). These words conclude this song of powerful testimony to the need for God and to the desperate love that makes surrender possible.

As we saw earlier, the idea of being at the lord's feet, or entering there, is very common in *Tiruvāymoḻi*.[20] The lord's feet (*aṭi, pāta, caraṉ, tāḷ*) appear very frequently throughout *Tiruvāymoḻi*; the lord's feet are attractive, a place of safety, surrender and refuge; and they are the feet with which the lord has performed great deeds in the past, such as measuring the world. By the time the *āḻvār* enters beneath the lord's feet in this 10th verse, the preceding verses have already focused our attention on these same feet; thus,

> . . . *summon me, that this servant, descendant of an old clan, may reach your feet* (1)

> . . . *show me your grace, that this servant who loves you without end may reach your feet* (2)

> . . . *great one, just say, 'Ah, there he is!' and bring this servant to your feet* (3)

> . . . *unite with this sinner that I may deserve your feet covered with flowers.* (4)

> . . . *when is the day when this servant will reach your feet?* (5)

> . . . *when is the day when this servant will reach the truth, touch your feet?* (6)

> . . . *I cannot wait a second to see your feet, though I've done no penance.* (7)

> . . . .*alas, this servant cannot be away from your feet even for a moment.* (9)

> *. . . with no place to enter, this servant has entered right beneath your feet.* (10)

When the speaker enters beneath those feet, the reader has already been prepared, at length and with great emotion, for the decisive action.

As for the larger meaning of this "entrance beneath the feet," a connection between devotion and being at the lord's feet is drawn frequently enough throughout *Tiruvāymoḻi*. For example, these verses from VIII.10 are particularly clear:

> *If I should gain the three wide worlds, if I should become him himself,*
> *would it be the same as enjoying the fruit of reverencing the holy feet of those famous in victorious service beneath the feet of my lord . . .*
>
> *When my rulers still move about here,*
> *great and small human beings still not at His feet,*
> *not entered beneath the fresh blossom of those feet which waft the fragrance of my holy short one with red-lotus eyes*
> *—would it be right for me?*
>
> *If I get the grace to worship, to move about gaining the pleasure of the flood of shining light,*
> *to move about and curl beneath the lovely flower feet of that wondrous one . . .* (VIII.10.2, 3, 5)

Several times we find the fuller performative expression "*entering beneath* the feet:" "casting off my body, *entering beneath* his feet, I love him;" (III.9.8) "the bright eyed lord who abides so that the one who receives his grace and anger can *enter beneath* his feet . . .;" (III.6.6) "be gracious, make this servant your object, make me *enter beneath* your feet" (IX.8.8). The reference to entering perhaps accentuates the ritual act that is undertaken in seeking refuge. To enter *beneath* the lord's feet appears to indicate a more certain and more total conjunction. It is Śaṭakōpaṉ's own preferred situation (II.9.7, III.2.4, III.9.8, V.8.9, VIII.3.8, VIII.5.7, VIII.7.1, IX.8.8) and the ideal location of all devotees (III.6.6, III.7.7, V.1.11, VI.10.11, VII.5.10, VIII.8.11).

A final noteworthy and distinguishing feature in VI.10.10d is the use of the past tense: I *have* entered: the deed *has* been done, the entering-beneath *has* been accomplished. On that basis alone one might be willing to afford the verse an important position in *Tiruvāymoḻi,* as a real turning point—as do the *ācāryas,* as we shall see in chapter 3. Yet VI.10.10 is by no means the only place where a definitive past tense occurs. Similar apparently decisive terminations are mentioned both earlier and later in the text:

> *I have reached you—so can I let you go, lord of the three worlds?* (II.6.10)
>
> *I've seen this visible radiance, I've reached your feet.* (IV.9.10)
>
> *You have finally given me refuge at your feet as my way . . .* (V.7.10)
>
> *He has ended up as me himself.* (VIII.8.3).

None of these instances seems less decisive than VI.10.10d, and on the face of it—unless we take other factors into account (e.g., the important place, Tiruveṅkaṭam)—nothing demands that we attribute particular import to VI.10.10d; it only becomes decisive, as it does in the Śrīvaiṣṇava tradition, when an audience confers such importance upon it. Though this investment with importance is not merely arbitrary, it is still a claim that must be confirmed by the choices and judgments of the audience.

C. Finding a Context: Total Surrender. We have already seen that the emphasis on the lord's feet in the prior verses in VI.10 prepare for this moment of entering. But do preceding songs also prepare for this moment? This is a different question, and an affirmative answer is more difficult since the dynamic seems again to be that expectation will find its own reasons. Once one has honored VI.10.10d as a definitive act of surrender—as one can, although one does not have to—it is then almost inevitable to read the earlier parts of VI.10 and earlier songs too as somehow preparatory for this act. Its definitive quality becomes a measure by which to reread earlier songs, looking for clues for the coming surrender.

By way of example, let us briefly consider VI.5, the now familiar song with which we began this book, and then, also very briefly, V.7, 8, 9, 10, four songs which the Śrīvaiṣṇava tradition privileges as the crucial antecedents for the decisive entrance beneath the lord's feet in VI.10. Is VI.5 a way of talking about the inner life of the person about to surrender in VI.10? Does the achievement of VI.10 depend in part on failures expressed in V.7–10?

If we ponder the relationship of the desperate young woman in VI.5 who is unable to put her life back together after visiting Tirutolaivillimaṅkalam with the person who is desperate for union with the lord of Tiruveṅkaṭam and who surrenders beneath the lord's feet there, two things seem evident. First, there are no clues in either song that would indicate that the woman in VI.5 is a persona of the speaker in VI.10; nor is there any evidence which demands that we connect her evident distress with the intense longing which comes to a head in VI.10. Second, however, it is quite easy to make such connections if one wishes to do so. The reader could read VI.5 first, and thereafter VI.10, understanding the latter in light of the former; or, more likely, read backwards from VI.10.10 to antecedents in VI.5 for what one has designated as the key act of surrender at Tiruveṅkaṭam. In a work like *Tiruvāymoḻi* which delights in unexpected shifts in mood and image, which continually, even in single songs, puts things together unexpectedly, even an apparent lack of connection between the young woman's plight in VI.5 and the yearning of the narrator in VI.10 invites the reader to fill in the gap with some connection and, most easily, with a psychological one, the desperate emotions of the poet as a persona active in the songs. In the end, the helpless, distraught young woman becomes the very model for the person who surrenders in VI.10.10.

At a still greater remove, we have songs V.7–10, four songs identified by the *ācāryas* as important moments in the *āḻvār's* search for the best way to find God. The sense of search, frustration and yearning communicated by these songs is taken by the *ācāryas* as conducive to the moods found in the "later" VI.5 and VI.10. Consider V.7, for instance:

I've done no ascetic deeds, I have no subtle knowledge but still
I cannot bear to leave you even once, lord with the snake bed.
Father, enthroned in Cirīvaramaṅkalanakar where lotuses bloom
in the mud amidst the ripening paddy,
apart from you, there, I am nothing.

You have ended up giving me the refuge at your feet as my way,
but I have nothing to give you in return, my life belongs to you
cool flowering fragrant tulasi in your hair, living in
Cirīvaramaṅkai full of abundant ripening paddy and sweet
sugar cane,
chieftain of the gods. (V.7.1,10)

One *can* read V.7 as privileging the *āḻvār's* search for God and his growing helplessness, and one can understand it (along with the three subsequent songs) as preparatory to VI.10; and then one can find in VI.10 a real climax in the forward movement of *Tiruvāymoḻi,* prepared for by the vain inquiries undertaken and abandoned in V.7–10: because the *āḻvār* finds God in neither temples (V,7,8 and 9) nor myth (V.10), he reaches both the necessity and realization of total surrender as his only way.

Yet here too it is true that were the songs given in a different order, one might just as well become content with another set of connections, highlighting other verses and parts of verses as conclusive, and thus successfully affording significance to another sequence of songs; e.g., VI.10.10 could seem a quite reasonable prelude to V.7.10, had we found them in that order:

"I cannot be away even for a moment," says the Maiden on the
flower who dwells on your chest;

you are unmatched in fame, owner of the three worlds, my ruler,
O lord of holy Veṅkaṭam where peerless immortals and crowds
of sages delight:
with no place to enter, this servant has entered right beneath
your feet. (VI.10.10)

You have ended up giving me the refuge at your feet as my way,
but I have nothing to give you in return, my life belongs to you,
cool flowering fragrant tulasi in your hair, living in
Cirīvaramaṅkai full of abundant ripening paddy and sweet
sugar cane,
chieftain of the gods. (V.7.10)

Though the *antāti* does firmly fix the songs in the particular order in which we find them, one is not compelled to invest this de facto sequence with any thematic significance. There are no further instructions, beyond the *antāti,* which tell us that the given order marks the internal meanings of the songs, each contributing to the emerging final meaning of the whole.

This modest conclusion, that it is possible to find meaning for words, verses and songs in their contexts, but that any such discovery will inevitably have an arbitrary element to it, can of course be extended to other parts of the *Tiruvāymoḻi.* Whichever part we take up, we will be confronted with the ordering effect of the *antāti,* the inviting imaginative possibilities of verses and songs, and the openings and hints which leave it to the reader to determine larger patterns of meaning. With this balance of suggestion and construction, we reach the limits of what can be done in a preliminary exposition of what it means to read *Tiruvāymoḻi* and find meaning in it.

At its best, this reliance on internal context—repetitions, patterns, sequences of words, verses and songs—serves not so much to determine the text fully as to offer a partial remedy for our not having memorized the whole text in the first place. By this search for proper contexts, illustratively sketched here, one begins to compose incrementally the resonances and correspondences which come into play as the whole text is interiorized. One submits to the text, finding ways to understand it, but one also takes control of it, putting it in place. The final determination of the meaning of the songs seems then to lie with the reader—and indeed this seems to be the intent we must construe from the way in which *Tiruvāymoḻi* was composed, with its particular combination of thematic and imagistic diversity and its formal fixedness. The greater the significance found in the songs, the greater must be the engagement of the reader in the construction of that singular meaning. As we shall see in the next several chapters, the *ācāryas* of the Śrīvaiṣṇava tradition carry through on one reading of the whole in a brilliant and convincing way—and yet, in light of the nature of the project of giving meaning to *Tiruvāymoḻi,* their reading too must accommodate moderate and bold alternatives to it.

V. Theologizing Tiruvāymoḻi

1. Boundaries

At what point then do these carefully composed songs and the attentive, constructive readings of them become open to theological formulation, assertions in which the meaning of the whole can be defined, asserted, and presented for scrutiny, consensus and criticism? Two factors must be kept in balance.

On the one hand, we must always begin with the recognition that *Tiruvāymoḻi* is clearly a Vaiṣṇava text, and Śaṭakōpaṉ a devotee in the Vaiṣṇava tradition. His creativity and imagination, though powerful, do not transgress the boundaries of his community's theology in any decisive fashion. The thematic, formal and directive elements we have examined are varied, but in the end they still describe a fairly specific religious space: *Tiruvāymoḻi* is theistic, devotional, Vaiṣṇava, south Indian, Tamil, distinguished by a number of myths and holy places and literary genres, emotional and intellectual. It is oriented to a personal relationship that can be characterized as that of lord and servant, mother and child, lover and beloved.

Tiruvāymoḻi is sufficiently specific to insure a strong measure of definition and exclusion, and most other religious ideas and religious attitudes are excluded by it: e.g., it is not a text in honor of Śiva, it is not compatible with Buddhist ideas, and Śaṭakōpaṉ's love of Viṣṇu cannot be equated with a Christian's love of Jesus Christ. *Tiruvāymoḻi* works within the boundaries of a definite theology, though it remains poetic and doctrinally underdetermined. Through it one comes to a certain kind of knowledge of God: as it were, one sees God in a particular way through this text:

> *When there was nothing, gods, worlds, life, nor anything else at all,*
> *he made the four-faced god and the gods with him, and the world and life,*
> *this first lord who dwells in tall Kurukūr, its jeweled terraces like mountains:*
> *apart from him, do you seek another deity?* (IV.10.1)

On the other hand, because *Tiruvāymoḻi* is good poetry, its verses and songs resist complete determination of their meaning. We have seen this point above, in considering how *Tiruvāymoḻi* expands and exceeds its own religious world.[21] However orthodox *Tiruvāymoḻi* is by Vaiṣṇava standards, it unsettles the very orthodoxy it upholds, for it always remains open to a variety of readings according to the expectations, mastery and sensitivity of its readers. Images and evocations overflow, jostling against one another, each echoed but never quite replicated somewhere else in *Tiruvāymoḻi*. It takes doctrinal positions quite seriously, and plays with them too: it is theologically as well as stylistically ironic. The dynamics of this internal contextuality compel us to move continually from any given detail (word, image, thematic, vocative) to its direct and indirect correlates throughout the whole, in a way that both appreciates the consonances we discover and yet at the same time, because more connections are always possible, always destabilizes the particular ways in which we may thus far have fixed the meaning of the text. *Tiruvāymoḻi* is composed with enough continuity, formality and indeterminacy that it invites efforts to determine its meaning; and yet, at every such point of conclusion, it also overflows the boundaries of such determinations. How one imagines these elements and composes them into one or another whole with determinate meanings is up to the reader. Śaṭakōpaṉ's poetry does not bear within it a completely stable systematic or sectarian theology, and cannot be successfully reduced to one:

Thinking, thinking, but even if you keep thinking about this
state below, within, above, beyond form,
it is still hard to know the lord's state, people;
so keep thinking, keep speaking of him who is called "Ari, Ayaṉ,
Araṉ,"
keep thinking, propounding, and then worship:
what you are thinking of is One. (I.3.6)

Since Śaṭakōpaṉ resists speaking any last word about God, and seems deliberately to unsettle even the firmest and most pious of determinations, we can say that it is part of the theology of *Tiruvāymoḻi* to remain open to new interpretations.

True Vaiṣṇavism, truly open and unsettled at its edges: it seems to me that we need to maintain this tension. *Tiruvāymoḻi* is amply coherent with Vaiṣṇava theology and not inimical to systematic views of that theology, yet as a subtle and innovative poetic work, it is never just a prose theology rendered poetically. In composing the full, broad array that is presented across the whole of *Tiruvāymoḻi*, rich in diverse meanings while yet firmly located within the regularity of form, Śaṭakōpaṉ has in effect presented the reader with more of ideas and sentiments than it is possible comprehend at any given time, while yet still encouraging the reader to comprehend the whole as integrally as possible. Perhaps, one hopes, this book enables the present reader to begin to make such correlations and personal determinations within the boundaries of the text.

2. Tiruvāymoḻi *as Map*

Particularly as we attend to the dynamics of reading instead of those of listening—the visual instead of the aural—it may be helpful to think of the whole of *Tiruvāymoḻi* as a kind of spectacle, something to look at, to see through. The dynamics of learning, hearing and realizing are enabled and represented across the surface of the 100 songs of *Tiruvāymoḻi*. They mark off a large panorama, words (and images, memories, names, places, deeds, concepts) that are broadly displayed in a pattern which approximates an object of vision so large that it cannot be viewed all at once, at any given moment. It is a text which both delights and distresses its audience—the spectators?—because one is always drawn to grasp it in its details, while yet finding over and over that one cannot grasp them together or all at once. One looks at particular verses and songs, one looks elsewhere and then back again, eye and memory moving back and forth across the songs and verses. This we have attempted, for instance, in our inquiry into the meaning of "tall one."

Each insight encourages the viewer—listener, reader—to peer more intently here and there within the circled garland of verses, playing one's eye across the text, tending toward a comprehensive vision of the world, yet without replacing that vision with an abstracted verbal rendering of it. *Tiruvāymoḻi* is neither merely a barrier nor simply a medium, but rather a extended, dispersed field of localities among which a kind of (in)direct encounter with God becomes imaginable. One must be *there* and *there* and *there*—to see and taste, to make present now and for oneself whatever it may be that attracts one from this text. One can do this religiously, of course, or simply in accord with one's own requirements of careful reading.

Tiruvāymoḻi as complete text does not tell us this about itself in any straightforward way. Rather, in its play of content and form, it verbally (re)presents a world we must negotiate, it is a place in which the charting of one's religious memories and commitments becomes possible and can become actual, as one (re)constructs these in trying to make sense of *Tiruvāymoḻi* and find one's position in relation to it. An immediacy is fashioned from and in these words, in which the reader finds intimacy through a mastery of the text which both obscures and makes present the religious reality into which it leads the hearer, who is in turn mastered. The reader is given much, but much more is demanded in return.[22]

Tiruvāymoḻi might also be thought of as a kind of window, a finely polished, slightly opaque glass which first stands as the object of our vision, but thereafter serves only as its medium. Our eyes, accustomed to its surfaces, learn to see through it to what can only be imperfectly surfaced, reflected, and mirrored in the individual verses and songs. The text is an obstacle, it dazzles and obscures, yet it is the very location of an otherwise unavailable vision.

To hear or read *Tiruvāymoḻi* is therefore to engage in a project that must be seen through, patiently, and deliberately. It is to be introduced not simply to an idea or ideas, but to begin and continue—and not to finish—traversing a rich and complex world of words which in turn replicates in a (continually) transitional and oblique fashion the world in which the songs were composed. *Tiruvāymoḻi* represents a studious combination of form and indeterminacy, and its power resides in that tension.

Living by the songs of *Tiruvāymoḻi* certainly located its original audience(s) within a "Vaiṣṇava world," but in their persistent presence, the songs leave open how the Vaiṣṇava is to act in regard to myths, temples, love, images of God, individual choices and communal intentions. This underdetermination is itself another kind of window, for it allows even the outsider a passageway into the realities of the text, a way that is not locked behind doctrinal and communal certainties; and so *Tiruvāymoḻi* remains powerful today even for those not interested in any formal, systematized belief.

3. Desire in the Text

The preceding attention to how *Tiruvāymoḻi* both fixes and overflows its boundaries brings us to the question of desire, for *Tiruvāymoḻi* is the occasion of desire, it is opened to those with desire and those who want to learn how to desire. It has a great deal to say about desire, and is itself a place where nearness to God is possible, in part because it both announces, and reproduces in itself, the elusive, receding possibility of any satisfying presence. This is, after all, the ground of desire: one knows what one does not have, one experiences what does not remain surely present. Instantiated desire—in every *this*, in every desire for *more than this*—is the organizing "drive" behind *Tiruvāymoḻi*, giving the text its direction. The *āḻvār* is constantly expressing his desire for God, not because he lacks experiences of God, but because the experiences he has had substantiate his original desire, and inevitably evoke a desire for more.

It is instructive then that the great conclusive claim about how desire ends,

> *Surrounding, inside, filling, uplifting every thing, unlimited*
> *great Matter;*
> *surrounding that, and greater still, the highest blossoming flame;*
> *surrounding that, and greater still, the fiery knowledge and bliss;*
> *surrounding that, and greater still, my desire for you, but that*
> *you finish too, you surround me.* (X.10.10)

is nevertheless followed by the subtly unsettling summation we have already seen, where Viṣṇu (Kṛṣṇa, Ari, Hari,) seems—

perhaps, maybe—to be just one among three, along with Araṉ (Śiva) and Ayaṉ (Brahmā):

> *Those who know this ten in the desirous antāti style*
> *which completes the thousand in desirous antāti style sung by*
> *Śaṭakōpaṉ of Kurukūr*
> *who has destroyed desire and gained release, who calls on Ayaṉ,*
> *Araṉ and Ari surrounding, finishing desire—*
> *they are born above,* (X.10.11)

Is it only Ari—Kaṇṇaṉ, Kṛṣṇa—who surrounds and finishes desire or, as is possible in the Tamil, all three of these Gods? In turn, too, this unsettled yearning (re)turns to the resounding announcement of a single lord:

> *Who possesses the highest, unsurpassable good? that one;*
> *who graciously gives the good of mind which removes confusion? that one;*
> *who is the chieftain of the unforgetting immortals? that one:*
> *so bow down at those radiant feet that destroy affliction*
> *and then rise up, my mind.* (I.1.1)

The whole includes within itself a subversion of its own ending; completed, it sees that completion is merely one more beginning: always, every time the text is heard or read, a kind of rebirth occurs, enflamed by desire. One is never done, desire is never sated. *Tiruvāymoḻi* is a kind of ecstasy in and from words.

This desire brings the thematic and formal elements to life as it pulsates through them, as this elegant composition of one hundred songs is always being stretched to its limits by the desire for more. This desire underlies the variations of the text, and is embodied in each of its elements; it gives direction to the whole of the work, which is reaffirmed and expanded in each song, on each different occasion. While various instantiations of desire are prominent—eating (mentioned at least 80 times), mingling (25 times), tasting (12 times)—and while we must not discount the whole range of possibilities related to the tactile, still the most common references are either to the desire to reach the lord's feet (*aṭi*) and perform service (*aṭi-mai*) there, or to the desire to see the lord. By my rough count, about 200 verses contain references to the lord's feet, particularly regarding their beauty and the value of being near them; there are likewise almost two hundred more references based on same root—*aṭi*—with the range of meanings, "serve," "servant," "service," etc. Similarly, I have counted 350 verses which contain altogether more than 511 words related to vision. Formally, one can take the two impulses of desire as parallel, for both emphasize nearness, in service, in sight. Indeed, the desire for one often shifts over into the desire for the other, and service seems at times to be held up as satisfying the need for vision, at times as a substitute for it when the latter is not yet possible. In any case, we are on solid ground if we give special attention to the desire to serve and the desire to see; let us examine each.[23]

A. The Desire to Serve. Some of the references to the lord's feet are purely descriptive, falling into the category of "the beautiful;" some are descriptive of past events, particularly worship of the lord's feet either by the āḻvār or by the gods; some are injunctive, summoning the listeners to worship at the lord's feet; some are prayers, wherein the *āḻvār* seeks from the lord union with the lord's feet, i.e., a life of devotion and therefore of service:

I do not ask for Release, though it is great in all ways,
instead I quickly place my head at your great, red lotus feet.
Lord who ended the elephant's sorrow, master:
that is all your servant wants.

For this I grasp you every day,
my jeweled-colored dark, pure light, master,
that I might reach your unreachable feet:
grant me the helping hand of knowledge, do not delay.

You have not granted that I dwell beneath your lotus feet
without ever separating,
you have not satisfied me, putting yourself inside me:
come to me always, for all time.

Conqueror of the seven bulls, lofty flaming light who reduced
lovely Laṅkā to ashes,
don't trust me,
join me to your golden feet quickly,
never let me go elsewhere. (II.9.2, 3, 7, 10)

As we have already seen, this theme of reaching the feet of the lord recurs in every verse in VI.10, forcefully directing the audience's attention to this goal, to be fulfilled at Veṅkaṭam, in the heart and spirit. The rich diversity of other thematic elements in the song is subordinated to the practical desire for union *now,* whatever else may vary. Though the song portrays both the speaker and the lord in various ways, the point is the reality of service, putting one's head at the lord's feet: if one must be somewhere in a human body, let it then be there, at the lord's feet, whether these be in the temple, the heart, the community—or in the song.

B. The Desire to See. The desire to see—balanced with a strong emphasis on what has already been seen—is equally important in giving the whole of *Tiruvāymoḻi* its direction. Keeping VI.5 in mind, where sight is so important, let us note V.5, another striking song where vision is emphasized:

> *Women, how can you be angry at me?*
> *after I saw our master who lives in lovely Tirukuṟuṅkuṭi,*
> *my heart has united with his conch, his discus, his lotus-eyes, his incomparable red fruit mouth.*
>
> *See the world with the eyes of my heart, don't be angry at me:*
> *after I saw our master who lives among the cool lovely groves of Tirukuṟuṅkuṭi,*
> *then his splendid thread, his earrings, the emblem on his chest, his four firm, adorned arms have come, they are everywhere.*
>
> *Mother won't let me see him, she says, "Time passes, her unique love keeps growing;"*
> *but after I saw our master who lives in flawless, praiseworthy Tirukuṟuṅkuṭi,*
> *his incomparable form rising up in a flood of light, where hosts of gathered gods worship—it has risen within my heart:*
> *this knowledge is precious for anyone.* (V.5.1, 2, 10)

IV.4 too is about the effects of seeing:

> *Confused, she looks about, wanders about, searching far and wide;*

she sweats, hot sighs, tears raining from her eyes;
her body droops, and agitated, she cries, "Kaṇṇaṉ!" she calls,
"Great one, come!"
What can this sinner do for my poor foolish girl,
dazzled by her great love? (IV.4.10)

Some verses, such as the following, seem almost meant to document vivid moments of sight, as if in a moment of vision in a temple, a vision of the sacred divine image there, a *darśana*:

Lustrous eyes, full ripe red lips, white bright teeth within,
crocodile earrings, shaking and shining,
four arms, bent bow, bright conch, club, discus, sword:
that peerless one is inside me at his feet. (VIII.8.1)

As the verse indicates, though, the desire to be at the feet, to serve, and the desire to see converge, since he sees, and yet is at the feet of the one who is now inside him (for each kind of desire must be internalized). Both service and vision pertain to proximity. One must be near to serve, yet service preserves a hierarchical structure in its increasing degrees, until in the end it opens into intimacy. Seeing, even if possible from a greater distance, can be blocked in various ways, limited to surfaces; yet across its distance it stimulates a different kind of intense nearness, as it opens up a freer movement back and forth, seeing and being seen.

These two desires function within the songs, and only from there do they compete with other desires and concerns in *Tiruvāymoḻi*; so one must remain slightly skeptical about any definitive identification of these as *the* central elements in *Tiruvāymoḻi,* as if to say, "What Śaṭakōpaṉ really had in mind was a dialectic of service and vision." A focus on these, if taken too literally or thematically, might in the end skew our reading and render us less attentive to what else is going on in Śaṭakōpaṉ's composition as a whole.

Still, it is fruitful to designate the desires for service and vision as the epicenters of the text, giving the whole its balance and plotting its tendencies toward completion in proximity, interaction, clarity. Although, as we shall now see in chapter 3 (which primarily opens the question of seeing and its limits) and chapter 4 (which primarily opens the question of surrender, in service), the *ācāryas* do not explicitly mark serving and seeing as the two privileged themes in the text, they do in fact rely heavily on the language of vision as marking the core problem of the āḻvār (chapter 3) and the language of service (chapter 4) as marking what *Tiruvāymoḻi* is really *for*: to learn to serve, to learn to be like the *āḻvār*, to learn to (come near to) vision.

We conclude with one more analogy, which returns us to the idea of a temple nearness to God. The themes of being at the lord's feet and of seeing seem to suggest temple theology: not a theology *about* temples, but rather a replication in words of the experience to trying to see Viṣṇu *in* the temple. This of course again brings to mind songs such as VI.5 and VI.10 where temples seem key, but even apart from such obvious formulations, *Tiruvāymoḻi* serves to replicate the possibilities and impossibilities one encounters in the temple: to hear or read *Tiruvāymoḻi* is a process of entering a holy place, peering about, seeing and then seeing through, and then being seen, seen through. To hear or read *Tiruvāymoḻi* is a kind of temple *darśana*, satisfying in its nearness and frustrating in its opacity; one has to keep looking, as near, nearly, as possible. Yet because *Tiruvaymoḻi* has become a written text, it is available to all, there is no exclusion from this moment and place of nearness to the sacred.

VI. Reading, Alone or with Others

In this chapter I have discussed *Tiruvāymoḻi* in terms of how it works as a whole text comprised of one hundred songs, how it invites complete, integral responses from readers. Without pretense to completeness and without denial of further, outstanding questions, this description has, I believe, touched on key points which need to be taken into account in a study of the whole, as we make our way into this very large text. Insofar as possible, I have sought to maintain a descriptive stance regarding what we read and how we read it, prescinding from favoring some responses over others. The main point is that the possibilities are multiple, and that it is the reader who must decide how to control them in responding to *Tiruvāymoḻi*. Since the songs are richly imaginative, underdetermined and at times even ironic, *Tiruvāymoḻi* is available only to the reader willing to get involved—but it is indeed available.

But as stated at the beginning of this chapter, this engagement is an exceedingly difficult task for the modern reader who approaches it without the specific resources of language, culture and memory expected by Śaṭakōpaṉ. The modern reader does not learn the songs and practice them in the expected fashion, and often enough will not even read, or be able to read, the entirety of the work. But since memory and desire and commitment are at stake in every case, in the end it will be the reader's actual memories and desires and commitments that matter, as these are placed under observation, even if they seem to diverge significantly from those more directly expected by the songs. To take a look at *Tiruvāymoḻi* as a primary text from another religious tradition is ultimately a costly endeavor in which one has to look at oneself too. The tension between the activities of service and the meditations of vision is also that of the reflective reader, who must similarly weigh the possibilities of the one against the advantages of the other. And none of this will occur, of course, except where the desire is strong enough. As the *Vedānta* theologians of the Sanskrit tradition have said, there must first of all be the desire to know, the *jijñāsā*. Some readers desire nothing more than to see God, some are just interested in learning about India or in the methods of religious studies.

Insofar as reading provides us with a mirror, we could intervene at this point in order to raise a series of parallel issues: how, for instance, have readers in the Jewish and Christian West devised habitual and fresh ways of reading the Psalms and the *Song of Songs* in the Bible? How do our expectations about poetry and how it has meaning affect the way we are likely to read *Tiruvāymoḻi*? What are we looking for when we read a poem—and what are we looking for when we read a "religious poem"? Such questions need to be raised, and we shall look at aspects of them in chapter 5, but it is premature to concern ourselves too much with answers to them. For *Tiruvāymoḻi* has not stood by itself all these years. Its possibilities were explored, tested and fixed early on; choices were made, the songs were passed down in context, their meaning and uses fixed and stated and applied. So we must read again, this time with the *ācāryas,* the master readers from early on in the Śrīvaiṣṇava tradition, who deciphered the songs in a vital and integral fashion. As we read with them in chapters 3 and 4, we will be preparing ourselves to return in chapter 5 to more basic questions: if we read *Tiruvāymoḻi* today, do we do it as they did, or do we do it differently? Does our reading lead us to the same locales, deeds, and insights that their reading led them? What else do we see, when we see *Tiruvāymoḻi*?

Chapter 3

Tiruvāymoḻi as Meditation, Narrative and Drama: Reading with the *Ācāryas*

> Once there was a man who wanted to learn just a little. He kept his mind open as far as the third song of *Tiruvāymoḻi,* thinking, "A person who is freed from passion should concentrate on these songs, for they pertain to reality." But when he came to the fourth song, he complained, "This song is merely about lust," and went away. Now this was his lack of good fortune, for such songs really indicate the desire for the Lord that is enjoined by the text, "The Self must be meditated on." [*Īṭu* on I.4.0][1]

The 100 songs and 1102 verses of *Tiruvāymoḻi* open up a rich range of possible interpretations; they invite listeners to participate in fixing their meaning in one way and then another, according to what seems fit, consonant with the vivid words of the songs and the wider contexts. Even if one respects the strictures imposed by the fact of *Tiruvāymoḻi*'s location within a Vaiṣṇava worldview—there are limits to what the songs can mean. The range of opportunities is very wide, as the songs, individually and all the more so when taken together, invite the completion of their meanings according to the particular memories and needs of the audience.

It is striking then to see how the meaning of *Tiruvāymoḻi* has been focused and finely articulated in its Śrīvaiṣṇava tradition. Over the centuries, its audience has in fact been educated to read it in a certain way, toward the accomplishment of certain moods and effects within listeners and readers. A process of determination began early on, as Śrīvaiṣṇavas gradually began to read the songs according to a certain problematic and in response to certain questions generated by that problematic.[2]

In the next two chapters we will trace the major components of the Śrīvaiṣṇava reading, insofar as the earliest commentaries tell us about it. As a Śrīvaiṣṇava text, *Tiruvāymoḻi* is preserved in a community where the learned teachers, the *ācāryas*, read it carefully, in their own way, imposing upon it the form of its author (chapter 3), and the form of its community, as they formulate this according to the meaning of the songs as deciphered and refined (chapter 4). By understanding these formations, it will also be possible to understand the expected and unexpected options available to the contemporary reader, as we shape our own response(s) in light of the openings suggested in chapter 2.

It is our task here to recognize and appreciate the exegetical and systematic commitments of the *ācāryas*. Throughout their commentaries, they offer a reading that carefully balances fidelity to the songs with fidelity to a specific set of theological views which accompanies and to some extent precedes their reading of them. In particular, they balance the *āḻvār's* very diverse expressions of his intensely personal delight and distress with his endeavor to articulate and confront the most basic religious problem, the capacity and limits of being human: i.e., to be human is to be oriented toward a union with God that cannot be fully consummated in this life, while yet in the body. The resultant interpretation of *Tiruvāymoḻi* is a highly refined exegetical theology in which literary and theological concerns deeply inform one another and neither is shunted aside for the sake of the other. As long as we pay attention to both their careful exegesis and their resolute theology, they will serve us well. The text is opened up, explained, and revealed as a source of practical nourishment and guidance for the community of believers.

A word of caution is in order about the inevitably limited, artificial and even arbitrary selection that comprises these two chapters: they do not tell us everything we need to know about *Tiruvāymoḻi,* its contexts and its place in the Śrīvaiṣṇava community, nor about the full and systematic presentation of the Śrīvaiṣṇava faith which was to develop in subsequent generations. I have worked with just the five primary commentaries, those of (Tirukkurukaippirāṉ) Piḷḷāṉ, Nañcīyar, Vaṭakkutiruvītippiḷḷai (who is said to have faithfully recorded Naṃpiḷḷai's discourses in the *Īṭu,* and whose record I shall refer to by the shorthand of reference to "Naṃpilḷḷai's commentary"), Periyavāccāṉpiḷḷai (who crafted Naṃpiḷḷai's discourses into a formal commentary), and Vātikesari Aḻakiya Maṇavāḷa Cīyar, along with several subcommentaries. These are not unsubstantial works to limit oneself to; altogether, they total over 4,000 pages, written in that difficult linguistic mixture known as the Śrīvaiṣṇava *maṇipravāḷa*—a splendid but intricate combination of the gem (*maṇi*) and the coral (*pravāḷa*) of the Tamil and Sanskrit languages taken together.[3] Though I have read major portions of these commentaries, I must admit that I have not read every word. There is a great deal of preliminary research yet to be done, just to state and make clear the meanings of various interpretations, to set forth the developments and differences among the *ācāryas'* views, and to trace the development of ideas from commentary to commentary.

These commentaries are interesting in part because we see in them the ongoing and still incompletely systematized theology of the Śrīvaiṣṇava community; yet their pre-systematic state means also that they are going to be all the more difficult to appreciate and summarize in their exegetical intent, their inventiveness and their provisionality. To catch them in the act of reading and to make sense of their interpretations must be a meticulous and tentative enterprise; it has a great deal to do with finding and selecting apt, illustrative citations from one or another of the various commentators, to make points which seem, in important ways, to pertain to all of them—and to do this without anachronistically anticipating later systematic theologies, or denying the differences that occur from commentary to commentary, or by way of summary replacing their commentaries with my own. As we listen in on their conversation, we are therefore venturing to read with them, alongside them, and to do this somewhat impetuously, before knowing everything, correctly and exactly as the good Indologist might wish. Everything that follows is therefore admittedly provisional, open to complement and nuance, although my goal is ambitious: to understand how the *ācāryas* read the individual songs and the whole of *Tiruvāymoḻi* and, by reading with them, to understand better the range of ways in which the songs in their tradition can be available to us today. Let us now turn to a delineation of their basic understanding of what is going on in the songs.

I. Śaṭakōpaṉ: Anguished Soul, Best of Theologians

In chapter 1 we reviewed the hagiographical account of Śaṭakōpaṉ, his extraordinary infancy, his 16 years of meditation under the tamarind tree, his awakening at the instigation of Maturakavi, and his sudden but perfect utterance of *Tiruvāymoḻi* (and his other three works) for his disciple. That pious account holds that the whole text was completely worked out and perfected in the mind of Śaṭakōpaṉ before he uttered one word of it in his recitation to Maturakavi. Prior to any normal temporal process of composition, the songs are removed from space as well; Śaṭakōpaṉ never goes anywhere, and even his vivid portrayals of temples rely on visits from deities who informed him about the temples under their protection.

Although this popular account may have a long oral heritage that precedes the written texts, in their commentaries the *ācāryas* neither repeat it nor deny it. Although there are several passages which seem to indicate another tradition on the matter of the *āḻvār's* life story, one in which he was more actively engaged in the world and with his audience during the time of composing his songs,[4] the *ācāryas* have almost nothing to say about Śaṭakōpan̲ the author "outside the text." But they do have very much to say about him *inside* the realm of the songs. For them, *Tiruvāymoḻi* is filled with his anguished plight, while it yet sparkles with his acute intelligence; his words tumble forth, yet they yet manage to state with refined precision everything that needs to be known if one is seeking after God.

Let us introduce these two basic components: the plight of Śaṭakōpan̲, and his perfection as seeker, thinker, author—and, by extension, the integral emotional and intellectual power of *Tiruvāymoḻi* as a whole.

1. The Plight of Śaṭakōpan̲

Each song is taken as representing a moment in the *āḻvār's* psychological development. The commentaries are filled with vivid descriptions of the *āḻvār's* desire, distress, and depression but also (always, at the last minute) his restored hopes. Indeed, these movements of soul serve to bind the interpretations together from song to song. Every experience the *āḻvār* has is enough only for a moment, every perceived limit seems fearfully like a hopeless dead-end, every delay a life-threatening torment. The *ācāryas* do not water down the vivid expressions of extreme feeling that are so much in evidence in *Tiruvāymoḻi*. Though, as we shall see, they locate such feelings within a larger pattern where they have their specific, legitimated meanings, the *ācāryas* are quite willing to repeat in their own words the extremities to which the *āḻvār* is prone, and even to accentuate them.

By way of example, let us turn to Nañcīyar (whose comments, here as elsewhere, have the two great virtues of relative brevity and completeness) and examine a few of his introductions to individual songs, where his diverse feelings are faithfully recorded. To begin with, the *āḻvār* can be filled with delight, even to the limits of his capacity to bear it:

> The *āḻvār* has meditated on his own state of existing for the sake of the Lord, after experiencing, by the Lord's

> unprompted favor, His beauty, good disposition, etc. He is exceedingly delighted . . . (VIII.9)

> The *ālvār* is exceedingly delighted, having meditated on how the Lord holds him in service, such that he is exclusively the Lord's. Now, due to the abundance of his delight, he does not stop there but goes farther, to the state where he exists solely for the sake of serving the Śrīvaiṣṇavas who are immersed in the Lord's beauty and good disposition, etc. (VIII.10)

But such moments of pleasure are usually accompanied by an intense desire for something more extended, more enduring:

> In saying, "When will my eyes see the sounding ankle bracelets of the Lord who once drove the chariot?" (III.6.10) the desire which arose earlier—"Red lotus-eyed Kaṇṇaṉ ate the seven worlds: see him! He became one with the most lustrous light, the form of the Three"[5] (III.6.1) has ripened. Although in III.7 he meditated constantly, still he has not been able to see as he has desired, and so he is exceedingly depressed. Therefore the *ālvār's* senses cry out one by one, each desiring the involvement of all of them: "We must see our Lord!" By saying that his senses experience desire, and that each sense desires the objects of the other senses, the *ālvār* thereby expresses the limitlessness of his own desire. (III.8)

Desire of such magnitude is predictably prone to frustration when its object remains elusive, so the *ālvār's* desire is quite often matched by depression:

> Thus in III.8 the *ālvār* and his gathered senses have cried out for a long time, desiring to see the Lord. Unable to do this, in III.9 the *ālvār* becomes exceedingly depressed. (III.9)

The *ālvār* is prone to dark loneliness, as in V.4, set in the dark of night:

> *The city sleeps, all the world is intense blackness,*
> *all the waters calmed, one long night stretches out.*
> *our lord who ate the whole earth, who lies on the snake bed,*
> *does not come.*
> *Alas, who will protect the life of this stubborn sinner now?* (V.4.1)

Remaining here, it's as if I melt away,
the lofty sky too melts in gentle dew, night continues;
no one wonders, "Once the lord came and measured the earth,
but now he does not come;"
the whole world sleeps. (V.4.10)

Nañcīyar observes how her sense of God does not protect her, but drives her to the extreme:[6]

> Now, in V.4, the young woman describes how night comes and all living beings sleep. Her relatives too are overcome, unable to share her suffering, and they sleep. She remains alone and disturbed in this state, and describes that night in detail. It seems many ages long, a great blackness, a night which rolls along and gives her no opportunity for escape. She describes her cruel fate which is the cause for her depression, but describes too that best of all males who should be helping her in her condition, and she mentions His gentleness and other virtues. After saying all of this over and over, she becomes completely depressed because no one notices how she does not pity herself or cry out in this state, nor how she does not break down and say, "This is wrong!"
>
> She reaches the point of dying. But she survives, saying, "He created that cosmic sleep solely with the thought of protecting the world; surely He will not neglect me in this depressed state! In order that everyone might reach His feet and thereby break their bond to material nature, the Lord created this world and undertook many descents into it. But all this has done nothing for me. At present I lack the means to terminate my relationship with material nature and thus to gain the Lord."

The *āḻvār's* feelings shift quickly, swinging this way and that, as joy itself leads to greater sorrow:

> After becoming afraid at the Lord's aloneness, the *āḻvār* has meditated on His valor, heroism, etc., and dispelled the fear which had been born within him . . . He desires then to see the Lord with his own eyes, to embrace Him intimately, and to converse with Him, but he is unable to do so.
>
> So the unsurpassable delight that had previously arisen deserts him. He then meditates on the Lord as present in

> both the Heavenly City and Tirucceṅkuṉṟūr, and cries, "The depression I have experienced from the beginning until now is but a small particle of my present depression!"
>
> Thus engulfed in the burning conflagration of his great depression, all his senses grieve and burn even more than he himself does. He experiences a great desire to see the Lord, and he keeps crying out that the Lord must reveal Himself in ways that refresh the *āḻvār* and end his anguish. Those who hear his anguish find it hard to endure the sound of it. (VIII.5)

The commentaries are filled with such accounts of the *āḻvār's* deepest, shifting feelings. In the following pages we shall have occasion to dwell on certain theological and more systematic concerns of the *ācāryas,* but this engagement of theological issues occurs without a sacrifice of sensitivity to the emotional depth of the songs. For it is in that depth, however bewildering it may be, that there lies the creative source of their theology.

2. The Perfect Theologian

The second starting point of *ācāryas'* interpretation is their view that *Tiruvāymoḻi* is theologically perfect in all its parts and as a whole: Śaṭakōpaṉ is the most vulnerable of lovers, but also the most acute of theologians. Though they are certain that *Tiruvāymoḻi* is born out of Śaṭakōpaṉ's inner experience, the *ācāryas* nevertheless do not read it as a series of momentary inspirations composed tentatively, in different moods and settings as ad hoc occasions might demand. Rather, from its creation—before it is recited—it is a complete, perfectly thought out and composed work of theology, informed from its first to last words with correct guidance to truth and right practice. It is a kind of theological *antāti,* beginning to end, end to beginning: no word is ever the first, no word ever replaces those that precede it; no part of *Tiruvāymoḻi* stands in contradiction to any other, but each confirms and enhances all the rest. Though necessarily linear, its meaning remains fully simultaneous in all its parts.

Of course, the claim to the perfection of the sacred text is a common feature of many religious traditions. What is striking here is that the view is maintained along with a positive appreciation of diversity within *Tiruvāymoḻi,* and especially without denying the *āḻvār's* very personal, creative role in composing the text: it is this human, anguished author who has accomplished the perfect text. Śaṭakōpaṉ stands in a self-conscious, reflexive relationship to his own experience, deliberately expressing it in a particular way so as to instruct the Vaiṣṇava community and all those who will listen. *Tiruvāymoḻi* (in continuity with his three other, earlier works that lead up to it, psychologically and theologically) perfectly reflects the full experience of the *āḻvār* that took shape in dialogue with his lord; the *ācāryas* understand this experience to be edifying, worth knowing, a complete guide to spiritual progress.

Of course, the main testimony of the *ācāryas* to their reverence for *Tiruvāymoḻi* is the very considerable energy they invest in teaching it; one learns best how they revere the text and its author by reading as much as possible of their commentaries: "Study the entire *Īṭu* three times with your teacher," they say even today, "and you will then have some understanding of it." But here we take a short cut to understand their estimation of the author and *Tiruvāymoḻi,* by following Nañcīyar's general introduction in its account of the excellence of text and author.[7] Nañcīyar makes weighty claims regarding the special character and authority of the *āḻvār:*

> Śaṭakōpaṉ possessed the essential nature of the Lord, His form, His qualities, and His entire glory: all of this is now made manifest in the *āḻvār* by the grace of the Lord . . . The *āḻvār* was the high point of all those wise ones whom the Lord mentions when He says, "The wise man is my own Self, I declare" [*Bhagavad Gītā* VII.18] . . . His nature was such that he could not for a moment endure separation from the Lord, for from his birth he was like Lakṣmaṇa,[8] he had the Lord as his sustenance . . . In him all worldly characteristics were eradicated, and by his inner nature he grew alarmed at the mention of any human goal other than the Lord . . .
>
> Three constituents of his being—the conscious, that lacking in consciousness, and the Lord—were consumed by his desire, which grew greater and greater like the ocean, so

> that it could never be satisfied even if he were to experience the Lord for all time . . . The *āḻvār* was in each and every way the standard for everyone, just as Prahlāda was the standard for all good people.[9] By his mere presence he banished all that darkness of ignorance in the form of "I" and "mine;" his proper nature was such that he brought about knowledge and devotion in people and established them in that freedom which is characterized by service of the Lord.[10]

Tiruvāymoḻi comes forth perfectly from this perfect author:

> When the time was ripe, he was unable to hold within himself his experience of the Lord's good qualities, and so were born his *Tiruviruttam, Tiruvāciriyam, Periya Tiruvantāti and Tiruvāymoḻi,* works so excellent that they destroyed doubts found both in the *Vedas* and in those epics and ancient *purāṇas* which confirm the *Vedas.* This the *āḻvār* graciously did, singing, "Composing these 1,000 verses in desirous *antāti* . . ." [*Tiruvāymoḻi* X.10.11][11]

To the objection that it is highly unlikely that a work coming forth spontaneously and unedited could be already so perfect, Nañcīyar responds by boldly comparing *Tiruvāymoḻi,* along with Śaṭakōpaṉ's other three works, with the revered epic, the *Rāmāyaṇa*:

> Look at how Vālmīki's *Rāmāyaṇa* was endowed by Brahmā's grace with all these perfections. As it says, "Niṣāda, may you never attain the unchanging state, for you have killed one love-struck Krauncha bird from a pair!" [*Bāla Kāṇḍa* 40.15] and, "By my [Brahmā's] pleasure alone, brahmin, you have spoken eloquently; therefore, best of seers, tell all the deeds of Rāma," [ibid.] Similarly, none of these perfections is impossible for these works that are born of the Lord's grace.[12]

Nañcīyar then gives eight reasons in justification of the excellence of *Tiruvāymoḻi*:

1. Among works intended to illuminate the goal of human life, these are the primary ones;
2. They came about in order to put into words that powerful abundance of delight which was born of his experience of the good qualities of the Lord;

3. By their sound, utterance and enunciation, we know that their foundation is a "divine eye" given by the grace of the Lord;[13]
4. They have the highest authority, because they are acceptable to all those learned people who have knowledge of the meaning of the *Veda,* and because we see in these works all that meaning of the *Veda* which must be known by those who are born in the torrent of this world;
5. The object of these discourses is the husband of Śrī, who is the highest goal for everyone;
6. The person with the right to read these works is anyone who lacks all taste for this world and who believes that it is necessary to do every kind of service at the feet of the Lord;
7. Those desirous of freedom, those who have been freed, the eternal ones, and our Lord who is the husband of Śrī—all will enjoy these works;
8. These works were composed in order to make known the unsurpassable human goal of service of the Lord, the object of description here.[14]

Thereafter Nañcīyar vigorously defends *Tiruvāymoḻi* against a series of seven objections which can be summarized briefly: 1. the songs cannot be taken seriously, since they are written in a vernacular tongue instead of sacred Sanskrit; 2. women and low-class *śūdras* are well-versed in them, although they are barred from access to real sacred texts; 3. they were composed in this worst age of the world by a man of the lowest class, who has no access to knowledge; 4. *Tiruvāymoḻi* is a regional text, not available everywhere; 5. people from outside the Vedic tradition accept it; 6. the songs judge inferior those states of lordship and isolation which scripture and tradition describe as legitimate human goals; and 7. the songs speak frequently of sexual desire, but such talk is contrary to both scripture and tradition.

Nañcīyar's response to the objection about the erotic content of the songs is emblematic of the innovative and bold approach of the *ācāryas:* "The songs are using the terminology of sexual love to speak of that devotion which in the *Upaniṣads* is spoken of as either knowledge or meditation." As is indicated by the anecdote cited at the head of this chapter, about the man who is offended by the sexual language in *Tiruvāymoḻi,* the *ācāryas* value this language deeply: the vocabularies of love and knowledge converge, desire and meditation cooperate. While the text is deeply imbued with the tumult of desire, it remains at the same moment also a theological discourse. It is a text of desire and passion, and sound, reliable theology, all at the same time.[15]

In chapter 4 we shall have occasion to examine another example of how Śaṭakōpaṉ is understood to model perfect theology in his personal experience, when we see what the *ācāryas* have to say about the two ways to the Lord, the ways of cultivated devotion (*bhakti*) and total surrender (*prapatti*). The songs chronicle the *āḻvār's* personal discovery that no path but total surrender can bring him to God, and they also give a refined and adequate theology of the virtues of *bhakti* and *prapatti,* and the superiority of the latter. As here, the point in chapter 4 remains the same: *Tiruvāymoḻi* ought to be read in two ways at once, as a vivid psychological portrayal of an ongoing series of mood-shifts, and as a straightforward, well-ordered theology that, despite its poetic form, is thorough and complete. However tumultuous, the songs are not an experimental diary of the *āḻvār's* emerging consciousness, a daily transcription of the utterances of a struggling self. Rather, all the parts of *Tiruvāymoḻi* presuppose the whole of his inner experience and are integrated perfectly into the whole, every verse enlightened by every other. Yet, as we shall see, the *ācāryas* take advantage of the chronological form of the text; for the sake of listeners, the *āḻvār's* progress is represented as a narrative which illustrates its theological exposition. We shall examine this narrative reading of the songs below.

But first, if we are to appreciate fully how the experiential and theological aspects of *Tiruvāymoḻi* are to be kept together—

in more than a pious gesture or generic claim—we must examine the root theological problematic which the *ācāryas* see as operative in the songs, at the point at which theology and psychology coalesce in the reading of the text: *the goal of this life is to see God, yet it is impossible to see God in this life.* Śaṭakōpaṉ feels most deeply the desire to see, and understands most fully the impossibility of doing so, here.

II. The Theological Problem of Vision

The problematic of the limits on the possible human vision of God in this life is founded by the *ācāryas* in the Sanskrit theology of their great *ācārya,* Rāmānuja. In the following sections we read the operation of the problematic of vision in the *ācāryas'* interpretation of the songs against the background of the formal expression of the problem of vision in Rāmānuja's theology. In the course of this, we will gain a better sense of how *Tiruvāymoḻi* is anchored in one specific theological worldview, which in turn is used as a tool in exegesis.

1. Rāmānuja on the (Indirect) Experience of God

The basic problem of the knowledge of God is set forth in Rāmānuja's *Śrībhāṣya,* his great commentary on the key *Vedānta* text, *Uttara Mīmāṃsā Sūtras.* In the introductory section of the *Bhāṣya* (particularly in "the brief exposition" [the *laghu siddhānta*] of his position at I.1.1), Rāmānuja introduces the basics of his *Vedānta* theology: the nature of the self (*jīva, ātman*), the transcendent reality (*brahman*), the distinction between what is real and what is illusory, plus the basic rules by which one can discern these truths which are revealed only in scripture. At I.1.3 he distinguishes three kinds of knowledge which appear to be in competition with scriptural knowledge: *perception,* based on the senses, *perception,* based on special yogic intuition, and *inference,* based on the reasonable assessment of whatever information is available about the constitution of the world, its origins, etc. Though not discounting entirely the possibility of direct knowledge that is not dependent on scripture—in the end, eschatologically as it were, such is possible—Rāmānuja denies to perception in its three forms the power to inform about religious realities:

> Of ordinary perception there are two sub-species, depending on whether the perception takes place through the outer sense-organs or through the internal organ. Now the outer sense-organs produce knowledge of their respective objects, insofar as the latter are in actual contact with the organs, but they are quite unable to give rise to the knowledge of the special object constituted by a supreme Self that is capable of being conscious of and creating the whole aggregate of things.
>
> Nor can internal perception give rise to such knowledge; for only purely internal things, such as pleasure and pain, fall within its cognizance; it is incapable of relating itself to external objects apart from the outer sense-organs.
>
> Nor is perception based on yoga able to give this knowledge; although such perception, which springs from intense imagination, implies a vivid presentation of things, it is after all nothing more than the reproduction of objects perceived previously, so it does not therefore rank as an instrument of knowledge; it has no means of applying itself to objects other than those perceived previously.[16]

There follows a much longer consideration of the real but limited value of inference as a means to knowledge of the origins of the world, with the same result: although reason is valuable, it must be firmly subordinated to that knowledge which is gained from scripture, the upaniṣadic texts.[17]

How scriptural texts are useful toward the acquisition of knowledge is stated in *Śrībhāṣya* I.1.1. All Vedāntins, including Rāmānuja, agree that the scriptures are necessary for salvific knowledge, but Rāmānuja debates his opponents, most conspicuously the Advaitins (the Non-Dualist Vedāntins), regarding the nature of liberative knowledge and the means to that knowledge. By Rāmānuja's account, his disagreement with Advaita has to do with what counts as knowledge of texts. He charges that the Advaitins so strongly insist on the sheer power of the words of the *Upaniṣads* that they seem to be suggesting that merely knowing words is the same as knowing what words communicate.[18] For Rāmānuja, the mere knowledge of the words cannot be liberative; still, though, there is something to be learned *through* the texts, when they are used properly, in the process of meditation:

> "Meditation" means steady remembrance, i.e., a continuity of steady remembrance, uninterrupted like the flow of oil; in agreement with the scriptural passage which declares steady remembrance to be the means of release, "on the attainment of remembrance all the ties are loosened." (*Chāndogya Upaniṣad* 7.26.2)[19]

Rāmānuja does not explain his emphasis on memory, or even what it is that is to be remembered.[20] But it is clear that he is emphasizing a process of internal clarification, whereby the reader personally appropriates the texts; one meditates under the guidance of texts, and brings new, vivid life to what one has already learned in some initial fashion.[21] He goes on to evaluate this remembering as an approximation of vision: "Such memory is of the same form as seeing, because the above passage has to agree in meaning with this passage, 'When He who is the highest and the lowest is seen, the knot of the heart is broken, doubts are all shattered, and his deeds perish' " (*Muṇḍaka Upaniṣad* II.2.8).[22] If so, then the texts one uses, however revered or efficacious they are in themselves, must become the material for a proper course of meditation: "That this is the case is known from another passage: 'The self, my dear, has to be seen, [heard, reflected upon, meditated upon . . .]' [*Bṛhadāraṇyaka* II.4.5]. We can be certain then that steady meditation has the same character as seeing. Moreover, memory has the character of seeing because it is [simply] an intensification [of the process] of mental conception . . ."

Rāmānuja then weaves together memory, seeing and perception, situating each in relation to the others:

> Such memory is declared to be of the same form as seeing; and for it to possess the nature of seeing is the same is to have the character of direct perception. Scripture thus

> specifies that memory which has been proved to possess the character of direct perception, and so to be the means of final release . . .[23]

No form of perception, no form of seeing, can be the source of knowledge of God. Only memory, informed by a knowledge of the sacred texts one has learned and meditated on, approximates vision. Rāmānuja makes one further, important correlation:

> Scripture makes a further determination, in the passage *Kaṭha Upaniṣad* II.23: "That Self cannot be gained by the study of the *Veda*, nor by thought nor by much hearing; whom the Self chooses, by him it may be gained; to him the Self reveals its being." This text means that mere hearing, reflection, and meditation do not suffice to gain the Self; it then declares, "Whom the Self chooses, by him it may be gained." Now a "chosen" one means a most beloved person; the relation being that he by whom that Self is held most dear is held most dear to that Self . . . . Therefore, the one who possesses remembrance marked by the character of immediate presentation, and which itself is dear above all things since the object remembered is such; he, we say, is chosen by the highest Self, and by him the highest Self is gained. Firm memory of this same character is denoted by the word "*bhakti*" (i.e., "devotion")—for "*bhakti*" is synonymous with "*upasanā*" (i.e., "meditation").[24]

The relationships among text, memory and (the approximation of) vision are remarkable, but still, in the end, there is still no sure path, and the outcome remains a matter of grace.[25]

In his small work known as the *Śaraṇāgatigadya,* Rāmānuja introduces a threefold distinction which the *ācāryas* use in describing the *āḻvār's* progress in meditation: superior devotion (*para bhakti*), superior knowledge (*para jñāna*), and highest devotion (*parama bhakti*). In verse two, he prays for . . .

> that satisfaction derived in all forms and kinds of service always suited to the conditions and circumstances of the moments and which is the result of boundless intense devotion born out of the experience of enjoyment of the lord; that is, the unbounded limitless love for no other end but

> that of service directed to him: a perfect love, enjoyed fully in all his manifestations, not only now but continuously with no interruption; and this again promoted by sincere one-pointed and ever intense superior devotion, superior knowledge and supreme devotion at the lotus feet of the lord.

And at verse 15 he adds,

> Endow me with constant superior devotion, superior knowledge and supreme devotion . . .

and, in the divine response in verse 16,

> By my mere mercy you will be freed completely from the obstructions to superior devotion, superior knowledge and supreme devotion and their causes. You will also by my grace obtain superior devotion, superior knowledge and supreme devotion and be favored by the direct vision of me, my form, my attributes, my glories and also the fundamental Nature . . ."

Though Rāmānuja does not explain the three terms—superior devotion, superior knowledge and supreme devotion—the commentators on the *Gadya* do. In his Sanskrit commentary, Śrutiprakāśikācārya gives definitions: superior devotion is the desire for ever greater, more immediate and manifest knowledge; superior knowledge is immediate, manifest knowledge; and supreme devotion is the desire for ever greater experience. In his *maṇipravāḷa* commentary, Periyavāccāṉpiḷḷai offers a distinctively Tamil gloss on the same terms: superior devotion is a variety of love in which one has the delight and sorrow due (respectively) to union and separation; superior knowledge is the immediate knowledge which comes with the ripening of that love; and, in terms of the mood that follows union, supreme devotion is the state in which one is unable to bear separation for even a moment. At verse 16, Periyavāccāṉpiḷḷai correlates increasing devotion with increasing clarity of vision: then, as devotion grows, it becomes clear (*viśada*), clearer (*viśadatara*) and most clear (*viśadatama*). We shall see below how the *ācāryas* correlate the stages of devotion and stages of clarity with the progress of *Tiruvāymoḻi*.

We conclude our brief consideration of Rāmānuja's contribution of a theological background for *Tiruvāymoḻi* by stressing the basic points: the knowledge gained through texts is fundamental, since direct experience (perception, vision) is not possible here; this textual knowledge is not in itself final; through the appropriation of textual knowledge, one gets beyond texts, as one learns to "see through" them. Rāmānuja is committed to a process of meditation in which texts are central but not sufficient. Clarification of knowledge through texts occurs in a process of meditation carried out over a period of time. The carefully demarcated and self-sufficient *Veda* of the Mīmāṃsakas and Advaitins is respected, but made to depend on a process that leads beyond it (and that, as we shall see, is also communal, because learning is communal). One uses words patiently, over a long term, in order to reach, by grace, an experience that goes beyond words; by texts, one gets beyond them, one sees God through them.

2. The Ācāryas' *Reading of the Problem of Vision in* Tiruvāymoḻi

For the *ācāryas,* all of the preceding is what Śaṭakōpaṉ is singing about: he reaches the frustrating, inevitable limits of vision, within the context of a remedial process of actions that stand for vision and bring one near by different means. In the view of the *ācāryas, Tiruvāymoḻi* records how this patient commitment works, what it costs, and what happens along the way: one learns, remembers and as it were, begins to see.

A. Looking for God. The *ācāryas* shared Rāmānuja's view of the problem of vision, that is to say, direct experience of God. Humans innately desire to see God, but cannot achieve vision in this life. Perception is not sufficient, inference is not a viable substitute for direct experience, and even the all-important *Upaniṣads* offer only a textually-mediated knowledge which approaches perception, something like vision. This position stands in the background of their reading of *Tiruvāymoḻi* as they interpret the apparently disparate claims made by the *āḻvār*—his desperate separations and deep moments of unity—according to the principle that vision can be approached but not gained in this life: the āḻvār wants to see, he sees, he doesn't see. God has been tangible and visible in the poet's life, God is nowhere to be found, now.

The concern for vision, evident throughout the commentaries, receives clear expression early on:

> *Accessible to those who love him, hard to find for others,*
> *the amazing one in whom the lady in the lotus delights,*
> *he whose feet are so hard for us to gain*
> *is bound to the grindstone, his firm waist is tied because he stole*
> *the butter from the churn:*
> *what is this? how pitiful, how vulnerable!*
>
> *Accessible by nature, born again and again without any limit in*
> *nature,*
> *by his nature bestowing radiant, complete goodness,*
> *beginningless, imperishable Release,*
> *the eternal lord of all without end, giving clarity;*
> *protecting, gracious, he is inside, he is outside.* (I.3.1–2)

Nañcīyar gives this rationale for the descents of the Lord by which he makes himself accessible:

> In this world, when one sees something with the eye, one can then enjoy it by touching it. So how can we, who are so utterly lowly, enjoy this Lord of everything—who is beyond the senses and can neither be seen nor touched?
>
> Just to hear that our Lord is the unsurpassable object of enjoyment gives birth to a desire to see Him. In order that people might see Him, and while remaining perfect in His qualities—excellence of character, etc.—the Lord by His own choice becomes like ordinary human beings. He descends in every age, with the forms of Rāma, Kṛṣṇa, etc., in order to protect those who take refuge in Him by His supernatural, divine body, and in order to destroy whatever might be an obstacle to their reaching Him. (I.3.0)

Naṃpiḷḷai puts it this way:

> Many times we hear it said, 'Be devoted to Him.' But there is no way to be devoted to Him without seeing Him with

> one's eyes; there is no way of seeing Him without being devoted to Him—so how then can one take refuge?
>
> It says, "He is seen, who is high and low," (*Muṇḍaka Upaniṣad* 2.2) and "By devotion one knows Me as I really am; after knowing Me as I really am, immediately thereupon he enters Me." (*Bhagavad Gītā* 18.55), Thus there is a devotion-as-means which culminates with some pain in manifestation, and that is what is being referred to here (in I.3). He is easily accessible to those who cry out with desire, "I must see Him!" (I.3)

Naṃpiḷḷai's comment gives later *ācāryas* the occasion to correlate the dynamics of *bhakti* with movement toward a vision that is "mental" but real, parallel to and in substitution for direct vision. In commenting on Naṃpiḷḷai, Āttāṉcīyar[26] makes some terse correlations that are in part based on Rāmānuja's threefold distinction of superior devotion, superior knowledge, and supreme devotion:

Meditation	*Perception*
1. the mind	1. the eye
2. the knowledge gained by devotion	2. superior vision
3. devotion, as a form of meditation	3. superior vision
4. superior devotion	4. the desire for further experience
5. superior knowledge	5. perception, experience
6. the supreme devotion	6. the inability to bear separation
7. direct manifestation	7. true knowledge

The dynamics of meditation match step by step the ordinary, exterior process of meditation, and both perception and meditation, at their hypothetical end point in perfect clarity, eventuate in true knowledge. Āttāṉcīyar concludes his comment on this section with an (unidentified) quotation that grades the process of meditation according to the three stages of devotion: "Superior devotion is the desire to have perception of an unseen object; superior knowledge is the bursting-forth manifestation of that [object]; supreme devotion subsists in the fear of ever being separated again." This is simply Rāmānuja's terminology applied to *Tiruvāymoḻi*: real manifestation and real union occur through the mental processes of meditation.

At the beginning of the next song, I.4, Piḷḷāṉ captures the theological dynamism of *Tiruvāymoḻi*:

> In this way the *āḻvār* has experienced the Lord by a knowledge which has the same form as seeing but, for this very reason, there is born in him a desire for exterior union. So now in I.4 he focuses on that. When this is not available, he becomes exceedingly depressed. He meditates on the qualities of the Lord, His tolerance of all sins, etc., but he thinks that He who has such qualities has abandoned him. He makes a presentation of his desire to the Lord by the words of messengers.[27]

B. On Not Quite Seeing God: Some Examples. To sharpen our understanding of the *ācāryas'* theological expectations regarding vision, in this section I will consider verses which appear to indicate actual vision, words spoken by a narrator within a song, or by the young woman bereft of her beloved, or by Śaṭakōpaṉ, as an inscribed first-person narrator. Such seemingly conclusive verses test the *ācāryas'* double commitment to careful reading and to the principle that there can be no direct vision in this world, even for the author of *Tiruvāymoḻi*. Let us review the most interesting examples, noting the pattern of reinterpretation which moves toward a doctrinally consistent reading of the verses.

In a first instance, commenting on "I saw my Kaṇṇaṉ, whose color is like a dark cloud" (II.8.10), Nampiḷḷai seems simply to repeat the *āḻvār's* claim as a testimony to how the lord makes himself accessible:

> When the *āḻvār* says, "I saw Kaṇṇaṉ," he means: not only does the Lord abide with the world as His body, but He who has a lovely body like a raincloud in the heavenly Śrīvaikuṇṭa, so that His activity is manifest there, has also came down as Kaṇṇaṉ, so that I have gotten to experience Him, seeing Him right before me—here for me to touch. (II.8.10)

Periyavāccāṉpiḷḷai suggests rather vaguely that the *āḻvār* must mean, "I have gotten to experience Him as my helper." Neither he nor Naṃpiḷḷai gives any further significance to the apparent direct contact between the *āḻvār* and Kaṇṇaṉ.

When Śaṭakōpaṉ says, "He who is hard for the eyes to see," (III.6.11), Naṃpiḷḷai emphasizes the tension inherent in this desire for what is impossible, and interjects the compromise position suggested by Rāmānuja:

> The *āḻvār* says, "the Lord cannot be grasped merely by the eyes, but only with difficulty. He is hard to see with the eyes, but still one cannot forget Him and so one complains, 'He can't be seen.' Yet He is very much in my heart." The *āḻvār's* separation is the mental confusion he experiences due to his desire for external experience; his union with the Lord is manifestation—knowledge *which has the same form as perception.* [my emphasis]

In commenting on "My eyes desire to see you truly" (III.8.4), Naṃpiḷḷai says that to see truly, completely, is to see in such a way that mental experience becomes just like perception, due to the power of the experience. Similarly, at IV.9.9,

> You whose bed is on the snake, this servant knows you: that I might go about bearing your feet, leaving behind all shame, you have brought me near to your hard to approach feet: I've seen this,

Naṃpiḷḷai says that the *āḻvār's* claim to vision is his way of talking about a very powerful *inner* experience.

In the third verse of V.1 Śaṭakōpaṉ claims, "Now I've ended up seeing you," (V.1.3) but the fourth verse manifests a quite different feeling: "I am a stubborn sneak, speaking such words." (V.1.4) In explanation of this seemingly abrupt shift, Naṃpiḷḷai records that some earlier *ācāryas* interpreted verse 3 to mean that the *āḻvār* has achieved a mental acquisition of the lord but that, as before, the *āḻvār* is depressed when he tries to convert this mental vision into an external vision and then union; verse 4 represents his feelings of failure in his effort to attain direct vision, external union, and his blaming this on himself.

Similarly, when Śaṭakōpaṉ says, "One day give my eyes a steady form to see" (V.10.7), Naṃpiḷḷai says that he is really talking about what he experiences in meditation and his desire for more than that:

> The *āḻvār* says to the Lord: Lest I melt away with this merely mental meditation, graciously act so that I can experience you with my eyes . . . You tell me that you give me mental experience which is of the same form as perception—but that is not what I want! You must turn it into steady perception—which mental experience can never be, for it is like a dream. (V.10.7)

At VI.3.1, the *āḻvār* claims to have seen the lord: "I have seen him at Tiruviṇṇakar." But Naṃpiḷḷai says that while there is a kind of seeing that can be achieved by visiting temples the *āḻvār*, who remained stationary at the foot of the tamarind tree,

> cannot have that kind of vision which could have occurred only if he had taken a different body and had gone to some different place; rather, here he is getting experience due to his act of desire, and this is like finding food in a place where one is hungry . . .

It is simply the intensity of inner experience that is being symbolized by comparison to the vision one has in a temple. Of course, VI.5, the song with which we began this book, is all about what happens when one "sees" God in a temple, and it too can be taken analogously as indicating the kind of experience the *āḻvār* has.

Finally, when the *āḻvār* says,

> *The one who is the complete content of all six philosophical*
> *systems in all their forms,*
> *who is the inner form of all things, who is the first one,*
> *who is the cause of all the gods, Kaṇṇaṉ:*
> *him I have seen* (IX.4.8),

Naṃpiḷḷai qualifies this claim by emphasizing that real vision is a spiritual achievement:

> Although he was born after the Lord's descents, the *āḻvār* says, "I have seen." What he means is this: the Lord can be seen by those who love Him, not by those who merely live in the same time period, such as Śiṣupāla.[28] The Lord, who cannot be reached through other religions, is the inner self of all and controller of all, He is the originator of Brahmā, etc. He is easily accessible to those who take refuge with Him, and in that way I have gotten to see Him. (IX.4.8)

Here, nearness to the Lord's feet, in service, substitutes for nearness in vision; these two epicenters, highlighted in chapter 2,[29] complement and also substitute for one another.

C. Visualization. One particularly important case in which the *ācāryas* deflect the *āḻvār's* apparent claims to have seen God is their appeal to the practice of *uruveḷippāṭu,* "exteriorizing (*veḷippāṭu*) the form (*uru*)," which here I shall abbreviate as "visualization." This practice is introduced to explain a song or verse which seems to present a visual experience so vivid that it cannot be explained as merely "meditational." That is, when the *āḻvār* is very much distressed at his inability to see the lord, he "conjures up" an exterior vision that is so vivid that the lord appears visible, even tangible; the intensity of the experience is such that the *āḻvār's* anguish is for the moment alleviated. For the *ācāryas,* this visualization is the best possible approximation to that direct religious experience which, according to the *Vedānta* of Rāmānuja which they follow, must elude viewers in this life.

Thus far I have found mention of the practice of visualization in the commentaries on five songs in *Tiruvāymoḻi.*[30] Here I will focus on only the two instances, V.5 and VII.10, whole songs which are understood to exemplify visualization. In *Tiruvāymoḻi* V.5, the young woman seems to be insisting that she has seen God in lovely Tirukuṟuṅkuṭi; in one of the few clear refrains in a song in *Tiruvāymoḻi,* every verse voices the same insistence in its second line, as these first verses show:

Women, how can you be angry at me?
after I saw our master who lives in lovely Tirukuṟuṅkuṭi,
my heart has joined
his conch, his discus, his lotus eyes, his red fruit mouth.

See the world with the eyes of my heart, don't be angry at me.
after I saw our master who lives among the cool lovely groves of Tirukuṟuṅkuṭi,
his splendid thread, his earrings, the emblem on his chest, his four firm, adorned arms have come,
they are everywhere. (V.5.1–2)

Since the *ācāryas* seem committed to the notion that Śaṭakōpaṉ—here, the young woman—does *not* actually visit temples but rather imagines them intensely, Naṃpiḷḷai interprets this claim to vision to be evidence of a deep theological appreciation:

> You women do not see what is being shown to you, you do not know this object as it really is. But I am not like that, for when He has shown Himself—"He graciously gives the good of mind which removes confusion" (I.1.1)—I see, I have seen Him as He really is, so I am caught in the beauty of my Lord's form, the beauty of His appearance, the beauty of His ornaments, the beauty of His greatness. So your well-meant words won't reach me!

He goes on to explain that although the young woman rejoices when she remembers the lord, because she cannot repeat the experience, she then grieves; caught between joy and sorrow, she improvises, imagining him so powerfully that she can say, always just for a moment, "I have seen him in lovely Tirukuṟuṅkuṭi."

Naṃpiḷḷai does not explain the practice of visualization—he introduces the term only in comparing the song with VII.7 to which we will turn in a moment—but Āttāṉcīyar offers a simple definition: "Visualization is an appearing which is like perception . . ." He then takes up an objection: "If all the songs up to *Tiruvāymoḻi* X.10 are mental experience, how are they different from visualization ?" He responds that mental experience in general proceeds according to changing moods, "as one forgets what was experienced previously and proceeds to a different mood." By contrast, "visualization generates attention to a new mood according to a previously experienced one [and not on the basis of forgetfulness of what preceded]."[31]

Āttāṉcīyar cites an example of visualization from the *Rāmāyaṇa*—the terror of Maricha who, as he testifies to the demon king Rāvana, cannot stop seeing Rāma. Vālmīki puts it this way:[32]

> Having somehow got back my life, being spared by the shaft of Rāma, I have been forced to turn a recluse here. Calm and collected, I have taken to the practice of yoga, adopting an ascetic life. But in each and every tree I actually perceive Śrī Rāma clad in the bark of trees and the black antelope-skin, wielding a bow and resembling Death with a noose in his hand. Terrified, Rāvana, I even behold thousands of Rāmas. To me the whole of this forest appears as having turned into Rāma. (*Āraṇya Kāṇḍa* 39.15)

By contrast to this visualization based on dread, *Tiruvāymoḻi* V.5 offers a vision which proceeds from affection; yet both are kinds of visualization.

In VII.7 the young woman meditates serially on the aspects of the Lord she sees—eyes, nose, mouth, brows, smile, ears, forehead, face, hair, head—moving from one to the other, immersed in each in turn, grieving at the unattainability of each of them:

> *Are they double Death eating the spirits of the wretched? I do not know;*
> *are they the eyes of lovely lord Kaṇṇaṉ with the discus? I do not know;*
> *see, they come and appear all around me, like fresh lotuses:*
> *friends, women, what should I do, I am afflicted?*
>
> *Shaking, reviling, continually—women, what's the point of your torturing me?*
> *is it a creeper from the karpaka tree, climbing nearby, or is it a shoot? I do not know;*
> *the nose of the one who ate the stolen butter shines,*
> *a fierce blazing fire deep in my soul.* (VII.7.1–2)

In introducing the song as a whole, Naṃpiḷḷai poignantly describes the impact of visualization:

> [Previously, in VII.6.6] he has meditated on the beauty of the Lord's form; he has rooted the beauty of that form in his heart and experienced it, and due to his superabundant experience, it is of the same form as perception. Then, thinking, "This is [real] perception," and meditating on how near it is, he stretches out his hand to grasp it—and when he cannot grasp it, his condition becomes unbearable. He expresses this suffering by the verses of a young woman who, now separated after union, suffers due to this visualization . . .

In the same introduction he also anticipates an objection: "The *āḻvār's* true nature is expressed everywhere in *Tiruvāymoḻi*—his desire for the lord's qualities, his mental experience [of them], his desire to experience qualities other than those he is experiencing, his inability to get these one after the other, his efforts to forget each past experience. In light of all this, what is specially added by these songs of visualization?" Naṃpiḷḷai's response, recalling his comment at V.5, clarifies the nature of visualization: "When he considers all the clarity he had previously gained, yet beyond that desires more—that's when visualization occurs. In other songs, he desires more only after leaving aside clarity previously gained." Memory—Rāmānuja's *smṛti,* remembering-through-meditation, is the basis for visualization.[33]

On the whole,[34] Naṃpiḷḷai's references to the practices of visualization, instead of actual seeing, emphasize the intensity of the desire to see, the impossibility of vision in this life, and the persistence of the *āḻvār* in trying to achieve the impossible. *Tiruvāymoḻi* is understood to record this necessary desire, and the necessary failure to satisfy it. Previous experiences and their expression in song become possible starting points for new experiences of the lord and, in memory, the basis for visualization. But the further delay of vision always enhances the dramatic thrust of the text, as postponement makes desire grow. The *āḻvār* is made to test the boundaries of the rule that meditation is the nearest approximation of direct vision in this life.

D. As Near as One Can Get to Vision. To sum up, let us return to the basic objection, raised finally at X.4, that all of these practices and intense feelings are still only in the mind—and therefore not qualitatively different from the rest of *Tiruvāymoḻi* where vision is not claimed. The song itself proclaims the nearness of the lord:

The feet of Tāmotara help on the path of asceticism,
dark cloud-colored, lotus-eyed,
the bearer of the discus, water, sky, earth, fire, wind,
the heaven-dwellers never stop talking of his names' greatness.

Greater than the heavenly unwinking ones, difficult for those not holding him within,
Māl, red lotus eyes, on whose chest Tiru forever dwells,
destroying both kinds of deeds each day, here he rules me.

He bears the discus, he rules me, from whom do I need anything?
I have no need to be saved, I have ended the sorrows of death:
I have fixed my eyes on the feet of the husband of chaste Piṉṉai whose eyes shine, a sword, a keṇṭai fish,
I adorn my head with them. (X.4.1–3)

As the *ācāryas* read the song, it is with this gracious approach of the lord that the relation of lord and *āḻvār* is resolved—it will end happily, in union—but also the problem of vision is resolved through sure reliance on the lord and steadfast dwelling at his feet. In introducing the song, Naṃpiḷḷai identifies Śaṭakōpaṉ's intense devotion, which culminates in a meditation that in turn culminates in direct manifestation. Meditation on the lord's qualities leads ultimately to the lord: "If a quality is the object of meditation, then the one qualified by that quality is also present in the meditation." Āttāṉcīyar elaborates more dramatically: "Attainment is perception; by saying 'meditation which has the same form as manifestation,' he means a specific mental experience which appears as perception, and does not appear merely 'in the same form as perception.' "

Naṃpiḷḷai adds that by the time one reaches X.4 the proximity to real vision is very intense, and Āttāṉcīyar again elaborates rather strikingly:

> Previous texts [which claimed direct vision—II.8.10, IV.9.10, V.1.3 and IX.4.9] referred to that mental meditation which has the same form as perception. Compared with those, however, this song is very near to X.10, so here there is a special clarity to the mental experience. Even if previously there had been meditation on the goal, there was still going to be depression connected with separation, and the experience of the goal could only be partial. But here the experience of the goal is complete, because of how many times it has already occurred.

At X.4.9, in commenting on the words, "I have seen his lotus feet," Nampiḷḷai says:

> The *āḻvār* says that he has gotten to see the Lord solely due to His grace—that Lord who has been attained so many times by that devotion which is defined by its object. As it says, "By means of austerities, meditation and contemplation on the Lord, in thousands of other births, the sins of human beings are annihilated and devotion to Kṛṣṇa born." (*Laghu Atri Smṛti*)

The *āḻvār's* desire to see, and claims to have seen, are made coherent with a continuing insistence on the sure impossibility of vision in this life and the insistence on surrender and service:

> Though elsewhere he had proposed devotion [*bhakti*, which is cultivated over time] as an alternative to the total surrender [*prapatti*, which is caused by the Lord alone] expounded here, now he says here that the Lord is the cause even for devotion; he says that he has no need for anything, and he explains how he accomplished his achievement.[35] The *āḻvār* says, "I have seen:" i.e., what he had always heard about, he now gets to see. He explains how this fits with his proper goal, how he has now gotten direct manifestation—i.e., direct manifestation in that knowledge which has the same form as perception.

Whereas today one might tend to read all these songs simply as variously expressive of different moods which are not meant to be harmonized, the *ācāryas* forcefully represent *Tiruvāymoḻi* as consistent in its testimony to the doctrine that one cannot see God while in the human body. Though the *āḻvār's* verses—and hence his experiences—are revered and minutely analyzed, even at their most joyful they are not allowed to transgress the boundaries of good theology, nor are they, at the *āḻvār's* moments of worst depression, allowed to mean that vision will always be impossible. In his best and worst moments both, Śaṭakōpaṉ remains always the best of theologians: *his* experience is *universalized*. The human condition is examined without romance, yet infused with the clarity that comes from understanding it. Vision is the only satisfying human goal, but this vision must occur later.

III. Tiruvāymoḻi *as Meditation*

The *ācāryas* are also following Rāmānuja when they read *Tiruvāymoḻi* as a text of meditation which describes and responds to the problem that direct vision is both necessary and impossible here, and as a record of how meditation, traversing the gap between word and vision, leads to the proximate resolution of that problem. Śaṭakōpaṉ's internal search is correlated with the ongoing act of meditation; the search and the process of meditation are captured in the words of the songs, which then become an imitable guide for others, surpassing even the *Upaniṣads.* Here, again, a close reading of the songs and a theology about them are closely integrated.

1. Tiruvāymoḻi *as the Act of Meditation*

We have already seen how Rāmānuja argued against those who thought that a direct salvific experience was possible without textual mediation, and those who thought that somehow the texts themselves, by their mere words, contained the salvific element required. In its positive version, his argument is that a patient, longterm reflection on texts—on what has been heard (*śruti*) and what has been remembered (*smṛti*)—is the reliable means toward this life's closest approximation of vision. *Tiruvāymoḻi* is taken by the *ācāryas* as confirming Rāmānuja's text as cited above: "Meditation [on upaniṣadic texts] is of the form of a succession of memories, which is unbroken like a stream of oil. For firm memory is declared to be a means of final release . . ." Śaṭakōpaṉ is understood to mark this meditational path, although it is evident that he does not undertake meditation exactly according to Rāmānuja's expectations: he does not use the sacred texts, since his primal meditation, "heard" directly from the lord, is the source of the texts he composes. But he is a seeker, he fails to achieve by interior meditation alone the direct experience which yoga promises (which Rāmānuja denied it could deliver), and he survives by potent acts of memory which both assuage his tormenting thirst and make him desire more.

Let us now see how the *ācāryas* read *Tiruvāymoḻi* as a text from and for meditation. In his general introduction, Naṃpiḷḷai traces the origins of *Tiruvāymoḻi* to the *āḻvār's* experience of the lord. He indicates that the experience which occurred within the *āḻvār* before any words were uttered was a process of increasing mental clarity:

> Śaṭakōpaṉ thus experiences clearly, more clearly, most clearly the Lord's proper form, His forms and qualities and manifestations; all of this cannot be held inside him, it overflows and is uttered outside, resulting in these works.

These stages of clarity—clearly, more clearly, most clearly—parallel the stages of devotion Rāmānuja expressed in the *Śaraṇāgatigadya*: a gradually dawning clarity, in the ascent from superior devotion to superior knowledge to supreme devotion. Meditation is the source of the songs, which in turn trace meditation's growth toward fruition.

In commenting on the words of Naṃpiḷḷai just cited, Āttāṉcīyar adds two observations which make the preceding points clear. First, Śaṭakōpaṉ "attains that specific knowledge which is established as superior devotion, superior knowledge and supreme devotion, and which is accompanied by that loss of desire for other things which arises due to the Lord's gracious glance." Second, these three steps parallel Śaṭakōpaṉ's works, grouped in three parts: superior devotion, clear knowledge characterized by joys and sorrows, is the topic of all the verses from the beginning of *Tiruviruttam,* through *Tiruvāciriyam* and *Periya Tiruvantāti,* up to and including

Tiruvāymoli X.8.11; superior knowledge is treated in *Tiruvāymoli* X.9; supreme devotion, the inability to endure without God, is treated in *Tiruvāymoli* X.10. Śaṭakōpaṉ's four works thus document and illustrate meditation as understood by Rāmānuja.[36] By this correlation the ācāryas are suggesting that the good devotee—Vedāntin, Vaiṣṇava, Śaṭakōpaṉ—just tread the path of meditation. Acts of reflection, reading, focus, remembrance, perseverance over time, a gradual learning to love more steadfastly, will lead one as far as one can go toward direct vision, as vision and love-with-knowledge are clarified. For Śaṭakōpaṉ, all of this occurs internally—without books, teachers, etc.—but the dynamics are the same.

Meditation is not a one-time event; it must be repeated, it advances slowly, its benefits occur only gradually, after some time. We recall that in the hagiographical account of Śaṭakōpaṉ (described in chapter 1) he is said to have meditated for 16 years before saying anything at all. Although the *ācāryas* do not mention that account explicitly in their commentaries, they read the songs as interior meditations undertaken by the *āḻvār*. *Tiruvāymoli* is used to reflect the long process in which the *āḻvār* came to an understanding of his inner self, his restricted situation in the body, and the nature of God. It is therefore theological, but it is also a living record of meditation, the process toward the real goal of full, direct vision:

Thinking, thinking, but even if you keep thinking about this
state below, within, above, beyond form,
it's still hard to know the lord's state, people;
so keep thinking, keep speaking of him who is called "Ari, Ayaṉ,
Araṉ,"
keep thinking, propounding,
but then worship:
what you are thinking of is One. (I.3.6)

Will the people who truly know all this serve anyone
but the one who made the good waters, made the Fourfaced one,
mixed within himself every old thing, and made every
thing appear anew after that long period when every thing
of every sort had perished
—after they have meditated on these skillful exploits?

Will the people who have meditated on these skillful exploits
embrace the feet of anyone
but the marvellous one who took the form of the boar when the
earth was drowning in the great deep waters and he held it
on his horn so that it wouldn't sink
—after they have heard and thought about all this? (VII.5.4–5)

In his general introduction Nañcīyar summarizes the dynamics of this kind of meditation:

> Union of the sort he had with the Lord is a direct manifestation of knowledge in the same form as perception. Separation is what occurred when he desired external union but could not obtain it, and so experienced mental confusion. The Lord is omniscient, omnipotent, all-controlling, and by nature imbued with flawless mercy; so what was His purpose in making this cleavage, so that His union with the *āḻvār* would not ripen?
>
> Just as happened during the separation experienced in Ayodhyā [Rāma's home] and Kuruvai [Kaṇṇaṉ's home], the separation made the *āḻvār* experience a great, ever greater thirst to make his own those qualities which he had experienced. When desire ripens and yet one does not obtain what one desires as hoped, grief and confusion come about. The state of the *āḻvār* that arises due to this consummation and subsequent separation is expressed through the words of the young woman.[37]

Fully half of Nañcīyar's introductions to individual songs refer to meditation as either the source for the song or as a response to what was learned in meditation. Such references are, of course, handy exegetical tools, for any shift in topic and mood can be accounted for. References to shifts in the moods of meditation provide a reliable and clear rationale by which to bridge the gap between one song and another, as the intervening silence is invested with various meanings.

Here are just a few examples of how Nañcīyar uses this appeal:

> After thus meditating on the transcendent nature of the Lord in I.1, due to the abundance of his delight born in that

experience, the *āḻvār* reaches the state of mind wherein he can no longer endure except by addressing at least a few others . . . (I.2)

By the ruse of sending messengers in I.4, the *āḻvār* has reminded the Lord that He tolerates sins. Immediately after that, the *āḻvār* meditates on the Lord's uniqueness and his own lowliness, so that the Lord will look favorably on their union. (I.5)

Singing "Kaṇṇaṉ the jewel, Kaṇṇaṉ of the heaven-dwellers, a jewel even to himself," [I.10.11] the *āḻvār* has meditated on the accessibility of the Lord, His greatness and His beauty, and has been excited toward external union. But this turns out to be impossible. Because he is so far immersed in the Lord's qualities but is now separated, he does not send a messenger as in I.4. Instead he meditates on the fact that like himself all things are grieving in separation from the Lord. He is confused and is depressed, and expresses his condition indirectly, in the woman's voice. (II.1)

The young woman's mother meditates on how the Lord graciously undertook descents, coming as Rāma, Kṛṣṇa, etc., taking suitable forms, so that all can see. She meditates on His nature, how He protects those who depend on Him, and on what has happened to her daughter who suffers so greatly due to the lack of help for her. She then speaks to the Lord about this . . . (II.4)

The Lord becomes radiant due to His union with the *āḻvār*. He shows the *āḻvār* the glories and qualities and forms of His proper form, His divine ornaments, His divine deeds, and all the other divine pleasures within Him. Thus the Lord has done all there is to do. Meditating on all this, the *āḻvār* is filled with delight and astonishment; in speaking about it, he experiences the same flourishing within himself. (II.5)

The *āḻvār* rejoices in seeing how the Lord's abundance of love for him cannot be contained within himself, how it floods ever increasingly even among his relatives. Delighted, he says, "This is even more than His making me His own!"

> He meditates on the qualities and deeds appropriate to the Lord's making him His own, and by speaking of them he experiences too the names which express those deeds. (II.7)

Meditations are always concrete and specific within the *āḻvār's* experience; it occurs within the context of specific encounters where old ideas are stretched and tested and new possibilities opened up. While the rich diversity of images and themes in the songs is respected, however, for the *ācāryas Tiruvāymoḻi* is understood ultimately as one complex, single act of remembering the lord and seeking after him.

At the beginning of this chapter I pointed to the sharply varying emotions evident in the songs, especially the delight aroused by awareness of God, the desire for more experience, the depression caused by the inability to attain or keep hold of God, the anguish prompted by the prolonged experience of the combination of great desire and lack of satisfaction. I noted too the fidelity of the *ācāryas* in recording these emotions in their comments; they did not ignore the flux of emotions for the sake of a theological correctness. Here we can add that in describing the disparate and shifting emotions in the context of meditation, the *ācāryas* also emphasize the interconnections among moods, how one leads to another, even when a mood seems abruptly different, unhinged from the one preceding it. The moods frequently occur in studied contrasts which are psychologically and theologically revealing.

The kind and direction of fluctuation depend on what the *āḻvār* is meditating on. For instance, when he thinks on the lord's reliable power and ability to bring about union, he is encouraged (I.10.0), whereas discouragement sets in when he considers the prolonged separation he suffers along with other beings (II.1.0). In II.5.0 the lord comes to the *āḻvār* in this way, as Nañcīyar recounts it:

> The *āḻvār* reflects on the following theme. When the Lord heard the pained cry of the elephant Gajendra, He Himself was into tumult, so He rose up and ended Gajendra's pain, making him very happy. Now the Lord who is an ocean of mercy has heard the *āḻvār's* pained cry and is Himself once

> again exceedingly pained. The Lord thinks, "I have not maintained the world very well!" He thus censures Himself in light of His own proper role as protector, and then He comes exceedingly quickly, ending the *āḻvār's* grief so that he is very satisfied.
>
> The Lord becomes radiant due to His union with the *āḻvār*. He shows the *āḻvār* the glories and qualities and forms of His proper form, His divine ornaments, His divine deeds, and all the other divine pleasures within Him. Thus the Lord has done all there is to do. Meditating on all this, the *āḻvār* is filled with delight and astonishment; in speaking about it, he experiences the same flourishing within himself. (II.5.0)

The result is a new burst of delight—"meditating on this the *āḻvār* is filled with delight and astonishment, and experiences and puts into words the prospering now born in himself"—which in turn is the object of further meditation all the way to song III.1. In his introduction to III.2, Nañcīyar catches nicely the interplay of delight and depression:

> When someone who is very thirsty sits down next to some very pure, cool water, he is agitated, if he is sick and cannot drink it. Likewise the *āḻvār* suffers because he is near to the object of his enjoyment and his desire has increased greatly while, due to that object's greatness, he is not only unable to swallow that which he desires, but he sees that he is bound by the causal restrictions which in turn rest on their relation to material nature.
>
> The *āḻvār* is therefore greatly depressed and says, "In order that all might reach His feet and thereby break this relation to material nature, the Lord created the world and undertook many descents into it. But all this has done nothing for me. At present I lack the means to destroy my relationship with material nature and so gain the Lord." He therefore comes close to ending in despair.
>
> But then he sees the Lord revealing to him that He abides on the temple-hill of Tirumalai, so that those who missed His descents might not perish. So the *āḻvār* instead ends up revived and joyful. (III.2)

Each good experience of the *āḻvār* provokes him to want more, but each experience of loss and separation serves only to make his desire all the more anguished, as this particularly poignant image shows:

> Therefore, each of the *āḻvār's* senses, one by one, desires the activity of them all. They cry out, "We must see our Lord who possesses divine ornaments, weapons, a body which is completely extraordinary and beyond the natural, all auspicious qualities, who does many deeds for the sake of those who take refuge in Him!" It is just as when, in time of famine, a poor man who has many children cries out for the appeasement of his children's hunger as well as his own. By saying that his senses experience desire, and that each sense desires the objects of the other senses, the *āḻvār* thereby expresses the limitlessness of his own desire. (III.8)

Another striking example is found at VIII.5, already cited above, where the heights of delight and depths of depression are strikingly proximate:

> Beginning with the 7th verse of the previous song he has been meditating deeply on the beauty and manliness of the "Lord at the holy stream" [VIII.4.7], and has become exceedingly joyful. He realizes, "The delight I have experienced from the beginning until now is but a small drop of this delight!"
>
> So he desires to see the Lord with his own eyes . . . But he is unable to do so, and the previously risen and unsurpassable delight deserts him. He meditates on the Lord as present in both the Heavenly City and Tiruccеṅkuṉṟūr, and says, "The depression I have experienced from the beginning until now is but a small particle of my present depression!"
>
> He is thus engulfed in the burning conflagration of his great depression; his senses all grieve and burn even more than he does himself. He experiences a great desire to see the Lord, and keeps crying out that the Lord must reveal Himself in ways that refresh the *āḻvār* and end his anguish. Those who hear the sound of his anguish find it hard to endure. (VIII.5)

So too, in his introductions to IX.4 and IX.5 Nañcīyar highlights this striking interplay of moods:

> He thus meditates on how the Lord has a noble disposition and how the fact that He is the spouse of Śrī is the cause for that noble disposition. Therefore, he and his senses both are filled with desire, crying, "We must see Him!" But because he cannot attain this vision, the *ālvār* is sorely afflicted. He meditates on how the Lord will end his anguish just as He ended the suffering of Prahlāda inflicted by Hiraṇya, by appearing from the pillar. So the *ālvār* ends up delighted. (IX.4)

But the mood immediately shifts:

> In the previous song he was delighted, for he had experienced the Lord directly, and was excited toward external union. But, unable to gain his desire, he is now greatly depressed. He decides that he must not only endure his depression, but must endure it by making his heart intent on something else—by reflection on worldly things. So he begins to meditate on them, but is greatly grieved even by them, because they remind him of the Lord. (IX.5)

It is illuminating to note that Nañcīyar, and the other *ācāryas,* weave together this extended, continuous interplay of emotions by linking it with the standard yogic term "endurance"—*dhāraṇā*: persistence throughout emotional upheaval, finding strength to bear it by still further acts of meditation. In the classical account of yogic concentration, endurance (*dhāraṇā*) and focused meditation (*dhyāna*) are the penultimate stages in concentration before the culminating, unitive *samādhi.* In the schema of Rāmānuja's yoga imaginatively applied by the *ācāryas,* this endurance is steady, committed perseverance in love, a commitment to the desire to see God despite insurmountable obstacles and extreme fluctuations of mood. Endurance allows the meditator to "keep at it" over the necessary time required for meditation to come to fruition, and the cycle of emotions must be endured, so as to be completed in meditation. Endurance keeps one on course until every superfluity is swept away and all that is left of the meditator is the sheer compound of unlimited desire and the limited body: if one endures, focused in meditation, union—the true, desired *samādhi*—will follow. By endurance, the *āḻvār* is able to sustain his self (*ātma-dhāraṇā*) and to engage again and more deeply in that process of meditation which is both consoling and yet also the source of further frustrations and greater desires.

The verb "endure" (*tari*, the Sanskrit root *dhṛ, dhāraṇā*) figures regularly in Nañcīyar's introductions to the songs, indicating the various successful strategies by which the *āḻvār* perseveres in meditation and keeps open the on-going process. The time spent in meditation is in part just endurance, and in part a gradual deepening and strengthening of a commitment to the Lord. In II.1, for example, the young woman meditates on the condition of other beings, and thereby doubles her own grief; but she then alleviates it by speaking out of it, for "just as one endures by speaking with others who grieve, she speaks with them and likewise endures." At IV.9, the *āḻvār* "is on fire with separation and depression, and looks at the whole world, saying, 'We will endure, crying out with all those who suffer.'" At V.5 and 6, Nañcīyar recalls how the cowherd girls, bereft of Kṛṣṇa, found a way to endure in separation:

> The young woman was thus terribly depressed throughout the night in V.4; but her distress eases a bit as dawn breaks, and she is able to endure for a while by remembering the beauty, etc., of her Master, which she had experienced in the past . . . (V.5)

> In the previous song her affliction came to a head and she was unable to sustain her own self. So she said, "I will endure by imitating all the deeds, etc., of Kṛṣṇa, His holy acts of creating the world, etc., as did the cowherd girls." (V.6)

The same emphasis on endurance recurs elsewhere too:

> He is unable to endure except by serving at the feet of the One who dwells in Veṅkaṭam . . . (VII.2)

> The Lord says, "We have ended your inclination toward the objects of the senses, sound, etc.; we have made it such

> that you can't survive without us. Is there still anything we haven't done for you?" The *āḻvār* meditates on this, dispels his doubts, and so is able to endure patiently . . . (VIII.1)

Just how *Tiruvāymoḻi* replicates and transforms the project of meditation—for the *āḻvār*, for the reader—appears most memorably in Nampiḷḷai's introduction to I.4, cited in part at the start of this chapter. He notes that from I.4 to the end of X.10 the songs represent the interior, mental experience in the *āḻvār's* mind, who keeps meditating (and yet, Āttāṉcīyar adds) always concludes by desiring more. He indicates that all these songs, however erotic, are actually the stuff of meditation, *nididhyāsanā*, the stage in the process of gaining spiritual knowledge that, in the calculus of the *Bṛhadāraṇyaka Upaniṣad* 2.4.5, follows after hearing (*śravana*) and thinking (*manana*), and culminates in seeing (*darśana*):

> Once there was a man who wanted to learn just a little; he was open-minded just as far as the third song of *Tiruvāymoḻi*, thinking, "The person who is freed of passion should concentrate on these songs, for they pertain to reality." But when he came to the fourth song, he said, "This song is merely about lust," and he went away. But this was his lack of good fortune, for such songs indicate the desire for the Lord that is enjoined by the upaniṣadic text, "The Self must be meditated on," [*Īṭu* on I.4.0]

Tiruvāymoḻi is about desire, love, lust; it is meditation, strength for endurance, the fruit of this fidelity, and a guide to yet further and deeper acts of meditation. It leads the way to that limit experience which is full vision, *darśana*.

IV. Tiruvāymoḻi *as Dramatic Narrative*

In the previous sections we have watched the *ācāryas'* weave together deep emotion and refined theology, the experience and theory of human desire and human limitation, and an understanding of meditation as experience and practice.

Our final step takes us in a slightly different direction, for the fundamental emotional and theological thrusts of the songs are retold in a single, extended narrative; as implied in the emphasis on the psychological, meditation itself is given a personal history. The narrative is, of course, something more too, since in it the *āḻvār* and the lord find each another; the bodily boundaries of time and space are finally overcome. With reference to Rāmānuja's theology, the songs had been organized in terms of the theological problem of vision, theoretically; with reference to meditation, they had been given a significance as a practical project undertaken in response to that problem; with reference to this narrative of *āḻvār* and lord, they are made imaginatively accessible to the broad audience of Śrīvaiṣṇavas. *Tiruvāymoḻi* becomes a drama: *it happens.*

The *ācāryas'* version of *Tiruvāymoḻi* as an interaction between the *āḻvār* and the lord in the course of meditation divides naturally in two parts: the action of the āḻvār is emphasized up to VI.10, the action of the lord thereafter. This division seems evident, although the *ācāryas* recognize the interaction of the two throughout *Tiruvāymoḻi,* the absolute priority of the lord from beginning to end. Let us now examine these emphases in turn.

1. The Preliminaries

At I.4.0 Piḷḷāṉ introduces the plot, so to speak, by observing that Śaṭakōpaṉ's initial, graced experience of the lord sets off in the *āḻvār* the cycle of increasing desires, satisfactions and then new desires. He wants more, he has to figure out how to get it, based on who he is and who the lord is, and nothing he gets is enough. His stubborn quest to gain the lord moves forward in the course of their dialogical interaction, in a process of meditation and purification that leads toward clear vision and intimate union. At the beginning of I.5, Naṃpiḷḷai offers a striking dialogue in amplification of this basic dynamic, and his words are worth citing at length:

> The *āḻvār* decides to go away, thinking, "My approaching the Lord is like cutting off a branch and throwing it down a well, or like throwing poison into ambrosia. So what's this idea of my entering—and thus destroying—the one who is the object of enjoyment, even for eternal beings?"

> The Lord realizes, "We are going to lose him!" so He asks, *"Āḻvār!* are you thinking of going away?"
>
> The *āḻvār* responds, "Yes, your servant is thinking of going away."
>
> The Lord replies, "You are thinking of going away because you think that coming near me will cause some flaw in me; but if you do that, then we will get no one at all, since everyone will think, 'This object is only for the select few.' But if you who are thinking this way—about going away—come near me, then it will be evident, 'This object is for everyone.' So it is only your going away that will cause a flaw in me."
>
> Then the Lord shows how accessible He was as the one who measured the earth, and says, "Where no one belonged to us, now there is a well-worn path; for we do not take into account qualities and lack of qualities, we place our feet on the heads of everyone."
>
> Even so, the *āḻvār* will not reconsider and say, "If so, then we will come near." He still seeks to go away, saying, "Does the Lord need more good qualities? Our quality is not needed by Him."
>
> So the Lord says, "We do not want some increase of our qualities by your coming. The question is rather whether I want you to come or not. Your going away with the idea that you are unworthy means that I lose my existence, and your coming near is what sustains me. Even if you go away thinking that you are unworthy, union with you is really what sustains me, just as butter sustains the cowherds. If you go away now, it would be like someone entering the cowherd place and barring me from the butter—that would mean my loss of existence."
>
> . . . So the Lord wonders what to do, and becomes all the more intent on union, and concludes by uniting with the *āḻvār*. (I.5)

Thereafter, the songs are read as a series of encounters in which the initial psychological and spiritual conflicts and possibilities are worked through. By the time we reach the songs of the Fifth Hundred, the anxiety and depression of the *āḻvār* have become desperate; he gropes wildly this way and that for ways to overcome his distance from the lord. Each song there is understood as a bursting forth of his inner turmoil, the venting of his inner feelings, and as yet one more desperate effort to act in some better way: V.4, a sense of dark desolation; V.5, the practice of visualization in order to assuage that desolation; V.6, the practice of imitating Kṛṣṇa, for the same purpose. By the time we reach the last songs in the Fifth Hundred, the *āḻvār* is focused most intensely on finding a permanent resolution of his problem, as Naṃpiḷḷai's introductory comments indicate:

> In the preceding song he endured by imitation; but though he became confused by the idea that he must imitate Kṛṣṇa in order to endure, the Lord does not come and show His face. The *āḻvār* reflects: "What is the reason for this? What is the reason for His delay regarding us, this Lord of all who must protect us, showing His face to those who love Him?"
>
> This is the situation: though by our very nature we cannot endure without the Lord—it is like going without one's own self—the Lord does not recognize this as our very nature, but He thinks of this merely as a means. Realizing this, the *āḻvār* makes known to the Lord that he has nothing in his hands, and then takes refuge at His feet. (V.7)
>
> The *āḻvār* fell like a rootless tree at the feet of the Lord who lives at Cirīvaramaṅkalam, and with nowhere else to go he entered refuge there. Though he entered refuge there and cried out with great angst, the Lord does not come and show His face. He endures, thinking, "Up to now, He has been rejecting my errors in thinking, 'There is another way,' and 'Going to another place, one can call out." Yet he endures, with the idea of going to yet another place, to Tirukuṭantai. This is just like when someone falls into the ocean and grasps at anything floating by. (V.8)
>
> He has not gotten his desire even after entering into Tirukuṭantai, yet he still hopes to go to Tiruvallavāḻ. Here he expresses his depression in the woman's voice, speaking of how difficult it is to reach Tiruvallavāḻ, how he cannot fulfil his desire there. (V.9)

> He started to go to Tiruvallavāḻ, after deciding that he must talk with the Lord who lives there. But he could not endure the walking, fell on the way, and lay there crying out. He realizes that he could survive by experiencing the Lord's qualities, but when he cannot do even that, his weakness increases. So he falls at the Lord's feet and asks, "Graciously grant that we become able to experience your qualities, so that we can survive even in separation from you, in all circumstances!" (V.10)

At VI.1.0 Naṃpiḷḷai summarizes the failure of these efforts to reach the lord:

> Beginning with V.7 he tried in four ways to enter into places of refuge, but he did not thus gain what he desired. Why is he left without what he desired, even though he embraced the means which is supposed to give results without delay? The reason is that the plan of the Lord, who was committed to the good of the world along with the good of the *āḻvār*, has not yet reached its completion. (VI.1)

Thereafter, the helplessness of the *āḻvār* continues to increase, and the *ācāryas* seem to take the predominance of songs about the young woman (VI.1, 2, 5, 6, 7, 8) as a sign of the increasing difficulty and turmoil. This of course is where the song with which we began this volume belongs, as the young woman suffers distress when she cannot stop thinking of the lord she has seen in the temple at Tirutolaivillimaṅkalam; according to the narrative, this distress and heightened consciousness mark yet another stage in the young woman's increasing desperation, loss of independence.

But it is at VI.10, according to the *ācāryas*, that the *āḻvār* has finally run out of options; in desperation he simply surrenders without reservation. Piḷḷāṉ puts it briefly:

> The *āḻvār* has thus cried out so as to be heard in the highest heaven, because he cannot get to see Him. He realizes, "There is no other means to seeing Him than entering refuge underneath His feet." He mentions the Lord's compassion, tenderness and other qualities, as his refuge; and so, with the Lady as his mediator, he takes refuge at the feet of

the one who possesses Tiruveṅkaṭam, the place of refuge
for all. (VI.10.0)

The process of search, loss, surrender—of meditation as far as the meditator is concerned—is now complete insofar as it is something that the *āḻvār* can undertake. He sees total surrender as the only course open to him, so he makes just such an act of surrender:

"I cannot be away even for a moment," says the maiden on the
 flower who dwells on your chest;
you are unmatched in fame, owner of the three worlds, my ruler,
O lord of holy Veṅkaṭam where peerless immortals and crowds
 of sages delight:
with no place to enter, this servant has entered right beneath
 your feet.

The limits of human activity have been reached, there is nothing more to do, the chronicle of human effort is finished.

2. Interpreting the Divine Silence: A Brief Theodicy

It is important to note that although surrender is idealized by the *ācāryas* as the *āḻvār's* only sound response, they do not propose it merely as a case of good theology, effective simply because it is true to the dynamics of human nature and divine grace. Rather, surrender is a response to the situation the *āḻvār* finds himself in; something has happened, the *āḻvār* has reached his limit, and therefore something must happen from elsewhere, there must be a response to his helplessness if the surrender is to mean anything, in reality. According to the *ācāryas*, then, from VII.1 on *Tiruvāymoḻi* is primarily the expected drama of the free divine response to the *āḻvār's* surrender, the lord's initiative and their subsequent exchanges as they reach toward a graced, freely chosen, inevitable union.

If there is going to be anything more to be talked about, it must come from the other actor, the lord. Yet, in the short run, he is silent. The scene at the beginning of VII.1 is dramatically effective because the complaint underlying the song is that the lord not only does not respond well, but seems content to leave the *āḻvār* entrapped by his body, symbolized by the five senses:

Tormenting me with the five living inside me,
you mean to torture me further
and keep me away from your lotus feet—
worker of great marvels beyond reckoning, praised by the gods,
owner of the three worlds, ambrosia, father,
master who rules me. (VII.1.1)

Even though I call out to you as my brightest flame
when I am ready to melt with love over your two lotus feet,
you weigh me down with this burden, this body,
and these five lay on me heavy loads, dragging me in every direction and tormenting me,
divine form that once churned the ocean and took out ambrosia. (VII.1.10)

After his (apparently) perfect act of surrender, the *āḻvār* finds himself still mired in the body that blocks vision, the cruel separation that had been torturing him, drawing him away from the lord. Why? The reason could simply be that the desired union is not possible, or that the lord could, but will not, respond in this particular case. Since these are not acceptable alternatives in the *ācāryas'* eyes, some other reason was required. It is in this context that at VII.1 the narrative takes a dialogic turn, as a debate about divine response and responsibility. Each *ācārya* seeks reasons for the delay in the lord's response, and the analyses which introduce VII.1 are more than usually inventive. Let us survey their explanations of divine inaction.

Piḷḷāṉ suggests that the lord desires two things: his own continued enjoyment of the body of the *āḻvār*, and the completion of the singing of *Tiruvāymoḻi*:

> Because he is greedy for the *āḻvār's* body, and because He intends to complete *Tiruvāymoḻi* with him, the Lord refuses to let the *āḻvār's* body be discarded. The *āḻvār* sees himself immersed in the senses as before, even though he had turned away from the senses and inclined toward the Lord.

Nañcīyar raises the possibility that the lord had been testing people by trapping them in their bodies:

> Even when he has taken refuge with the Lord with great desire, the *āḻvār* is still unable to get what he desires, so he is dejected. Even though he has conquered his senses, he sees how others, bound to nature, are unworthy of the Lord because of things that must be rejected, because they are inclined toward those other things. So they suffer greatly from the senses which are opposed to experience of the Lord. He himself suffers affliction due to the same senses, for he too is still connected with nature.
>
> To get rid of his own suffering, he affirms that the Lord is the protector of all who are accustomed to place on Him the three constituents of their nature—lucidity, passion, inertia—plus the senses and their objects. He also affirms that the Lord has power sufficient to protect him, and that He is actually engaged in this protection. The *āḻvār* makes all this understood here: "He and the flawless immortals now seek to loose the bonds of those whom He had tormented by binding them to their senses, so that they could not get away, due to the three constituents."

Despite this confidence, in the end, Nañcīyar leaves the situation dramatically open:

> The *āḻvār* then asks the Lord, "If you are the most merciful one and are attached to the task of protection, why do you merely watch this suffering?" Unable to endure, he cries out with a great cry.

Periyavāccāṉpiḷḷai dares to portray the *āḻvār* as thinking that the lord is laughing at him:

> The *āḻvār* sees that although the Lord is the protector of all and knower of everything, including what others suffer, and although He is the one able to ward off such sufferings and is perfectly accomplished, still He does not end his suffering. As usual, the senses still restrict him. He thinks that the Lord, in His eternal glory along with the eternal beings has bound him by the three constituents and is

> laughing at him, tormenting him, watching how he is bound by the senses.
>
> The *āḻvār* says, "Do you who are the most merciful and the protector just afflict me here—and just look at me?" He cries out in a manner that is hard for those who hear it to bear. His interpretation is such that he attributes his suffering, which is actually due to his own deeds, to the Lord: "He is afflicting me: what I get is due to Him, what I lose is due to Him!"[38]

Naṃpiḷḷai develops the problematic more fully and vividly:

> The *āḻvār* becomes afraid, thinking that perhaps the Lord is cruel by nature, sending His henchmen—the five senses—against those who would take refuge. He considers how he needs the Lord's mercy, how this miserable world is to be avoided, how the Lord is extraordinary—and yet also, how nothing has happened after his surrender. When he sees that there is no result from his surrender, he cries out, "He has blunted the greatest weapon, i.e., total surrender, that I had to throw at Him!"

Naṃpiḷḷai then introduces two *Bhagavad Gītā* passages which highlight the divine role in human destiny: "These haters, cruel, the worst of men and unholy, I hurl continually into the cycles of birth and death, into none other than demoniacal wombs," (*Bhagavad Gītā* 16.19), and "To them who are uninterruptedly united with Me and who lovingly adore me, I give that union of mind by which they draw near to me." (*Bhagavad Gītā* 10.10) The *āḻvār* is portrayed as pondering his fate as someone who experiences the first of these verses, the hurling into endless cycles of rebirth, but not the second—the gift; and he is not sure why this has happened. He speculates, Naṃpiḷḷai says, on his own deficiency and the lord's affection for his body, but dismisses those reasons as inadequate. Perhaps then the lord has simply decided to abandon him:

> The *āḻvār* meditates on what he himself is like, on how the Lord lacks nothing as protector, how the Lord's very nature is to protect, how attaining His feet is the cause for

> protection—and yet how he himself is not connected with that protection, etc.; he meditates too on the three constituents, lucidity, etc., and at the root of them the qualities, the body, the senses, etc., and at the root of them Material Nature, the Great Material Principle, the Ego, and their productions, objects, and the desire and traces of ignorance and deeds that are dependent on them. He realizes, "He made this miserable world and objects and the senses, and has planned to put us in the middle of them; so we are in the midst of these things, as it says, "These haters, cruel, the worst of men and unholy, I hurl continually into the cycles of birth and death, into none other than demoniacal wombs." (*Bhagavad Gītā* 16.9)

Naṃpiḷḷai concludes by noting a more moderate difference of opinion between the lord and the *āḻvār:* the former argues for patience, saying that knowledge matures over time, while the latter holds that knowledge instigates an intolerable and unsatisfied desire. Or, to cast the dispute in a different light: the *āḻvār* sees this world as a prison, while the lord and the heaven-dwellers see it as the place of divine delight.

It is of great importance, emotionally, theologically, narratively, that VII.1 is taken to portray this moment of divine inactivity and human doubt, just after the great surrender in VI.10. Nothing is taken for granted, the feelings involved are realistic and justified, the concept of grace refers to the unpredictable and open-ended nature of the divine-human relation; God does not have to act—and the narrative, as a good story, may or may not have a happy ending. The *ācāryas'* exegesis comes into full flower at this point.

For the reader who approaches these issues from outside the tradition, the suspense of this moment is useful, by way of analogy. At stake here are not the sure consequences of predictable first principles, as if a sound grasp of *Tiruvāymoḻi* would itself be the means to salvation. Rather, the process is open: something may come of this appropriation of *Tiruvāymoḻi,* but neither Śaṭakōpaṉ nor the *ācāryas* seems to think that what they are talking about ought to be taken for granted. Something must happen, the lord must choose to be gracious.

3. Resolution and Union

The remainder of *Tiruvāymoḻi* is dedicated to the resolution of this situation, the revelation of divine graciousness. Strikingly, the lord is portrayed as having to work through his own ambivalences and to decide whether to leave the *āḻvār* in his body or to set him free. Throughout, the *ācāryas* give the lord a voice. Beyond the few divine words cited in the songs, they freely read the divine mind and voice divine words, attributing to him the same problematic shared by the *āḻvār*: the problem of this world, a love-hate relationship with the human body. Even time is an issue, since *Tiruvāymoḻi* can be recited, heard, enjoyed, only over time, while time is still painful, since things take so long, and union is only gradual. After VII.1, the *ācāryas* narrate the ongoing and ever more intense negotiations between the lord and the *āḻvār*, as the former seems to be finding a balance between his desires and the desires of the *āḻvār*, his own desire for the continuation of the body and the *āḻvār*'s desire to be free from it. The last part of the story, after the *āḻvār*'s "final" act, his surrender, is the story of the increasing entanglement of the lord who is irretrievably smitten with the beauty of the *āḻvār*. And so it is also the story of the *āḻvār's* desperate realization that the lord may not let go of him—here, in the body.

The account of this interplay between lord and *āḻvār*, as they work through the physical, psychological and interpersonal issues which have kept them apart, goes well beyond the explicit script of *Tiruvāymoḻi*. Especially at this point, the *ācāryas* discover connections by appealing to what occurs between songs, in response and preview to them. Let us note a few examples of this, following Nañcīyar and Naṃpiḷḷai.

At VIII.1, Nañcīyar records how the lord and the *āḻvār* argue over whether the āḻvār's unworthiness is a legitimate obstacle or not:

> The *āḻvār* has seen this Lord in Tiruvāṟaṉviḷai, in VII.10, and desires to serve Him. But because he was unable to accomplish that desired goal then, he is grievously afflicted. In the divided condition in which he finds himself, he wonders whether what he has known thus far is all false: "The

> Lord is exceedingly favorable toward those who take refuge in Him, He is the Lord of all, He is the protector of all, He is the source of the my own exaltation."
>
> But the Lord says to the exceedingly depressed *āḻvār:* "I have brought it about that you have spurned any inclination toward sound and the other objects of the senses, and hence you no longer function except on account of me—so is there anything I haven't done for you?" The *āḻvār* meditates on this, banishes his doubts, and is able to endure patiently. (VIII.1.0)

At VIII.4, the lord is portrayed as convincing the *āḻvār* of his nearness and, touchingly, of his divine safety even though he has ventured into the world. Naṃpiḷḷai spells it out in this way:

> The *āḻvār* worries, "Concerned about the needs of people of this miserable world, the Lord of all came down all alone into this miserable world; but after getting what they need, the people of this world may think of Him differently, and no longer support Him. What will happen then? To end the *āḻvār's* fear, the Lord shows the nature of His people, saying, "We do have people who support us; besides, we are strong enough that we don't need support!"

And,

> lest this fear return, the Lord shows him His strength and virility, His amazing deeds such as creation, etc., His power to rip out by their roots obstacles that get in the way. Moreover, He shows how there are three thousand brahmins[39] who are His supporters. The *āḻvār* sees all this and is satisfied, delighted, experiencing in his heart the Lord's beauty. (VIII.4)

At VIII.5, the *āḻvār* increases the pressure, as Nañcīyar tells us:

> After becoming afraid at the Lord's aloneness, the *āḻvār* has meditated on His valor, heroism, etc., and dispelled the fear which had been born within him . . . He desires then to see the Lord with his own eyes, and to embrace Him intimately and converse with him, but he is unable to do so—so the unsurpassable delight that had arisen previously leaves him. Then he meditates on the Lord as present in

> both the Heavenly City and Tiruccenkunrūr, and says, "The depression I have experienced from the beginning until now is but a small particle of my present depression!"
>
> Thus engulfed in the burning conflagration of his great depression, all his senses grieve and burn even more than he does himself. He experiences a great desire to see the Lord, and keeps crying out that He must reveal Himself in ways that refresh him and end his anguish. Those who hear the sound of his anguish find it hard to endure the sound. (VIII.5)

The lord's persistent reassurance makes some headway, though only slowly; he argues both his general power and his compassion, and keeps pointing out all that he has done for the *āḻvār* in the past. In the end, the lord decides on a more conclusive, though still gradual intervention in response to the *āḻvār's* intense suffering:

> The Lord is deeply distressed when He hears the sound of the *āḻvār's* affliction; to end this affliction He undertakes to come and graciously unite with him. But just as Lord Rāma stayed a while at the *āśrama* of lord Bharadvāja before entering the city of Ayodhyā, in order that Bharata might become accustomed to his delight at Rāma's gracious return, and just as Vasudeva's son Kṛṣṇa did not enter directly into Hastinapura when He came as a messenger, but stayed first in Kuśasthala, so too the Lord does not come directly to the *āḻvār* and enter him. Rather, in order that he might grow accustomed to the delight which is arising within him at the Lord's coming, the Lord first enters into Tirukkaṭittāṉam before graciously uniting with the *āḻvār*. The *āḻvār* sees how the Lord will thus mingle with him, and rejoices. (VIII.6.0)

Once the lord's intention to unite with the *āḻvār* is ascertained to be definitive, the forward movement of the text quickens. In the *ācāryas'* reading, VIII.7 marks the lord's irreversible commitment:

> That dwarf inclined toward me when I begged unceasingly for many days,
> "Put astonished me beneath your golden feet," and

> now he himself has entered me, he holds my mind as his own,
> *he reigns there, he watches constantly.* (VIII.7.1)
>
> In his stomach he holds all three worlds which hold
> in their stomachs everyone who holds anything
> in his stomach and this dark lord who is the sort to stay
> *in my stomach when I've placed him there with his*
> *consent.* (VIII.7.9)

Piḷḷāṉ states in this way the *āḻvār's* amazement at what the lord has now achieved:

> Thus the Lord has graciously entered into my heart; all that I might suffer in separation from my own self is nothing at all compared with this. He is now graciously, completely filled, having seen and held and entered me. Being the sort that He is, He is depressed in separation from me. Can anyone have such affection? Can this be fitting? (VIII.7.0)

Nañcīyar speaks more expansively:

> The Lord has Himself brought an end to what blocked the *āḻvār's* way to reaching Himself, and He is exceedingly affectionate, not noticing even briefly the *āḻvār's* sins. The *āḻvār* meditates on this, and on how the Lord has from time without beginning exerted many efforts to gain him, how He has desired to attain him, and how He is acting as if He has gained some unattainable prize. The *āḻvār* considers how the Lord acts, and reflects on how his own entreaties were slanderous. He is ashamed, and cries out, "What have we done!" just as did Vibhīṣaṇa when he saw Lord Rāma's nature and became immersed in him. The *āḻvār* is astonished to see the Lord's infatuation, he rejoices and plunges into the ocean of the Lord's qualities of compassion, etc. (VIII.7.0)

And, finally, let us note Naṃpiḷḷai's emphatic comment:

> Everything preceding this song has been cultivation in preparation for what is acquired here; everything that follows is only a hedge around this acquisition. What goes on in this song? Here the *āḻvār* forgets all the obstacles which He had consciously been putting forward for ages without beginning, and a sense that things are now suitable arises

> within him. He sees everything that had been in error, he now strives for his goal, and reaches union, quenching the thirst that has arisen within him. He reflects on how the Lord has helped him, but more than that, on what he has now gained. He is embarrassed, thinking, "What have we done, crying out night and day to the one who has come and mingled with us so as to satisfy His own desire too? The Lord of all has made Himself subject to the understanding of a person in this world!"
>
> At first he doubted whether it was all a mistake or a dream, but then he rejoices when he clearly realizes that it isn't, that it is all true: "The Lord has overcome our hostility, He has turned us toward Himself and brought it about that we cannot exist without Him. What a response! Without care for His own excellence, He has humbled Himself and come and mingled with us! Such is His dependence on His devotees! Such is His nature!" Thus he reflects on the Lord's ways and is delighted. (VIII.7.0)

In VIII.8 and thereafter, the project is simply that of nurturing and deepening in the *ālvār* this awareness of what is happening to him. Śaṭakōpaṉ begins VIII.8 with this sense of deeper unity:

> *Lustrous eyes, full ripe red lips, white bright teeth within,*
> *crocodile earrings, shaking and shining,*
> *four arms, bent bow, bright conch, club, discus, sword:*
> *that peerless one is inside me at his feet.*
>
> *Inside me at his feet, inside my body, inside the cosmic egg,*
> *inside what's outside:*
> *you may say "He is like this," but he isn't;*
> *higher than the highest, his is that great unceasing joy which by*
> *nature destroys joys and sorrows:*
> *honey with pervasive fragrance,*
> *the peerless one, beyond thought.*
>
> *Beyond thought, the peerless one, by his grace*
> *in my thought I have placed him, to hold him,*
> *but that too is his sweet grace.*
> *All mind, all breath, all body, the infinite are mere waste*
> *he makes me think*
> *and in the end, he ended up as me himself.*

He ended up as me himself; before everything and everyone
he himself is the peerless first one,
expanding himself as Śiva, Brahmā and himself;
as sweet as honey, milk, cane, ambrosia,
he abides in my body, in my breath, in my mind:
I'm always thinking of him. (VIII.8.1–4)

Nañcīyar puts it this way:

> The Lord has gained union with the *āḻvār,* and is exceedingly delighted with him, more even than with His own self. Lest the *āḻvār,* as in I.5, meditate on his own unworthiness and go away, letting their now accomplished union be disturbed, He begins to reveal to the *āḻvār* the uniqueness of the *āḻvār's* own self, in order to make their union firm. But He realizes, "If I first make him meditate on the proper nature of his self, he may say, 'What is there to this miserable thing?' and he will despise his own self." In order then to make him desire to see his self, He first reveals the qualities and forms, etc. of His own proper self which is the unsurpassable object of enjoyment. In this way, the *āḻvār* rejoices, meditating on how it is revealed to him, "My self is oriented solely to this Lord!" and "My self possesses a uniqueness which gives luster even to the Lord!" (VIII.8.0)

In this context, it is interesting to note, the *ācāryas* develop here their reinterpretation of Vedāntic non-dualism (*Advaita*) as a seamless unity which is achieved through grace, not as a given, ontological reality. Just as the yogic goal of *samādhi* is to be gained through patient and loving perseverance, so too the highest state of non-dualism is a question of grace—and thus both more unpredictable and more steadfast than ontological oneness.[40]

We have already seen that at X.4 the *āḻvār* becomes certain in his own knowledge of this graced non-dualism, and knows for sure that the path of total surrender was the right one to take. Thereafter, the narrative is almost entirely the lord's:

The discus-bearer has decided to give his grace to me who serves
his servants who have received his grace, such is my fate:
I do not wish to be born again in this darkening world,
so abandon your confusion, gentle heart,
and worship at the feet of Tiruvāṭṭāṟu's lord. (X.6.1)

Tiruvāṭṭāṟu, cool land where splendid Tirumāl dwells with the pure woman on his splendid chest,
mounted on his glorious eagle, destroyer of the clan of evil devils:
he is always in my heart, he never leaves it. (X.6.9)

The lord pursues the *āḻvār*, and all that matters is his gracious initiative. Even at this point the *ācāryas* insist that the conclusion is not merely a predictable deduction as to what will occur. Grace must be real, a real gift, and not a sure eventuality premised on good theology. Nañcīyar says:

> The Lord who dwells in Tiruvāṭṭāṟu reflects on how the *āḻvār* has taught the essential nature of devotion and has destroyed his dependence on others, so he now cannot exist apart from Him. The Lord is eager to have the *āḻvār* enter into heaven as a help toward the *āḻvār's* having an uninterrupted and essential union with Himself, so He attentively seeks any opportunity for this, thinking, "I must give him what he asks for." The *āḻvār* reflects on this causeless infatuation of the Lord who has now become dependent on him and is astonished; with great delight he says to himself, "See what we have gained!" (X.6)

Naṃpiḷḷai forcefully emphasizes the novelty of the situation at this point:

> From the beginning of *Tiruviruttam* to here, the *āḻvār* has been seeking after the Lord. Beginning here, it is the Lord of all who is seeking after the *āḻvār*. (X.6.0)

Still, as Nañcīyar observes at X.7, the pursuit continues, as does the debate:

> Thus the Lord, completely absorbed in the *āḻvār*, wants to do as the *āḻvār* commands Him to do. He is very much absorbed with having the *āḻvār* enter heaven even with his body, swiftly. He realizes that if the *āḻvār* knows this he will not want it, but still He wants the *āḻvār* to mingle with him even with his body, and He enters him again just as He did when He sang *Tiruvāymoḻi* through him.
>
> But when the *āḻvār* sees how the Lord is intent on having him rise to heaven even with this body, he says, "If the

> Lord is intent on this, then there will be no means of my separating from this nature, never; it is necessary then to make Him destroy my connection with this nature which is opposed to experience of Him." So the *āḻvār* prays, "Destroy my connection with this nature made up of the twenty-four elements—let me go!"
>
> The Lord responds, "Apart from your body, what else is my goal?" The *āḻvār* responds, "Are you intent on this body for any reason other than because it is my dwelling place? Then for my sake let it perish!" He begs to be able to take refuge with the Lord who consents, "Let us do this!"
>
> The *āḻvār*, exceedingly delighted, plunges into the qualities of the Lord, His generosity, etc. In the superabundance of his delight he says, "If you serve Him, you cannot escape because His generosity etc. are so abundant; if you wish to preserve yourself, serve—but without getting caught in His qualities." (X.7.0)

The narrative concludes dramatically, with the final, complete, irrevocable union with the lord which finally satisfies the *āḻvār*. The *ācāryas* treat this conclusion rather soberly, though, without any of the pictorial enhancement one finds in the hagiographical accounts or in the temple rituals even today. After describing the ascent of devotees (and not his own ascent) to the heavenly Vaikuṇṭa in X.9, in X.10 the *āḻvār* compels the lord to commit Himself to permanent union, under oath:

> *Silent sage, the four-faced one, three-eyed lord, flawless jewel,*
> *lips red as berries, eyes like lotuses, my thief, full self for me who am alone—*
> *you have come upon my head,*
> *and now I will not let you go:*
> *don't tantalize me anymore.*
>
> *Do not surprise me:*
> *I place under oath Śrī who lies on your holy chest, garland, lady,*
> *her hair adorned with fragrant flowers,*
> *and see, I place you under oath too:*
> *if you have loved me without reserve and made my life one with*
> *yours without any another,*
> *then come, call, hold me.* (X.10.1–2)

What does Śaṭakōpaṉ experience at the end of *Tiruvāymoḻi*? There is still some pain of separation. At the beginning of X.10 Piḷḷāṉ says,

> Thus the *āḻvār* who is "with devotees possessed of great, endless bliss" [X.9.11] calls out groaning, "Look at me, still caught in this material nature!"

Or, as Nañcīyar puts it,

> In this song [X.10] the *āḻvār*, who is "with devotees possessed of great, endless bliss," [X.9.11], still shares that state only through meditation founded in knowledge. He realizes that he is still connected with nature, and thus still lacks external union. Although he has been established as exceedingly happy and without sorrow, (as if) on the top of Mount Meru, he is depressed like one who is sunk into a very deep ocean in which there is no firmness anywhere, which can be crossed only with difficulty and much suffering. He realizes how the Lord came to him before, and how he lacks any other means for gaining Him other than the Lord Himself. He also reflects on how there is no protector other than the Lord—for anyone. Because he cannot gain that Lord at that very moment, he is no longer satisfied with reflecting on his proper nature. As in I.5, his anguish is so great that even people with hard hearts become compassionate
>
> It is like when a breast-feeding child calls out due to the greatness of its anguish, weakened with hunger and thirst, unable to see its mother.
>
> Disturbed, he summons under oath the Lady who by nature can never be separated from the Lord. He now spurns his custom of placing his words into the mouth of others by addressing messengers, and calls out with a voice of great lamentation which cannot be put off. He is like one caught in a forest fire. Unwilling to be patient any more, he calls out with a voice of great anguish, that he might be in that Holy Place with the Lord apart from whom he has no refuge. And so he takes refuge.

At last, there is a swift response:

> The greatly compassionate Lord, along with his Lady, comes riding Garuḍa and graciously and fully reveals what He Himself is—just as the *āḻvār*, at his feet, had desired—and so He breaks the *āḻvār's* connection with nature. Thus they are united, the *āḻvār's* thirst and his own thirst are satisfied; the Lord has thus graciously accomplished everything that the *āḻvār* had desired. (X.10.0)

In the end,

> *Surrounding, inside, filling, uplifting every thing, unlimited great Matter;*
> *surrounding that, and greater still, the highest blossoming flame;*
> *surrounding that, and greater still, the fiery knowledge and bliss;*
> *surrounding that, and greater still, my desire for you, but that too you finish, you surround me.* (X.10.10),

Naṃpiḷḷai simply echoes the finality of the verse:

> The *āḻvār* adjures the Lord along with the great Lady, so that He cannot abide without doing what the *āḻvār* wants. The *āḻvār* cries out with great anguish, and as he prays, the Lord, the most full, graciously comes and unites with him. The *āḻvār* says, "You have mingled with me, you have ended my thirst which is greater than the infinite Material Nature, greater than the self, greater than your knowledge in the form of will. I have gained everything I desire, all at once.
>
> As it says, "Rising fully from his seat and drawing to himself Bharata, whom he was seeing only after so very long a time, Rāma joyfully embraced him," [*Yuddha Kāṇḍa* 127.41].[41] (X.10.10)

The *ācāryas* thus characterize Śaṭakōpaṉ and his lord as a pair of actors inside the drama of *Tiruvāymoḻi*, bringing them together only at the very last moment, just as the songs end. Desire is satisfied, meditation is complete, theology proven, union consummated, *Tiruvāymoḻi* completed. The text is larger than its author who appears as just one player in these songs which both map his raw experience and delineate a most refined theology.

By playing his part—talking with the lord, addressing various human audiences, reflecting on the experience of visiting various holy places, re-using the shifting emotions of the songs of the young woman—his drama signals the general, whole human condition; the ways and problems that emerge as any human being seeks to find God, see God, be united with God, even while in the body. By their interpretation, the *ācāryas* inscribe Śaṭakōpaṉ's lord in the text as well. Even the lord, the very prime mover of the entire sequence of events, acquires a new identity after and according to the songs; in a sense, the songs not only reveal but also shape the identity of the God whom it praises.

The *ācāryas* read *Tiruvāymoḻi* as a narrative of meditation, as the fruit of meditation and, insofar as its words replicate the path of meditation, as an important guide to progress in meditation. The *ācāryas* see the *āḻvār* as working through his deepest yearning, paying the terrible cost that the desire for God entails; as personally embodying the theological doctrine, enunciated by Rāmānuja, that one cannot see God in this life; as resolving the tension as best he could, gaining through experience a gradually clarified vision; as waiting until the last moment, for the lord to do something. The theology remains exegetical, close to the words of the songs—psychological, sensitive and detailed—while the songs are given a theological credibility that explains their unusual emotions and transitions. *Tiruvāymoḻi* is thus explained, and made ready for lived appropriation by its listeners.

It is evident that the *ācāryas* are very fine interpreters of the text, aware of their presuppositions and concerned to ground their views in the songs themselves. Even when they are using Rāmānuja's theology of vision and meditation, this usage is moderate, generated from within the songs, not merely superimposed on them; this is exegesis disciplined by theology, theology brought to life in exegesis. Their interpretation reflects their basic attitude. *Tiruvāymoḻi* is a text on the edge, opened, words at their best, and therefore at every point opening into an exhaustion of words in the face of unutterable mystery; *Tiruvāymoḻi* is a dazzlingly complex reconstruction of vision through words, a wall of words that turns out to be a window: the reader who is positioned properly by and in relation to this text, can *as it were* see God—with one's outward looking eyes blocked by the text. Śaṭakōpaṉ and his songs show the most revered theological points of the community, in a way that can be imitated by those who are not theologians.

Of course, the *ācāryas* accomplish these interpretations by making important choices about how to read *Tiruvāymoḻi.* They choose to emphasize internal experience, to deny significance to exterior experience, even in forms as simple as visiting temples, etc. In their chosen portrayal, *Tiruvāymoḻi* happens entirely in the *āḻvār's* head, before any word of it gets out of his mouth. It is thus simultaneous; yet, when uttered, *Tiruvāymoḻi* assumes a linear form, each song building on the meaning of those before it, the sequence reflecting a real beginning and real ending for the *āḻvār* and for *Tiruvāymoḻi.*

As for the contemporary reader who comes from outside the tradition: in chapter 2 we encountered in an initial way the abundant possibilities latent in the songs themselves; here we have encountered some specific and defining decisions about how one can respond to those possibilities. Limits notwithstanding, we are surely given access to *Tiruvāymoḻi* through the *ācāryas'* reading of it, even if we might have chosen to read otherwise. The concrete, optional decisions made by the community present us with ways of thinking about the songs. We cannot think in the same ways, since at the start we share neither the memories nor the skills requisite to such understandings; yet possible and successful decisions about the songs' meaning and purpose are placed before us by the *ācāryas.* There is a story for us to listen to, a story based on a view of human nature and an attitude toward religious practice; it is a story we might perhaps choose to become part of.

Of course it clear that this choice need not be a straightforward, simple affair. Experience and theology are intertwined here, and either may be the starting point, though more likely there will be a mix of affective and theological responses from the beginning. We may simply read the songs and work from there as our initial understandings prompt us; or we may read with the *ācāryas,* engaging in a dialectical understanding with them, of songs that we and they both seek to understand. On the whole, it seems that while we must surely learn to read the songs on our own, we would be quite foolish to ignore the powerful interpretation the *ācāryas* fashioned over several generations.

So too, such choices are not merely theoretical. There are supposed to be practical effects to how one reads the songs. The *ācāryas* are not content with speculation nor with inspiring spectacle. They go further, they insist on the practicality of the songs, their paradigmatic and enabling roles as guides to the community's self-understanding and religious practice. How the *ācāryas* do this, and what further questions are then posed to us, are the topics addressed in chapter 4.

Chapter 4

Five Ways to Think about *Tiruvāymoḻi:* Following the *Ācāryas'* Practical Response

> The first song sums up the whole of *Tiruvāymoḻi*; its first three verses sum up the first song; the first verse sums up the first three verses; the first line sums up the first verse. What is this like? It is the same as where it says, "The Vedic verses and whatever else is made of word: all of that is in the 'Eight Syllables [the *Tirumantra*.]'" Thus, the Tirumantra sums up all the *Vedas; Aum* sums up the mantra, and the 'a' sums up *Aum*. Other works—the *Rāmāyaṇa, Mahābhārata,* etc.—serve as various summaries and expansions. [Third Introduction to the *Īṭu*]

> Among our predecessors, one Vaiṣṇava asked another, "Tell me how to think of God." The second replied, "I will tell you how—if you can tell me how to forget God." (*Īṭu,* III.4.4)

In the preceding two chapters we have been assessing the major features of *Tiruvāymoḻi,* the possibilities of engagement in this text, what is expected and required of the reader, what is gained and lost, as one articulates one meaning or another for these one hundred interwoven songs. In chapter 2 we examined ways in which *Tiruvāymoḻi* affects and involves those who would read it, engaging them in the process of mastering and being mastered by the songs. Though *Tiruvāymoḻi* is inviting, even enticing, it remains elusive and difficult to understand; thus it encourages its readers to construct its meaning(s) as they (re)read it (or, *hear* it) once and again. For example, after much hesitation we ventured to highlight the "desire of the text," and proposed thinking of the paired desires, to serve and to see, as the defining epicenters of the complex whole: it is a text about desire and nearness and the approximations of satisfaction. Yet *Tiruvāymoḻi* tends to surge past any such explanations, opening new possibilities and so inviting its readers to try to organize it one more time, over and over. In the process, one's skills and sensitivities are refined, and it is a changed reader who chooses to return to the songs each time. Yet in the end there can be no perfect masters of the text, no finished reading, no final explanation.

Still, there certainly are readers who have persuasively brought definition to the text, living by it, and enabling others to live by it. For the Śrīvaiṣṇava community, the *ācāryas* were precisely these ideal readers.

It was to them that we turned our attention in chapter 3, listening in on the communal conversation which arose in and around their expositions of the songs. We saw how they balanced sensitivity to intense emotion with a concern for theological precision, how they appealed to the dynamics of meditation and making meditation possible and, finally, how they wove a dramatic narrative through and around the songs. We began to appreciate the capacity of the text, when read by such masters, to be engaged by its audience in a coherent, imitable and effective fashion, so that each reader/listener could see in the *āḻvār's* problem, progress and solution, something of his or her own journey. According to the *ācāryas'* reading of *Tiruvāymoḻi,* it describes the *āḻvār's* extraordinary path, while yet also being a guide to life for everyone, the path to be travelled by all. *Tiruvāymoḻi* was taken as a text of practice, reaching its fulfillment when mastered—memorized, recited, meditated, taught, lived—by those who hear it and ponder it, surrendering to its songs, to the lord speaking in them—and, intermediately, to those who correctly interpret them.

In this chapter we extend our consideration of these practical and participatory possibilities by examining how the *ācāryas* highlighted for their community *Tiruvāymoḻi*'s virtues as a text of practice, attending to five of the most important ways in which the *ācāryas* open up *Tiruvāymoḻi* according to the requirements of its practical orientation. This selection of five ways is simply indicatory, offered with an awareness of how each of the five requires fuller attention and can be complemented by the identification of still other ways. The five serve simply to suggest the kind of responses careful readers have made to the songs over a millennium, which too are the kinds of practical responses devotees make even today in seeking to understand, imagine, be informed and educated by *Tiruvāymoḻi*. We begin by examining two rather abstract approaches by which the *ācāryas* formulate and systematize the songs. First, we see how they read *Tiruvāymoḻi* in correlation with the three sacred mantras of the Śrīvaiṣṇava tradition, three revered prayers, highly valued in themselves, which were understood to form a profound but easy distillation of the 1102 verses (section I). Second, we examine the summation of *Tiruvāymoḻi* by the 11th century theologian Periyavaṅkippurattunampi, a summation which is the earliest extant effort to formulate *Tiruvāymoḻi* as a systematic presentation of the entire program of right action and right salvation (section II). We turn then to three ways of approach more evidently attuned to the affective and personal commitments required for the desired appropriation of *Tiruvāymoḻi*. To begin, we examine the pattern by which the *āḻvār* is portrayed as personally exploring and experiencing deeply the ways and non-ways of finding God and, at the same time, formulating this knowledge as the two paths of *bhakti*—studied, effective love which reaches toward God by the best of human efforts, and *prapatti*—sheer and utter surrender to that divine grace to which no human effort can be commensurate (section III). Fourth, we turn to the *ācāryas'* practice of citation and their composition of the "intertext," examining how citation from the Sanskrit-language epic *Rāmāyaṇa* enables the audience to imagine more vividly its roles and behavior according to *Tiruvāymoḻi* (section IV). Fifth, we listen-in as the *ācāryas*, conscious of their place in a tradition of hearers and expositors of the songs, speak of themselves, their predecessors and their own community, instantiating by appeals to these exemplary lives the most immediate and accessible opportunities for living in conformity with the text (Section V).[1] This then is the plan of the chapter:

I. The first way: *Tiruvāymoḻi* in correlation with the three holy mantras

II. The second way: *Tiruvāymoḻi* as a guidebook to the right means to union with God

III. The third way: Śaṭakōpaṉ as exemplar and teacher of surrender

IV. The fourth way: Imagining the *Rāmāyaṇa* and *Tiruvāymoḻi* as a moral scenario

V. The fifth way: Living *Tiruvāymoḻi* in the community

These five ways are at the core of the Śrīvaiṣṇava reading of *Tiruvāymoḻi*, and must be highlighted in any full interpretation of the tradition. Yet they have the potential to matter also for the reader from outside the tradition, insofar as they offer practical avenues of approach which may, under certain circumstances, typify what *any* reader can do in response to the songs and the commentaries. Once we have understood the five ways of approach, we are inevitably invited to assess how they serve to prompt such new readers to think more amply and imaginatively of comparable resources—creed, system, virtues, imaginative parallels, exemplars—in their own home traditions. When we read these songs, what are the avenues of access by which we can understand them, imagine their meanings, connect them with what we already know and believe?

I. The First Way: Tiruvāymoḻi *in Correlation with the Three Holy Mantras*

The first way taken up by the *ācāryas* is to be observed in their effort to demonstrate the close connection, in a very concise, even mathematical equivalence, between the songs and these three highly revered mantras of the Śrīvaiṣṇava community:

- The *Tirumantra* ("the holy mantra"): *aum namo Nārāyaṇāya*; "Aum, reverence to Nārāyaṇa;"[2]
- The *Dvaya mantra* ("the double mantra"): *Śrīmān-Nārāyaṇa-caranau śaraṇaṃ prapadye, Śrīmate Nārāyaṇāya namaḥ,* "I take refuge at the feet of Nārāyaṇa with Śrī; reverence to Nārāyaṇa with Śrī;"
- The *Carama Śloka* ("the last verse" of the *Bhagavad Gītā*, 18.66): *sarvān dharmān parityajya mām ekaṃ śaraṇaṃ vraja, ahaṃ tvā sarvapāpebhyaḥ mokṣayiṣyāmi mā śucaḥ;* "Giving up all dharmas take me alone as your refuge; I will free you from all your sins; do not grieve."

The *ācāryas* do not explain the mantras in their commentaries on *Tiruvāymoḻi*; such information is presumed to be known from elsewhere, in the life of the community. Certainly the object of close attention prior to the *Īṭu* (Parāśara Bhaṭṭar had written his *Aṣṭaślokī* on the Tirumantra a generation before) it is only in the generations after the *Īṭu* that the three mantras become the object of comprehensive writings, most illustriously as the topic of Piḷḷailokācārya's *Mumukṣuppaṭi* and as the organizing element in *Vedānta* Deśika's *Śrīmadrahasyatrayasāra.*[3] Here, I offer a simple summary of their meaning.

All three mantras are understood to deal with the relationship between God and the human person as a dynamic, living reality, the central orientation and project which makes sense of human life. The first two mantras, the Tirumantra and the Dvaya mantra, are addressed to the Lord; by reciting them the devotee enters into communication with God in a way that is both heartfelt and theologically profound. The third, Kṛṣṇa's famous words to Arjuna near the end of the *Gītā*, is indicative of the kind of life the devotee is to lead because of who God is and what God does. The mantras encapsulate manageable answers to three basic questions: What is *Tiruvāymoḻi* about? It is about the deepest human need, to praise God (as occurs in the Tirumantra). What does *Tiruvāymoḻi* say to us? It tells us that we should cast aside all obligations and resources and depend on God alone (as is stated in the Carama Śloka). What does one do who understands

Tiruvāymoḻi? One surrenders to Nārāyaṇa with Śrī (as is described in the Dvaya mantra). Such wisdom is the essence of the mantras and, for the *ācāryas*, the essence of *Tiruvāymoḻi*. To recite the mantras is to imbibe this wisdom and at the same time to appropriate the songs in a succinct, easy and profound fashion. The mantras serve as credal distillations of the faith of the Śrīvaiṣṇava community and, on that basis and in their succinctness and iterability, as practical resources for worship: do the mantras, do the songs, do one's faith. Within this rich and fascinating topic, our analysis is restricted specifically to the mantras' function as instruments of exegesis to be used in correlation with *Tiruvāymoḻi* in the interpretation of the songs.

1. Smaller Correlations

In the course of their exegesis, the *ācāryas* occasionally use the mantras in the explanation of individual words, verses and songs. At first, such correlations may seem rather artificial, and sometimes so obscure as to make understanding more rather than less difficult. Yet the purpose is rather to make the essence of *Tiruvāymoḻi* available in a concise form, conducive to easy grasp and reproduction. Correlations with the mantras serve to bring out and illumine the meaning of particular words. These references are often obscure from the point of view of the contemporary reader; sometimes it seems that pious delight in the fact of the correlation itself is the fruit to be gained: the things I believe are all connected with one another. At VI.1.10, for example, Naṃpiḷḷai mentions the *ācāryas'* preference for the Dvaya over the other mantras, giving as his reason that the Dvaya has six [metrical] feet, as do the bees mentioned in the verse:

> *I have begged you specially, fragrant swarm of bees,*
> *speak to that mighty bull of a warrior who rejoiced in pulverizing the walls of that demon unparalleled in war, who dwells in Tiruvaṇvaṇṭūr on the north bank of the cool Pampai river,*
> *tell him I exist.* (VI.1.10)

Superior even to the bees, the mantra is a reliable messenger for the devotee who recites it knowledgeably and piously.

In commenting on the words, "my love, who loves the woman on the lovely flower," (X.10.7) Naṃpiḷḷai recalls how Bhaṭṭar, when dying, emphasized to Nañcīyar the value of thinking always of the Dvaya mantra:

> To meditate on the verse, "My love, who loves the woman on the lovely flower," (X.10.7) along with our Dvaya is to meditate on how He loves us who have been grasped by Her, for He is in love with that great lady.

At IV.6.11 reference is made to "rich Kurukūr of ancient, unerring praise;" in explicating this richness, a comment on the mentality of Śrīvaiṣṇavas prompts reference to one of the mantras:

> When they were ignorant, their contact with other gods and with their devotees was the cause of their destruction. Now, the "praise" mentioned here is that Śrīvaiṣṇava glory by which the Lord's name and contact with his devotees come to sustain their existence; if one hears someone who is a Vaiṣṇava say, "The Lord of all is protector," but engages in contact with other gods and people who are not the Lord's—then his way is not the true Vaiṣṇava way.

This social reality—the shift from wandering among troubles and obstacles to clinging solely to the lord—is paralleled by the two-part structure of the mantra:

> If one reflects on the first part of the mantra, then one sees that all of this [world] is a barrier as far as he is concerned, preventing him from reaching the goal. If one reflects on the second part of the mantra, then one can become like Lakṣmaṇa who would not even sleep [because he was ever alert to the opportunity to perform some act of service]. As it says, "If their love has grown through seeing, can their eyes ever close?" (*Tiruviruttam* 97) If one knows that this being with the Lord is one's proper nature but still does not undertake behavior conformed to this proper nature, nor give up contrary behavior, then true knowledge has not truly been born in that person. (IV.6.11)

The mantra is thus used to elucidate the verse. Which mantra? It is striking that Āttāṉcīyar, in interpreting what Naṃpiḷḷai means by the "first part" and the "second part" of the mantra, leaves undecided which mantra Nampiḷḷai has in mind when he makes this important practical correlation with one or the other. Āttāṉcīyar suggests that the two parts of the Dvaya are meant—or perhaps the two lines of the Carama Śloka; either will do, since both mantras serve to distinguish wrong and right attitudes and behavior. This insistence that either mantra can pertain here emphasizes all the more directly how deeply commitment to thinking about the mantras is intertwined with the commitment to understand *Tiruvāymoḻi* itself, in its details.

2. Larger Correlations

When broader correlations are at stake, we find yet more ample examples. The second of the *Īṭu*'s three interpretations of VI.10.10 is essentially a gloss on the Dvaya mantra. Unsurprisingly, much is made of the echo of the Dvaya in VI.10.10, since both the verse and the mantra are taken to exemplify complete surrender:

> *"I cannot be away even for a moment," says the maiden on the*
> *flower who dwells on your chest;*
> *you are unmatched in fame, owner of the three worlds, my ruler,*
> *O lord of holy Veṅkaṭam where peerless immortals and crowds*
> *of sages delight:*
> *with no place to enter, this servant has entered right beneath*
> *your feet.*

and,

> I take refuge at the feet of Nārāyaṇa with Śrī;
> reverence to Nārāyaṇa with Śrī.

The correlations are closely worked out. Thus, the words of Śrī at the beginning of the verse,

> *'I cannot be away even for a moment,' says the maiden on the*
> *flower who dwells on your chest,*

is correlated with the mention of Śrī in the second line of the mantra:

> reverence to Nārāyaṇa *with Śrī*

The middle of the verse likewise conforms to the Dvaya, as the words beginning with "you are unmatched in fame," up to "O lord of holy Veṅkaṭam where peerless immortals and crowds of sages delight," is taken to express the meaning of the word connected to "with-Śrī" (Śrīmān), i.e., "Nārāyaṇa." So too, the last line of the verse and the Dvaya also conform, word by word:

> *with no place to enter, this servant has entered right beneath your feet.*
>
> I take refuge at the feet of Nārāyaṇa with Śrī.

To read VI.10.10 is to understand the mantra, and vice versa; what is dramatically portrayed in the song is distilled to its essence in the mantra. The painstaking and grammatically detailed correlation reinforces the audience's sense of the reality of the claims in both the song and the mantra, and to recite one is to capture the other.

Some correlations are more dramatic, for example, the use of the Tirumantra in the interpretation of V.9. We have seen in earlier chapters that this song expresses the longing of a young woman who is separated from her lord at Tiruvallavāḻ, while yet close enough to the town as to remain entirely captivated and tormented by the sights and sounds and smells she cannot quite reach. The *āḻvār's* earthly experience of longing for the lord and the young woman's longing for the temple at Tiruvallavāḻ exemplify the fundamental orientation of the human to the divine, and this dynamism is captured in "*Aum namo Nārāyaṇāya,*" where "*Aum*" represents the human, "*Nārāyaṇa*" the divine, and the dative "*-āya*" the dynamic tendency of the one to the other.[4] Nampiḷḷai and Periyavāccāṉpiḷḷai see the Tirumantra as marking the intellectual structure of the song, as the young woman's existential situation is captured in the words of the mantra. The Tirumantra—wherein the "*Aum*" is always near to, yet never one with "*Nārāyaṇa*"—is used to elucidate and heighten the tension in the song, replicating the same distance-and-nearness so graphically depicted there, as the spaces of grammar and geography replicate one another. Thus we have,

Ontology	*Song*	*Mantra*
God	the Lord in Tiruvallavāḻ	"Nārāyaṇa"
human	the young woman	"Aum"

Expressing both the distinction of the self and lord and the intrinsic orientation of the former to the latter, the Tirumantra is a shorthand expression of the tension of closeness and distance which characterizes human religious experience; it articulates the young woman's state theologically without doing away with the existential tension at the heart of it.[5]

3. Correlations with the Whole

A still broader use of the mantras occurs when the *ācāryas* seek to distill the meaning of the whole of *Tiruvāymoḻi* to a manageable formula, intelligible and useful, when they translate the songs into the mantras, as it were. As cited at the beginning of this chapter, the first song and first verse of *Tiruvāymoḻi* are recognized to stand in parallel to the Tirumantra. Mirroring one another, each encapsulates the complete truth that is required by Śrīvaiṣṇavas:

> The first song sums up the whole of *Tiruvāymoḻi;* its first three verses sum up the first song; the first verse sums up the first three verses; the first line sums up the first verse. What is this like? It is the same as where it says, "The Vedic verses and whatever else is made of word: all of that is in the 'Eight Syllables, the Tirumantra.' " Thus, the Tirumantra sums up all the *Vedas; Aum* sums up the mantra, and the 'a' sums up *Aum.* Other works—the *Rāmāyaṇa, Mahābhārata,* etc.—serve as various summaries and expansions. [Third Introduction to the *Īṭu*]

The Tirumantra is used also in summation of particular sections of *Tiruvāymoḻi,* as the following examples show. In introducing VIII.10, Nampiḷḷai says this:

> In the previous two songs, VIII.8 and VIII.9, the *āḻvār* has said that the self belongs exclusively to the Lord, indicating

> that this is not bad for others, nor bad for himself. He has expressed this point with reference to the middle "letter" ["*u*"] in *Aum* and to "reverence" [*namas*]. The limit for "exclusive belonging to the Lord" is his own belonging to the Lord. In the two previous songs, the expression of these points was implicit, but here the meaning is explicit, when he speaks of belonging to other devotees. (VIII.10.0)

At the beginning of IX.3, Naṃpiḷḷai follows the (oral) teaching of Naṭuvil Tiruvītippiḷḷai in order to re-read rather elaborately the preceding songs according to the *Tirumantra*. The result is a rather intricate correlation that can be tabulated as follows:

i. Regarding *Aum*
   - VIII.8.1–3a = the "a" [in *Aum*];
   - VIII.8.3b–4 = the meaning of the dative [*-āya, to* Nārāyaṇa], and the middle letter ["u"] and the third letter ["m"];
   - VIII.8.5–8 = "m;"
   - VIII.8.9–10 = against false views which are not based on meditation on the *Aum*;

ii. Regarding *namas*:
   - VIII.9, VIII.10 = respectively, the linguistic (*śābda*) and substantive (*ārtha*) meanings of *namas*

iii. Regarding *Nārāyaṇāya*
   - IX.1 = the meaning of *Nārāyaṇa*
   - IX.2 = the dative ending (*-āya*).

iv. In summation
   - IX.3 = a summary of all eight syllables in the Tirumantra

The Dvaya mantra too is used to measure the whole of *Tiruvāymoḻi*. For instance, at the beginning of IV.1, a song which rebukes kings bent on material gain and power, Naṃpiḷḷai says that the second half of the Dvaya explains *Tiruvāymoḻi* I-III, while the first half explains *Tiruvāymoḻi* IV–VI:

> By the previous three hundred verses (I.1–III.10) he has given the meaning of the second half of the Dvaya; now, in what follows (IV–VI), he gives the meaning of the first half of the mantra. In this song (IV.1) he gives the means to the human goal that was taught in the first three hundred verses, warning that those who don't know this means will go after prohibited means . . . (IV.1.0)

At VII.2.0 Naṃpiḷḷai says, "In VII.1 the *āḻvār* has meditated on the meaning of 'namas' in many ways, culminating in the complete dependence expressed in VII.1.11: 'Śaṭakōpaṉ, servant of the servants of the servants of the servants.'" Āttāṉcīyar observes that the first part of the Dvaya is explained in VI.10, while in VII.1 the *āḻvār* gives the meaning of the "*namas*" from the second part of the Dvaya, while here, in VII.2, the *āḻvār* is explaining "*Nārāyaṇa;*" in VII.2.9 ("my Lord on whose chest is the sacred lady . . ."), he adds, "with *Śrī*" is explained. Thus, to summarize,

VI.10	=	I take refuge at the feet of *Nārāyaṇa* with *Śrī*
VII.1	=	reverence to
VII.2	=	*Nārāyaṇa*
VII.2.9	=	with *Śrī*

The second Introduction to the *Īṭu* refers to the mantras rather broadly, echoing Naṃpiḷḷai's statement at IV.1. After hearing first of five aspects of the process toward the goal (lord; self; goal; obstacle; means) we are then told how *Tiruvāymoḻi* can be divided into four parts according to the structure of the Dvaya:

> By *Tiruvāymoḻi* Śaṭakōpaṉ explains the Dvaya. In it, the first three hundred verses [*Tiruvāymoḻi* I–III] explain the second half of the mantra; the next three hundred verses [*Tiruvāymoḻi* IV–VI] explain the first half. In the next three hundred verses [*Tiruvāymoḻi* VII–IX] after that, he gives the qualities connected with the means and how he desires nothing of his self or what belongs to it . . . In the last hundred verses [*Tiruvāymoḻi* X], he reaches his conclusion, explaining how he has attained what he desired.

Thus we have,

Tiruvāymoḻi I–III	=	"Reverence to *Nārāyaṇa* with *Śrī*;"
Tiruvāymoḻi IV–VI	=	"I take refuge at the feet of *Nārāyaṇa* with *Śrī*"
Tiruvāymoḻi VII–IX	=	the discourse on means
Tiruvāymoḻi X	=	the discourse on attainment

At the conclusion of his entire commentary, Vātikesari Aḻakiya Maṇavāḷa Cīyar[6] offers the most detailed and elaborate summary correlation of the mantras and the songs:

> In the first and second hundred verses he explains the Lord's proper nature as the one to whom everything belongs, and who is distinguished by being protector, and object of enjoyment.
>
> In the third and fourth hundred verses he explains the proper nature of belonging to the Lord, in the form of having that one experience and taking delight in that one alone. When he explains, in these four hundred verses, the uniqueness of the Lord's being the one to whom all belongs, and the human state of of belonging to the Lord, it is with reference to the first letter ("a") that he explains all things as belonging to the Lord. It is with reference to the third letter ("m") that he explains how the Lord is the one to whom all belongs; with reference to the emphatic "u," he explains that state of service which connects "a" and "m," Lord and self. Thus the *āḻvār* has expounded *Aum*.
>
> Then, in the fifth hundred verses he explains the proper nature of means, in the sixth hundred verses the choice of that means, in the seventh hundred verses the proper nature of obstacles to it, in the eighth hundred verses the ending of those obstacles. Thus he explains how the Lord is the means, in terms of the act of reverence (*namas*) and His being its object, with reference to both the word "*Nārāyaṇa*" and its meaning. He explains the proper nature of taking refuge, which is the act of reverence, and the proper nature of the obstacle, which is "I" and "mine," and "*namas*" as the prohibition of "I" and "mine".

> In the ninth and tenth hundred verses he explains the last syllable (the dative "*-āya*" in "*Nārāyaṇa-āya*") which expresses the acquisition of the result that is distinguished by being connected with service and all kinds of relationship. Thus the *āḻvār* had expounded in detail throughout *Tiruvāymoḻi* the meaning of the Fundamental Mantra (Tirumantra) which is explained succinctly in the summary first verse, and which is the summary of all the Scriptures. (X.10.11)

That is,

Tiruvāymoḻi I–II	= the Lord's nature as the one to whom all belongs = "*m*"
Tiruvāymoḻi III–IV	= human nature, as belonging to the Lord = "*a*"
Tiruvāymoḻi I–IV	= the relationship of Lord and humans = "*u*"
Tiruvāymoḻi V	= the means to reach the Lord
Tiruvāymoḻi VI	= choosing the right means = *namo*
Tiruvāymoḻi VII	= obstacles to the Lord
Tiruvāymoḻi VIII	= the removal of obstacles = "*Nārāyaṇa*"
Tiruvāymoḻi IX–X	= achieving the results = "*-āya*," to [*Nārāyaṇa*]

As concise as this correlation is, according to Vātikesari Aḻakiya Maṇavāḷa Cīyar the *āḻvār* also had the other mantras in mind when he composed *Tiruvāymoḻi*:

> He speaks also of the Dvaya mantra: in the first song, after expounding "the Lord of *Śrī*" and "being *Nārāyaṇa*," and thereafter the many qualities, such as *Nārāyaṇa's* virtue and easy accessibility, knowledge, etc., he expounds the achievement of service to the Lord which is the highest human goal and which is devoid of all obstacles, and the proper nature of that taking-refuge—all of which is found in the two sentences of the Dvaya.

> Moreover, he speaks also of the Carama Śloka: after expounding the Lord Himself as the means, and the cessation of all else except the choosing of this means, and how the

> Lord is without a second, the *āḻvār* then expounds the cessation of all obstacles—that cessation which is the object of means—and that purposefulness which is connected with the accomplishment of the fruit. Thus he makes clear the meaning of the Carama Śloka.
>
> He thus elucidates in their various aspects all three secret mantras which must be known by every suitable person who has no other purpose, who has no other means, who belongs to the Lord, the possessor of all modes.

Let us sum up. Though such efforts to distill the meaning of *Tiruvāymoḻi* according to the mantras are found only occasionally in the commentaries and await the formal systematization which will be composed elsewhere, in subsequent generations, they are already important resources for the conceptualization and practicalization of *Tiruvāymoḻi.* On the theoretical level, the *ācāryas* distill the elaborate, richly dispersed truth of *Tiruvāymoḻi* down to the pure, "mathematical" truth of the mantras. The mantras themselves are grammatically dynamic, they are relational, the words standing in need of one another, no single word able to replace the rest. From this perspective, we can say that the reduction of the songs to the mantras is not a process of abstraction, but rather the simple claim that the songs are ultimately about the intrinsic orientation of the human to the omnipotent and gracious divine.

On the more practical level, that *Tiruvāymoḻi* is understood to be in exact correlation with the three mantras serves to make manageable and available the full meaning of *Tiruvāymoḻi* for those who cannot memorize or fully appreciate the 100 songs in all their detail. They can now appropriate this large meaning just by reciting one of the mantras; to know the mantras is to know the text in essence, to utter the mantras is to voice, ever so briefly, the entire truth of *Tiruvāymoḻi.* And, as one recites the hundred songs, their full yet single meaning is brought home through recollection of the succinct truth of the mantras. Later texts make clear that the mantras increasingly serve a credal function, with the truths of Śrīvaiṣṇavism indicated by the parts of the mantras.[7]

It is possible that the contemporary reader from outside the tradition might gain some access to *Tiruvāymoḻi* through these mantras, by venturing to think through the concomitant understandings of the order of *Tiruvāymoḻi*: repeating the mantras may help the reader to pay better attention. More likely, though, attention to the mantras in correlation with *Tiruvāymoḻi* will prompt the reader to think of similar correlations and distillations in his or her own tradition, and also open the way for a comparison of communal creeds as strategies by which communities formulate their rich scriptural traditions for the sake of catechesis and worship. Though it will not be as productive merely to compare the ideas contained in the three mantras with, let us say, the Christian Nicene Creed, it will certainly prove to be fruitful to trace the posited parallel paths from *Tiruvāymoḻi* to the mantras, and from the New Testament to Nicea.[8] How do we make precise and memorable the many things we believe?

II. The Second Way: Tiruvāymoḻi *as a Guidebook to the Right Means to Union with God*

The project of correlating *Tiruvāymoḻi* with the three mantras marks the effort to understand the text as a whole, though by the nature of the correlation, it occurred only in the most succinct of forms. For more elaborate summations of the songs—putting aside the commentaries themselves, as a particularly ample way of approach—one must wait a generation after the *Īṭu*, for Aḻakīya Maṇavāḷa Perumāḷ Nāyaṉar's great *Ācārya Hṛdayam* and its thorough summation and reorganization of *Tiruvāymoḻi*.[9] But we do find a complete summation at the end of the first and longest of the three introductions to the *Īṭu*. Attributed to a disciple of Rāmānuja, Periyavaṅkippurattunampi,[10] this summary is the earliest comprehensive reading of *Tiruvāymoḻi* available to us. Practical in its concerns and structuring of the text, it establishes in great detail that *Tiruvāymoḻi* is a text about the right goal of human life, and the right way to that goal. Periyavaṅkippurattunampi finds latent in *Tiruvāymoḻi* a complete framework for the spiritual life, including its essential features. His exposition of the songs according to the major features of the way to salvation sets the course for the later expositions of the Śrīvaiṣṇava way;[11] his work may be understood as answering these five questions:

1. What is the topic of this work, *Tiruvāymoḻi*?
2. What human goal is most appropriate to our proper nature?
3. What are the obstacles to this goal?
4. How is renunciation to take place?
5. What is the result of renunciation?

Since this summation is highly important yet not readily available, I will present Periyavaṅkippurattunampi's text almost in full.

After a rather abstract introductory analysis of the divine self, material nature, and human nature, Periyavaṅkippurattunampi begins with an exposition of: a.) *Nārāyaṇa* as transcendent lord; b.) the meaning of "*Nārāyaṇa*;" c.) the relationship of *Nārāyaṇa* to *Śrī*; d.) the human self as belonging totally to the lord:[12]

> a.) What is the topic of this work, *Tiruvāymoḻi*, which this *āḻvār* composes? In the first song, beginning with "*Who possesses the highest, unsurpassable good*" [I.1.1], and "*This one is all good and understanding, there is no one like him past, present or future; he is my good life, there is no one greater than him,*" [I.1.2], and then graciously says, "*He bears all forms in earth and heaven, but has no form.*" [I.1.3], "*He became all of them, that one,*" [I.1.4] and, "*that highest one who abides as wide sky, fire, wind, water, earth, as fine sound, vigor, strength, cool affection, patience.*" [I.1.11] he explains the meaning of the word "*Nārāyaṇa,*" and thus too states the transcendence of Nārāyaṇa. The meaning of Nārāyaṇa is this: He is superior to all things, He is possessed of all auspicious qualities, He is the Lord of both realms. The *āḻvār* explains what belongs to this Lord in IV.10 and II.2.[13]

b.) When, in the second song, he says, "*The unceasing, shining praise, Nārāyaṇa,*" [I.2.10], he is actually giving the holy name which expresses the meaning given previously, giving this meaning among other ways of naming Him. After expressing precisely what it means, he impresses this form in his own mind by stating, "*Nārāyaṇa our Treasure,*" [I.10.8] and, "[Meditate on the feet of] *Tiru's Nārāyaṇa,*" [IV.1.1]; by noting that "*when they see the people of Nārāyaṇa who live praising him,*" [X.9.1] is said during the [heavenly] ascent, he fills out the meaning of this name.[14]

c.) Next, by the following verses, beginning with "*In whom the Lady in the lotus delights, he whose feet are so hard for us to gain,*" [I.3.1], "[Reverence each day] *the lovely ornamented feet of Śrī's Lord,*" [I.3.8], "*Joy for us and for the woman in the flower,*" [IV.5.8], "*Shall I then not be joined to you and the great, holy, lovely maiden?*" [VI.9.3], "*I place under oath Śrī who lies on your holy chest,*" [X.10.2], "*my love, who loves the woman on the lovely flower,*" [X.10.7], he expresses the transcendence of Nārāyaṇa-with-Śrī. The significance our *ācāryas* have attributed to these two words, "*Nārāyaṇa*" and "*Śrī,*" when they explicate the Mystery, has its basis in what this *āḻvār* says here. In the course of his taking refuge he says, "*In whom the Lady in the lotus delights, he whose feet are so hard for us to gain,*" [I.3.1]; while in the time of enjoyment, he says, "*my love, who loves the woman on the lovely flower,*" [X.10.7]. Yet in the times of taking refuge and of enjoyment, he is actually expressing the same referent, the pair of them, without difference. Thus the proper nature of the transcendent is defined.[15]

d.) What then is his own nature which is correlate to the proper nature of the transcendent? First he meditates on his nature as being the Self in the body by saying, "*Become all this, the soul in the body, though hidden, everywhere he pervades, he is within,*" [I.1.7]; when teaching it to others he teaches this nature as the Self in the body, saying, "*Surrender your life's breath to him who owns all surrender,*" [I.2.1]. In regard to the fullness of this nature as the Self in the body, as belonging to the Lord, he says, "*He makes me exist for himself,*" [II.9.4], and "*Within me at his feet, within my body,*" [VIII.8.2]. But he does not stop by expressing

> this state of belonging to the Lord; rather, he expresses the perfection of his belonging to the Lord to the limit. In III.7 and VIII.10 he states this concisely. By praying, "*When will I join the crowd of his devotees?*" [II.3.10] and then, in accordance with what he had prayed for, stating emphatically, "*With devotees possessed of great, endless bliss,*" [X.9.11], he is explaining that his own state of belonging to the Lord reaches its limit in belonging to those who belong to the Lord.[16]

Second, after this exposition of the lord and human self (and community of human selves), Periyavaṅkippurattunampi identifies service as the highest human goal:

> What human goal is appropriate to our proper nature? The *āḻvār* specifies that service is the human goal, when he says, "*He makes me exist for himself,*" [II.9.4], "*It is our desire to abide for time without end and offer perfect service,*" [III.3.1], "*This dark jewel who holds me as his servant, unfailing in service,*" [IV.8.2], and "*If you will not come then call me to you, to be beneath your flower feet,*" [VIII.5.7], etc. Yet he also makes the point that service is not just what is enjoined by the *śāstras*, nor just what is appropriate to human nature, but also what is appropriate to desire; he mentions which qualities are to be achieved when he says, "*Who possesses the highest, unsurpassable good,*" [I.1.1]. He expresses the object of enjoyment as specified by those qualities, when he says, "*My lord, lord Kaṇṇaṉ, the sweetness of my ambrosia, husband of Śrī,*" [I.9.1], and, "*Again and again I drink his pure ambrosia,*" [I.7.3]. He also shows how this pleasure is ever new, when he says, "*For every moment, day, month, year, every age upon age—for all that time, he is my insatiable ambrosia,*" [II.5.4], and, "*My ambrosia, I can never get enough of you,*" [V.8.1], and, "*You are the food I never get enough of,*" [X.10.5]. He also states how the human goal, service, is achieved in that pleasure in the self which is born in the experience of these qualities, when he says, "*I have gained you, in joyful service I have gained your feet,*" [X.8.10]. In order to emphasize that this is the true human goal which pertains to the self, he expresses the joy which is achieved in the pleasure born in the experience

> of the qualities of the Lord, saying in summary, "*Such is now and always what I have desired, Father!*" [X.8.10][17]

Third, Periyavaṅkippurattunampi describes obstacles to the goal of reaching and serving the lord:

> In the second song, he expresses succinctly the obstacles which impede the goal, beginning with "*Surrender everything,*" [I.2.1]. Thereafter, he expatiates on this point in three songs. What is to be renounced? In III.9 he mentions kinds of service that ought not to be undertaken; in IV.1, the inferior goals of lordship and isolation; in IX.1, the things that are connected with one's relation to the body.
>
> But ought he speak in this way? Surely lordship and isolation are certified by scripture as legitimate goals. He insists that these things must be renounced by anyone who seeks liberation "*because their delight is puny*" [IV.9.10] in comparison with the experience of the Lord, even if such goals are "*hard to know,*" [IV.9.10] and unlimited for the one who seeks that liberation which is characterized as the highest goal. Thus he emphasizes what must be renounced.[18]

Fourth, Periyavaṅkippurattunampi explains the requirements of renunciation, in a longer section which I have divided into three parts: a.) the nature of renunciation; b.) the means of renunciation; c.) the identity of the renunciant.

> a.) One may ask how renunciation is to take place. If renunciation is letting go of things, isn't it necessary to know how renunciation is to take place? Yes, it is necessary. Ought one transcend things while remaining among them? Or must one live only having gotten rid of things?
>
> Neither is possible. If one thinks of transcending things, one would have to go beyond this world; but to think of getting rid of them in that way would be to destroy the Lord's glory, i.e., this world. If one were to live apart, still near to things but in a forest with no people, leaving everything and being there among the animals—even then, mental confusion would be sure to arise. For example, Saubari went into the water, saw fish having intercourse, and became infatuated with things again—so moving away or getting rid of things is not the means to renunciation.

> Is there any means, then? In saying, "*Pull out by the roots 'you' and 'yours,'*" [I.2.3] he teaches others the true means of renunciation, saying that one must renounce the confusion of the self with the body, and the sense of owning the things connected with the body. In saying, "*When I did not know myself I said, 'I, mine,'*" [II.9.9] he meditates on this himself. As the text says, "*The house of one whose lust has ceased—that is the house of asceticism,*" [*Itihāsa Samuccaya* 13]. The solitary place of asceticism is the home of someone in whom lust has ceased. Where have we seen this? Just look at King Janaka; look at Lord Kulaśekhara. Real renunciation is renunciation in the mind.[19]

Periyavaṅkippurattunampi then identifies *bhakti* and *prapatti* as the two means to the goal:

> b.) What is the means for ending these obstacles and accomplishing the human goal? The means as certified in the *Vedānta* is twofold: *bhakti* for competent members of the three upper classes, and *prapatti* for those with no such competence. In his exposition of means, the *āḻvār* expounds both means, but concludes that *prapatti* is his own means.
>
> He speaks [on the subject of means] beginning where he says, "*I've done no ascetic deeds*", [V.7.1], and "*You have finally given me your feet as my refuge, my way,*" [in V.7.10], "*Who has as his refuge the feet of the one who sucked the life from the breasts of the big-boned demoness,*" [V.8.11], "*Śaṭakōpaṉ of souther Kurukūr whose protection is at the feet of the lord with a thousand names,*" [V.9.11], and, "*Our refuge is the feet of the lord on the snake,*" [V.10.11]. Then he sums it all up by saying that the Lord's feet alone are his means: "*Except for you I have no support to which my self can cling,*" [in X.10.3].
>
> In teaching this to others, he sings, "*So seize the moment, meditate on the feet of Tiru's Nārāyaṇa and be uplifted,*" [IV.1.1] He expounds the fullness of means by saying, "*Your feet are my refuge, my way,*" [V.7.10], "*Who has as his refuge the feet,*" [V.8.11], and "*His feet are our refuge,*" [V.10.11].[20]

Periyavaṅkippurattunampi next describes the identity of the person who can undertake this path and surrender to God:

c.) Who is competent for this means? In saying *"He graciously gives the good of understanding which removes confusion"* in I.1.1, the *āḻvār* stresses that the Lord was gracious to him; he thus brings helplessness to the fore, because he is not able to see the Lord. When he specifies the means, he expresses helplessness, which is unconnected with the means for which the three classes are competent; he says, *"I've done no ascetic deeds,"* [V.7.1]. At the moment of taking refuge he says, *"This servant who has no other place to enter,"* [VI.10.10]. In the time of delight, in order to express what he has gained by the Lord's grace, he says, *"Wretched me had no fullness,"* [III.3.4]. To express his barrenness, he says, *"He uplifted me whose evil deeds are beyond compare,"* [VII.9.4]. By making it clear to all sinful beings that they should enter refuge, he indicates that everyone is competent for taking refuge.

Regarding the competent person: even if the means is sure, insofar as this means is not appropriated, the person will not survive. So, on the topic of this appropriation he says, *"Who has as his refuge the feet,"* [V.8.11]; in the time of performing it with its subsidiary aids, he says, *"I have entered right beneath your feet,"* [VI.10.10]; regarding the fact that this appropriation is due to the Lord, he says, *"You have given your feet alone as my refuge,"* [V.7.10], and *"This too is his grace."* [VIII.8.3]; in regard to the decisive moment in this appropriation, he says, *"You destroy my affliction, never stop destroying it, I have no other destroyer . . ."* [V.8.8], and "[noble Śaṭakōpaṉ of Kurukūr] *who at all times has only one thought,* ['Our refuge is the feet of the Lord on the snake']," [V.10.11].

When he teaches this means to others he mentions how easy it is by saying, *"See, this thought is enough, not even a little more is needed,"* [IX.1.7]; in explaining it and its adjuncts he says that surrender is not an subordinate part of *bhakti*, but rather an independent means. With *"Refuge [for all those who reach his feet], he gives them Vaikuṇṭa when they die,"* [IX.10.5] he indicates its completion, up to complete attainment. If you ask how one who has fixed on this means is to pass the time, the *āḻvār* has graciously explained that the way to pass the time is *Tiruvāymoḻi* itself: *"That his servants might eat ambrosia I have spoken this garland of words."* [IX.4.9][21]

Fifth, Periyavaṅkippurattunampi describes the results of refuge-taking:

What result will follow for the one who undertakes this means? He describes the result of the means which begins with the control of the senses and concludes with the perfection of service. In the beginning, the meditator must gain control of the senses first; for this competent person, control of the senses is the fruit accruing from the means.

When he controls his senses—as it says, "*You destroyed my mind's evil,*" [II.7.8] and "*You gave me a mind to come near you,*" [II.7.7]—and gains control, at that point do devotion, etc. still help him toward experience of the Lord? As it says, "*He graciously gives the good of understanding which removes confusion,*" [I.1.1]: the Lord gives that knowledge which is proximate to devotion, and so too He prompts the origination of devotion. Who then increases the devotion that has been thus originated? As it says, "*In the field of my heart, He planted love great enough to fill the ocean, Kaṇṇaṉ whose body is so dark;*" [V.3.4]. It is therefore the Lord who increases devotion.

Is there a limit to this increase? The *āḻvār* explains how the Lord increases devotion so as to flood all three realities [the Lord, the self, the world] by saying, "*Surrounding, inside, filling, uplifting every thing, unlimited great Matter; surrounding that, and greater still, the highest blossoming flame; surrounding that, and greater still, the fiery knowledge and bliss . . .*" [X.10.10a–c]; with his own mouth he says, "*Surrounding that, and greater still, my desire for you, but that too you finish, you surround me.*" [X.10.10d], and thus explains how in the end the Lord has finally broken the bond of the body and brought him to that special Place [Vaikuṇṭa], uniting with him there.[22]

Periyavaṅkippurattunampi then summarizes his analysis:

Therefore: these [five] points are expounded in *Tiruvāymoḻi*, other points having come in only incidentally. What five?

> 1.) divine transcendence—Śrīmān Nārāyaṇa, and total belonging to him as one's proper essence; 2.) that service which is achieved in joy born at the experience of his qualities, as the human goal; 3.) "I" and "mine" as the obstacles; 4.) the feet of the Lord who is easily available to all, ending obstacles and bringing about service, as the means; 5.) beginning with the conquest of the senses all the way up to service—all of this as the result.[23]

The text ends with this coda:

> In this way Periyavaṅkippurattunampi has explained the meaning of *Tiruvāymoḻi* in its five aspects, the purport of all the *Vedas*. As it says,
>
> "Sages, great-souls, those who know the *Vedas* and the meaning of the *Vedas*, and all the *Vedas* along with the epics and *Purāṇas*: they all explain the nature of *brahman* which is the goal and of the individual self which seeks the goal; the means to the goal and the result thereof, and the obstacles to the goal." [*Hārītasaṃhitā* 11.152][24]

For Periyavaṅkippurattunampi and his systematizing successors, *Tiruvāymoḻi* was a complete, intricately encoded system, where everything required for right understanding and right practice is present, albeit in a way that is evident only to a master of the songs. When read carefully and comprehensively, *Tiruvāymoḻi* sets up the framework for the spiritual journey modelled on that of the *āḻvār*. *Tiruvāymoḻi* maps perfectly the goal for the devotee, rooting this in the nature of Lord and self, and even predicts the obstacles to this path. Going beyond a theoretical resolution, the text offers a perfect and practical resolution to life's troubles, the satisfaction of one's deepest desires. One simply has to "do *Tiruvāymoḻi*."

When I first read this small treatise, I was surprised that Periyavaṅkippurattunampi did not pay more attention to the dramatic elements of the *āḻvār's* quest, even to his surrender at VI.10.10, cited only as one among many verses. But it is clearer to me now that this is exactly what is to be expected; this systematization of *Tiruvāymoḻi* prescinds from authorial experiences and focuses on the perfection of the teaching; though it does not deny the experiences, it explains what they mean, so that one can follow them properly and, thereafter, do as Śaṭakōpaṉ did. Of course, this systematization claims to capture the existential core of the human condition, yet this is done without personalizing it. As was the case with the mantras, narrative gives way before system in this explanation of who humans are and what they ought to do.

His work opens yet another way to begin to engage the Śrīvaiṣṇava tradition: his system is a (small) step away from the immediacy of the songs, it invites rational study, a consideration of the theoretical and practical doctrines involved. It is an excellent catechesis, valuable for newcomers from inside and outside the tradition. Since it is richly exegetical, it can also be an avenue into the songs themselves, a map for the reader.

Obviously, the theory and practice of such transitions between commentary and system, tradition and a rational or even rationalized exposition, are not absent from the religious and philosophical traditions of the West. Though artificial in its own arrangements and local patterning, Periyavaṅkippurattunampi's systematization may in its own way be more accessible to the outside observer, appealing as it does rather directly to the mind and common sense of the reader: there is a goal, there is a way to get there, and both of these are mapped out in this particular understanding of the human and divine natures, etc.; you just have to know how to read the map. Periyavaṅkippurattunampi the theologian invites dialogue with his theological colleagues in other traditions, particularly those systematic theologians who value maintaining scriptural roots for their neatly ordered presentations. Though it is worthy of the attention even of those not interested in comparison per se, his practical theology should be of interest also to those engaged in a comparison of systematic theologies.

But such systematizations are never enough. They need to be complemented by still other ways of approach which emphasize those human and dramatic factors which appeal to the heart and spirit more directly. To these we turn in the next three sections, as we consider in turn three exemplars: Śaṭakōpaṉ himself, as the teacher who lived what he taught; characters from the *Rāmāyaṇa* who, by their right living, exemplify ideal aspects of Śaṭakōpaṉ's life and teaching; and the *ācāryas* themselves, who in the community's own time exemplify the integral union of right understanding and right practice. If system remains too difficult, imitation on such varying levels may not be.

III. The Third Way: Śaṭakōpaṉ as Exemplar and Teacher of Surrender

The third point of entry into *Tiruvāymoḻi* is in essence a practical formulation of the issues considered in chapter 3, the mutually illuminating experiences and teachings of Śaṭakōpaṉ. This way of approach focuses on how one is to respond to the lord's overwhelmingly complete, gracious initiative, and how the life and songs of the *āḻvār,* responses to that initiative, were seen by the *ācāryas* as powerful complementary invitations to similar acts of listening and responding. Through the articulation, in the course of interpretation, of a practical doctrine in which total surrender is superior to all other forms of response, the *ācāryas* invite their listeners to learn from what Śaṭakōpaṉ experienced, composed and taught, to verify the doctrine in the man, and to act likewise.

As we saw, the *ācāryas* hold that *Tiruvāymoḻi* teaches the way to God that is rooted in the *āḻvār's* own experience. His way, though intensely direct and personal, is complex and consonant with tradition, and so he expounds a way to God that distinguishes two kinds of devotion, *bhakti* as a way of good works and right intentions, and *prapatti* as a way of total surrender, the latter of which is his own preferred and chosen way. The way of *bhakti* is a nurtured, long prepared-for and patiently refined love which takes a long time to mature and which requires certain human activities, preparatory, purificatory. The way of *prapatti* is a desperate longing beyond all bounds, which impatiently violates all schedules of implementation and culminates in a surrender so unconditional and helpless that even *bhakti* has no place anymore: *prapatti* is a way that is a nonway. The *āḻvār* understood both ways, but lived the latter.

The brief analysis which follows emphasizes the exegetical and exemplary components of this teaching as they appear in the *Īṭu*. As in our earlier presentation of the mantras, we are interested here not in the larger debates related to *bhakti* and *prapatti*, but specifically in how the distinction between the two affects the way the *ācāryas* read *Tiruvāymoḻi*, explain the songs, and draw the audience into participation in the *āḻvār's* religious journey.[25] The *ācāryas'* distinction between *bhakti* and *prapatti* is inextricably intertwined with their presentation of the story of Śaṭakōpaṉ himself; he is the person who tests every means but finally, at VI.10, abandons them all and surrenders to his lord. What he learns, he teaches; how he lives is his most convincing teaching.

In the midst of the various complications that inevitably accompany exegesis, the *ācāryas* are on the whole suggesting that the *āḻvār* is making three points in *Tiruvāymoḻi*, in regard to the topic of the way to God. First, he is setting forth two distinct and venerable ways of union with the lord, the way of *bhakti* and the "(non)way of *prapatti*;" both are taken seriously and given due consideration. Second, he is announcing that *prapatti* is his personal way, or (non)way, to the lord, because of his own acutely experienced helplessness. Third, by example and exposition he is finally making it clear that *prapatti* is also the better path for his audience to follow. By way of illustration, let us note the five key places at which these themes are announced and illustrated: I.1.1, I.2.0, V.7.1, VI.10.10, and X.4.0.

1. I.1.1

Since the first verse of *Tiruvāymoḻi*, I.1.1, is said to contain implicitly everything that follows in the 100 songs,[26] the *ācāryas* find, as expected, important indications of *prapatti* right there at the beginning:

> *Who possesses the highest, unsurpassable good? that one;*
> *who graciously gives the good of mind which removes*
> *confusion? that one;*
> *who is the chieftain of the unforgetting immortals? that one:*

so bow down at those radiant feet that destroy affliction
and then rise up, my mind. (I.1.1)

Although Naṃpiḷḷai's lengthy comment on I.1.1 does not introduce any systematic discussion of *bhakti* and *prapatti*, the topic is raised prominently in his comment on the *āḻvār's* words, "who *graciously* gives the good of understanding which removes confusion." (I.1.1) Grace is signalled here, the gift is free, the songs begin in the gift of realization, *Tiruvāymoḻi* is entirely the fruit of *prapatti*. This sense of grace remains primary throughout. When one realizes how unreservedly generous God is, one needs only to receive and enjoy that grace, without reserve. The lord provides reliable ways for the devotee to find him, but once one recognizes the lord's insatiable desire for union, to find and to be found, that divine spontaneity becomes first the main thing, and then the only thing: the lord himself is the sufficient means for salvation, *prapatti* the proper human response.

Since the lord's grace is primary, the *ācāryas* believe that when the *āḻvār* speaks of his own "devotion" and his own efforts, he must always be understood to be referring to *prapatti*, and not to the more elaborate *bhakti* of the brāhmaṇical tradition. Naṃpiḷḷai's rule is clear: "Instead of that devotion [a first *bhakti*] which is achieved through ritual actions and meditative knowledge, for the *āḻvār* there is the lord's favor; the *āḻvār's* was that devotion [a second *bhakti*, i.e., *prapatti*] which grows up in the very instant before complete service." (I.1.1) Śaṭakōpaṉ is the one who surrenders completely; he is a *prapanna*, the "performer" of *prapatti*:

> People asked Empār, "Was the *āḻvār* a *prapanna*, or was he established in *bhakti*?" Empār replied, "The *āḻvār* was a *prapanna*, although *bhakti* was of help during his bodily journey. You may wonder what this is like. We are all supposed to be *prapannas*, yet for six months of the year we pursue our livelihood. But for the *āḻvār*, Kaṇṇaṉ was everything—'the food he eats, the water he drinks, the betel he chews.' (VI.7.1)."

> For the Lord has been so gracious, without cause. The *āḻvār* thinks of himself as having been non-existent before the

> Lord made him His own, and this sentiment culminates in his saying, "He who graciously gives . . ." (I.1.1) The *āḻvār* does not even plead; it is like breast-feeding, where the mother gives her milk spontaneously . . ."

Everything that follows is, for the *ācāryas*, infused with this understanding: the *āḻvār* knows the several ways to the lord, but in his own experience knows only one way, the way of surrender.

2. I.2

In I.2, a song which strongly urges renunciation, the *āḻvār* preaches what he has experienced and knows with certainty within himself:

> *Surrender everything, and after surrendering that,*
> *surrender to the one who holds your life, at your surren-*
> *der.* (I.2.1)[27]

Since the song is both the product of experience and a message to others, the appeal is understood by some *ācāryas* to refer to *prapatti*, and by others, to *bhakti*: "Tirumālai Āṇṭāṉ, following the interpretation of Āḷavantār, explained this song (I.2) as referring to *prapatti*. At first Rāmānuja agreed with this, but after finishing the *Śrībhāṣya* he decided that this song was about *bhakti*. Afterwards, Empār agreed with Rāmānuja." Both *bhakti* and *prapatti* lead to the Lord, and so it is possible that the *āḻvār* might be recommending one or the other. As Āttāṉcīyar observes, in both cases the lord is still the goal and the means to the goal. But how could the *āḻvār* be understood by some as putting forward *bhakti* as the means, if *prapatti* is superior on experiential and theological grounds? The difference of opinion among the *ācāryas* pertains not so much to the *āḻvār's* own view of the options and his personal choice, which must be for *prapatti*,[28] but rather to what he has deemed advisable to teach to others, given their presumed capabilities here at the beginning of *Tiruvāymoḻi*.

Nampiḷḷai's introductory comment on I.2 concludes with a summary of the *āḻvār's* message on devotion:

> He sees that other things are to be avoided, that the Lord of all is to be sought, and that if this was known to them they would have to leave behind those other things and grasp Him alone. So he begins to teach them, explaining the goodness of the Lord of all, as well as the flaws of transitoriness and insignificance in the things they now have . . ., [he urges] that they should develop a loss of taste for other things, grow in devotion to the Lord, and then take refuge. (I.2.0)

3. V.7–10

We saw in chapter 3 how the *ācāryas* identify songs V.7 to V.10 as the place of the *āḻvār's* personal testing and evaluation of all available means of gaining the lord. It is not surprising that they find here further instruction on *bhakti* and *prapatti,* and particularly in light of the *āḻvār's* underlying experience. V.7 begins with the words,

> *I've done no ascetic deeds, I have no subtle knowledge but still I cannot bear to leave you even once . . .* (V.7.1)

According to Naṃpiḷḷai, the *āḻvār* is here confessing that he has not done any approved, efficacious deeds, and hence is not in the position to gain their fruits; that he has not practiced upaniṣadic meditation and so cannot have that "assured" knowledge of the lord which begins with knowledge of the self and ends in manifestation; and, moreover, that he does not have *bhakti* either.[29] The goal of the *āḻvār's* quest is to reach God; the contribution of V.7 to V.10 is his realization that all efforts are likely to fail, that even *bhakti* itself must be inadequate. The *āḻvār* learns to live by grace and to depend on grace alone, and by his example he shows this, and shows it to be the better option for his listeners too.

4. VI.10.10

VI.10.10 receives the most extended comment of any verse in *Tiruvāymoḻi,* and the *āḻvār's* exemplification of surrender is very clear and direct here, as Naṃpiḷḷai indicates:

> The *āḻvār* sees the generous nature of the Lord: how one may take refuge with Him without any requirements, such as restrictions on who is eligible, or restrictions on time, or restrictions on what else is required. He then makes known his resolve to enter refuge at the feet of Śrī Veṅkateśvara after making known before the great Lady that he has nowhere else to go . . . All his obstacles are gone, there is nothing missing in his acquisition of all that he desires, so he enters at the feet of the one who possesses Tiruveṅkaṭam, the one who is always most near. In this way, one must take refuge near the object of refuge, where the fruit of taking refuge will be given.[30]

In his first explanation of VI.10.10, Naṃpiḷḷai gives special emphasis to the mediating role of the divine consort Śrī in ensuring that *prapatti* is entirely reliable. He examines at length the circumstances under which Śrī, mentioned in the first words of VI.10.10 ("the maiden on the flower who dwells on your chest, saying, 'I will never leave you for an instant'"), mediates perfect, sure salvation. Naṃpiḷḷai stresses that true surrender must be total and deep, in accordance with the last words of VI.10.10, "this servant who has no place to enter has entered right beneath your feet." Naṃpiḷḷai strikingly illustrates Śrī's role in the implementation of *prapatti* by contrasting the fates of Kāka and Rāvana, two characters in the *Rāmāyaṇa* who seriously offended Rāma (the lord) and Sītā (Śrī). The crow Kāka sinned grievously by actually wounding Sītā, pecking at her breast; although Rāvana committed the grievous wrong of kidnaping her, he never touched her. Yet it was Kāka who was able to escape death, because he took Sītā's advice and threw himself down helplessly at Rāma's feet, in an act of surrender, whereas Rāvana ignored her advice, refused to surrender even when faced with defeat, and so inevitably perished.

In his second explanation of the verse, Naṃpiḷḷai emphasizes how factors related to right means—the *āḻvār's* surrender, the role of Śrī—are inextricably related to the goal of this practice, the lord who is the real topic of VI.10.10. Surrender is not primarily a sensible rationalization of the human condition, it is a response to who the lord is, an act which makes sense only when one takes into account both the nature of the one who surrenders and the one to whom one surrenders.

Still, if all that mattered was the lord's nature, then there would be nothing to prevent everyone from being saved; but one must learn, and choose, to live according to the reality of the lord: "The Lord's proper nature is that He Himself is the means; these two qualifications (having nothing, having nowhere to go) are the *āl̲vār's* proper nature. Otherwise, if the *āl̲vār* lacked these, the consequence would be universal liberation based solely on the Lord's nature."[31] Hence too the need for the songs: listeners must be guided to see that the truth of the *āl̲vār's* experience is the truth of their own.

Naṃpiḷḷai's third and longest explanation of VI.10.10 is meant, Āttān̲jīyar says, precisely to excite a taste for *prapatti*. After a long introductory portion on the interrelations among ritual action, meditative knowledge, *bhakti* and *prapatti*, Naṃpiḷḷai examines the nature of the person eligible for complete surrender and elaborates on the relationship between *prapatti* and other religious considerations.

> The first *ācārya* himself, Śaṭakōpan̲, was great in that knowledge which he possessed by the Lord's grace; he became perfect by grasping the point that everything is from the Lord. As he says, "He has graciously given the good of understanding which removes confusion." (I.1.1) There are others inside and outside our community who, though grasping this same means, still cling to other goals. And there are those who take the Lord as their goal only after taking hold of some other means. Unlike them, the *āl̲vār* determined the Lord to be both the goal and the means. Such was his excellence. But, even if the Lord is the goal, what harm is there in undertaking other means? The harm is this: those means have to be accomplished; they are numerous, difficult; they are not in conformity with one's proper nature.[32]

After discussing the limits of ritual action and meditative knowledge and the efficacy of the holy name, Naṃpiḷḷai concludes his exposition in this way:

> The aforementioned means (ritual action and meditative knowledge) are difficult and touched by ego, so they are listed among what is to be abandoned. By contrast, because *prapatti* is single, already accomplished, easy and pertinent to all, there is no means beyond it. This verse expresses what has been said elsewhere: "Therefore, they say that surrender is different from all these ascetical practices."[33]

The *āḻvār*, again, is seen to be cognizant of two ways to union with the lord, *bhakti* and *prapatti*. He admits that both are valid, but holds that *prapatti* is his personal way; by implication, it is also held up as the best way for everyone else who seeks a sure way to God. Out of his personal experience of search and frustration, the failure of means, the *āḻvār* has been able to describe the easier, better path—one that others can take too.[34]

By the end of VI.10, *prapatti* has been set out with all its dramatic entailments—the search, the failure to find the right means, the desperation, the unconditional surrender; its virtues have been adequately narrated. What lies in the background—ritual action, meditative knowledge, devotion as the culmination of a traditional set of practices, etc.—has also been set forth and ranked accordingly. Three truths are inseparable—who the *āḻvār* is, what he does, and what he teaches—and one can profitably begin with any of the three, in order to end in union with the lord.

5. X.4

After VI.10 (though only as understood in light of the continuing problems faced in VII.1 ff., as we saw in chapter 3) all that remains at issue by the time we reach X.4 is to emphasize how *prapatti* relates to *bhakti* in the overall view of things, and how this theme is intrinsic to *Tiruvāymoḻi* as the *āḻvār's* personal testimony and as refined theology. As we saw in chapter 3, X.4 is understood to mark the end of the *āḻvār's* self-questioning, at least insofar as theological issues are at stake; the song offers decisive assurance that vision and union will be achieved:

The feet of Tāmotara help on the path of asceticism,
dark cloud-colored, lotus-eyed, the bearer of the discus, water,
sky, earth, fire, wind,
the heaven-dwellers never stop talking of his names' greatness.

Greater than the heavenly unwinking ones, difficult for those not
holding him within,
Māl, red lotus eyes, on whose chest Tiru forever dwells, destroy-
ing both kinds of deeds each day,
he rules me here.

He rules me, he bears the discus;
from whom do I need anything?
I have no need to be saved,
I have ended the sorrows of death:
I have fixed my eyes on the feet of the husband of chaste Piṇṇai
whose eyes shine, a sword, a Keṇṭai fish,
I adorn my head with them. (X.4.1–3)

In his introduction to the song Naṃpiḷḷai recalls the basic point that is woven into his reading of *Tiruvāymoḻi* from the start:

> . . . In I.2 and I.3, the *āḻvār* spoke of *bhakti* and how the way in which it is consonant with his own goal, and in those two songs he meditated on the qualities which increase *bhakti*. In this song he makes his summation, speaking of that *prapatti* which had been mentioned in I.1, and which is his own means to attainment.

He then reaffirms Śaṭakōpaṉ's own preference for *prapatti*:

> Although both ways are available to him, the *āḻvār* thinks that *prapatti* is the cause for his own acquisition of the Lord. One may wonder whether there is some word indicative of *prapatti* in the first song. Yes there is, for he said there, "who *graciously* gives the good . . ." [I.1.1] His devotion is not the *bhakti* enjoined in the *Vedānta*, for the exclusory rule enunciated in the discussion about *śūdras* [*Uttara Mīmāṃsā Sūtras* I.3.33–39] would raise the problem that *bhakti* could not apply to him [who is a *śūdra*, and thus excluded from the very *bhakti* he would be recommending]. One may ask whether that *bhakti* could not have been conceded to the *āḻvār* due to his glory. But that would contradict what he says in passages such as "who *graciously*

> gives the good . . ." [I.1.1] To be sure, there is a kind of devotion born in an inner mind prepared by ritual action and meditative knowledge . . . But here, instead of ritual action and meditative knowledge, there is only the Lord's grace, upon the receipt of which there was immediately born in him superior devotion, etc.

Still, a kind of participation is required, for the lord's grace must be answered with desire:

> Even if the Lord is the means, the *āḻvār* has a desire for the accomplishment of the goal. If there were no desire, that goal would not be the human goal; the Lord is the one who makes possible acquisition by one like the *āḻvār* who has a flawless desire for the goal, who praises the Lord, saying, "This is the goal." The *āḻvār* thus offers an option between *bhakti* or *prapatti*. After explaining the way in which the *bhakti* taught to others in I.2 and I.3 has been an instrument for his own acquisition and how it is connected with his own goal, he summarizes his position here.

After some clarifications, Naṃpiḷḷai returns to *prapatti* and finds it expounded in X.4:

> Here, in X.4 and X.5, he reemphasizes that both *bhakti* and *prapatti* are conformable with his goal. When he says, "the feet of Tāmotara help on the path of asceticism," (X.4.1) by the word "asceticism" he means *prapatti*. For *prapatti* is the greatest asceticism, as it says, "Therefore, renunciation is unequalled among these ascetical practices." When he says, "In the ways of the highest one of old I have seen his lotus feet; when I see them my deeds completely cease." (X.4.9), and "destroying both kinds of deeds he rules me here" (X.4.2), he is explaining [what is said in the *Bhagavad Gītā* 18.66,] "Take refuge with me alone; I will free you from all your sins."

X.5 adds just one major point regarding true devotion, that it flourishes best when it depends on the holy name of God:

> *If you plan to approach the feet of Kaṇṇaṉ,*
> *the holy name worth reckoning is surely "Nārāyaṇa"!* (X.5.1)
>
> *If you keep chanting "Mātava" over and over,*
> *no evil will stick to you, no suffering will touch you.* (X.5.7)

Suffering will not touch anyone
who chants the names of the rain-cloud-colored lord
who never dies. (X.5.8)

Nañcīyar's summary here nicely summarizes the *ācāryas'* understanding:

> The *āḻvār* had previously defined *bhakti yoga,* and stated that one must know the manner of this *bhakti yoga.* He now realizes that it cannot be lost, and so in this song he teaches the holy name which is its foundation. He says, "Reflect on this name, and in accord with what has been said here, incline your mind and speech and body toward the husband of Śrī. From your delight, perform worship ceaselessly with flowers and all the other helps; worship Him who himself graciously removes all obstacles to devotion toward Himself."
>
> The *āḻvār* thus graciously describes the essence of the *bhakti yoga* which he had praised in many places. Reflecting on the fact that the Lord has decided to allow him to go to the Holy Place, he realizes that afterwards there will be no further opportune moment to teach them; so he sums up what he has been teaching for the sake of others.

At this, the *ācāryas* have completed what needed to be said about *bhakti* and *prapatti.* All that is required to show their relation to the *āḻvār's* experience and to his teaching in *Tiruvāymoḻi* is complete, including their portrait of the *āḻvār* as the teacher who embodies his teaching. The *āḻvār* is the one who has learned by trial and error the path of perfect surrender and who has surrendered without qualification; he is the teacher of two reliable paths, though always offering the advice that total surrender is the better way. The teaching is adequate, but for many, his life itself and the drama of his personal surrender may be the point of access to the path he lays out. The *ācāryas* make the case that *Tiruvāymoḻi* is not only about the goal and the way to the goal, but also that it focuses specifically on *prapatti,* complete surrender, as an option available to all Śrīvaiṣṇavas. The profound truths of the songs are practically, socially open to all members of the audience, not just the elite, and the songs open the way, intellectually and emotionally, for the experience recounted in the songs. The listeners learn that *prapatti* is not merely an ideal, a theory; it is founded in the human experience of the *āḻvār* who stands as a sign of hope, inspiring those who appropriate *Tiruvāymoḻi* seriously to see him as their exemplar and follow his path of total surrender. The saint himself is indeed the medium of his message.

Here too, of course, a reader versed in the traditions of the West will be on familiar ground. Figures such as Socrates among the ancient Greeks, or Jesus among Christians, exemplify the unity of life and teaching, and the generation of wisdom from life. Their teachings are powerful in part because of the witness of their lives; most of us discover the former only through the latter. The rhetorical power of such appeals even across cultural boundaries is not to be underestimated, as respect for the exemplary life makes possible a way to understand the teachings that accompany it. Though the technicalities of *prapatti* in relation to *bhakti* may not be understood clearly, the deed of total self-surrender may nonetheless speak eloquently. By admiring Śaṭakōpaṉ, the observer may discover a way to understand what *Tiruvāymoḻi* and the Śrīvaiṣṇava tradition are really about: entering a theological discourse by way of its believers, seeing through a teacher's life what he or she is trying to say.

IV. The Fourth Way: Imagining the Rāmāyaṇa *and* Tiruvāymoḻi *as a Moral Scenario*

The fourth of the *ācāryas'* ways of making *Tiruvāymoḻi* accessible and intelligible to the Śrīvaiṣṇava audience is to open it in a more broadly imaginative fashion, so that moral imitation becomes an easier, more likely mode of response. This is achieved by various acts of citation and contextualization which link the songs with other texts known and loved by the community—with parts of the *Mahābhārata*, the *Bhagavad Gītā,* the *Upaniṣads,* and myths from the Vaiṣṇava *Purāṇas*—but especially by reading the songs along with the famous *Rāmāyaṇa* narrative. The abstract principle is that texts from the Sanskrit tradition are in theological and dramatic parallel with *Tiruvāymoḻi*; this principle was concretely realized through the very many specific citations which occur so frequently in the *Īṭu*. Instances of citation serve in part to clarify what is meant in any given verse of *Tiruvāymoḻi*, in part to legitimate the thoughts and words of the songs, and in part simply to increase the enjoyment of the listeners, as one favored text prompts a pleasurable recollection of another from somewhere else. But all such purposes function within a still broader framework: theoretically, all Śrīvaiṣṇava texts were understood to form a single great Context. Practically, the project was to place *Tiruvāymoḻi* as deeply and firmly as possible in the minds and imaginations and affections of the community, interconnecting it with everything else devotees would know, particularly the models by which they lived their daily lives.

The aspect of this project of contextualization that I will explore here is how the virtues of Śaṭakōpaṉ are made yet more persuasive by correlations which link his person with characters from the *Rāmāyaṇa*. For the *ācāryas*, *Tiruvāymoḻi* and the *Rāmāyaṇa* represent a single, extended moral panorama, a doubled story of love and devotion wherein grace is the beginning and surrender the fitting conclusion.

The plot of the *Rāmāyaṇa* can be recounted briefly.[35] Rāma, the prince of Ayodhyā and heir to the throne, renounces his claim and goes into exile for fourteen years, in order to honor two promises his father had unwisely made to his second wife, who draws on them at an inopportune moment. It is also the story of Sītā, Rāma's wife, who goes with Rāma into exile, and of Rāma's three younger brothers: Lakṣmaṇa, who follows Rāma and Sītā into exile in order to serve them there; Bharata, who reluctantly stays behind to run the kingdom; and Śatrughan, who remains ever by the side of Bharata. During the forest exile, the story builds slowly toward its great climax: Sītā is kidnapped by Rāvana the demon king of Śrī Laṅkā, and Rāma, with the help of the monkey people in the south of India, invades Śrī Laṅkā, and defeats Rāvana, thus fulfilling his princely and marital obligations by winning back his wife.[36]

The *Rāmāyaṇa* is cited very frequently in the *Īṭu,* as it is in the later Śrīvaiṣṇava tradition as well.[37] The effect is familiarity, a cumulative, cultured sense of how the songs and the epic fit together. As one reads the many interpretations of *Rāmāyaṇa* texts in the *Īṭu,* one is impressed by the erudition behind the citations, the skilled and sensitive choices which the *ācāryas* make; for they have internalized the entirety of *both* texts, reading them in light of one another, bringing them to life together. As one reads the *Īṭu,* one becomes increasingly attuned to the resonance between *Tiruvāymoḻi* and the *Rāmāyaṇa,* even if this is at first a cultural resonance to which one must grow accustomed, rather than one which is urged upon the reader by *Tiruvāymoḻi* (which gives priority neither to the Sanskrit tradition nor to the *Rāmāyaṇa*). One begins to imagine together the dramas of Śaṭakōpaṉ and Rāma, and to find oneself a place in that extended dramatic context. Let us examine one example first, and then focus on how the moral exemplarity of Śaṭakōpaṉ is enhanced through parallels with the *Rāmāyaṇa.*

1. Paralleling Tiruvāymoḻi *and the* Rāmāyaṇa

In chapter 2 we saw that V.9 is a song in which loss, separation and distance are keenly suffered.[38] Tiruvallavāḻ is the temple town where the young woman's beloved lord lives; she is near to it, but she cannot get there. The song is all about that tantalizing closeness and unattainability. Unsurprisingly, the song reminds the *ācāryas* of the similar plight of Sītā and Rāma, who are tortured by their separation from one another after she has been kidnapped. The *ācāryas* repeatedly cite *Rāmāyaṇa* scenes which evoke the agony of separation, drawing particularly on Sītā's viewpoint. Let us notice just a few of these evocative parallels.

At verse 1, we are reminded that she constantly suffers the pain of separation, yet with great strength, whereas the monkey Hanumān has trouble enduring separation even for one night;[39] there too we are reminded that just as the town of Ayodhyā wilted in the absence of Rāma, so too Sītā wilts.[40] At verse two, we are told that for Rāma it is enough that Sītā simply exists on the same earth as he does.[41] At verse three, when we hear that even the fragrant breeze torments the young woman near Tiruvallavāḻ, we are reminded that Hanumān likewise seems to hurt Sītā simply because she thought him to be Rāvana in disguise;[42] there too we are reminded that everything in the town, even the recitation of the *Vedas*, seems to have something to do with Sītā.[43] At verse four, the poisonous snake who guards the cosmic ocean where Viṣṇu enjoys his primordial rest is compared with Lakṣmaṇa who guards Rāma and Sītā;[44] here too we have a starker contrast: Rāma and Sītā can survive by thinking of one another, but the young woman in the song has no memory of togetherness which could help her survive this time of separation.[46] At verse five, we are asked to appreciate that whereas Sītā's whole body suffered due to her love, the young woman singles out her eyes as specially tortured, and so specially deserving of compassion.[46] Some comparisons focus on Rāma more than Sītā. In commenting on verse six—"where fresh breezes carry the songs of bees everywhere"—Periyavāccāṉpiḷḷai cites the beginning of the *Kiṣkindhā Kāṇḍa,* where Rāma visits Śabarī's *āśrama* and then proceeds toward lovely Lake Pampā. Periyavāccāṉpiḷḷai evokes the following passage to speak of the bittersweet experience of beauty in this sorrowful world:

> Far from Vaidehī, whose eyes are as long as the petals of the lotus, who ever loved the water-lilies, life has no attraction for me. Perfidious Kāma, now that I am no longer able to rejoin her, you seek to evoke in me the memory of that sweet lady, whose speech was a thousand times sweeter still; it were possible to bear the love I feel for her, if the Spring with its flowers and trees did not increase my torment! Those things that enchanted me, when I was with her, in her absence, have no further charm for me. On seeing the petals of the lotus cup I say to myself: "These resemble Sītā's eyes," O Lakṣmaṇa. The fragrant breeze, blowing through the stamens of the lotus flowers and the trees, resembles her breath.[47]

Rāma sees clearly the beauty around him, yet that very beauty heightens rather than assuages the agony of his separation from his beloved Sītā, of whom everything reminds him, on whom beauty itself rests. So too the young woman outside Tiruvallavāḻ, and the *āḻvār* too: both are tortured by the inaccessibility of what is near, the elusiveness of what they can almost taste.

The densely composed feelings of the young woman near Tiruvallavāḻ are opened and enjoyed across the vast panorama of the *Rāmāyaṇa*. The Sanskrit and Tamil texts come to echo one another. As the listener moves back and forth from one to the other, one learns to feel more deeply the absence, loss and tangible desire of the characters, as the song is brought vividly to life in this alternative imaginative universe. Since, as we have seen, these verses have also been enhanced in parallel to the Tirumantra, we now have this more complex chart:

Ontology	*Song*	*Mantra*	*Drama*
God	the lord in Tiruvallavāḻ	*"Nārāyaṇa"*	Sītā
human	the young woman	*"Aum"*	Rāma[48]

Beginning anywhere, one makes sense of the rich and diverse components of the whole.

2. Characters in Parallel: the Āḻvār *and his Soulmates*

The larger practical motivation for citations of the *Rāmāyaṇa* is to constitute *Tiruvāymoḻi* and the *Rāmāyaṇa* as a single broad moral paradigm wherein every kind of person can find a model for right human living in the presence of a gracious God. The *Rāmāyaṇa* provides many larger and smaller examples of how to live rightly, near to the lord, Rāma. Let us first introduce this general paradigm and then, in the next section, focus on one example, the presentation of Lakṣmaṇa, the younger brother of Rāma, as an ideal figure whose life highlights part of the *āḻvār's* identity as conceived by the *ācāryas*. The expectations behind a moral exegesis of the *Rāmāyaṇa* are most fully spelled out in Naṃpiḷḷai's introduction to III.7, a song about devotion to the lord among his devotees:

Highest ruler, Kaṇṇaṉ, himself the lord with the discus,
my pure jewel-colored one with the marvellous four shoulders:
see, those who worship him, joining hands and feet,
are the lords who rule me in all my births, every day.

See, they are my rulers in all the births I can sing of,
those who reverence those able to honor
the feet of the lord whose tulasi leaves are so fragrant,
whom heaven and earth praise,
my father with the broad shining discus. (III.7.2–3)

In introducing the song, Naṃpiḷḷai says this about the *Rāmāyaṇa*:[49]

> The Rāma-*avatāra* has primarily to do with right behavior. In the *Rāmāyaṇa,* Rāma is the one who obeys the general rule that one must always honor the word of one's father. Indeed, he firmly sets it on an unwavering foundation, with the firm norm, "A son must do what his father says." His younger brother Lakṣmaṇa obeys the rule, "One must do what is fitting to one's appropriate object of attention." His half-brother Bharata obeys the rule, "One must perform whichever acts of service are pleasing, according to one's assigned place." Bharata's younger brother, Śatrughan, in turn obeys the same rule, but to the extreme of being of service to those who belong to the Lord.

Or, a bit more simply,

> Rāma acts with the idea, "I must do what my father says." Beyond that, Lakṣmaṇa acts instead with the idea that one must do what one's chosen master wants. Beyond that, Bharata, who cannot speak Lakṣmaṇa's words, "Kindly make me your attendant," (*Ayodhyā Kāṇḍa* 31.24), acts with the idea that one must perform acts of service even if they are not pleasing to oneself, as when Rāma cannot be persuaded to stay, but instead says to him, "Stay here in the kingdom." Beyond that, Śatrughan is obedient to the extreme; as it says, "He was led along by Bharata who was going to his uncle's house." (*Ayodhyā Kāṇḍa* 1.1)

Rāma directly obeys his father, Daśaratha; Lakṣmaṇa obeys his brother Rāma, rather than their father Daśaratha; Bharata obeys Rāma by not going with him into exile, instead remaining behind in the city; Śatrughan stays with Bharata, thus serving the one who serves the absent Rāma. Though one might imagine it most desirable to be with Rāma, as were Sītā and Lakṣmaṇa, the distanced and mediated activity of Śatrughan is very highly praised, for it is he who exemplifies the *āḻvār's* claim, "See, they are my rulers in all the births I can sing of, those who reverence those able to honor the feet of the lord."

Naṃpiḷḷai reinforces the general point, celebrating the diversity of roles in the community:

> In the same way, being a Vaiṣṇava is in essence one thing only: to be immersed in Rāma's beauty, qualities and deeds. But some devotees are immersed in the beauty of His form, others in His qualities, still others in His great deeds. Thus they are different from one another, though they all desire the same union with Him. "All these devotees are my lords," says the *āḻvār* in this song.

The *Rāmāyaṇa* puts on display the various ways of acting to which Śrīvaiṣṇavas can aspire, depending on their capabilities, circumstances, preferences. Each way exemplifies some aspect of devotion, while all of them together represent the truth that is contained so concisely in *Tiruvāymoḻi,* in Śaṭakōpaṉ who himself represents the whole range of devotees within the songs.

Most parallels between Śaṭakōpaṉ and characters from the *Rāmāyaṇa* are drawn with an exemplary goal in mind: act thus in this life, and so live a little more the truth of *Tiruvāymoḻi.* Thus we saw above how at VI.10.10 Naṃpiḷḷai explored the role of Sītā (Śrī) as the mediator of salvation by introducing a comparison between Kāka and Rāvana; the former, though the more grievous offender, was saved because he took to heart Sītā's advice to surrender to Rāma, thus giving support for the *āḻvār's* "surrender-with-the-intercession-of-Śrī." The rhetoric of the situation emphasizes both the sinfulness of the human condition and the possibility of forgiveness. Likewise, as we saw, the lengthy exposition of VI.10.10 concludes with a consideration of Sītā's discourse on the universal human condition of guilt and need. The general themes and moral virtues are emphasized by the recurrent evocation of representative figures from the *Rāmāyaṇa*—Lakṣmaṇa, Bharata, Sītā, Vibhīṣaṇa, etc.—who gradually, through the cultivation of sentiment and imagination in the audience, become characters in the broader story told in and around *Tiruvāymoḻi,* and therefore points of access to the *āḻvār's* drama. Doors are opened through which the listeners too may imagine their own more or less humble entry into Śaṭakōpaṉ's world, not as the *āḻvār,* but perhaps as some aspect of him, as a little bit of Hanumān who gets angry, or of Sītā who suffers in captivity or, as we shall now see in some detail, of Lakṣmaṇa who wants nothing but to be with Rāma and Sītā, serving them.

3. Parallel Lives: Śaṭakōpaṉ and Lakṣmaṇa

Lakṣmaṇa is portrayed in the *Īṭu* as the model for the active devotee whose only goal is service of the lord. He is not quite the quintessential practitioner of *prapatti,* since he is privileged by his innate and de facto closeness to his brother Rāma, who allows Lakṣmaṇa to come with him into exile. By comparison, the destitution of other characters and the true helplessness of their act of surrender will appear greater. Nonetheless, Lakṣmaṇa's example is favored as particularly illustrative of Śaṭakōpaṉ's distinctive identity: for both, to exist is to exist for the lord; to serve is to be unable to exist separately. There is no character, it seems, to whom Śaṭakōpaṉ is compared more frequently.[50]

In his introduction to the whole of *Tiruvāymoḻi,* Nañcīyar makes a direct comparison of Lakṣmaṇa's and Śaṭakōpaṉ's commitments to their lord:

> The *āḻvār* was like Lakṣmaṇa who from his birth had Rāma as his sole support. As the text says, "From childhood Lakṣmaṇa was exceedingly affectionate, increasing in good fortune, always with Rāma, his world-pleasing elder brother" [*Bāla Kāṇḍa* 18.27–28], and as Lakṣmaṇa says, "Neither Sītā nor I can survive even for a moment without you, Rāghava; we would be like fish taken from the water" [*Ayodhyā Kāṇḍa* 53.31]. His nature was such that he could not for a moment endure separation from the Lord.[51]

Like Lakṣmaṇa, Śaṭakōpaṉ had no other goal:

> In the *āḻvār* all worldly characteristics were eradicated, and due to his inner nature he became terrified at the mere mention of any human goal other than the Lord. As it says,

> [in a verse addressed by Lakṣmaṇa to Rāma], "I would choose neither ascending to the world of the gods nor being immortal nor being the Lord myself, without you" [*Ayodhyā Kāṇḍa* 31.4–5][52]

The first introduction to the *Īṭu* adds that, like Lakṣmaṇa, Śaṭakōpaṉ too satisfies all his needs for relationship simply by his relationship with the lord:

> He was the very apex of exclusive focus on the Lord, saying, "Now he has become girls with slender fish-eyes, great wealth, my people, my excellent mother and father." (V.1.8) He is like Lakṣmaṇa, who took the Lord as his everything, saying to Daśaratha, "I do not see you, great king, as my father; Rāghava [Rāma] is my brother and lord and friend and father." [*Ayodhyā Kāṇḍa* 58.31][53]

Like Lakṣmaṇa, Śaṭakōpaṉ is totally dedicated to service of the lord:

> He could not bear to refrain from doing whatever service needed doing, as it says, "I will do everything for you, whether you sleep or are awake; you with your Vaidehī [Sītā] will rejoice on the mountain plateaux." [*Ayodhyā Kāṇḍa* 31.24–25] . . . as the verse says, "I, his younger brother, have entered his service because of his good qualities" [*Kiṣkindhā Kāṇḍa* 4.12], the *āḻvār* has surrendered to the Lord's good qualities: "Who possesses the highest, unsurpassable good? that one! . . . so bow down at his radiant feet that destroy affliction and then rise up, my mind!" (I.1.1)[54]

We shall see below how the *Ayodhyā Kaṇḍa* quotation echoes throughout the *Īṭu*.[55]

In the course of their expositions of the individual songs, the *ācāryas* frequently compare Śaṭakōpaṉ to Lakṣmaṇa. At I.5 the *āḻvār* says:

> *He is the source of the seven rich worlds and lord of the heaven-dwellers,*
> *but still, doer of harsh deeds that I am, I accused him,*
> *"Brazenly you stole and ate the butter, thief!"* (I.5.1)

This contrast of the lord and "the doer of harsh deeds" is taken to imply that the *āḻvār* has decided, "It is not right that I, caught in this world, should pollute the lord who is the unique object of enjoyment—as if one might pollute ambrosia with poison." Periyavāccāṉpiḷḷai compares this with a decision taken by Lakṣmaṇa, who risked his own well-being for his lord's sake:

> It is like the time when Lakṣmaṇa interrupted Rāma and the messenger from heaven while they were in consultation, in order to make known the arrival of the sage Durvāsa; for he was afraid that Durvāsa might curse Rāma. Lakṣmaṇa disregarded the fact that he might be banished according to Rāma's command against any interruptions. As he says to Rāma, "O king, descendant of Raghu, punish me without hesitation if you love me and are favorable to me; in that way advance the cause of righteousness." (*Uttara Kāṇḍa* 106.4)

Similarly, when the *āḻvār* says,

> *"Serve me always," he says,*
> *he enters my mind and abides there without interruption,*
> *he makes me exist for himself:*
> *to hold Kaṇṇaṉ for myself, that is my glory.* (II.9.4)

the *ācāryas* liken him to both Lakṣmaṇa and Bharata, because he is "unable to live except in dependence on the lord."

At the climactic last line of VI.10.10—"this servant has entered right beneath your feet"—the *āḻvār* is compared to Lakṣmaṇa, because both took refuge with the lord in the presence of Śrī (Sītā):

> All this must be understood according to this verse: "The illustrious Lakṣmaṇa, who had already arrived there, could not bear the grief of impending separation, and his face was covered with tears. Tightly pressing the feet of Rāma his brother, Lakṣmaṇa, the delight of the Raghus, spoke to Sītā who enjoyed great celebrity, and also to Śrī Rāma, who had undertaken a great vow." [*Ayodhyā Kāṇḍa* 31.1b–2].[56]

Lakṣmaṇa goes on to beg Rāma to let him be with him during the exile in the forest, not to leave him behind. The terror experienced by Lakṣmaṇa resonates with that of the *āḻvār* at his moment of surrender. The listeners can look back and forth between the two prostrate figures, enjoying a doubled opportunity to understand the utter depth of holy misery.

Familiar, beloved, deeply evocative citations are woven into the *Īṭu* everywhere, and they are repeated regularly enough so as to inculcate them and their moral analogies deeply into the minds and hearts of the audience. The attentive listener can hardly avoid internalizing their suasive encouragement, and so begin to act like one or another figure from the *Rāmāyaṇa,* and hence like Śaṭakōpaṉ in some aspect of his personality.

By way of example, let us trace just one quotation,[57] in which Lakṣmaṇa entreats Rāma to allow him to come along to the forest and offer total service there:

> Therefore kindly make me your attendant; there will be no unrighteousness in it. I shall thereby have accomplished my object and your purpose too will be adequately served. Taking my stringed bow and carrying a spade and a basket I shall walk ahead of you showing you the way. Nay, I shall procure for you from day to day wild roots and fruits and other products as well fit for being consigned as oblations into the sacred fire. You will sport at will with Sītā [Vaidehī] on mountaintops. I will do everything for you whether you are awake or asleep. [*Ayodhyā Kāṇḍa* 31.24–27]

The words "I will do everything for you whether you are awake or asleep," are cited at least fourteen times in the *Īṭu.*[58] To be with the lord and to serve him and his spouse, all the time, everywhere, is the highest human ideal, the *ācāryas* repeatedly inculcate this ideal by echoing the words of Lakṣmaṇa. Whenever Śaṭakōpaṉ speaks of his desire to serve, Lakṣmaṇa's words are heard too:

> "Will there be a day when this servant reaches there?" [IX.8.2] When he consorted with the Lord and Lady in their time of dwelling in the forest, Lakṣmaṇa focused on doing all service; as it says, *"I will do everything for you whether you are awake or asleep."* [*Ayodhyā Kāṇḍa* 31.27] Similarly the *āḻvār* focuses on doing every act of service for the Lord

> here. For him, just as for Lakṣmaṇa, there is no deficiency in the object which compels service. (IX.8.2)

Both Śaṭakōpan̲ and Lakṣmaṇa savor possible future acts of service, like a very hungry man who anticipates a meal:

> [When Śaṭakōpan̲ turns his attention toward Veṅkaṭam in III.3.0,] he thinks, "Because those qualities of generosity, etc. are manifest there at Veṅkaṭam, now even those in heaven come down here to serve. If so, we too must enter Venkaṭam, and serve there." Think of how a hungry person feels when he takes food in his hand and contemplates it before eating it, or how a man who has been thirsty feels when he sees water or even a mirage. In the same way, Śaṭakōpan̲ hungers to serve. For one who seeks to serve the Lord, this is all he can think of, and every prior intention is lost. As Lakṣmaṇa says, *"I will do everything for you whether you are awake or asleep."* [*Ayodhyā Kāṇḍa* 31.27]. His desire for service is single-minded, just as the man who wants to eat focuses on food.[59] (III.3)

Śaṭakōpan̲'s desire to serve the lord is as extravagant as Lakṣmaṇa's:

> "They praise you . . . from all eight directions" [IV.7.8]—i.e., in accordance with the object and in accordance with my affection. This is in accord with his own desire, for "one must have everything one desires." This desire extends in all directions, for these are the words of one who hungers for service; as a hungry man says, "I must eat every bit of rice," so here he says, *"I will do everything for you, whether you are awake or asleep."* [*Ayodhyā Kāṇḍa* 31.27]

The concentration of the *āl̲vār* on service is like that of Lakṣmaṇa:

> "In that time when I did not know you:" [II.3.3a] i.e., in my infancy when I had no knowledge, as it says, "From childhood Lakṣmaṇa was exceedingly affectionate, increasing in good fortune, always with Rāma, his world-pleasing elder brother," [*Bāla Kāṇḍa* 18.27]. . . . And, as it also says, *"I will do everything for you whether you are awake or asleep.,"* [*Ayodhyā Kāṇḍa* 31.27]. Didn't you then connect me with that "recompense" which belongs to the heavenly beings who are not tainted with any scent of this miserable world?

> . . .As it says, "Therefore kindly make me your attendant" [*Ayodhyā Kāṇḍa* 31.24]. He means, "If I don't get to serve, I will die." (II.3.3)

Since the *āḻvār* and Lakṣmaṇa have perfect devotion, they lack nothing at all:

> "When I was saying, 'I, mine'—all the day long . . ." [II.9.9] I felt no burden, for I had accomplished everything I wanted to do. As it says, "This doer of evil deeds was completely without purpose," (*Periya Tiruvantāti* 82); that is, I was completely like one who had nothing else to do, who had achieved his goal. As it says, *"I will do everything for you whether you are awake or asleep."* [*Ayodhyā Kāṇḍa* 31.27]

"I will do everything for you whether you are awake or asleep:" the refrain again and again punctuates the lessons given by the *ācāryas*. It invites the audience to imagine Śaṭakōpaṉ, to imagine Lakṣmaṇa—to imagine the two together and then to imagine themselves standing near these figures and thus to near the lord, ready to surrender themselves too into unlimited service. This imaginative appeal, particularly when intensified and complicated by its inclusion in the wider array of correlations with other characters who are marked by deep union with the lord—Sītā, Bharata, Vibhīṣaṇa—becomes very persuasive, inviting and appealing. By acting out the *Rāmāyaṇa*, one interprets and appropriates the songs.

4. Multiple Dramas, One Ending

The mutual inscription of *Tiruvāymoḻi* and the *Rāmāyaṇa* stands as the exegetical, poetic complement to the linguistically and theoretically more refined distinctions achieved by the three mantras and the theologies of right means and *prapatti*. Such patterns of mutual enhancement, moral correlation and mirroring, the merging and distinction of characters and their ways of being and acting together indicate the theological and dramatic finality of *Tiruvāymoḻi*. One of the very last images given in the entire *Īṭu* is a brief but powerful evocation of the *Rāmāyaṇa*'s climax as converging with the climax of *Tiruvāymoḻi*:

> *"Greater still, my desire for you, but that too you finish, you surround me,"* [X.10.10]: the *āḻvār* means, "He has now done as I had been begging him to do!" So too, upon his return from exile Rāma came near to Bharata, rejoicing, and drew him to his chest and clasped his head. As it says, "Rising fully from his seat and drawing to himself Bharata whom he caught sight of only after so very long a time, Rāma joyfully embraced him," [*Yuddha Kāṇḍa* 127.41]. Here too the Lord mingles with the *āḻvār* just as he had craved.

Śaṭakōpaṉ is welcomed into lord's arms just as Bharata was drawn into Rāma's. The narratives, travelling their own paths, converge on the same reality which the *ācāryas* discover within both texts: the long-sought and totally satisfying moment of union with a lord who has taken the initiative, tenderly. That these texts are consonant is no surprise, since the doctrine that all scripture is coherent means that all stories must ultimately have just one ending. But here the doctrine is given affective force, and one is meant to enjoy with great savor the union of Rāma and Bharata, the union of the *āḻvār* and his lord.

These parallels between the *Rāmāyaṇa* and *Tiruvāymoḻi* run the range from similarities in plot to the comparison of moral and spiritual character traits. Each parallel is in its own way nuanced and subtle, inviting the reader into a larger correlation of the Tamil verses and the correlated *Rāmāyaṇa* passages. *Tiruvāymoḻi* is played out on a larger stage by its contextualization with the *Rāmāyaṇa,* which by its ampler and more vivid narrative encourages the listener to live *Tiruvāymoḻi,* to act and feel according to its songs, and so become participants in its dramatic truth.

When outside readers approach *Tiruvāymoḻi* and find it richly interwoven with the *Rāmāyaṇa,* the first feeling may be that this is too much, that the epic and the songs are obviously quite different, and *Tiruvāymoḻi* ought to be appreciated according to Tamil paradigms and allusions, not Sanskrit ones. Most readers who are coming fresh to *Tiruvāymoḻi* will not have strong memories of the *Rāmāyaṇa*. For most, the epic will not be part of the fabric of their being, as is the *Rāmāyaṇa* for so many Indians, including the Śrīvaiṣṇavas; many readers will not find it helpful to explain unfamiliar poetry by references to an unfamiliar epic. Here again we are faced with the question of memory: the reader may lack the expected treasure of memories traditionally been brought to bear on the songs, and must learn something of these connections before becoming really able to appreciate the *ācāryas'* interpretations. We must walk alongside Rāma and Sītā and Lakṣmaṇa, at least for a time, if we are to feel the full power of Śaṭakōpaṉ's vision of life. But one can learn at least a little, one can begin to get inside the conversation, to imagine along with the Śrīvaiṣṇavas, feeling something of stories the members of the community live day and night. And then, as scholars, we can see how the *Rāmāyaṇa* illumines *Tiruvāymoḻi.*

So too, the general model may be useful. The reader from outside the Śrīvaiṣṇava tradition surely has other memories and is attuned to other resonances, with other great texts and cultural memories; the reader brings to the reading of *Tiruvāymoḻi* a store of other imaginative possibilities, other interplays, other enhancements, other exemplars of moral and religious sentiment. Even if unintentionally, for example, a reader may remember the Biblical *Song of Songs* when reading of the young woman in search of her beloved, or the life of some Christian saint when learning of Śaṭakōpaṉ's desire to serve; though necessarily arbitrary, such memories and echoes may serve as the affective bridge to the songs, so that *Tiruvāymoḻi* finds new life, again, and begins to draw together a new community, with these new readers and the texts they bring to their reading. Such possibilities open a way into the world of *Tiruvāymoḻi* that is imaginative and intuitive, while remaining intellectually responsible and mindful of tradition. For some, the imaginative retelling of our own ancient narratives together with these narratives we have just learned may be *the* way into the Śrīvaiṣṇava world: my story, our stories.

V. The Fifth Way: Living Tiruvāymoḻi *in the Community*

The fifth approach I wish to highlight leads into the heart of the living community,[60] to the *ācāryas* themselves, as they remember their own revered teachers and how they read and lived and shared the songs. In this communal memory, ancient and lofty paradigms are demonstrated as immediately, locally relevant, here and now, in *this* community. In anecdotes passed down in the commentaries, community members are enabled to see how the songs have been lived among themselves, by people like themselves. Throughout, of course, Śaṭakōpaṉ's own story remains the prime exemplar as the audience is invited to enjoy the stories of the *ācāryas* as extensions of the *āḻvār's* story, and now as their own stories too.

In the *ācāryas'* view, Śaṭakōpaṉ remains always human (a *saṃsārin*); his story typifies the story of every embodied being, his experiences are a highly polished and illuminated mirror in which one can see oneself. *Tiruvāymoḻi* is rooted in his experience and is the convincing utterance of his experience, the fact and necessity of surrender as he discovered this at the limits of his experience. Consequently, the songs are a "school" in which one is educated to become like him, and the *ācāryas* are the graduates par excellence of this school. Skilled expositors of *Tiruvāymoḻi,* they have mastered the text and been mastered by it, so that in the end their lives and their teachings represent the songs perfectly. The *ācāryas* stand before their audience as their own people: neighbors, relatives who have done what they themselves can do.

Like everything else in the commentaries, this familial, inspirational role-modeling begins in exegesis, for the exemplars are first of all people who interpret well. The text is subtle and demanding, it requires attention, understanding, memory, sensitivity, and an appreciation of what matters in the larger context. To read it properly engages the whole of the persons involved; the best readers are the best people. Most recollections of the *ācāryas* preserve their inspiring interpretations of verses and words, as earlier interpretations are remembered and applauded, even if subsequent interpretations are also offered and implicitly valued as superior. Sometimes the skilled exegete from an earlier generation is not named, sometimes he is.

Here are two examples of the latter. Nañcīyar is remembered as having given four interpretations of I.2.1, which I have translated,

Surrender everything, and after surrendering that,
surrender to the one who holds your life, vīṭu.

For a moment I leave the *vīṭu* untranslated, since the point is that it has multiple appropriate meanings: "dwelling place" or "surrender" or "liberation." Nañcīyar's four interpretations are as follows:

> First interpretation: *vīṭu* as "dwelling place," the body:
> *Surrender everything, and after surrendering that,*
> *surrender to the One who holds your life and its dwelling place.*
>
> Second interpretation: *vīṭu* as "dwelling place," the life, spirit:
> *Surrender everything, and after surrendering that,*
> *surrender to the One who holds your life as His dwelling place.*
>
> Third interpretation: *vīṭu* as "surrender"—of the body, at death:
> *Surrender everything, and after surrendering that,*
> *surrender to the One who holds your life, at your surrender.*
>
> Fourth interpretation: *vīṭu* as "liberation:"
> *Surrender everything, and after surrendering that,*
> *surrender to the One who holds your life, as its liberation.*

No great issue is at stake here, and all four meaning can be accepted, linguistically and theologically. Once they are all displayed, the audience is likely to embrace *all* of them. The point of the recollection is to make them available and to honor Nañcīyar for this laudable virtuosity and his skill in disclosing the wealth of possible meanings latent within the simple verse. He has surrendered himself to the verse, he is at home there, and so its wealth of meanings becomes evident to him.

Our second example recollects the views of three *ācāryas* as to why IV.2 (where the mother describes the strange condition of her daughter), is followed by IV.3 (where the young woman seems content and happy):

> *My foolish girl, my child, doesn't pay attention,*
> *no matter what I say or tell her, gentle women;*
> *all she does is say, "For my soft breast, adorned with golden red ornaments,*
> *I want that tulasi on the feet of Kaṇṇaṉ whose chest is adorned and dazzling!"*
> *and then she fades.*
> *What should I do?* (IV.2.10)

For the sake of the woman whose mouth is like kōvai fruit you smashed the bulls' teeth;
to destroy the king of walled Lankā you bent your bow;
you broke the tusks of the elephant of fine clan;
even if I do not sprinkle water and fresh flowers,
the sandal paste for rubbing on your flowered body
is my heart. (IV.3.1)

The shift from song to song might be jarring for the reader who is expecting continuity in mood, but the record of several interpretations has little to do with doctrinal issues.[61] In the first interpretation recorded by Nampiḷḷai, Empār is remembered as suggesting that between IV.2 and IV.3 the lord has distracted the *āḻvār* and made him think of qualities other than those he desired in IV.2, satisfying him by a kind of substitution:

> To the child who cries, "Grasp and give me the moon!" the mother gives a coconut to stop his crying. So too, the *āḻvār* graciously says, "Having revealed various qualities which make me experience Him, He has made me feel that I have experienced Him."

Tirumālai Nampi is remembered as saying that the lord has promised a response, and that this favor is sufficient for the *āḻvār*, just as a subtle favoring was enough to satisfy Rāma's mother, Kauśalyā:

> If a person desires something, and if someone agrees to give it, then the person gives no sign of his previous want. So [in response to desperation evidenced in IV.2] the Lord says, "We will act thus," and then, as one who has gained all, [the *āḻvār*] forgets his previous experience of loss. When she came to Rāma, Kauśalyā said, "I have only one son; I cannot bear to be separated from you, so take me with you." Rāma replied, "Dear mother, what you say is injurious to *dharma*." But in speaking to her he thus showed her his face, so she forgot her loss and blessed him and recovered. So too, when Kṛṣṇa said, "Do not grieve" [*Bhagavad Gītā* 18.66], Arjuna was sustained, saying, "I am made firm, my doubt is removed" [*Bhagavad Gītā* 18.73].

In a third view, Bhaṭṭar is remembered as suggesting that the lord has indeed given the *āḻvār* exactly what he wants, not just a substitution or a promise:

> The *āḻvār* means this: just as the Lord who bears time as his wheel has overcome the limits of time and has brought about in the present moment that experience in one who is so thirsty as to feel, "I must gain now what exists in all three times," [IV.2] so now [at IV.3] He makes me experience time passing by as just the present moment, in a way that accords with that desired experience.

All three interpretations are recorded for the listeners' sake, without any further comment. Three wise men, three wise readings, and the community is invited to enjoy this handed-down wisdom. The naming of the interpreter allows teacher and disciples to remember gratefully persons who have read rightly, and it also encourages imitation of them; and, even those who are not capable of making skillful interpretations by themselves can, at least, take to heart what they hear, and live according to the fruits of such wise interpretations.

The interior qualities of the *ācāryas* are also cherished, and there are numerous anecdotes which highlight their vulnerability, their acquired ability to be emotionally carried away by what they recite and hear with deep emotion and many tears. Such accounts too seem intended to inspire the audience to imitation, the cultivation of interior sensibilities and sentiments.

Let us recall just a few of the many examples we find in the *Īṭu*. At VI.7.1 Naṃpiḷḷai recalls that when Piḷḷaitirunaṟaiyūr Araiyar would explicate certain verses he would grow faint and weep continually. Those tears were all that Nañcīyar, who heard him, could remember from the explications:

> "her eyes flowing tears" [VI.7.1]: Just to see her face is sustenance for those around her. So when she goes off to the temple for her own sustenance, should she carry away our sustenance with her?
>
> When one person weeps with knowledge of the Lord's qualities, it is enough just to see him weeping . . . As Nañcīyar

> observed, "I studied three songs with Piḷḷaitirunaṟaiyūr Araiyar; but not even one word comes back to me. All I remember is that when he recited these words, he grew faint and tears flowed."

Similarly, Āḻvār Tiruvaraṅkaperumāl Araiyar is remembered for shedding tears when he began to sing *Tiruvāymoḻi* III.3.1. All he could do was keep singing a few words, "for all time without end, for all time, all time," [III.3.1], and he was unable to finish the verse.

When Śaṭakōpaṉ says, "Starting then, her eyes have rained like clouds, she is amazed, " [VI.5.5], we hear the following remembrance:

> See how there is a flood of tears like rain as soon as she sees the Lord! When Āḷavantār heard about the Lord in the presence of Maṇakkālanampi, he exclaimed, "There is no way higher than this—isn't there a way to make this known to all, right now?" Tears came in a flood.

In another place Naṃpiḷḷai recalls Nañcīyar's own emotion at the words, "He grieved when the cowherd woman reluctantly bound him to the mortar," [VI.4.4]:

> When Nañcīyar began to sing this song, how beautiful it was when he came to "He grieved;" when he sang, "He grieved," it was as if someone had tied the rope to his own body.

At VI.7.5,

> *Desiring, fading more and more, she will not play, my little*
> *goddess;*
> *she's gone and seen Tirumāl's temple and tanks and groves*
> *fully in flower in Kōḷūr*
> *and her inner life has been chilled:*
> *so how can she be happy?*

Nañcīyar is remembered as recounting his vicarious experience of his teachers' experience of the words, "She's gone and seen Tirumāl's temple and tanks and groves fully in flower in Kōḷūr, and her inner life has been chilled:"

> When Piḷḷaitirunaṟaiyūr Araiyar and Bhaṭṭar were going around inside the temple, I followed behind them. I enjoyed watching how they looked as they stood there, as if drinking with their eyes, unable to move even a step. (VI.7.5)[62]

Some anecdotes record the intense desires of those who live according to the songs: one must be greedy for God, as Kṛṣṇa was for the butter (I.3.0); waiting for God is like anticipating a fine meal, where the anticipation itself is part of the enjoyment (III.3.8). Nañcīyar hungered for God alone, yet could satisfy this hunger simply by bowing down and touching the feet of the lord's devotees (VI.1.2). At IV.4.9—"when she sees great dark clouds, she flies up"—we are told of a Vaiṣṇava so sensitive to reminders of Kṛṣṇa that he could barely live an ordinary life; he would faint every time he walked out to inspect his fields and saw a dark rain cloud in the sky, because that reminded him of Kṛṣṇa.

Anecdotes which raise the prospects of death constitute a revealing genre:

> "*Consider the day when your body will depart*" (I.2.9): on Rāmānuja's birthday, Kuṉṟattu Cīyar came to bow at his feet. Rāmānuja said, "Siṅkapirāṉ, isn't today my birthday?" But Cīyar said nothing, because he did not know what was running through Rāmānuja's mind. Rāṃānuja then explained: "When this body falls away, then one gains the flawless goal. Of the days standing in the way as an obstacle, one more year has now passed away—don't you think this something gained?"
>
> In the same context, Empār observed: "If the cause is thus finished, won't the effect also come to an end, by itself? Isn't the goal then at hand? So how can there be any cause for anxiety?"

At I.4.5 Naṃpiḷḷai explains why respectful language is so important, i.e., why the young woman in the song uses the word "graciously" when addressing mere birds in that messenger song. In explaining this holy courtesy, he gives the example of how one is to say that a Vaiṣṇava has died:

> When they told Bhaṭṭar that Nampi Eṟutiruvuṭaiyāṉ Dāsar had died—"gone to the holy country"—Bhaṭṭar rose trembling, and said, "One must not say it that way—rather, one must say, 'He has graciously ascended to the holy country to commune with Śrīvaiṣṇavas there.'"

And,

> When Piḷḷāṉ was dying, Nañcīyar was weeping, but Piḷḷāṉ kept repeating, "Won't you call me . . . and thus shorten the time?" (VI.9.9) Nañcīyar heard this and still wept, but Piḷḷāṉ replied, "Cīyar, why do you lie there weeping? Isn't it clear that getting to go there is better than staying here?" (VI.9.9)

Finally, as cited earlier in this chapter:

> When Bhaṭṭar was dying, he said to Nañcīyar, "To meditate on the verse 'my love, who loves the woman on the lovely flower,' (X.10.7) along with our Dvaya mantra is to meditate on how He loves us who have been grasped by Her, for He is in love with that great lady." (X.10.7)

To live and die with *Tiruvāymoḻi* on one's lips and in one's heart and imagination: such was the practice of the *ācāryas*, and such the ideal held up before the community as something they too should emulate.

Interpretation and conversation do not occur in a vacuum, and anecdotes often illuminate the educational context in which they were received, thus indicating how the audience ought to learn. There is ample praise for good students who are deeply immersed in the text. When discussing how striking it is that the mother in VI.7.9 is so reverent toward her daughter—she doesn't say simply, "She's gone [*pōṉāṉ*] to Kōḷūr," but uses the more honorific, "She has progressed [*naṭantāṉ*] to Kōḷūr"—the *Īṭu* relates an anecdote to illustrate how the elder can reverence the younger:

> One day Nañcīyar greatly praised Naṃpiḷḷai in the assembly, and others commented, 'See how he praises his own student!' As it says, "He counts as his own child the little one who worships Tirukaṇṇapuram." (*Periya Tirumoḻi* 8.2.9) Likewise, Ammuni Āḻvāṉ would prostrate himself before

his student; when asked why he did this, he replied, 'One must recognize other Vaiṣṇavas by their conduct; when I know who these are, I honor them as Vaiṣṇavas.'

But some anecdotes deal quite directly with those who do not measure up to the standards of the community. It is the paradigmatic "bad student" who lacks patience and trust and who closes his mind and leaves off the learning process too soon. As we have seen, Naṃpiḷḷai introduced I.4 with the story of a student who, because he lacked sufficient respect for Śaṭakōpaṉ and for his own teacher, stopped studying *Tiruvāymoḻi* at the end of the third song; for he thought that the next song, on the young woman in love, was too lustful.

Some students are more clever, but even more deficient, like the one who finds in *prapatti* an excuse for doing nothing at all:

> One man who had taken refuge at the feet of Nañcīyar said, "If the Lord is the means, I see no reason then even for *prapatti*!" Nañcīyar covered his ears and said, "From Nāthamuni until now our *ācāryas* have taught the highest mystery, in a continuous tradition. But now I, a great sinner, have taught this to you who do not appreciate its excellence." He slapped his head, and retreated into the sanctum of the temple. (VI.10.4)

At III.7.3—"See, those who reverence those able to honor his feet rule me in all the births I can sing of"—two students are shamed into reconciling their differences:

> Vīrapiḷḷai and Pālikaivāḷippiḷḷai were devoted to the service of Nañcīyar, and very close to one another. Once they were going somewhere together, but since they had quarreled, they were no longer on speaking terms. Looking at them Nañcīyar said, "Children, aren't wealth and pleasure to be given up? isn't the topic of the Lord sufficient? aren't we to reject the idea of two Śrīvaiṣṇavas not speaking to one another?" The two of them got up, fell prostrate before one another, and became one again. (III.7.3)

Those who hear these songs cannot live by lesser standards; the community must embody the ideals it sings.

The commentaries also contain insights into how respect is both resisted and learned. In commenting on Śaṭakōpaṉ's verse which concludes with the words, " . . . see, those who reverence those able to honor his feet are my rulers in all the births I can sing of" (III.7.3), Naṃpiḷḷai tells this anecdote of how respect gradually dawns:

> There was a very good man named Piḷḷai Āttāṉ. He came to the feet of Nañcīyar and said, "Graciously teach me some songs from *Tiruvāymoḻi.*" Nañcīyar said, "You can study with Naṃpiḷḷai who will make it clear for you; go ask him." "But I would have to show him signs of honor!" "Why, what about it? Do so only if you want to." So Nañcīyar called me [i.e., Naṃpiḷḷai] and said, "Teach him some songs, insofar as he is capable." Naṃpiḷḷai recalled, "When he had listened with me up to this point [III.7.3] the man ventured to show me signs of respect, but I would not allow it. So the man went back to Nañcīyar and said, 'I spoke as I did before because I did not know the excellence of this truth. Now graciously allow me to honor him as I wish.' And so he did." [III.7.3]

When one is led into the songs by a skillful teacher, one's life is liable to deep transformation. One anecdote illustrates both the *ācāryas'* sense of the strong obdurancy that can occur even among religious people, and the power of *Tiruvāymoḻi* against that stubbornness. At the words, "She grieves all day long, her face alarmed, tears splashing, crying, 'Jewel colored one!' so even the trees pity her . . ." (VI.5.9) Naṃpiḷḷai comments,

> See how the girl opens her mouth and cries, how she removes the difference between the consciousness and nonconscious [i.e., so that even trees are thought to be compassionate]! But someone asked Empār, "How is it possible for trees to be compassionate?" He responded, "Beginning when He graciously acted in that way, into how many mouths lacking in mental purity this has entered, one cannot say. [But we know of the power of the Lord to change hearts:] if one seeks to soften hearts by the steps of yoga, they still do not melt, but remain hard like rock. Yet now you see them 'destroyed' [just by a few words of *Tiruvāymoḻi*]. If so, can't we say that even the trees were compassionate?" (VI.5.9)[63]

Though learning is admired, sometimes it is the humblest who are praised most highly, as most sensitive to the songs. Āttāṉcīyar records how Bhaṭṭar would treat with scant respect a learned brahmin who used to come to his house, while at the same time he would go out of his way to praise a simple devotee who would also come by. When Bhaṭṭar is asked why he reverses the expected protocol and treats the first as last and the last as first, this exchange follows:

> Bhaṭṭar replied, "The next time they come as usual, you watch as usual; I will speak with them both." So he watched the next day when they came. After the brahmin came and reverenced Bhaṭṭar, Bhaṭṭar asked him, "Who do you think is the highest one?" He replied, "Some authorities suggest that it is Brahmā; some, Viṣṇu; some Rudra. So how can we decide?" Bhaṭṭar replied, "Thank you."
>
> When he left, the simple Śrīvaiṣṇava came up and reverenced Bhaṭṭar who gently asked him, "Who do you think is the highest one?" He replied, "You, your reverence, have said that the highest one is Nārāyaṇa, husband of Śrī. Your servant knows nothing but that." Bhaṭṭar asked, "What do you think of as your treasure?" The Śrīvaiṣṇava replied, "You have said that the Lord's feet are both the goal and the means, so they are for me too my treasure." Bhaṭṭar rejoiced, and said, "Wash, and come into my house." He then turned to the man who was watching and said, "You see the difference between the two? Would you reverence this one or the first one? Such are people's natures." The observer went away satisfied. (I.9.6)

Scholarship is not an ideal, unless it is imbued with wisdom; much learning is not a prerequisite for reaching the right conclusions, since simple folk often know best:

> Though adept in all the scriptures, the learned man never gets to a definition, "Transcendence is such and such." And does one really need a big knife to cut through a small plant? Could there be some other object of worship for us? People go about bowing their heads everywhere they look, and they still don't get the point! But think of how uneducated women, unversed in Rāmānuja's theology, still know enough to use other gods as bricks for cooking! (IV.10.0)

As this last anecdote suggests, the generous, open and heartfelt sense of the Śrīvaiṣṇava community developed by the *ācāryas* is balanced by a deeply felt abhorrence of the world, those who are not Śrīvaiṣṇavas, and their gods. Above we have already seen the sharp demarcation announced at IV.6.11, where the Śrīvaiṣṇava has made a decisive shift from worldly to communal values, as well as this example of the women who use idols for cooking stones.

To escape the world with its gods and its values is good in itself. At VI.4.10—"and then he returned to his dwelling beyond the sky"—Naṃpiḷḷai remembers how Āṇṭāṉ and Empār embraced when the festival ended and the festival image was carried back into the temple sanctum, because once more the lord had escaped the rude and selfish crowd:

> How He has managed to destroy His enemies and moreover return to His place where they do not exist! . . . At the evening of a festival, Āntāṉ and Empār met and embraced, saying, "For ten days He graciously moved about, with His lovely fresh body exposed, in the midst of millions of people spoiled by 'I' and 'mine;' but see how He has now managed to return safely, without danger." Nañcīyar himself heard this. (VI.4.10)

Sensitivity regarding what belongs to the community and what is alien to it is deeply ingrained, as is shown by the following anecdote recounted at IV.6.6, "If you would make the effort to touch the dust at the feet of the devotees of the Marvellous one:"

> When king Akaḷaṅkanāṭṭāḻvāṉ showed two men named Vaṇṭar and Coṇṭar a lion in the courtyard of a Jaina temple and told them to worship there, they worshipped at the lion's feet, believing the king's word. But when Akaḷaṅkanāṭṭāḻvāṉ admitted to them, "This is a Jaina temple," they fainted and collapsed. When Piḷḷai Uṟaṅgāvillidāsar sprinkled them with the dust from his feet, they revived and got up. (IV.6.6)

Of course, there is always the steady example of Rāmānuja. Here, as Āttāṉcīyar recollects, Rāmānuja sets forth in terms that are very clear—though rather unbalanced, genderwise—the boundaries of *his* faith and his determination never to pollute himself with false gods:

> Once Lord Raṅganātha was being carried in procession, when it began to rain. For shelter, the Lord was carried into the premises of another temple, the temple of Jambukeśvara. Rāmānuja and the other elders who had accompanied the procession remained outside the premises, in the rain. Someone asked Rāmānuja, "Sir, if the Lord has taken shelter inside, why do you not do the same?" Rāmānuja answered, "Fool, if the emperor elects to make love to a courtesan, does this mean that his Queen should imitate her Lord and make love to a courtier?" (X.2.1)

Even to be thought little of by outsiders is a compliment to the Vaiṣṇava. At X.9.4, "The waiting, unwinking ones distribute places for resting," Naṃpiḷḷai comments on the plight of devotees in this world:

> To those people here, in this world, who do not get their share because they are Vaiṣṇava, those there, in heaven, distribute places of honor. Thus it was that Miḷakāḻvāṉ went to the king in his capital. The king said to him, "You are in-between, there is no share in my wealth for you." Miḷakāḻvāṉ replied, "But tell me, is there something lacking in my virtue?" "Deficiency in virtue is not the reason [for my refusal to give you anything—rather, it is that you are a Vaiṣṇava]." Miḷakāḻvāṉ thought, "Even were we not really Vaiṣṇavas in our hearts, still we have managed to be abandoned, just by their calling us 'Vaiṣṇavas.'" So he left the capital dancing for joy. (X.9.4)

The ideal community of teachers and students is marked by an unusual challenge which links the search for God—admirable in itself—with the yet more powerful preoccupation with divine presence:

> Among our people one asked another, "Tell me a way to think of our lord." He replied, "I will tell you that, if you can tell me a way to forget him." (III.4.4)

The sequel shows that the issue is not simply a virtue of the privileged few, but rather a cultivated awareness of the ways things simply, really are; Naṃpiḷḷai adds

> For nothing apart from the Lord has substance or name without Him; whenever anything appears, it manifests Him first. Just as substances and their qualities [respectively] lack permanence and perceptibility if separated, even if something is substantial it lacks permanence and perceptibility apart from Him. [III.4.4]

So too, it is possible to define membership in the community at a fundamental, seemingly non-sectarian level:

> To love God is to be compassionate toward this world. As Nañcīyar said, "We can be sure that we are in relation to the Lord if the misfortune of someone else is unbearable to us; but if one says, 'He deserved it,' a person can be sure that he has no relation to the Lord—let him go away!" (VI.10.4)[64]

This compassion also reaches out to other living beings: for example, Nallār scolds Śrī Sēnāpatidāsar just for bruising a reed (VI.3.2); Āḻvāṉ is admired because he faints in sympathy with a frog caught by a snake, realizing how God must feel at the human plight in this world (IV.9.0).

In the end, membership in the community is recognized to be a matter of grace and nothing else. Self-congratulation is not warranted, and credit must be given where it is due:

> When the words "making known what is not known" [II.3.2] were being discussed in Empār's class, the question arose, "Who is the first guru for the human person?" Some present said, "Isn't it the *ācārya*?" Others said, "It is the Śrīvaiṣṇava who meets you and invites you saying, 'Go, take refuge at the feet of the teacher.'" But Empār responded, "Neither of those. It is the Lord of all who enters within and makes one unable to say no; as it says, 'You made me desire you . . .' [V.8.9]. So the Lord is the first guru."

The lord is the ultimate *ācārya*; *ācāryas* and disciples, along with Śaṭakōpaṉ, stand in a specific relation, directly responsible to the lord.

One could go on recounting such anecdotes, but the basic point is clear. Nearer to home than Rāma and Lakṣmaṇa, more fluid and yet in a different way equally compelling than the ontological-linguistic calculus of the three mantras, memories of the *ācāryas* present the community with imaginative moral access to *Tiruvāymoḻi*. They represent perfect transparency to the text, for they appropriated it and lived according to it, totally surrendered to its pull on them. Disciples who revere and admire their teachers could then be drawn into the same dynamic of imitation, where total surrender to the text, to the teacher, to the community, lead to a complete restructuring of one's consciousness and behavior.

Insofar as we appreciate the depth and power of the *ācāryas'* appeal to exemplars and anecdotal representations of the values imbedded in *Tiruvāymoḻi*, we can appreciate all the more fully then what is happening when we meet representatives of a tradition such as the Śrīvaiṣṇava community, men and women who have been formed and transformed according to the songs, who bear within themselves the full power of the tradition. We meet individuals, and in them a millennium of learning and wisdom. If so, a key point in research will be to become sufficiently aware of the tradition so as to be able to recognize what is present in the Śrīvaiṣṇava today; the texts and the persons who read the texts are mutually implicated realities. When I had the opportunity to read the *Īṭu* with Sri Sampat Kumaran, for instance, I was in touch with the tradition in a direct way, and not simply for the obvious reason that I was listening to a Śrīvaiṣṇava who knew the texts very well, with deep understanding and emotion. To meet him was to meet his teachers, and theirs, all the way back, and to encounter in this one person the community's memory and its treasuring of its heritage. Such personal encounters do not, of course, replace reading the text, but they too provide a way to see through them, to remember.

Of course, one is also invited by extension to look more broadly for similar guiding stories of the masters. One thinks here of people such as Francis of Assisi or Bonaventure (whom we shall meet in chapter 5), vivid examples of the quest for the union of knowledge and love; or people who are known for having crossed cultural boundaries, beginning with the candidates usually mentioned (in Catholic circles, at least), missionaries such as Mateo Ricci in China and Roberto de Nobili in

India; or even some modern scholars who exemplify the sympathetic understanding of the traditions they study. Such persons, because they represent the traditions in which they have been formed, provide meeting points for longer and deeper encounters. If text and person and then community thus intermingle in such cases, one can also predict that this kind of study across religious boundaries will proceed not only by the valuing of individuals and their traditions, but also by the formation of communities in which the virtues of comparative studies are cultivated, and the values of traditions learned together are remembered and passed down. Comparative study itself must find its *ācāryas* as well as its doctrines and stories and ways of proceeding, people whose lives speak for the wisdom of the work to which they have committed themselves.

VI. On the Threshhold of Participation

By the five ways of approach reviewed in this chapter—and, of course, by others—the *ācāryas* opened *Tiruvāymoḻi* as a participative drama, so that the community is drawn into the drama which first included the *āḻvār* and his lord. The drama is opened for response and engagement as it is encapsulated in the mantras, systematized as a guidebook to salvation, modelled according to the *āḻvār's* experience of *prapatti,* retold more broadly according to the *Rāmāyaṇa,* and paradigmatized in wise, earlier teachers. *Tiruvāymoḻi* is clearly presented as a text constitutive of a world wherein one can live one's life, individually and in community.

These practical representations of *Tiruvāymoḻi* successfully establishes an intermediate place where the outsider can join the insider in engaging the songs, even if lacking a complete understanding or mastery of them. The extremes of banal universality—"*Tiruvāymoḻi* tells us what we already knew"—and a ponderous particularity—"a lifetime's study cannot be a sufficient preparation for saying anything about this complex material"—can now be avoided by attention to this middle ground where values are instantiated in local situations and yet at the same time opened for participation.[65]

Great challenges as well as opportunities are therefore placed before the audience of *Tiruvāymoḻi*. Listeners and readers are asked not only to learn or memorize *Tiruvāymoḻi*, or to visit temples, or to understand it as a grand narrative flow, but also to delve as deeply as possible into the songs and into their own selves. To hear, to hear properly, and then to live according to what one has heard: these are the duties to be undertaken, so one will be ready for an opening into wider realities: perhaps before a God who, in an unexpected but free dramatic turn, graciously chooses to be unable to live without the company of such persons as live the drama of *Tiruvāymoḻi* completely.

One can say that the goal of the Śrīvaiṣṇava appropriation of *Tiruvāymoḻi* is to learn "to live, act, read like a *prapanna*," surrendered to the lord, opened to the songs, constantly corrected and transformed by them:

> *In thought, word, and deed Śaṭakōpaṉ of splendid Kurukūr*
> *reached the point of calling the lord of the gods his mother and*
> *father;*
> *whoever masters these ten pure Tamil verses about*
> *Tolaivillimankalam from his venerable thousand verses*
> *will serve Tirumāl.* (VI.5.11)

It is time then to assess what we have achieved by the analyses undertaken at length in these three chapters. In chapter 2 we explored the possibilities presented to us by the songs themselves, recognizing the wide range of ways in which they are open, inviting, demanding, perhaps for a few, perhaps for many listeners and readers. In chapter 3, we examined the narrative structuring of *Tiruvāymoḻi* by the Śrīvaiṣṇava *ācāryas*, their re-presentation of *Tiruvāymoḻi* in a narrative and drama which, however theologically particular, are evidently in response to basic human experiences and plausible theological positions about what it might be like "to see God." In this fourth chapter, we have traced five practical ways, each of which can, potentially, be a path we can not only observe, but also follow.

Our goal in the fifth and final chapter cannot be to work out all the implications of what we have done thus far, but simply to lay the foundations for this wider, more inclusive reading of *Tiruvāymoḻi*—it will be our way of rethinking the outside and the inside of the traditions we find ourselves near, so as to share something of Śaṭakōpaṉ's own productive dilemma:

I am not here, I am not there,
but I am fallen into the desire to see you,
so I am nowhere
destroyer of Laṅkā, my lord:
you live among the lofty buildings of Cirīvaramaṅkalanakar
    with their jewels fit for the moon,
you hold the conch and discus,
but I,
I am alone—
so be gracious to me. (V.7.2)

Chapter 5

Seeing through Texts: Some Marginal Insights, Presented in Reflections

This girl with her sweet nectar
words has entered
Tirutolaivillimaṅkalam
noisy with the deep din
of festivals,
so have no hopes regarding her;
transformed, she stands
speechless, crying,
"lord, God of gods,"
her mouth twisted about,
her eyes welling tears,
she bends, she breaks,
she comes apart.

Is she Piṉṉai born here? or
Nīla? or the Maiden?
what marvel is this? she
stands calling, "My tall lord!"
To hear the name of that
town, to bow before
Tollaivillimaṅkalam
where he who came before
stands, sits, dwells—
that is her only
thought. (VI.5.2,10)

Let us, then, die and enter into this darkness. Let us silence all our cares, our desires, and our imaginings. With Christ crucified, let us pass out of this world to the Father, so that, when the Father is shown to us, we may say with Philip, "It is enough for us." (*The Journey of the Mind to God*)

I. The Prospect from Here

1. What We Have Seen

We began this book with the song about a young woman who went with her neighbors to visit the temple in Tirutolaivillimaṅkalam deep in south India. Unlike the other women who visit the temple and return home without any particular bother or further ado, the young woman is entirely captivated by what she saw there, the lotus-eyed lord, Viṣṇu. Her plight—her altered state, made worse by their incomprehension—is recounted by her friend who urgently addresses the uncomprehending women of the town: leave the young woman alone, understand why she is in this situation—after all, you did it to her!

At *this* temple at Tirutolaivillimaṅkalam, *this* vision of God becomes completely engaging, overwhelmingly demanding, impossible to deny—for just a few of those who visit there, who *see*. Replicated, extended, explored, through the words of this song, the temple visit is meant also to become a provocative and troublesome possibility for at least some of the readers who listen to it, as the song begins to master those who master it, drawing them into the service of the lord who dwells in that temple and speaks in those words, transforming their own thinking, speaking, doing:

> *In thought, word, and deed Śaṭakōpaṉ of splendid Kurukūr*
> *reached the point of calling the lord of the gods his mother and*
> *father;*
> *whoever masters these ten pure Tamil verses about*
> *Tirutolaivillimaṅkalam from his venerable thousand*
> *will serve Tirumāl.* (VI.5.11)

In chapter 1 we pondered, somewhat abstractly, the effect of this song (alone, with the 99 others) on readers, as well as the conditions under which these words, as heard, recited, read, studied, lived, become words able to draw in an audience, to captivate the casual observer, to extend listening into seeing, and seeing into commitment. Taking up the question of boundaries and the endeavor to cross them, faithfully, we asked with special concern whether someone from outside the Vaiṣṇava tradition could be drawn into the world inscribed in the song, whether the study of the text—which is available for anyone's scrutiny, even if it is demanding—sets in motion a process leading to the brink of a dramatic change, wherein personal and communal loyalties, from the academic to the spiritual, might begin to expand or shift or dissipate.

In considering such possibilities, our purpose was not the cultivation of mere skepticism or mere piety, but rather the initiation of a more extended survey of the possibilities a large, complex, beautiful text such as *Tiruvāymoḻi* would open when resituated in relation to the expectations and requirements of new readers. We were therefore choosing not to engage in a kind of research which would separate scholarship from questions of personal commitment or which would replace the former by the latter. Surely, scholarship must involve some distance and some dispassion, research ought not to be undertaken as the means of personal fulfillment, and personal concerns must be disciplined by a commitment to understanding. Nevertheless, among the most interesting aspects of this study of religions is reflection on what one brings to the reading of religious texts and what one gets from that reading: the before and after of taking a first look.

Reading VI.5 from the definite time and place and concern of this reader, I responded in kind. In writing this book, the point was to try to produce conditions under which its readers might begin to do, redo, their theology among the Śrīvaiṣṇavas. In neither my reading nor writing was the goal to be entirely open; it was rather to make sure that our sympathetic reading would go forward with an acute awareness of our strictures of prior commitments, beliefs, attachments—according to linguistic community, profession, religion, etc. We have therefore studied *Tiruvāymoḻi* and its reception among the Śrīvaiṣṇavas with a growing awareness of our own commitments, imaginations, desires. Just as we did not want to short-circuit the discussion by denigrating one set of commitments simply in order to buttress or formulate a second, neither did we see any benefit in diminishing our distance from an evidently different tradition merely by pronouncing vaguely—theoretically, abstractly, sentimentally, perhaps with the best of intentions—that something could be gained from studying *Tiruvāymoḻi*.

Words stand in the way, words are a window, we see by seeing through words, and by seeing through our efforts to treat them as words. As we assess the diverse facets of this verbal mediation and consider the process of meditation on texts (one does things with words to gain more than words can tell us) it also becomes clear that the results of this inquiry are not to be simplified into straightforward claims regarding a clear, discrete set of results available to be experienced and subjected to ready assent. What this book means is a necessarily complicated thing. The words remain dense and opaque, and we must find our way through them. When we describe where we have ended up, our account ought to bear with it characteristics of this verbal opacity; without indulging in obfuscation, our account ought to resist the pretense of a completeness which would preclude anything new from taking shape, now. Yet we must also mark some progress toward an understanding of the dynamics of this kind of thinking that occurs across religious boundaries, when carefully chosen texts are brought into what is—or eventually becomes—a single conversation instead of two parallel monologues adorned by occasional reciprocal bows.

To *begin* convening this conversation is the goal of this final chapter. Section two will sketch the kind of context that is shaped from reading *Tiruvāymoḻi* along with texts from the Biblical and Christian traditions, while section three will consider the interior context—new words, old words newly displayed—that takes shape in the reader who ventures across the boundaries of tradition, and back.

Committed to a theology that is an engaged, reflective and open practice across religious boundaries, I began by looking for a way to engage this whole body of texts, *Tiruvāymoḻi* and commentaries both, as these could be understood apart, and together. We had to venture upon the study of both the songs and the commentaries on them, reading them distinctly, though in the end keeping them together. Though the cost of this focus is perhaps all the more evident now—too much has been done, too much has been left out—it still seems all the more to have been a worthwhile venture, in view of the possibilities that have been opened up.

Chapter 2 had to do with learning to read *Tiruvāymoḻi*, and this was a project of mastery: mastering the formidable 1102 verses while also admitting the value of being mastered by them through becoming the kind of person able to read, imagine, think differently, along with these 100 songs. I argued the necessity of dwelling with the particular details and images of the songs, patiently postponing generalizations and enjoying the possibilities opened up by their underdetermination, while yet also emphasizing the necessity of finding ways to appropriate *Tiruvāymoḻi* as a whole, realizing in a more than notional sense how songs work together and in mutual tension within the whole of the work. We had to recognize, and then take advantage of, the tension between formal and thematic elements, within the boundaries set by the desire(s) for proximity and vision. In doing this we had to test different ways of talking about how there is a unifying purpose to *Tiruvāymoḻi* as a whole, a kind of verbal desire that infuses the text without being reducible to what the text has to say about desire. Due particularly to the inevitable space between the clarity of the elements of the songs and their underdetermined full meaning, the reader is placed in the position of having to take steps to make sense of the whole, to manage it. He or she then becomes an active participant in its full composition, committed to it in the long run and unlikely ever to be finished with it definitively—and all of this for whichever purpose this reader proposes as his or her purpose. As we became involved in Śaṭakōpaṉ's play of memory and presence, the results were likely to be skewed, since we were only learning for the first time things that Śaṭakōpaṉ was already reusing anew in his effort to put religious memory at the service of his present religious possibilities; what he was doing was not fully present to us, his remembering could never become fully our memory. Much of our work then had the effect of setting *Tiruvāymoḻi* on its head, as we stayed very much on the surface of the text, only rarely venturing to imagine what was going on inside the author of the songs as we learned anew what for him was already old. Perhaps then we learned more about ourselves than about him. Still, involvement has grown, we and the songs have gotten inside one another.

In chapters 3 and 4 we turned to a study of the Śrīvaiṣṇava *ācāryas'* reading of the text, reading with them and learning from them about their encounter with *Tiruvāymoḻi* . In Chapter 3, we traced the main lines of their reading, following them in their effort to present *Tiruvāymoḻi* as the perfectly ordered theological production of the completely engaged, desperate, overwhelmed *āḻvār*. In my reconstruction of the elements of their reading, I showed them to be drawing attention to and resolving what they perceived to be the primary human dilemma: the inability to see God in this life, even though this vision alone is what satisfies human desire. We saw too how they smoothed out *Tiruvāymoḻi*, retelling it as a narrative defined by both psychological and theological positions, and how this narrative was one that was ultimately a drama, dependent on divine intervention for its completion. As an account of interior happening, *Tiruvāymoḻi* itself always requires something to happen, if it is to be finished. In turn, we have retold their retelling of the songs as a part of this book's own narrative, a narrative including a narrative including a narrative, each opening into its own dramatic dénouement.

If for the *ācāryas Tiruvāymoḻi* is a kind of drama where something unpredictable, never assured, must occur as the finale, it would be easy, perhaps facile, merely to suggest that the project of reading undertaken in this book concludes in drama, in something new, uncharted, able to be finalized only in the future, somewhere ahead of us or in the reader. We could simply leave it up to the reader to decide what the preceding chapters mean, ourselves concluding merely with some generalizations about the future of interreligious dialogue, etc.; we could also jump to conclusions and decide how religions fit together, or not.

Yet these appeals to drama are in important ways inadequate, and not only because they are at once vague and inspirational. They fail also because they does not take into account the strong investment traditions have in continuity—the "new" stands in relationship to the "old," and does not appear as something entirely disruptive, discontinuous, for otherwise it would be either unappealing or incomprehensible. Particularity is also at stake, for traditions care about very special things. So, whatever conclusions we draw must be continuous with tradition, and rooted in particularity; they must follow from the preceding chapters, and from what we bring to the project venured in this book.

As we saw, Śaṭakōpaṉ himself introduced very little new information in his songs—yet he was constantly putting everything in new arrangements, almost never repeating himself. His language was old, even in its details, but his speaking new. So it was too when (as we saw in chapter 1) Rāmānuja argued with Tirumālai Āṇṭāṉ and proposed his new reading, an interpretation that when beyond what his predecessors had noticed, yet without depending on a new set of presuppositions or drawing significant new conclusions from the exegesis. This indicates why, from the *ācāryas'* viewpoint, vision has always to be founded in remembrance, not in *ex nihilo* creativity.

Against this background, comparative theology—the endeavor to study a religious tradition other than one's own while still, and thereby, deepening one's commitment to one's own tradition, but perhaps then learning to speak from both—can be understood to offer something new primarily because of the specific practical possibilities it opens for us through its production of new relationships, and not because of the data it offers about another religious tradition which is, just for a time, very new. To see through texts is a reflexive activity, where the major changes occur in those who take seriously traditions other than their own while yet remembering where they are coming from. This book's narrative—about reading *Tiruvāymoḻi* from inside and outside its tradition—has then to be retold in a way that some contemporary audience finds familiar, if the desired self-transformation is to be effected.

In Chapter 4, we traced the *ācāryas'* effort to understand *Tiruvāymoḻi* and present it in an accessible form, by way of five practical ways of opening the text: their semi-mathematical and iterable correlation of songs with the three holy mantras; Periyavaṅkippurattunampi's pioneering systematization of *Tiruvāymoḻi* as an exposition of the goals, means and obstacles to salvation; their presentation of Śaṭakōpaṉ as the model and teacher of *prapatti* who tells us his own story and from there articulates and lives his own theology in *Tiruvāymoḻi*; their dramatic opening of *Tiruvāymoḻi* imaginatively through its interface with the *Rāmāyaṇa*; their illumination of the *ācāryas* themselves in the reflection of the songs, the *ācāryas* themselves being in turn mirrors to the community. These paths of access indicated to us what we might do with the songs, inviting various kinds of imitation, analogous theoretical and dramatic ways for outsiders to begin to participate in *Tiruvāymoḻi*, beginning, most effectively, from reading with a contemporary teacher, entering with reverence into a temple, tracing the patterns of one's own heart. Our theological peers, the *ācāryas* offer us wise advice, prompting us to think about who we are, where our community is to be found, what it is that we believe.

2. *Did the* Ācāryas *Notice Everything?*

But before introducing some signal examples from the Biblical and Christian traditions that invite our attention after this engagement of the Śrīvaiṣṇava tradition, something must be said regarding the possible evaluative implications of this study. Did the *ācāryas* get it right? The ordering of chapters—one on the songs, two on the *ācāryas*—may suggest either a polite and laudatory reading of the latter or, just as likely in the agonistic milieu of contemporary scholarship, the arrangement of a competition between my reading of *Tiruvāymoḻi* and that of the *ācāryas*, with an eye toward determining who understands the songs best, on the basis of what kind of erudition, etc.

It is certainly possible to proceed in either direction. But what has in fact happened here is somewhat different. In choosing first to survey the songs and develop an understanding of what is entailed in reading them, and then to read with the *ācāryas*, I was interested in the imaginative and practical strategies by which originally unfamiliar yet very powerful religious resources become available to new readers from outside the tradition, on their own, and with the help of others, in this case the *ācāryas*; we read twice, at least.

All things considered, we can admit freely that the *ācāryas'* reading of *Tiruvāymoḻi* is a complete and fruitful response to the songs which captures two key features in particular. First, how Śaṭakōpaṉ constructs a universe composed of the words and images of Vaiṣṇavism, while transcending the details he evokes through weaving them together in various combinations, and locating every memory against the background of his vivid, present desires. Second, how a full understanding of *Tiruvāymoḻi* is a very practical affair, a matter of desire, conversion, insight and service to be achieved in one's present moment, for this is a text to be performed, not merely admired. The *ācāryas* give a good sense of these basic possibilities that confront us in our reading of *Tiruvāymoḻi*.

It is striking, though, that even as a revered hierarchy of *ācāryas* and disciples (and then everyone else) is established, currently—and for centuries, perhaps since Rāmānuja ran into the hesitations of Āṇṭāṉ—there seems to have been little ongoing encouragement of the members of the audience to become interpreters themselves, to go back to the songs and reread them according to their own concerns and desires. The *ācāryas* are the recognized masters of oral and written interpretation, and it is sufficient and proper simply to hear the interpretations they have made, to be formed by them, and to live by the readings of the songs they have offered. Readings that were at first admirable and inspirational became canonical; even the *ācāryas* sought only to amplify what their predecessors had said, rather than to restate the meaning of the songs in new times, in light of new issues. As the tradition progressed, there was increasing reverence and decreasing originality—"return to the text itself"—in the commentaries; after the 14th or 15th century, though hinted at earlier, it became the *ideal* that very little in the way of new insight should ever occur, particularly if it proceeds by a new style or from new presuppositions. Even today, it seems to remain the highest praise of a Śrīvaiṣṇava speaker to observe, "He was magnificent, he said nothing new."

This is *not* to say that the *ācāryas* failed to appreciate the poetic excellence of the songs, but only that their devoted, loving reading of the text is ordered by theological and psychological principles which increasingly confine the songs within the established values and practices of the community, instead of reserving to them a capacity to reopen boundaries, to produce new imaginative combinations, to retrieve old memories for new purposes. As a result, ritual and popular usages notwithstanding, *Tiruvāymoḻi* has experienced little life apart from that which it has shared with its *ācāryas* in their powerful interpretive re-creation of it. The ability of *Tiruvāymoḻi* to generate new forms of religious imagination and action has, in the end, been submitted to the narrowing constraints of memory, and reduced to the minimum. Sacred memory has tended to foreclose the present, rather than to open it anew.

For us, though, the possibilities glimpsed in chapter 2 remain, and wider possibilities are apparent. Though as outside readers we are likely to remain amateurs—ill-versed, inarticulate—we do know differently, more, now; *Tiruvāymoḻi* has a life outside its original tradition, even in translation. The purpose of the detailed survey undertaken in chapter 2 was to retrieve some sense of how the text not only can speak to us, but also demands some response from us. *Tiruvāymoḻi* has to be determined once again in its meaning, by the affective and imaginative, practical and theoretical theological constructions of late 20th century readers. We read with the *ācāryas*, respond to their inspirations and insights, we remain endlessly indebted to them—and yet in the end we can and must complete *Tiruvāymoḻi* for ourselves, deciding how its set of possibilities communicate now, where they can be entered now, seen through now. Outsiders, we bring different memories, expectations, narratives, creeds, exemplars to bear on these ancient songs.

Thus, the songs are re-opened as we find a series of new partners for comparisons with *Tiruvāymoḻi*, ranging from options within the Indian tradition—e.g., ancient Tamil love poetry, Tamil Śaiva poetry, poetry in other Indian vernaculars—to various modern literatures, modes of literary criticism, different religious expectations, and systems of theology perhaps quite different from Rāmānuja's. Particularly on the level of practical response, we may opt to stress differences or similarities, and the latter is usually the better course; nevertheless, the options are there. In the end, we have therefore to hold a middle position: the songs *are* clear and approachable, they *have been* ready brilliantly by the *ācāryas, and* they resist full determination even when brilliantly interpreted, *so* more can be said by contemporary readers from outside the Śrīvaiṣṇava tradition, *even by us. Tiruvāymoḻi* deserves, and has, a global audience:

> *"He became the cowherd, he became the fish and boar;"*
> *as soon as you say this, he's become a million more.* (I.8.8)

II. Doing Things with Texts: Composing a Biblio/Biographical Self

The prospects for the articulation of our insight into *Tiruvāymoḻi* and what it means for us depend a great deal on our making use of the affinities and divergences—of culture, memory, class, literary and religious genealogies—which link and divide Śaṭakōpaṉ, the *ācāryas* and ourselves. In one sense, too much is possible at this point, and our theological comments scattered throughout chapters 2, 3, and 4 have hardly begun to exploit their possibilities. We experience something of what Naṃpiḷḷai said in commenting on the *āḻvār's* distress at the gap between what seems possible in general, and what is his capacity, now:

> If one goes to the ocean, one can look and drink it all in with one's eyes. But the *āḻvār* is not able to drink the Lord in that way, there is no single place where he can experience all the beauty of the Lovely One at one time. (III.2.0)

One must nevertheless try look to the whole, or at least look for an honest point of entrance. If we have spent much time examining the immediate and distant objects of vision—the commentaries, the songs, what we see through them, darkly—then it is worthwhile to balance that inquiry by sketching a more focused and precise profile of the self of the reader who attempts to read the old and the new together. Peering into the songs, one also needs to be able to see with a kind of inward searching eye, watching the theologian who stands near to *Tiruvāymoḻi*, venturing to enter upon the conversation spoken around the text, to do theology not about the Śrīvaiṣṇavas, but among them.

In chapter 1, I used myself as the proximate, handy example in order to take up the issue of the outside reader's self, in a preliminary, deliberately anecdotal and personalized fashion. I gave there an initial account of how it is that I have been reading these texts for a number of years, in certain contexts, within certain limits, etc. I now return to the theme of (my)self, this time somewhat more indirectly—for there is much more at stake now—by sketching a religious, literary context that has become evident in the course of this study. What does *Tiruvāymoḻi* remind me of, what do I read along with the songs, how do I now articulate something about myself, textually, biblio/bio/graphically? What can be remembered and reflected upon here, at the beginnings of one particular response to the songs?

In taking up these questions at the end of this study, my goal is by no means to establish a canon of the texts to be read along with *Tiruvāymoḻi*, but simply to illustrate how one's literary profile can matter when one ventures into comparative work. Though about texts, the following reflections are very personal, and it is taken for granted that the reader of this book will have other memories and can sketch other frames of reference.[1]

By way of example, I introduce six representative texts which merit attention in this context—texts which, because they productively open a (Christian) reader to affective engagement and commitment, accentuate some of the possibilities available after one has begin to read *Tiruvāymoḻi*. The first, the *Song of Songs*, raises issues regarding the management of a powerful text and the focusing of its multiple possibilities. The second, the *Gospel according to St. John*, is a prolonged exploration of how words obscure and reveal, reveal or banish darkness, making the meaning of deeds more evident and more uncertain, more mysterious and more accessible. The third, *The Journey of the Mind to God* by St. Bonaventure, shows how an author well-versed in older texts draws the reader to the very edge of direct experience. The fourth, the *Spiritual Exercises* of St. Ignatius Loyola, articulates practical strategies of memory and meditation which lead to a way of seeing God, here and now. The fifth, the work of the 20th century German theologian Hans Urs von Balthasar, reminds us how the constructive retrieval of these traditions is possible today. The sixth, the Indian works of the *Mīmāṃsā* and *Vedānta* schools of theology, highlight the way in which previous comparative studies also become part of what one brings to new comparisons. Given the extent to which I have labored in the preceding chapters to make *Tiruvāymoḻi* and the Śrīvaiṣṇava tradition accessible, the brevity and speed with which I introduce these great and deep texts will surely astonish some readers, and annoy others. Nevertheless, what follows is meant to be an extended suggestion, and what to make of it is left mainly to the reader. Occasionally in what follows, I juxtapose texts in columns, recollecting the textual/visual "collage effect"[2] so thoroughly illustrated by Jacques Derrida in his experimental writings. The possibilities opened by these experiments in juxtaposition are as broad as the reader may wish to make them, and I appeal simply to the advice Wolfgang Iser has given us as to what we might expect in this kind of situation, where strategic fictionalizing acts open new possibilities for us, in acts of "boundary-crossing:"

> In each instance, what has been overstepped is subjected to different qualifications: selection cancels out the organization of referential realities, combination relegates denotation and representation to latency, and self-disclosure makes the textual world unreal. In each case something determinate is cancelled, pushed into latency, or derealized in order to release the possibilities inherent in the given. Selection works on referential realities, whose relegation to the past adumbrates the motivation of such a shift. Combination works on convention-governed functions of denotation and representation, whose reduction to latency

> permits new relations as otherness. Self-disclosure, finally, sets itself apart from such realities, and through its "as-if" turns the textual world emerging from selection and combination into pure possibility. This embodies a radical alternative to the referential world of the text insofar as it cannot be extrapolated from the latter's reality, and may therefore stand as a model for the production of new worlds.[3]

According to Iser, the textual possibilities (of experiments such as those which follow) are so very rich and, indeed, functionally infinite:

> The clustering of texts adds to the complexity of the play space, for the allusions and quotations take on new dimensions in relation to both their old and their new contexts. Since both old and new always remain potentially present, there is a coexistence of different discourses that reveal their respective contexts as a play of alternating fade-ins and fade-outs. Whatever the relationship may be, two different types of discourse are always present, and their simultaneity triggers a mutual revealing and concealing of their respective contextual references. From this interplay there emerges semantic instability, which is exacerbated by the fact that the two sets of discourse are also contexts for each other, so that each in turn is constantly switching from background to foreground. The one discourse becomes the theme viewed from the viewpoint of the other, and vice versa. This iterative movement enables old meanings to become material for the new; it opens up long-established borders, and allows excluded meanings to enter and challenge the meanings that had excluded them. The more a text accumulates other texts, the more thorough-going will be the doubling process induced by the act of selection. The text itself becomes a kind of junction where other texts, norms, and values meet and work upon each other; as a point of intersection, its core is virtual, and only when actualized by the potential recipient does it explode into its plurivocity. The doubling manifests itself as a play space in which all the different discourses come together to form the matrix that enables the text to end up with a potentially infinite variety of relations to its surroundings.[4]

Let us now introduce in turn these six remembered texts, as the beginning of a practical response to *Tiruvāymoḻi*.

1. The Desires of the Song of Songs

The *Song* is a powerful and beautiful work of poetry, richly composed of vivid imagery, dramatic moments, deep passions and desires, and a complex set of interlocutive voices, especially those of the young woman and her lover:

> The voice of my beloved! Behold, he comes, leaping upon the mountains, bounding over the hills. My beloved is like a gazelle or a young stag. Behold, there he stands behind the wall, gazing in at the windows, looking through the lattice. My beloved speaks and says to me,
>
> Arise, my love, my fair one, and come away; for lo, the winter is past, the rain is over and gone. The flowers appear on the earth, the time of singing has come, and the voice of the turtledove is heard in our land. (2.8–12)[5]

Though not without its own obscurities, the *Song* speaks immediately to a very wide audience, religious and not. It is intensely physical, erotic, passionate, expressive of the desire of the woman and her lover. However powerful and vivid its expression, the *Song* is striking—it catches us, it begs for commentary—in part because of what it does *not* say. Despite its settled place in the Biblical canon, it says nothing at all about God, it does not tell us to give it a spiritual interpretation as we read it. Yet we do, its perceived indirection opens the way for us. Almost everyone expects the *Song* to have a spiritual meaning, even if, or perhaps especially when, it speaks of sexual passion; the expectation is that there must be some spiritual value to be gleaned for the benefit of the community. It grabs the attention of its audience, yet does not advise us clearly on what we are to do in response. Given its rich texture, the *Song* provides many varied opportunities—in relationship, dialogue, shifts in voice, scenario, mood—to taste the elusive fruits, and readers have responded accordingly. The *Song* has been singled-out in the Christian tradition for particular attention in spiritual and theological commentary, sermon and drama. As part of the canon of the Biblical scriptures, the text has received careful attention from early on, in the Jewish tradition and in the Christian tradition, even before the time of Origen in the 3rd century.[6] From and through the literal meaning, commentators have sought to draw out spiritual meanings for the nourishment of their audience. Key to this, in turn, was the intuition of most commentators that the meaning of the *Song* could best be deciphered when paired with a concomitant reading of human nature. As a spiritual meaning was sought in the "letter" of the text, this would both be guided by, and contributory to, the reader's transition from a "carnal" reading of the self to a spiritual one.

In the medieval era, there were many different readings of the *Song* in Latin and the vernaculars, drawing on typological references, most notably to the Virgin Mary. Various more or less indirect applications of the text in new contexts, including a variety of lyric and dramatic renderings, are at least implicitly indebted to the *Song*.[7] Most famous of the interpretive strategies throughout the history of the interpretation of the *Song* has been the impulse, datable at least to Origen, for the interpreter to move rather expeditiously from literal to spiritual meanings, finding in every word of passion and erotic detail of appearance some Godward indication. Yet this move to the spiritual was most often ventured *not* at the price of ignoring the literal meaning, but rather by a skillful, fine-tuned interpretation of the literal. Because the *Song* is both provocative and possibly out of place in a religious context, it stimulates both reader and exegete to imagine spiritual connections and so to profit from its inviting riches.

Most exegetes, seeing both human nature and sacred text as ultimately coming from God, were disposed to assume that the truth of the human was in some way indicatory of the divine truth, and thus to understand the *Song* as articulating a sacred pedagogy which, as gradually deciphered and understood, would little by little reveal the truth of the human person in encounter with God. The *Song* was a school of self-discovery and the nurturing of the human spirit, guiding individuals along the path of changing priorities and values with a strong emphasis on an affective, interior appropriation of the truth in a way that would make one change one's life, to begin to love and live in the way of the *Song*. The *ācāryas* might have been tempted to view it as *Tiruvāymoḻi* "descended" yet again, in Hebrew form.

Wilfred C. Smith devotes the opening chapter of his *What is Scripture?* to the *Song*, treating it as a paradigmatic scripture. He uses it to open a way of thinking about scripture that is more sensitive to its position in human usage, emphasizing the variability of the *what* and *how* of canonization and interpretation. Showing how the *Song* was productive of a rich variety of responses over the centuries, he discusses its reception as exemplary of the fact that "scripture" is in important ways—even primarily—a human deed, enacted over time, as an environment is composed in which written words achieve the status of *scripture*. Tradition is what we do, our handing down of what we love to remember; the tradition makes the scripture. At the end of his analysis of St. Bernard's medieval interpretation of the *Song*, Smith describes Bernard's commentary in a way that reminds us of Naṃpiḷḷai:

> Bernard reads the *Song*, then, and guides his audience to reading it, as invitingly affirming the glorious heights to which humanity may rise, and indeed is intended to rise. Yet in no wise does his exposition suggest that realizing these aspirations will be at all easy; let alone, in any manner automatic. The contrast drawn between the actual situation and the potential is stark. What the *Song* expresses, and encourages, in the midst of deeply troubled life, is constant yearning. What it offers is firm and unflustered hope. What it prescribes is rigorous discipline, for the journey from where we in mundane fact are to where rightly we should be and where God's flowing mercy and abounding love are ready, despite our own incapacity and unworthiness, to take us.

> Accordingly, for Bernard the message of this scripture, in addition to the vision of a final mystic oneness, is of careful

> moral refinement and realistic spiritual growth. These are ancillary, yet quite explicit, and integral to the whole: specific practical steps toward the ultimate goal . . . Bernard, then, was not that kind of mystic for whom union with the Absolute is a substitute for moral striving and conformity to obligation, nor even an alternative to them. For him it is, rather, their result, and their reward. *Transformamur cum conformamur*: we are transformed into God's likeness as we are conformed to His will. The *Song* is not only the depiction of a promised glory but also the details of the exacting route that will lead to it.[8]

Of course, the *Song* is obviously a text to compare with *Tiruvāymoḻi*. Scholars have frequently noted the parallels between the *Song* and south India love poetry,[9] and in the specifically religious sphere, the songs of the young woman in *Tiruvāymoḻi* very much invite comparison with the *Song*. The dramatic situation of the young woman, the absent lover, the search, all of these are highly resonant. Though the shifts in mood are not identical, a similar powerful passion pulses through all these songs. The Biblical theologian who approaches *Tiruvāymoḻi* reflectively and with a sense of memory may already be responsive to the *Song* and its commentaries—or become so, because of reading *Tiruvāymoḻi*.

As the familial resemblance of the two works is recognized, we can compare the questions, possibilities and demands which the two texts make together, as we read them together. Across religious boundaries sharply marked in other ways, a kind of recognition and easy transit becomes possible, and urgently so, as we move back and forth between what we remember and what is new, yet not entirely so. Readers of the *Song* become ready to read *Tiruvāymoḻi*, and to respond to the possibilities and problems evident there. The *Song* and *Tiruvāymoḻi* become mirrors for one another, in which we learn to see ourselves more clearly as interpreters opened to the demands of what we read. These are, after all, texts infused with desire—our own desire, too.

As mentioned above, here and in each of the following sections I introduce small experiments in comparison, juxtaposing verses from *Tiruvāymoḻi* with excerpts from the texts now under discussion, as it were (re)gathering the remembered Biblical and Christian traditions around *Tiruvāymoḻi*. I will offer these juxtapositions without much explanation, leaving it to the reader to do something with them.

First, the lover's advent illuminates every natural thing:

The voice of my beloved! Behold, he comes, leaping upon the mountains, bounding over the hills. My beloved is like a gazelle or a young stag. Behold, there he stands behind the wall, gazing in at the windows, looking through the lattice. My beloved speaks and says to me,

Arise, my love, my fair one, and come away; for lo, the winter is past, the rain is over and gone. The flowers appear on the earth, the time of singing has come, and the voice of the turtledove is heard in our land. (2.8–12)

Touching fire which everyone
knows is hot, she says,
"Imperishable one," and she
does not burn her body;
feeling the wafting cool breeze, she
says, "My Govinda," and
effuses the fragrance of his
cool tulasi.
Did she do these things only for my
eye, my little doe whose
forearm bears the thick
bracelet?

Pointing to the full moon, she says,
"He is the color of a shining
gem;"
seeing a steadfast mountain, she
calls, "Tall lord, come!"
when she sees a good rainfall
pouring down, she cries
"Nārāyaṇa has comes," and
she dances;
my young girl has done such
amazing things. (IV.4.3–4)

A second example places the *Song* near VI.5, accentuating the stubborn presence of love in places where love seems largely absent, resisted by the common view of how things work in life. I leave it to the reader to decide—according to his or her understandings of literature, tradition, and spiritual concerns—what can be done with this placement of texts:

I opened to my beloved, but my beloved had turned and gone. My soul failed me when he spoke. I sought him, but found him not; I called him, but he gave no answer.

The watchmen found me, as they went about in the city; they beat me, they wounded me, they took away my mantle, those watchmen of the walls.

I adjure you, O daughters of Jerusalem, if you find my beloved, that you tell him I am sick with love. (5.6–8)

She worshipped
Tirutolaivillimaṅkalam on the northern bank of the Porunal
where the perfect Vedas and sacrifices and great women mingle together;
from that first day until this day, that girl with eyes dark and wide keeps crying, "Lotus eyed one!" she weeps, she fades.

She grieves all day long, her face alarmed, tears splashing,
crying, "Jewel colored one!" so even the trees pity her;
ever since she learned the name of that city
all she does is join her hands in worship and say,
"Tirutolaivillimaṅkalam, home of the one who split the horse's mouth!" (VI.5.8–9)

2. *Encountering the Word in the* Gospel According to St. John

For a second example I turn to the *Gospel According to St. John.* Chronologically and self-consciously the latest of the four canonical Gospels, *John* retells the story and significance of Jesus recorded in the Synoptics, *Mark, Matthew* and *Luke.* Of course, *John* too has invited much commentary, including spiritual readings which find in it traces of the soul's pathway toward God. There are several core features which, for our purposes, distinguish its contribution.

First, it is explicitly, grandly aware of the identity of Jesus Christ, even to the extent of emphasizing that he is the preexistent Word, one with the Father. This is a Jesus who presides with authority in his encounters with strangers, his would-be disciples and his eventual enemies. Though he truly suffers and dies, it is solely by his own choice that he puts down and takes up his life again. *John* is about Jesus who is the Word of God, come for a time into the midst of humans, some of whom come to know who he truly is; and it is a narrative intended to draw readers into the same encounter with this Word spoken in human flesh, living on in the Spirit within the community.

According to these intentions, *John* self-consciously explores the power and limits of word, of vision, of signs in relation to what they signify; flesh and words both conceal and reveal. *John* presents the Word "made flesh," and so offers a series of signs whereby Jesus makes his presence evident to those around him, but where, often enough, the sign is lost sight of in the noise of arguments as to whether what one sees is really possible: whether water can really become wine, whether the eyes of the blind can really be opened, whether the dead can truly be raised, whether love truly conquers death. The series of encounters which comprise chapters 1 through 12—the wedding feast, the woman at the well, the raising of the dead boy, the multiplication of loaves, the curing of the blind man, the raising of Lazarus—are told simply, but they are accompanied by discourses which open up what is to be seen and accepted. The underlying point is perhaps simply a series of questions that can now be posed according to these scenes: if the Word takes flesh, with which words does one hear that Word? Why do some people come to see the Word while others remain blind to it? What is obscured and what is made stunningly obvious in these local enunciations of the Word?

Like Śaṭakōpaṉ, the author of *John* seeks to enable us to see, through words. Words mediate what words cannot express, the flesh reveals what bodily eyes cannot see. Though there are numerous literary and theological grounds which distinguish the encounters in *John* from the varied poetic reflections which make up the 100 songs of *Tiruvāymoḻi,* and though such differences must always be kept in mind, the following features make *John,* among Christians, and *Tiruvāymoḻi,* among Śrīvaiṣṇavas, stand also near to one another as kindred writings: the manner of encounter, the varied possibilities of perspectival interpretations, the location of the whole narrative in a present moment that is yet the product of memory and a venture in hope, and, as in chapter 13 ff. of *John*, the location of ongoing meaning in the "beloved community." They read well together, reading the one helps us to understand the other. It is easy enough to make fruitful comparisons here, reading back and forth between the two texts, because there are perceived theological similarities and because both texts invite, even provoke, the reader to expect present encounters with God, and in the meanwhile to examine the limits and obstacles by which words open up ways to actual encounters with God, in words.

For example: several years ago I had occasion to work out in rather full detail a comparison between *John* 4, the encounter of Jesus and the Samaritan woman, and *Tiruvāymoḻi* I.7, where the *āḻvār* is surprised by his lord, tricked as it were, and yet thereafter all the more stubbornly committed to the relationship:[10]

To destroy my confusion he dwells in my mind himself,
giving me soaring deeds, mass of resplendent flames,
source of the tireless immortals, chieftain—
could I ever talk of leaving my lord whose deeds suit me so?

Could I leave my light, my lord
who has entered right into my soul and uplifted me,
whose glance captivated the eyes of the flirting young cowherd girls,
my desirous lord?

The lord furrowed the wide earth, and then
his hair was garlanded with fragrant tulsi blossoms;
he marvelously pierced the Mara trees, if he says
he will not remain inside me, can I agree with him?

I never said I would agree to his being inside me, but he decided to,
he came and deceived my heart, joined with my body, mingled with my life's breath, that's his nature:
if now he wants to leave me, can I agree?

Even if he lets go of me, he cannot make my blameless heart leave his;
he is the one who grows great rejoicing in the slender bamboo shoulders of Piṉṉai,
he is foremost among all the ancient immortals.

Foremost among all the immortals,
the first, the ambrosia of the immortals, the chieftain of the
cowherds—
my soul is intimately united, mingled with him;
now that we are in close embrace, can we ever part? (I.7.4–9)

In *John* 4, a tired and thirsty Jesus meets a Samaritan woman by Jacob's well at noontime. Jesus breaks the restraints of both male-female and Jew-Samaritan relations by asking her for a drink of water. They begin to speak, they trade comments and questions, and the conversation gradually reveals that she is the thirsty one, she is the one who seeks an abundant supply of living water. Their conversation places in tension her profound longing and the barriers of place and history that divide Jew and Samaritan, her need and her presupposition that the Messiah will come, but not just now. Gradually she lets down her guard and opens up to this stranger. His words get inside her, for somehow he seems to know her, he speaks what is going on inside her, and so she cannot keep from telling everyone in the village about him. Her words in turn draw her neighbors out to see him, though eventually they come to appreciate him for themselves. By the end of her account, the townspeople—those who, like the readers of *John* have not seen but only heard—make their own claim and commitment:

> Many Samaritans from that city believed in him because of the woman's testimony, "He told me all that I ever did." So when the Samaritans came to him, they asked him to stay with them, and he stayed there two days. And many more believed because of his word. They said to the woman, "It is no longer because of your words that we believe, for we have heard for ourselves, and we know that this is indeed the Savior of the world." (*John* 4: 39–42)

This transition to responsible and direct encounter takes place even as Jesus is lecturing his disciples on how and when to speak the powerful words of the good news which will enable people to come personally into God's presence.

Jesus, then, is portrayed as getting inside them all, coming in small ways, yet quickly becoming irreplaceable, someone they cannot live without:

I never said I would agree to his being inside me, but he decided to,
he came and deceived my heart, joined with my body, mingled
with my life's breath, that's his nature:
if now he wants to leave me, can I agree? (I.7.7)

I offer just one juxtaposition, in three parts, for the consideration of the reader:

I never said I would
agree to his being
inside me, but he
decided to,
he came and deceived
my heart, joined with
my body, mingled
with my life's breath,
that's his nature:
if now he wants to
leave me, can I
agree? (I.7.7)

Just then his
disciples returned.
They marveled
that he was talking
with a woman, but no
one said, "What do
you wish?" or,
"Why are you
talking with her?"
The woman left
her water jar, and
went away into
the city, and said
to the people,
"Come, see a man
who told me all I
ever did. Can this
be the Christ?"

The poor thing, she
melts, her face shines,
for after entering
Tirutolaivillimaṅkalam
you showed her the
lord with the red lotus
eyes, the splendid
light;
starting then, her eyes
have rained like
clouds, she is amazed,
women,
her mind has gone
inside there, she keeps
on looking in that
direction,
worshipping. (VI.5.5)

Tiruvāymoḻi I.7 and *John* 4 echo one another, and together they affect the way we reread *Tiruvāymoḻi* VI.5. If we take into account the intentions that seem operative in the passages, the implied, presumed narrative and theological settings, the contrasting, complementary uses of 1st and 3rd person narrators, then together all these create an atmosphere wherein readers are encouraged to use words in a way that moves through those words to an encounter and intimacy which reach beyond them: from word to vision, promise to glory.

3. *Travelling the* Journey of the Mind to God

The *Song* invited us to consider the variability of interpretations which occur in response to a richly poetic and powerfully imaginative text that draws readers into a kind of verbal play and verbal intimacy. The *Gospel of John* invited reflection on what one sees, and cannot see, and on how words, with their obscuring, partial expressiveness, make possible a vision wherein one sees in and through words. In these ways, both texts serve us well in our reading of *Tiruvāymoḻi*, providing a background to that reading, and a location for further reflection thereafter, for most of us, in traditions and texts closer to home.

We now turn, again in a preliminary, merely indicatory fashion, to a third text, the *Journey of the Mind to God* by St. Bonaventure (1217–1274). Like *Tiruvāymoḻi*, the *Journey* bears strong rhetorical features, has a compelling spiritual appeal, and likewise maps out an intellectual and practical way to God. As a systematically planned work in prose, it is thus more immediately analogous to the (incipient) systematization occurring in the *ācāryas'* commentaries, particularly the *Īṭu*.

The opening passages of the *Journey* establish its range: after an invocation, Bonaventure identifies himself as a Franciscan theologian, a spiritual son of Francis of Assisi; he is a disciple who, like his master, has been graced with certain insights into the Crucified Lord:

> . . . it happened that, thirty-three years after the death of the Saint, about the time of his passing, moved by a divine impulse, I withdrew to Mt. Alverno, as to a place of quiet, there to satisfy the yearning of my soul for peace. While I dwelt there, pondering on certain spiritual ascents to God, I was struck, among other things, by that miracle which in this very place had happened to the blessed Francis, that is, the vision he received of the winged seraph in the form of the Crucified. As I reflected on this marvel, it immediately seemed to me that this vision might suggest the rising of Saint Francis into contemplation and point out the way by which that state of contemplation may be reached. The six wings of the seraph can be rightly understood as signifying the six progressive illuminations by which the soul is disposed, as by certain grades or steps, to pass over to peace through the ecstatic transports of Christian wisdom. The road to this peace is nothing else than a most ardent love of

> the Crucified, which so transformed Paul into Christ when he "was rapt to the third heaven" that he declared: "With Christ I am nailed to the Cross; it is now no longer I that live, but Christ lives in me." This love so absorbed the soul of Francis too that his spirit shone through his flesh the last two years of his life, when he bore the most holy marks of the Passion in his body. The figure of the six wings of the Seraph, therefore, brings to mind the six stages of illumination, which begin with creatures and lead up to God, in union with Whom no one rightly enters save through the Crucified.[11]

After this, the reader is exhorted to enter upon the *Journey* with the entirety of mind and heart. Bonaventure then leads the reader along this ascending path of intense wisdom and love, a way composed in an intricate configuration of scriptural texts, epistemological assumptions, metaphysical orderings of the world, spiritual and ascetical encouragements, all according to a sixfold schema: 1) the consideration of God in his vestiges in the universe and 2) in the visible world, 3) "in his image imprinted on our natural powers," 4) "in his image reformed through the gifts of grace," 5) as "the divine unity through its primary name which is 'Being,'" and 6) as "the Most Blessed Trinity in its Name which is the 'Good.' "[12] The path is an ascent through the universe toward God, yet also a journey into the inner self where God is to be found. Symbolically, it is also a holy pilgrimage which enters the inner sanctum of the Jerusalem temple, where God dwells in the inner darkness and Christ is present in mystery.

Among the many powerful and admirable features of this text the most notable is perhaps its comprehensiveness. With its careful distinctions and analyses of the constituents of physical, mental and spiritual reality, it demands of the reader complete intellectual attention, yet it appeals constantly to the heart, insisting on the interior, affective attitude which the reader must have to appreciate the text and glimpse its spiritual truths. Richly inscribed with Biblical texts, the *Journey* reflects the vitality and revitalization of a long exegetical tradition. Bonaventure has given a theoretically and pedagogically attuned order to his entire intellectual and spiritual heritage, and all for the practical purpose of getting the reader to tread this same path. Like Naṃpiḷḷai, Bonaventure sets as his goal a spiritual advancement that does not sacrifice sober and critical reflection on both world and tradition:

> After our mind has beheld God outside itself through and in vestiges of Him, and within itself through and in an image of Him, and above itself through the similitude of the divine Light shining above us and in the divine Light in so far as it is possible in our state as wayfarer and by the effort of our own mind, and when at last the mind has reached the sixth step, where it can behold in the first and highest Principle and in the Mediator of God and men, Jesus Christ, things the like of which cannot possibly be found among creatures, and which transcend all acuteness of the human intellect—when the mind has done all this, it must still, in beholding these things, transcend and pass over, not only this visible world, but even itself. In this passing over, Christ is the way and the door; Christ is the ladder and the vehicle, being, as it were, the Mercy-Seat above the Ark of God and the mystery which has been hidden from eternity.[13]

The *Journey* asks how one might organize, as far as one can, the desired encounter with God, in what intellectual and spiritual contexts, and for whom. It contains in itself a vision of an entire world and an understanding of things spiritual. It is a highly skilled retrieval of multiple older resources but, with its insistence on the directness of experience, mediated by words yet opening into ritual and visionary directness, it speaks in an intense, persuasive voice which draws the reader into the project of working through of the ultimate possibilities promised in the text. The *Journey* expects a great deal of its readers, while yet opening them to the possibilities of grace:

> He who turns his full countenance toward this Mercy-Seat and with faith, hope, and love, devotion, admiration, joy, appreciation, praise and rejoicing, beholds Christ hanging on the Cross, such a one celebrates the Pasch, that is, the

> Passover with Him. Thus, using the rod of the Cross, he may pass over the Red Sea, going from Egypt into the desert, where it is given to him to taste the hidden manna; he may rest with Christ in the tomb, as one dead to the outer world, but experiencing, nevertheless, as far as is possible in this present state as wayfarer, what was said on the Cross to the thief who was hanging there with Christ: "This day you shall be with me in Paradise."[14]

The virtues required of those who would travel this path can therefore be reduced to the bare essence:

> If you wish to know how these things may come about, ask grace, not learning; desire, not understanding; the groaning of prayer, not diligence in reading; the Bridegroom, not the teacher; God, not man; darkness, not clarity; not light, but the fire that wholly inflames and carries one into God through transporting unctions and consuming affections. God himself is this fire, and His furnace is in Jerusalem, and it is Christ who enkindles it in the white flame of his most burning Passion. This fire he alone truly perceives who says, My soul chooses hanging, and my bones, death. He who loves this death can see God, for it is absolutely true that Man shall not see me and live.[15]

And the result is total surrender:

> Let us, then, die and enter into this darkness. Let us silence all our cares, our desires, and our imaginings. With Christ crucified, let us pass out of this world to the Father, so that, when the Father is shown to us, we may say with Philip, "It is enough for us." Let us hear with Paul, "My grace is sufficient for you," and rejoice with David, saying, "My flesh and my heart have fainted away: you are the God of my heart, and the God that is my portion forever." Blessed be the lord forever, and let all the people say: so be it, so be it. Amen.[16] (37–9)

The *Journey*, a kind of theological homily, exemplifies the complete and integral appeal one learns if one is to understand what is required in reading Naṃpiḷḷai's homiletic commentary on *Tiruvāymoḻi*. It seems to me likely, other boundaries and blockages aside, that Naṃpiḷḷai and Bonaventure might well recognize in each other's works a shared concern for the whole of body, mind, heart, prayer, ritual practice, and receptivity to divine grace. What we see only in formation in the *Īṭu*—to be completed in later Śrīvaiṣṇava works—is achieved more systematically in the *Journey*. Yet we can say that the intent of both texts is much the same, particularly regarding where the reader is left at the end of the text's program of action. We might even see ourselves as standing nearby:

She worshipped
Tirutolaivillimaṅkalam
on the northern bank
of the Porunal
where the perfect Vedas and
sacrifices and great
women mingle
together;
from that first day until this
day, that girl with eyes
dark and wide keeps
crying, "Lotus eyed
one!" she weeps, she
fades.

She grieves all day long, her
face alarmed, tears
splashing, crying,
"Jewel colored one!" so
even the trees pity her;
ever since she learned the
name of that city
all she does is join her hands
in worship and say,
"Tirutolaivillimaṅkalam, home
of the one who split the
horse's mouth!" (VI.5.8–9)

If you wish to know how these things may come about, ask grace, not learning; desire, not understanding; the groaning of prayer, not diligence in reading; the Bridegroom, not the teacher; God, not man; darkness, not clarity; not light, but the fire that wholly inflames and carries one into God through transporting unctions and consuming affections. God himself is this fire, and His furnace is in Jerusalem, and it is Christ who enkindles it in the white flame of his most burning Passion. This fire he alone truly perceives who says, My soul chooses hanging, and my bones, death. He who loves this death can see God, for it is absolutely true that Man shall not see me and live. Let us, then, die and enter into this darkness.

Is she Piṉṉai born here?, or
Nilā?, or the Maiden?
what marvel is this? she
stands calling, "My tall
lord!"
To hear the name of that
town, to bow before
Tollaivillimaṅkalam
where he who came before
stands, sits, dwells—
that is her only
thought. (VI.5.10)

Let us silence all our cares, our
desires, and our imaginings.
With Christ crucified, let us
pass out of this world to the
Father, so that, when the
Father is shown to us, we
may say with Philip, It is
enough for us. Let us hear
with Paul, My grace is
sufficient for you, and rejoice
with David, saying, My flesh
and my heart have fainted
away: You are the God of my
heart, and the God that is my
portion forever. Blessed be
the lord forever, and let all the
people say: so be it, so be it.

Amen.

The reader is encouraged to tread this path because it is possible to do so, for it has already been tread before, and recently. Bonaventure refers at the beginning and end of the *Journey* to the example of Francis, whose holiness and deep experience of Christ signal for Bonaventure the perfect completion of everything he has elaborated in prose. Even if one has not seen God, one has been able to see how people change when entered by God. The reader is drawn into an increasingly deep and prayerful relationship with the Lord—whose grace alone brings the reader forward step to step along the path. Knowledge, spiritual awakening and worship converge in an encounter with God which is not merely described but, in a sense, is both inscribed in and enabled by the sacred narrative:

> This was also shown to the Blessed Francis, when, in a transport of contemplation on the mountain height—where I pondered over the matter that is here written—there appeared to him the six-winged Seraph fastened to a cross, as I and many others have heard from the companion who was with him at that very place. Here he passed over into

> God in a transport of contemplation. He is set forth as an example of perfect contemplation, just as previously he had been of action, like a second Jacob-Israel. And thus, through him, more by example than by word, God would invite all truly spiritual men to this passing over and this transport of soul.[17]

In this way Bonaventure is much like Nañcīyar, recollecting his own teachers' holy tears:

This was also shown to the Blessed Francis, when, in a transport of contemplation on the mountain height—where I pondered over the matter that is here written—there appeared to him the six-winged Seraph fastened to a cross, as I and many others have heard from the companion who was with him at that very place. Here he passed over into God in a transport of contemplation. He is set forth as an example of perfect contemplation, just as previously he had been of action, like a second Jacob-Israel. And thus, through him, more by example than by word, God would invite all truly spiritual men to this passing over and this transport of soul.

When Piḷḷai Tirunaṟaiyūr Araiyar and Bhaṭṭar were making their circumambulation within the temple, I followed behind them, I saw and experienced watching how they looked as they stood there, as if drinking with their eyes, unable to move even a step. (*Īṭu*, VI.7.5)

Or, drawing on passages from Nañcīyar (about Śaṭakōpaṉ, as we saw in chapter 3) and Nampiḷḷai (about the teacher who wept continually, as we saw in chapter 4), we can see the effect of reading Bonaventure with his new theological colleagues:

Śaṭakōpan̲ possessed the essential nature of the Lord, His form, His qualities, and all His glory, all this now made perceptible in the *ā̲lvār* by the grace of the Lord . . . His nature was such that he could not for a moment endure separation from the lord, for from his birth he had the lord as his sustenance . . . In him all worldly characteristics were eradicated, and by his inner nature he grew afraid at the mention of any human goal other than the lord . . . Three constituents of his being—the rational, the irrational and the Lord—were consumed by his desire, which grew greater and greater like the ocean, so that it could never be satisfied even if he were to experience the Lord for all time . . . His proper nature was such that he brought about knowledge and devotion in people and established them in that freedom which is characterized by service of the lord. (from Nañcīyar's Introduction to *Tiruvāymo̱li*)

It happened that, thirty-three years after the death of the Saint, about the time of his passing, moved by a divine impulse, I withdrew to Mt. Alverno, as to a place of quiet, there to satisfy the yearning of my soul for peace. While I dwelt there, pondering on certain spiritual ascents to God, I was struck, among other things, by that miracle which in this very place had happened to the blessed Francis, that is, the vision he received of the winged seraph in the form of the Crucified. As I reflected on this marvel, it immediately seemed to me that this vision might suggest the rising of Saint Francis into contemplation and point out the way by which that state of contemplation may be reached. (*The Journey*)

"Her eyes flowing tears" [VI.7.1]: just to see her face is sustenance [for those around her]. So when she goes off to the temple for the sake of her own sustenance, should she carry away our sustenance too? when one person weeps with knowledge of the Lord's qualities, it is enough just to see him . . . As Nañcīyar observed, "I studied three songs with Piḷḷaitirunaṟaiyūr Araiyar; but not even one word comes back to me. All I remember is that when he recited these words, he grew faint and tears flowed." (Naṃpiḷḷai, at VI.7.1)

Throughout this book, I have not attempted to claim that there must be an experiential basis for interreligious communication; even in chapters 2 and 3, I linked reflection on the experiences of Śaṭakōpaṉ to reflection on textual and theological expression. Indeed, I remain little interested in asking whether *Tiruvāymoḻi*, as a whole or in the songs of the young woman, refers to the same experience as the *Song*, or whether Bonaventure's ascent would have us end up in the same place as does Nañcīyar or Naṃpiḷḷai. My concern is more limited and practical, for the large questions about mystical experience can be answered, more or less easily or not at all, according to the linguistic, philosophical, and theological commitments of those who pose such questions. My concern here is to invite interested readers to enter into this project of reading back and forth across religious boundaries, with texts as powerful and inviting as these; these readers can then estimate the possibilities and limits of such commitments, in practice.

4. Working through the Spiritual Exercises *of St. Ignatius Loyola*

My fourth example is a text deeply engaged in the interplay of meditation, scripture and encounter with God, and also focused very precisely on the means of spiritual awakening. More practically than *The Journey*, the *Spiritual Exercises* of Ignatius Loyola (1491–1556) indicates a path of focused meditations, founded in acts of memory and (often) concluding in acts of visualization, a path which opens, at the end of its course, to a mediated vision of God, in all things.[18]

Grounded in the mystical experiences of Ignatius as a youthful seeker, the *Exercises* are a guide to a spiritual director or retreat master whose task is to assist the person making the *Exercises* to find out God's will for him or her in the particular circumstances of everyday life. Divided into four more or less equal "weeks," and planned to occupy, under ideal circumstances, a period of about thirty days, the *Exercises* move through four sets of meditations: sin and death, the life of Christ, the death of Christ, and the resurrection of Christ from the dead. In each week the exercitant is led through a series of different, largely scriptural meditations that share some regular features: opening and closing vocative prayers; three points which organize the selected text and render it manageable for meditation; gradually distilled repetitions which ask the exercitant to focus ever more closely on just where God speaks to him or her in prayer; finally, "applications of the senses" which invite the person who has spent time with a scriptural text to imagine himself or herself in that Gospel scene, with as vivid as possible an engagement of the five senses. Thus we have controlled, focused exercises premised on the gracious immediacy of God:

Many, many are his ornaments, many, many are his names, many, many his forms of light, if you reckon up his traits; many, many are the delights you see, eat, hear, taste, smell; many, many are the things we know about him who lies on the snake bed. (II.5.6)

This is the mental representation of the place. It will consist here in seeing in imagination the way from Nazareth to Bethlehem. Consider its length, its breadth; whether level, or through valleys and over hills. Observe all the place or cave where Christ is born; whether big or little; whether high or low; and how it is arranged. (*Exercises* 112–113)

It will be profitable with the aid of the imagination to apply the five senses to the subject matter of the First and Second Contemplations in the following manner: First point. This consists in seeing in imagination the persons, and in contemplating and meditating in detail the circumstances in which they are, and then in drawing some fruit from what has been seen.

In order that the *āḻvār* might enter that state of service which he had previously prayed for, the lord has graciously revealed to him how He is the Self of all. The *āḻvār* sees this and is excited. He meditates on all the elements and their derivative forms; the things which shine in lights; things of taste; songs sweet to the ears; all human goals, liberation, etc.; those gods who are chief in this world, Brahmā, Rudra, etc.; the Male and that Prime Matter which are the cause for the entire world; He meditates on the Lord who has all of this as His glory, and who pervades all this glory which is His body, as its soul—yet without the slightest touch of the imperfections pertaining to those things; who is excellent because of this unique body which is due to his glory; the Lord who is the husband of Śrī.

There is the joy experienced by the five senses, seen, heard, touched, smelled, tasted, and there is that hard to know, unlimited small joy:
but when I see you and the lady with shining bracelets, abiding as both;
then I've seen the visible radiance, I've reached your feet. (IV.9.10)

Second point. This is to hear what they are saying, or what they might say, and then by reflecting on oneself to draw some profit from what has been heard. Third point. This is to smell the infinite fragrance, and taste the infinite sweetness of the divinity. Likewise to apply these senses to the soul and its virtues, and to all according to the person we are contemplating, and to draw fruit from this. Fourth point. This is to apply the sense of touch, for example, by embracing and kissing the place where the persons stand or are seated, always taking care to draw from fruit from this. (*Exercises* 122–125)

When he thus meditates on the Lord's qualities, he is not content to stop in that service which is bodily. He realizes that the Lord is one who considers the words the *āḻvār* speaks to be entirely an act of service, and that a word about the glory is expressive of the Lord through reference to His glory, and that therefore to sing of the things which manifest that glory is to sing of the Lord who possesses them. So he undertakes that service which is made of words. (Nañcīyar, III.4.0)

The *Exercises* are deeply realistic: God is real, God deals really with the individual person, God has a discernible plan for human lives. They are also deeply committed to the power of texts, to the possibility of coming to intimacy with God through loving and reflective meditation on Gospel narratives—so much so that in the middle of the *Exercises,* the person is normally expected to be able to make an "election," to decide what to do with his or her life thereafter. One thinks here of Śaṭakōpaṉ's great and paradigmatic act of surrender in VI.10.10, with all that precedes and follows it. Outstanding differences aside, the *Exercises* might be understood as a further practical systematization of *Tiruvāymoḻi,* a practical step beyond Periyavaṅkippurattunampi's organization of the songs as a text of spiritual means.

There is a large bibliography pertaining to various aspects of the *Exercises*, exploring the various practices, their theological and mystical implications, etc.[19] Yet it is from outside the Jesuit tradition that Roland Barthes offers some of the freshest and most pertinent, though not uncontroversial, recent observations on the *Exercises* and its modern organization of religious knowledge.[20] He approaches the *Exercises* with particular attention to the instructional style of the text and the cumulative effect produced by obedience to the rules, and focuses on what he sees as the complex reorganization of knowledge being orchestrated by Ignatius whose plan, according to Barthes, was to strip the exercitant of language and imagery, and thereafter to return these to him or her with a reconstituted, invigorated religious purposefulness.

Barthes identifies two strategies of "assemblage" which come to the fore as the religious psyche is analyzed, deconstructed and recomposed. First, there is *repetition*, by which the exercitant continually "redoes" his or her meditations and his or her life as well, gradually focusing on what really matters in either. Second, there is *narration*, which "must be understood, in a formal sense, as being any discourse having a structure the terms of which are differentiated, relatively free (open to alternative and therefore to suspense), reductive (the resumé), and expandable (secondary elements can be infinitely intercalated)."

Ignatius' narrative is ordered according to the Gospel accounts, to which he constantly directs the exercitant's attention, a series of disconnected "scenes" in relation to which he or she "is to repeat what depresses, consoles, traumatizes, enraptures him in each narrative; he is to live the anecdote by identifying himself with Christ." The exercitant is taught to remember, to see anew, and so to gain opportunities to which he or she can respond in the newly acquired freedom which comes through imitation. The self is reviewed and reconstructed in these long periods of spiritual, imaginative, sensual exercise.[21]

Two other points in Barthes' perceptive and original essay are noteworthy. First, he describes the *Spiritual Exercises* as a text of desire, desire aimed at the material representation of spiritual realities. Every spiritual truth is clothed in images and forms, marked by times and places; this pertains to "the application of the senses" already introduced above. One cannot help but think of Śaṭakōpaṉ sitting with his eyes closed under the tree, when one reads Barthes' summary sentences on the desire of this text:

> Indeed, anyone reading the *Exercises* cannot help but be struck by the mass of desire which agitates it. The immediate force of this desire is to be read in the very materiality of the objects whose representation Ignatius calls for: places in their precise, complete dimensions, characters in their costumes, their attitudes, their actions, their actual words. The most abstract things (which Ignatius calls 'invisibles') must find some material movement where they can picture themselves and form a *tableau vivant*... This upward movement toward matter... is conducted in the manner of a conscious fantasy, a controlled improvisation ... : in the isolated and darkened room in which one meditates, everything is prepared for the fantastic meeting of desire, formed by the material body, and of the "scene" drawn from allegories of desolation and the Gospel mysteries.[22]

Second, Barthes points to a shift in late medieval thinking that is exemplified by the *Exercises*: from the privileging of hearing to a preference for vision, and for vision as implicated with touch, so that one seeks to have and hold what one sees. It is as if Ignatius has in mind a kind of visualization (*uruveḷippāṭu*), and these words could describe Ignatius' experience:

> The *āḻvār* has previously, in VII.6.6, meditated on the beauty of the lord's form; he has rooted the beauty of that form in his heart and experienced it, and due to his superabundant experience, it is of the same form as perception. Then, thinking, "this is [real] perception," and meditating on how near it is, he stretches out his hand to grasp it—and when he cannot grasp it, his condition becomes unbearable. He

> expresses this suffering by the verses of a young woman who, now separated after union, suffers due to this visualization . . ." (*Īṭu* at VII.7.0)

No longer is the divine simply beyond words, its transcendence is rather "worded" by a series of articulations of instantaneous perceptions, where specified images may yet open into a kind of illumination or rapture. For Ignatius, says Barthes, it is finally possible to "speak God," concretely naming and imagining every divine attribute as one becomes increasingly capable. Yet, in the end (as if to point to the dialectic of vision and service put forward by the *ācāryas*),

> the speculative mystic (John of the Cross, for example) is satisfied with something beyond language; Ignatian discontinuity, the linguistic vocation of the *Exercises*, are on the contrary in conformity with the mystique of "service" practiced by Ignatius: there is no *praxis* without code . . . but also, every code is a link to the world: the energy of language (of which the *Exercises* is one of the exemplary theaters) is a form—and the very form of a desire of the world.[23]

For Ignatius, the end point of the practices and reconstructions expected by the *Exercises* is not direct vision—Ignatius the theologian agrees with Rāmānuja on this—but rather an intellectual awareness of God in all things, which is articulated in total surrender, in a kind of *prapatti*, and thereafter in service. As Ignatius puts it:

> Take, Lord, and receive, all my liberty, my understanding, and my entire will; all that I have and possess is yours—for you have given it to me; to you, Lord, I return it. All is yours, dispose of it wholly according to your will. Give me your love and your grace, for that is sufficient for me.

Other echoes now become very obvious:

In return for the great gift of your mingling inside my self,
I ended up giving you my self—so now what other return can I make?
you are the self of my self, my father who ate seven worlds;
who is my self? who am I? it's what you've made it, you who gave it. (II.3.4)

I thought I would give my life to him in return for his help,
but then I reconsidered, for that too is totally his:
by me this father sings himself in sweet songs,
there is nothing at all that I can do for him, neither here nor there. (VII.9.10)

Take, lord, and receive, all my liberty, my understanding, and my entire will; all that I have and possess is yours—for you have given it to me; to you, lord, I return it. All is yours, dispose of it wholly according to your will. Give me your love and your grace, for that is sufficient for me.

Is she Piṉṉai born here? or Nilā? or the Maiden?
what marvel is this? she stands calling, "My tall lord!"
To hear the name of that town, to bow before Tirutolaivillimaṅkalam
where he who came before stands, sits, dwells—that is her only thought.

In thought, word, and deed Śaṭakōpaṉ of splendid Kurukūr
reached the point of calling the lord of the gods his mother and father;
whoever masters these ten pure Tamil verses about Tirutolaivillimaṅkalam
from his venerable thousand verses will serve Tirumāl.
(VI.5.10–11)

In these instances, a practiced and carefully achieved sense of empty-handedness is combined with a sense of wanting very much to respond in thanksgiving, by thought, word and deed. Neither Śaṭakōpaṉ nor Ignatius take this sense of gratitude for granted, for even to be aware of how much one needs God is itself a gift. Both are committed to an understanding of the farther reaches of spiritual need and desire; and, despite their very different settings, they are also committed to the development of strategies by which individuals can move toward these desired end points. The management and practicalities of desire are common to both traditions. Comparison then becomes a cooperative venture across religious boundaries, wherein practice is doubled, as one moves toward unsettlingly familiar-but-new insights through this juxtaposition of ways of spiritual exercise.

5. Hans Urs von Balthasar's Prayer

My fifth example can only be touched on lightly here, since the most important works of the contemporary theologian Hans Urs von Balthasar (1905–1988) are massive treatises and lengthy collections of essays—neither category lending itself to easy summation. Of the Catholic theologians of the modern period, von Balthasar is perhaps the most successful in bringing together exegetical, spiritual and systematic concerns, and his writings are richly imbued with a sense of literary, theoretical and practical concerns. When one reads von Balthasar, one finds a spirit kindred to Naṃpiḷḷai the exegete and mystagogue (and then, as well, kindred to the later *ācāryas* who would systematize and expand what is learned in the meditative reading of texts).

His major work is the massive, multi-volume project in three parts: *The Glory of the Lord: A Theological Aesthetics, Theodrama: Theological Dramatic Theory,* and *Theologik.* In these volumes he retrieves and explores the interrelationships among aesthetics, drama and theology, all of these woven together for the sake of a richer understanding of God who is beautiful, good and true. John O'Donnell offers a succinct summation:

> In his earliest *chef d'oeuvre, The Glory of the Lord,* Balthasar unfolds in seven volumes the theological nature of divine beauty. He explores how divine glory is reflected in the face of Christ especially in his cross and resurrection, and how the Christian tradition has sought to give creative expression to his aesthetic dimension of faith. In the *Theodramatik* in five volumes the accent shifts to the good.

> Here in the center of the discussion stands the problem of liberty, God's freedom and ours. The encounter of these two freedoms constitutes the drama of salvation history. Finally, in the last part of the trilogy, the *Theologik* in three volumes, Balthasar turns his attention to the problem of the truth of Being. Here he focuses on three questions. First, what is the philosophical nature of truth? Second, how is it possible to make the leap from a philosophical account of truth to Jesus' astounding claim to be the truth in person? Finally, how does the Holy Spirit lead us into the truth of Christ?[24]

This identification of "the good, the true and the beautiful" is hardly a surprising or novel theme in theology, but the breadth, detail and wholeness of von Balthasar's progress from one to the other is most valuable.

Typical of von Balthasar's writing, but on a much smaller scale, is his 1955 book *Prayer* (*Das Betrachtende Gebet*), concerned both with the possibilities of prayer in the life of the individual believer—though it is not a primer, the book is meant in part help people who want actually to pray—and with the larger context in which we understand prayer to occur. The first part of the book locates contemplation—prayer as an open, living encounter with God—in the context of the Christian tradition's lived, experienced understanding of God through the reading of the Bible, worship and community. The second part focuses on Christ as the object of contemplation, the embodied presence of God, the "Word made Flesh." The third part explores four pairs in tension—existence and essence, flesh and spirit, heaven and earth, cross and resurrection—which must be kept together if prayer is to be the fulfilling act of the whole person in encounter with God.

By way of example, let us see how von Balthasar makes use of the texts we have just examined. He quotes the *Song of Songs* when he considers the deep connections between community and devotion; it is hard to read the following passage without thinking of Naṃpiḷḷai's understanding of how community is inseparably integrated with the exemplary love, divine and human:

> Love neither divides nor dissipates. "My dove, my perfect one, is only one, the darling of her mother, flawless to her that bore her;" "A garden locked is my sister, my bride, a garden locked, a fountain sealed." (*Song* 6.9; 4.12) There is only one Bride of Christ; each and every thing which wishes to participate in the mystery of being loved by God must be *in* the one Bride. Everyone who is chosen to share this love is chosen *in* the Bride, as "part" of her or, better, as the embodiment of her, so that the Bride's unique mystery shines forth with ever more radiant truth at the very depths of the chosen soul to whom grace, faith and love have been given . . . The Church's unity of life comes about through the self-emptying and externalizing of God's unique spirit-life *beyond, in,* and *through* the individuals integrated in it.[25]

What is perhaps most attractive in *Prayer* is the way in which von Balthasar roots the entirety of his theology in an apprehension of the beautiful, thereby insisting from the start on the engagement of the whole believer, not just the mind or the will. For von Balthasar, though God can never become an object of ordinary knowing, there is a kind of human knowledge of God which begins in a captivating glimpse of the divine beauty in created things and just beyond them. In turn, this vision evokes a larger human desire for God, drawing even tentative believers beyond themselves into the deeper places of God, beyond mere spectacle into worship. Since it is God who reveals in the give and take of gracious encounter, in von Balthasar's view as in Śaṭakōpaṉ's, such human steps toward God must be recognized as responses, not initiatives. In turn, this participation in the divine-human drama becomes the foundation and location of reflection on the nature of God and the human: the experience, the ecstasy, the dramatic interchange, these are the resources and home for discourse about God.

What von Balthasar has to say about *The Gospel according to John* shows us his understanding of the foundations of theology in personal encounter with the Revealed Word:

> In all its major scenes we are shown the breakthrough from contemplation (an attitude which is somehow preliminary

> and neutral, as is appropriate to its abstract content, provisional, reserved and even distant) to direct adoration, at the point where truth suddenly moves toward the person contemplating and overwhelms him, not from outside but from inside, since Truth is a Person. Even the Prologue of John's Gospel depicts this movement: first of all the Word is with God; it is the absolute ground of everything in the world. But then it "comes," approaches the world, approaches man; it becomes flesh and thus can be encountered directly "among us," bringing grace upon grace out of its "fullness" and so showing itself to be the Word of the Father whom no one has seen.[26]

His comments on the scene from *John* which we reviewed earlier in this chapter engage the tradition of reading it as a text which makes present what it recounts—a kind of visualization, and thus too attuned to Ignatius' style of contemplation:

> To be sure, Jesus addresses a particular Samaritan woman at the well, but, at the same time, in her, he also addresses every sinner, woman or man. When Jesus sits, tired, at the well's edge, it is not for this one person alone: "quaerens *me* sedisti lassus!" Therefore it is not a mere "pious exercise" when, in spirit, I put myself beside this woman and enter into her role. Nor only may I play this part: I must play it, for I have long been involved in this dialogue without being consulted. *I* am this dried-up soul, running after the earthly water every day because it has lost its grasp of the heavenly water it is really seeking. Like her I give the same obtuse, groping response to the offer of the eternal wellspring; in the end, like her, I have to be pierced by the Word as it wrings from me the confession of sin. And even then I cannot make this confession in plain language; it has to be supplemented by the grace of the eternal Word and Judge, which—so incomprehensible is his mercy!—actually justifies me and puts me in the right: "You are right in saying, 'I have no husband;' for you have had five husbands, and he whom you now have is not your husband; this you truly said." (*John* 4.17–18) So it is not at all enough to see the dialogues and encounters presented in the gospel as mere "examples," like the instances of valor in a heroic

> tale, which a boy reads and feels inspired to emulate. For the Word which became flesh at that particular point in order to speak to us, on whatever particular occasion he addresses us, is concerned with every particular, unique occasion; in addressing this repentant sinner he addresses every sinner; in speaking to this woman listening at his feet he is speaking to every listener. Since it is God who is speaking, there can be no historical distance from his word . . .[27]

von Balthasar's observation on Ignatius himself tells us more again about his own view of the dynamics of religious knowledge; he too he seems to echo what we have heard in our consideration of the *ācāryas'* view of the integrity of the spiritual:

> . . . when [Ignatius] contemplates the gospel, he is not concerned with imagining some historical past event but with a personal encounter with the incarnate Word of God, who discloses himself in historical uniqueness and summons believers to discipleship. Thus the concrete object of contemplation is not meant to yield mere dry knowledge: what the contemplative is aiming at is a "feeling and tasting of things from within," that exercise of spiritual taste which is traditionally seen as our faculty of discerning the supernatural and the divine (for *sapientia* comes from *sapere*, "to taste"). Consequently, Ignatius demands more of the five senses in contemplation than a merely earthly functioning: they must discern the reality of God making himself present in the earthly activity of the imagination: "Smell the indescribable fragrance and taste the boundless sweetness of the divinity" (*Exercises* 124). Finally, in mystical experience, Ignatius has been touched by God in a way he describes as direct ("with no previous occasion,") i.e. not mediated by anything in the world) and hence free from the possibility of illusion. (*Exercises* 330, 336).[28]

At this point the experiment in comparative reading might take on this different tone:

Love neither divides nor dissipates. "My dove, my perfect one, is only one, the darling of her mother, flawless to her that bore her;" "A garden locked is my sister, my bride, a garden locked, a fountain sealed." (*Song* 6.9; 4.12) There is only one Bride of Christ; each and every thing which wishes to participate in the mystery of being loved by God must be in the one Bride. Everyone who is chosen to share this love is chosen in the Bride, as "part" of her or, better, as the embodiment of her, so that the Bride's unique mystery shines forth with ever more radiant truth at the very depths of the chosen soul to whom grace, faith and love have been given . . . The Church's unity of life comes about through the self-emptying and externalizing of God's unique spirit-life beyond, in, and through the individuals integrated in it.

Everywhere you see sugar cane, tall ripening paddy, and luxuriant red lotuses
at rich Tirutolaivillimaṅkalam on the north bank of the cool Porunal;
after seeing this she looks nowhere but that direction, all day, every day,
and the only word in her mouth is the name of the jewel colored one, women.

Women, this great lovely peahen, this little doe, has escaped our hands,
whatever you say she hears nothing but "Tirutolaivillimaṅkalam;"
is this the outcome of things she did before, or the magic of the cloud colored lord?
all she wants is to learn his signs, his names. (VI.5.6–7)

von Balthasar had no announced comparative agenda. Indeed, given the dour fashion in which he contrasts the vain ambitions of "Eastern religions" with the subtlety and profundity of the Christian mystery, one might justly judge him to be unsympathetic toward comparative work. Nevertheless, his integral understanding of theology in relation to aesthetics and narrative opens a surprisingly rich set of possibilities by which we can understand what happens in an encounter such as the one proposed in this book: a sense of tradition and responsible analysis combine with an appreciation of the centrality of personal, affective transformation, and this opens into the possibilities of resolutions beyond what, in the end, one is capable of. von Balthasar is then, and oddly enough, a most valuable ally in the effort to understand and appropriate *Tiruvāymoḻi* in a nonreductive fashion. One ought not to think about spiritual things, in reading words which express them, unless one is prepared to respond on multiple levels, from the most technical and abstract to the most personal and autobiographical. This is, of course, exactly what the Śrīvaiṣṇava *ācāryas* think; on these points at least, the differences of traditions seem to matter less and differently than one might have imagined.

6. Contexts on the Other Side: Mīmāṃsā *and* Vedānta

The situation I have been describing bibliographically is not so neatly arranged that I can still point only to texts from the Biblical and Christian traditions in describing the context in which my approach to *Tiruvāymoḻi* and the commentaries of the *ācāryas* has taken place. Perhaps there are still readers today who know only their own traditions, but I am not one of them.

My previous study of *Mīmāṃsā* and *Vedānta,* for instance, brings to the fore a number of features which affect the way I read, what I look for, how I articulate what is to be gotten from reading: e.g., the interconnection of texts and ritual performance (which *Mīmāṃsā* teaches us), the transformative power of reading (which *Vedānta* teaches us), and the real possibilities, values and costs of enclosing oneself in a world structured by (just some) words (which both *Mīmāṃsā* and *Vedānta* teach us).

Aside from the frequent instances where the *ācāryas* cite *Mīmāṃsā* and *Vedānta* texts—more the latter than the former—examples from *Mīmāṃsā* and *Vedānta* often came to mind during my reading of *Tiruvāymoḻi* and the *ācāryas.* For instance, in chapter 1 I discussed the need to refrain from excessively privileging the author, instead putting Śaṭakōpaṉ, even at his most intensely personal, back into his text, as a part of it. Perhaps it was the *Mīmāṃsā* which made it easier for me to suggest this move, the intensity of Śaṭakōpaṉ's own testimony notwithstanding. For the *Mīmāṃsā* thinkers quite readily dismiss investing the authority of texts in their authors, reducing this author function to the role of "exemplary expositors."

Thus, for example, in reviewing the ancient Vedic texts, the Mīmāṃsakas hold that despite the attribution of the title

"Kāṭhaka" to certain texts, this does not mean that their author is a man named Kaṭha; rather, he was just a brilliant expositor of texts he received from his teachers, and that is why he is thus honored. This surely is not what Śaṭakōpan̲ had in mind, but the combination is interesting:[29]

It has been urged by our adversary that such names of Vedic texts as "Kāṭhaka" and the like must be indicative of the author [i.e., "Kaṭha," etc.] Our answer to this is as follows. No such presumption of an author is justifiable. As people might call a text by the name of one who is not the author at all; it is possible that all "Kaṭha" and other persons (whose names are applied to certain Vedic texts) have done is such superior expounding of the text as has not been done by anyone else. For there are people who call texts by the names of such exceptional expositors. Then again, we are told that while Vaiṣanpāyana was a student of all the Vedic texts, Kaṭha taught only the one particular recension which is named after him. If someone concentrates on a single recension and does not study any other recension, he becomes an expert in that recension, and as such it is only natural that he should become specially connected in that recension which is then distinguished by its connection with him.

He has uplifted me for all time, day after day he has already made me himself;
Now he sings himself through me in sweet Tamil,
my lord, my First One, the abiding light: what can I say about him?

What can I say about him?
Become one with my sweet life, he sings in me these sweet songs which I sing in my own words,
he now praises himself in his own words, my marvellous one, the First One who sings in his three forms ahead of me.

He does not sing his song about himself by the sweet songs of the best singers,
but now joyfully he becomes one with me and through me
sings fine songs about himself:
Vaikuṇṭa's lord. (VII.9.1–3)

Though it is clear that the mere introduction of the *Mīmāṃsā* argument on the precedence of texts over their "authors" can hardly be taken as refutation of the claim of authorship made by Śaṭakōpan̲ and the *ācāryas*, the "counter-resonance" is there, for learned Indian readers, and for this Western reader at least: the human author is exceeded on the one hand by a tradition, on the other by an inspiring divine author. Knowledge of *Mīmāṃsā* enhances some positions and diminishes others that one might take in regard to how Śaṭakōpaṉ relates to the songs connected with his name.[30]

As for the *Vedānta*, there are numerous ways in which expectations formed according to the *Vedānta* might be shown to affect one's reading of *Tiruvāymoḻi* and its commentaries. Of course, the comments on Rāmānuja in chapter 3 are pertinent here, since it is through him that the *Vedānta* heritage is brought to bear on *Tiruvāymoḻi*. But other kinds of comparisons have a more striking literary effect. For example, Periyavāccāṉppiḷḷai cites this favorite *Vedānta* text, the ending of the great *Chāndogya Upaniṣad*, which proclaims the final cessation of the process of rebirth and ending of returns to this world:

> Brahmā proclaimed this teaching to Prajāpati, Prajāpati to Manu, Manu to the created being.
>
> He, who returns back to his home, from the family of the teacher, after the Vedic studies (carried out according to the rules) in the period left remaining after having done work for the teacher, he who pursues the study of the *Vedas* by himself in his own householder's place, in a pure region allowed to the Brāhmaṇas for abode, he who educates pious sons, who brings all his organs to a state of stillness in the *Ātman*, he who commits no violence to beings, excluding in the holy places, then he, indeed, when he has observed this conduct throughout the duration of his life, he enters into the world of Brahman and never again returns, never again returns. (*Chāndogya* 8.15.1)[31]

As one becomes familiar with the *Upaniṣads* and the values inscribed in those texts, both the world and transcendence of it are weighted differently, in theory and practice, as "non-return"—"liberation from this world"—becomes nearly identified with the highest religious goal. In chapter 3, we have seen how the *ācāryas* simplify the narrative of Śaṭakōpaṉ's quest by highlighting the problem of the body and the task of trying to escape from it.

Yet, precisely when such expectations have been established within the tradition and for readers who become familiar with it,

Periyavāccāṉpiḷḷai's citation becomes all the more effective, for he uses to it to reverse the expected *Vedānta* emphasis. What one expects to find *yonder* is actually *here,* liberation is in Tiruvallavāḻ:

Brahmā proclaimed this teaching to Prajāpati, Prajāpati to Manu, Manu to the created being.
He, who returns back to his home, from the family of the teacher, after the Vedic studies (carried out according to the rules) in the period left remaining after having done work for the teacher, he who pursues the study of the *Vedas* by himself in his own householder's place, in a pure region allowed to the Brāhmaṇas for abode, he who educates pious sons, who brings all his organs to a state of stillness in the *Ātman,* he who commits no violence to beings, excluding in the holy places, then he, indeed, when he has observed this conduct throughout the duration of his life, he enters into the world of Brahman and never again returns,
never again returns.
(*Chāndogya* 8.15.1)

Good, doe-eyed women, day by day this sinner wastes away:
when will this servant reach the feet of the king who dwells in Tiruvallavāḻ amidst honey-filled gardens where lovely kamuku trees fill the heavens and honey-rich mallikai trees send forth such a fragrance? (V.9.1)

The immobile things of Tiruvallavāḻ—the trees, flowers, etc.—are described here, as characteristic of the One who abides there. Because He decided to leave the highest heaven and by descent come here to be installed in a material object for the enjoyment of those seeking refuge, all those dwelling there, in heaven, decided that they would live on earth, in immobile bodies—trees, etc.—suitable to Him, just as bands of devotees live at Tiruvallavāḻ, without ever leaving their states of enjoyment. When these heaven-dwellers continue to abide there without drawing back, their lives thus take on the form indicated by the words, "He enters into the world of Brahman and never again returns, never again returns." (Periyavāccāṉpiḷḷai at V.9.1)

In general: given the lineage which connects the *Mīmāṃsā* and *Vedānta* traditions with Śrīvaiṣṇavism, the situation becomes all the more complex and interesting as these influences too combine and cross religious boundaries, back and forth. In my case, the reception of *Tiruvāymoḻi* happens to be mediated in part through my prior study of *Mīmāṃsā* and *Vedānta*—a development unlikely to be the case for many others who come to read *Tiruvāymoḻi* for the first time. Still, the principles involved, that influences multiply in number and effect across traditional boundaries, and that there are very few neat and ordered comparisons of "here" with "there," would seem to be true in most cases where comparison is accompanied by remembrance and attentiveness.

7. In Conclusion

The *Song of Songs*, the *Gospel according to John*, the *Journey of the Mind to God*, the *Spiritual Exercises*, a modern theology such as that of von Balthasar, Indian resources such as *Mīmāṃsā* and *Vedānta*: these are quite varied, and I do not wish to underemphasize the eclectic nature of my choices here by arguing for continuity among them. Yet the texts have at least three things in common: their engagement in action, or focus on eventual action, as information and description are implicated and intertwined with emotion and desire, engagement and commitment; their sense of how words both stand in the way of direct experience and yet, when used skillfully, assist in the reconstruction of human sensibilities so as to open the person to "experiences beyond words;" their demand for "whole readers" who engage the texts on their multiple intellectual and affective levels, responding to their whole meanings and not just to selected portions of them.

Of course, even classics occupying comfortable positions in the Christian tradition differ among themselves. The *Song* resists any particular signification, given its evident non-use of God-language; *John*, composed in conscious counterpoint with the synoptic Gospels, is powerful in part because it unsettles the narratives received from those earlier texts, transposing the past and present, making clear words puzzling so as to invest them with greater power; the *Journey* offers a clear idea about what the world is like and how to traverse it on the way to God; the *Exercises* recommend different paths to guide one's journey; von Balthasar, the systematician, seeks to encompass all of these, but in part he remains preoccupied with a European, Roman Catholic agenda that fits neatly in the middle of the 20th century; and none of these stands in continuity with *Mīmāṃsā* and *Vedānta* traditions.

In selecting these texts, I have envisioned a more complex composition which would take very considerable effort to complete, particularly were I—as I do not—to venture to weave a single narrative around it or a convincing set of reasons as to why these texts should be read together. For the moment, it is best taken as simply one imaginative, biblio/biographical response to *Tiruvāymoḻi* and the theology of the *ācāryas*.

But we do have to decide a little more clearly what it means to try to conceive of all these elements together: whether we can learn to see through these texts (the ones we begin with, the ones we find later on, the ones we return to) together, to read, write, teach our own theology among the Śrīvaiṣṇavas. Thus far, we have only created possibilities which require yet more attention—some of which are attractive, some demanding or too demanding, some worthy of resentment and resistance, and most of which cannot be comfortably described or governed according to any single, stable theological account. In lieu of making large and ambitious claims even on these points, in our final section let us look a just few steps ahead of ourselves.

III. Learning to See

1. Making Comparisons, Possibly

Once we have presented—mapped out, framed, put on display—this complex, composed place for religious thinking with *Tiruvāymoḻi* and yet also with the memories of our own traditions, we can begin to work through the combinations that have then become possible. We can pursue a further series of experiments, setting up tighter and neater comparisons with some precise theological focus and working them through, highlighting areas where similarity and difference stand forth prominently, judging the significance of what one then sees, and responding accordingly. Gradually, still larger and more complex issues can be engaged.

The turn to more elaborate thematic comparison is a promising path to follow in this case in particular, where it is Śrīvaiṣṇava and Christian scriptures and theologies, communities and spiritualities, that are placed together. As noted in chapter 1, we cannot help but notice the impressive similarities between the two traditions in doctrine, method, practice and goal, personal and communal sensibilities.[32] Encouraged by evident similarities, one might compare the role of tradition in each case, the origins, histories and formulations of creeds, the exemplarity of holy figures, the function of contemplation in relation to more narrowly defined intellectual pursuits. On the face of it, these similarities would be quite relevant, since a common goal seems to be operative in each case. In both traditions, theological positions are at the service of the ultimately practical, the transformation of the person who, for reasons that are ultimately undergirded by theological values, comes to the edge of human capability and awaits satisfaction from beyond. In the end, one must do and read everything with intense care, yet admit also that ultimately grace alone matters.

We might then spend some time comparing the distinction between kinds of devotion, such as *bhakti* and *prapatti,* and some comparable Christian doctrine, perhaps some version of the debate over how grace is to be balanced with free will and good works. Or we might compare Periyavaṅkippurattunampi's systematic account of *Tiruvāymoḻi* with Bonaventure's systematization of Biblical insights according to his metaphysical and epistemological concerns. If we retain a strong sense of the context in which these selected comparisons take place, we could travel quite far with such thematic and theological considerations.

From the very beginnings of such comparisons, though, we need to recognize that much will have already been done to make them plausible, likely to succeed, just by the prior decisions made in the identification of such possibilities. Any such comparison must be moderated by a lively sense of how each side of the comparison fits—theologically, textually, culturally, etc.—with its entire context, and where we are standing when we observe these materials together. It is helpful to undertake such comparisons with the expectation of always doing more of them, of trying other kinds of comparisons as well: of concepts, poetic texts, excerpts from treatises, ethical norms, ritual enactments, festivals, etc. If one crosses the religious boundary intelligently, no single comparison can be decisive, even if one determines with a rare degree of certitude that in this or that instance either similarities or differences are preponderant.

The larger values at stake therefore remain the skill and familiarity one gains and employs in constructing the series of comparisons, even by way of inevitable dead-ends and obstacles one encounters, by recognitions of the inappropriate as well as of the incomparable. The goal is a reflective one, to create "a comparative intertext," a detailed map of tried and true pathways back and forth, by which to see the texts and see oneself in relation to them, finding one's way, learning what works, what belongs together or doesn't, where one might take a worthwhile step, and the next one after that.

Though the identification of theological similarities and differences is important, and reflections upon system may be of significant heuristic value, these are not enough, since we still must ask: what does the comparison as a whole—of which the specific comparisons are moments—mean; what does it demand of us, where are we after we have undertaken it? The practical implications of our reading *Tiruvāymoḻi* along with the *ācāryas* still have to be confronted, in some way appropriate to the materials we have been considering.

In addition to specific acts of comparisons which give necessary substance to this conversation—lest we get mired in questions of method—we must seek, in ordinary circumstances, to bring coherence and overall intelligibility to the diverse elements we have linked across the expanse of some chosen terrain. We must explain the overall picture and articulate a meaning for the whole, we need to compose an account—a practical guidebook, a narrative, a systematic presentation—which supports and informs and justifies what one does in this regard.

2. *Toward a Systematic Theology—But Not There Yet*

One may therefore legitimately seek to make claims about the truth, the rationality and value of the situation in which one finds oneself. It is surely reasonable to insist that at some point, after doing many comparisons and on that basis, comparative study put forward not simply a series of practical examples, but also a comprehensive and systematic explanation. It may be, for instance, that Naṃpiḷḷai or Bonaventure is wrong on one or another point in theology, and we need not dismiss such possibilities; there must be room for judgments, and judgments must have sound and accessible bases.

Yet I defer also the systematic interpretation of the comparison undertaken in this book, not because such systematization is impossible—it will come, later—but for three specific reasons. First, and practically, the Śrīvaiṣṇava materials we have been studying are commentarial and remain largely pre-systematic. Commentaries, and particularly commentaries as pastoral as the *Īṭu*, are by nature diffuse, they deny us the certainty of a clear-cut, finished product, awarding us instead a clearer sense of the genealogy of particular issues than of their systematic completion. Lack of complete system in the materials studied is a very important pedagogical resource the theologian comes to appreciate, but this lack forecloses certain possibilities, for now. Though there have been good reasons for focusing on commentaries, a systematization of our understanding of them and of a comparative project based on them requires the study of the later, more systematic Śrīvaiṣṇava texts.

Second, the composition of a post-comparative, post-commentarial systematic theology is simply too large a task to be undertaken at the end of this project, and it merits postponement to a later, ampler context.

Third, insofar as it approaches the goal of doctrinal consistency, systematization too requires an integral communal context if it is to be persuasive; there must be a rich body of material, accepted and lived, that is systematized. However rationally coherent it may be, a good system will also be intertwined with the self-understanding of a community where creeds are professed, doctrines composed, systems put forth. Thereafter, systems may make sense independently, but only after, not before, the contexts of their development and articulation have been noticed. The systematization of a theology done across religious boundaries must occur as a service in the context of a community (even if only an incipient community) where inquiry is pursued on all its levels, with all its implications; for the project of a comparative systematic theology, such a community has not yet articulated identity for itself.[33]

Still, even if we do not put forward doctrinal positions which determine the significance of the traditions studied, we may still find ways of employing the dynamics of doctrinal formulations to guide our reading, just as the *ācāryas* made use of their mantras (as we saw in chapter 4) to distill the essence of what they were reading and teaching. We may bring together texts which successfully open up the possibilities of the several compared traditions within one new, imaginative framework, acutely, sparely written, so as to highlight the most telling features of each: a kind of rule book, a guide by which to know what one is to pay attention to first.

3. *Telling New Stories, A New Story*

In lieu of formal comparisons and completed systems, is it at least possible to compose a convincing narrative in which we can knit together what we have learned and remembered in this venture to understand *Tiruvāymoḻi* and the *ācāryas*? In Chapter 2 we saw how Śaṭakōpaṉ, though relying on old Vaiṣṇava accounts and various (partial) retellings of them, also incorporated notice of other religious traditions, taking into account Brahmā, Śiva and even village goddesses. In chapter 3 we saw the *ācāryas'* retelling of *Tiruvāymoli*, as they transposed it from a synchronic interplay of themes, images, desires, etc. into the diachronic narrative of Śaṭakōpaṉ's spiritual advancement. Though read onto the songs rather than demanded by them, this traditional and expanding, inclusive narrative is persuasive and useful, giving a sense of what *Tiruvāymoli* was for, how it was to be used, why people should and could care about it. In chapter 4 we saw how parallels with the *Rāmāyaṇa* and the recollection of stories about earlier *ācāryas* served to give the narrative a more intense presence and immediacy in the lives of its contemporary audience.

Of course, there are ample precedents in Christian tradition for the composition of encompassing narratives designed to locate "the others" within a world described by the Bible or Gospel, as these are understood in some particular way. For such narratives, the end goal has often been either the erasure of the other—by a denial of its legitimacy, by its subsumption through conversion—or its subordination, its incorporation into a Christian account of the world, as its foil or adornment or outdated predecessor. Even when aware of the varied and occasionally agonistic uses of narrative in pluralistic contexts, one may of course continue to recount these narratives, to set forth these encompassing religious frameworks for the exploration of religious traditions other than one's own. But to do this well will require a certain skill, the ability to distinguish productive constructions from those designed solely to exclude what might be seen through other people's texts and traditions, were one's eyes not closed. If done attentively, the composition today of a narrative to justify how one lives with one's religious neighbors is likely to be a messy and imaginative project where the rules and distinctions and limits are never entirely clear; the neighbors are really there, they are never quite what we think them to be, they have voices of their own, and we play parts in their narratives too.

But even if there is certain value to formulating coherent and comprehensive narratives, it may also be advantageous to postpone the completion of any such narrative, so as to leave open the possibility of other versions of the story, the enjoyment of other accounts, without undue concern where the stories conflict, move forward and backward, overlap, cohere or contrast. When the demands of a coherent narrative are held in abeyance, and the experience of learning from a different tradition is opened to the logic of imaginative connection, statements which at first appear to be in conflict may turn out to be mutually enriching, even when they do not fit together.[34] If every account, even the most novel, has precedents, it will always be possible to factor its value into the requirements of the present moment; something new or different may have to be said, the tradition may have to be remembered differently. Comparisons will then be fruitful in part because they are always relativizing the narratives we form, the stories we tell.

Thus, neither of the narratives offered by Naṃpiḷḷai and Bonaventure, for instance, will be able to succeed in completely mapping the religious horizon within which we now dwell. Neither discourse obliterates the other, and adherence to the one does not in fact preclude openness to the other. One looks back and forth, again and again, remembering both, each glance enriched by the preceding, yet opening again into the immediacy of the present moment. When, as in the previous section, one allows one's eye to play across a series of juxtaposed Christian and Śrīvaiṣṇava texts, all kinds of combinations become possible; if they are not immediately subjected to a rule of faith, the one text will be allowed to linger on the periphery of a credal commitment to the other. The reader will not forget *Tiruvāymoḻi* when reading the Bible, even if, as a Christian, one is totally committed to the Gospel. Or vice versa.

This kind of openness makes possible a wider and broader range of shifting positions, even for those who remain very much committed to their own traditions, if their commitments are strong enough that openness becomes interesting, and spiritually worthwhile. Though, in a theological context where communal responsibilities often loom practical and demanding, large decisions which specify narrative and commitment cannot be postponed permanently, further delays for the sake of the imagination will be worthwhile. We are *only* in the 20th century, after all.

During this deferral, one may also consider whether it would be a good idea to entertain a new, larger narrative which encompasses both traditions without (intentionally) privileging either one of them. Though early on this too may be an explanatory venture which aids future scholarly work, at a root level it may also be a step toward the composition of a new canon, the telling of a larger story—for, and in the formation of, a new community beyond both traditions.

Thus the theological theory of pluralism, if well-formed by knowledge of specific traditions, may offer this kind of new, encompassing narrative. Pluralism is the position in the theology of religions debate which, in the roughest terms, can be said to hold that all religions are equal in their meeting, perhaps because they are differing accounts of the same spiritual reality, perhaps because courtesy is the prerequisite, perhaps because we must remain agnostic about ultimate values.[35] When pluralism is more than a muted version of a Christian universalism or of a post-religious rationalism, it may be taken as a narrative strategy that speaks powerfully beyond what religious traditions have always said about themselves, in order to describe how the world coheres and has meaning when many religious traditions are noticed *together* within a new world narrative, and where all extant stories are subsumed into one greater story. Because this new narrative would explain traditions beyond themselves, it would have the advantage of relativizing specific obstacles and making compatibilities convenient.

But this option is more costly than it might seem at first. Given the deep commitments of religious communities to their own narratives, a pluralist narrative can well be taken as an aggressive act which religious communities are quite likely to resist. To find what one has thought to be the story of the whole world swallowed by yet another, ostensibly larger story will not be easy to accept, even if the pluralism is expressed tastefully.

Even if certain traditions were not previously in direct conflict, competing in one space, but were rather functioning in different environs, we create new problems as well as new possibilities by including their stories in a new, wider story. Integrating two traditions in a single coherent account formed according to the expectations of one of the two traditions—in tension with the other—is likely to put us in the situation where the different narratives no longer mesh properly, but instead compete, vying for predominance in this new story of the world and its religions. The temptation is to smooth out the new, encompassing narrative, leaving out the troublesome details of the subsumed traditions.

When differences are recognized, it is better to recognize the real resistances involved without too quickly moving to a compromised, third position. Indeed, the strength of a community is often marked by the vigor of its stance regarding outsiders; some communities are strong because they include, some because they exclude. As we saw in chapter 4, the Śrīvaiṣṇava community, like many other religious communities, is marked in part by whom it excludes, or passes over in silence, relegates to the edges of its story. Communities cannot be swiftly judged wrong in such exclusions; these instincts matter deeply, they are not merely mistakes.

Even a proposed new narrative would itself require roots if it is to be anybody's story or if it is to speak to anyone. Narration and community are always mutually dependent, mutually generative. With what resources, from where, is one telling the new story, and for whom?[36] There must be the gathering of a community which finds life in such an account and which carries it beyond a merely notional existence. If not one particular, long-recognized community, there must still be a community, not merely a theory or a position paper appealing for the creation of such.

Even if a pluralist narrative is coherent, interesting, and compelling, it may still fail to convince important players in the broader context comprised of members of the other tradition, along with other members of one's own community, unless it works on the level of spiritual practice. Traditions can of course be placed together in a way that is spiritually enlivening and creative—the promise is immeasurable, as I have attempted to show earlier in this chapter—but it is not clear that people actually want to live with those they are willing to visit, or that visitors would really be welcomed as new members of a community. Who are those who will wish to continue re-reading the Christian tradition in light of *Tiruvāymoḻi*?

To stay, to dwell, in a complex and unsettling comparative location requires a large commitment that must be more than clever; the excitement of the tourist is not the best model for this enterprise. Though the theologian who crosses religious boundaries is likely to be a venturesome sort of scholar, writing into a void is not a good idea. Cross-religious persuasion, such as is also convincing within traditions, is required if the new situation is to be one where spiritual flourishing occurs, where there can be told a new narrative which appeals effectively to all those involved.

4. The End of this Venture: Seeing It Through, Seeing Through It

Let us conclude, for now, with some reflections on the spirituality of this endeavor of thinking and reading religiously across boundaries, an endeavor which may, in time, form a community wherein narratives can be persuasively told and systems convincingly put forward. If sympathy and engagement are positive values that should accompany study and reflection, the study of a religious tradition other than one's own must include an openness, risk, the possibility of losing one's way in the presence of that other. One must recognize that this endeavor is really dangerous, really valuable.

The way one thinks about religious things is going to be transformed, and also one's religious practices, including ritual, prayer, worship. The Bible, Bonaventure, Ignatius: for a Christian who has studied the Śrīvaiṣṇava tradition, these are still there, still central, but they do not mean now what they did before. If so, then we must also notice how this process of change affects the substantive integration of what one has learned into one's conscious understanding of what one believes to be true, what one believes one ought to do. Beyond the formulation of encompassing and encompassed, revised or original narratives, and beyond the ways one might transgress the boundaries of narratives in relation to the communities which stand in mutual dependence with them, theologians must also inquire as to the limits of what one can and ought to do in this situation. If the theologian comes to stand in an in-between space, unaccounted for by either one's familiar narrative, or the one newly learned, then what happens during and after comparison? To what or whom do we now, still, make our commitments?

In the end, this book has perhaps provided some of the required resources for an insight by which one can begin to see—more clearly—through words, Tamil words, English words, ancient words, modern words, to the realities most of us claim lie beyond, after, within such words. Or has *Seeing through Texts* been an erudite but ultimately empty production, words about things which are better left unsaid?

It should be clear at this point that if one takes *Tiruvāymoḻi* to heart, even from outside its tradition, there is at least the possibility, perhaps the probability, that one is going to be drawn into what one studies, and changed by it. As the young woman at Tirutolaivillimaṅkalam learned, glances are not always casual. By studying *Tiruvāymoḻi* and the uses to which it is put by the *ācāryas*, and by raising the questions of wider context by attention to some powerfully evocative texts from the Christian tradition, I have therefore been urging more acutely the question of loyalties which has occupied us implicitly from the beginning of this book. If one worships, whom shall one worship, and where, with which memories, in which community? One may wonder about the end of comparison: if one takes *Tiruvāymoḻi* seriously, where does it lead?

Certainly, all the texts we have been considering envision the possibility of an eventual rupture, or rapture, where the sum total of deliberate possibilities neither accounts for nor predicts what comes next—the realization that everything is divine word, divine voice, the discovery that the divine desire for the human is greater than the human desire for God, and that things then get out of hand. Yet these texts also expect the ironic unsettling of any such faith, just as it becomes a sure thing: we worship Viṣṇu and not Śiva or Brahmā, says Śaṭakōpaṉ—or is it someone beyond the "three"?

> *Thinking, thinking, but even if you keep thinking about this*
> *state below, within, above, beyond form, it is still hard to*
> *know the lord's state, people;*
> *so keep thinking, keep speaking of him who is called "Ari, Ayaṉ,*
> *Araṉ,"*
> *keep thinking, propounding, and then worship:*
> *what you are thinking of is One.* (I.3.6)

> *"He became the cowherd, he became the fish and boar;"*
> *as soon as you say this, he's become a million more.* (I.8.8)

Whatever we might prefer, we should not exclude the possibilities of irreversible new involvements at the end of the comparative project, the possibilities of a different, real worship.

Or, to shift to another, older and much-burdened vocabulary, perhaps the conclusion might lie nearer to idolatry: a seeing through to something that is neither neutral nor benign, but which captures attention and then memory, realigning loyalties and prospects, bringing about a new kind of worship, and in a way that is compelling and to some unacceptable. Recall Śaṭakōpaṉ's own strong repugnance toward village goddesses.[37]

If we take seriously what we read—if we actually read, pay attention, learn to understand—we are confronted with what some believers, in whichever community, will view as the endangering and possible destruction of faith, a going over to false gods, a dalliance in the trappings of false cults. What one person thinks of as openness can be interpreted by another, often with great rhetorical effect, as an infatuation with foreign beliefs, even the worship of a false god. One starts as a tourist or scholar or dialogue partner, and ends up worshipping in a different place, belonging to a new religion: or is it religious discovery?

The young woman, worshipping at Tirutolaivillimaṅkalam, was enraptured by what she saw, she stepped beyond herself.

Her temple vision was a beginning, not an ending. It would be ironic if the scholar is preserved from this possibility of infatuation and from even the idea of idolatry because he or she is rather like the neighborhood women who visit the temple, think nothing of it, return home unchanged: casual readers, whose presuppositions are so comfortable and secure that nothing is ever really going to be threatening.

At what point does the simple claim—"I was just looking around the temple; I was just reading the text"—open into the possibility that one will not return home the same person, but instead become different "in thought, word and deed"? It is here that exclusivism, often criticized simply as narrow-minded and impolite—has its honest place. This is the position in the theology of religions debate which, in the roughest terms, can be said to hold that "only my religion is true, others are false; at most, let us pick and choose redeemable elements from them." This exclusivism takes very seriously the possibilities brought forward in comparative study; and because it takes them seriously, it rules them out. The exclusivist thinks that it is neither safe nor neutral to look around, to take things in, to assume that nothing is off-bounds: it is dangerous, after all, to go to (un)holy places and participating in (un)holy rites; as we have seen, it is not really much safer to mediate or soften such encounters by relying on words.

For words can be unsafe too. Both the Śrīvaiṣṇava tradition (as indicated throughout) and the Christian (as indicated earlier in this chapter) very much believe that just as real encounters can occur through visiting holy places, they can occur through taking words seriously; one does in fact see through words. If, as both the Christian and Śrīvaiṣṇava traditions agree, texts not only block but also mediate experiences that are vainly sought in a pure, immediate form, then attentive reading ought to be respected as a dangerous activity. The exclusivist at least realizes this, in saying that such encounters need to be excluded, from the start, for they are unholy, they horrify the lover:

Once lord Raṅganātha was being carried in procession, when it began to rain. The Lord was, for shelter, carried into the premises of another temple, the temple of Jambukeśvara. Rāmānuja and the other elders who had accompanied the procession remained outside the premises, in the rain. Someone asked Rāmānuja, "Sir, if the Lord has taken shelter inside, why do you not do the same?" Rāmānuja answered, "Fool, if the emperor elects to make love to a courtesan, does this mean that his Queen should imitate her Lord and make love to a courtier?" (*Īṭu* at X.2.1)

Contemplation starts at the point where the believing mind begins to perceive a dawning light in the abyss of the mystery, where the mystery begins to reveal itself in all its vast proportions. Not in the sense of doubt, of loosening the tautness of the dogmatic affirmation, but in an astonishment which reaches to the very roots of our being. For we must be aware, at every moment, that the mystery of Jesus Christ transcends all the experience of God accessible to natural man and man as he is in history. It transcends the realization that absolute Being can never be or become relative being. Finally, it transcends the impressive experience of God on the part of Old Testament Man, who is still haunted by the negative theology which merges into the natural knowledge of God. He is acquainted with the chasm which yawns between God and the creature; if God wills, of course, there can be a dialogue, a covenant, a mutual faithfulness between the two parties, but under no circumstances can they ever share a common Being. It would make the true God into a worldly image, the kind of idol which, on the the Day of his appearing, the Day of his wrath, he will smash into a thousand pieces. (*Prayer*, 158)

But the risk may also be put positively. When we try to see, when we read, when we begin to include, we are confronted with the possibility of ecstasy, where one's carefully composed and focused words get out of hand, overflowing with possibilities which go beyond one's expectation. One is thrust forward in a kind of ecstasy, always *from* one's home position but not limited within its boundaries anymore.[38] From where one is, one learns to include what one finds, to be included within its dynamic and vitality. One finally gets to see through texts—the texts of one's own tradition and of another, of both as a comparative intertext—and one finally reaches what Rāmānuja (as we saw in chapter 3) called a form of seeing "which in form is just like perception." This kind of holy vision can be where the project of including may end.

At the end of a venture across religious boundaries that is intellectually and pedagogically honest and careful, one might indeed experience what one has been talking about, and one might then have to respond accordingly, or at least consciously refuse to do so. The scholar, become a participant in the narrative he or she has been recounting, then stands opened to such an encounter, free in regard to what comes next. Then, there, one finally engages in true theology, *theoria* and *praxis*.

For now, both the fears and ecstasies which accompany study across religious boundaries are best seen with a sober glance, moderated by ongoing commitments to careful scholarship, to the mediating role of texts, and to ongoing conversation in old and new communities. It is important to focus not so much on dramatic options—ecstasies and so forth—but much more modestly on the habits of this person who expects, risks, and is willing to include further insight, without any guarantee that there is something further to be seen.

No depth of comparative study, no level of skill in words, can be sufficient to sort out in advance the dangerous possibilities of idolatry and the captivating ecstasies of worship. We must therefore be content to ponder the habits of comparison, how one is to act when one is caught at the end of one's abilities, finding neither the scholarly nor spiritual resources to take the necessary next step on one's own:

I've done no ascetic deeds,
I have no subtle knowledge
but still
I cannot bear to leave you
even once,
lord with the snake bed,
Father, enthroned in
Cirīvaramaṅkalanakar
where lotuses bloom in
the mud amidst the
ripening paddy,
apart from you, I am nothing,
there. (V.7.1)

. . . *With nowhere else to enter,*
this servant has entered right
beneath your feet. (VI.10.10d)

Thus, using the rod of the Cross, he may pass over the Red Sea, going from Egypt into the desert, where it is given to him to taste the hidden manna; he may rest with Christ in the tomb, as one dead to the outer world, but experiencing, nevertheless, as far as is possible in this present state as wayfarer, what was said on the Cross to the thief who was hanging there with Christ: "This day you shall be with me in Paradise." (Journey, 38)

I conclude simply by recalling, from the end of chapter 4, that perhaps the ideal reader can be described as one who reads like a *prapanna*—like someone who does *prapatti*, who surrenders completely, somewhat desperately, having run out of strategies and plans: surrendering to the text and its meaning after attempting and abandoning every skillful strategy by which to make something certain and safe of it. This *prapanna* would then speak and write from this simple, clear, unadorned learning.

This is a spiritual possibility, to be sure, but it can also be described as a carefully cultivated intellectual virtue which extends the scholar to the limit and which can profitably inform the whole comparative enterprise. It is the ability to suspend, for a time, the quest for practical and theoretical system, to plead a kind of helplessness, at least for now. It is the cultivation of an openness not only to questions, but also to events, encounters, inclusions, and without protection. It is to let slip the careful boundaries between what one thinks, how one feels, what one does, all without certainty about some ultimate coherence. It is letting one's beliefs intrude into scholarship, and risking them there, without having something ready and wise to say in summation. Everything gets included, eventually.

To say that the scholar might be a *prapanna* is certainly not a full job description, but it serves to highlight key virtues which have been identified in this particular comparative exercise, and which promise to serve well in other ventures too. After this, other, extended reflections can follow later, elsewhere, by which one can speak beyond the songs, the commentaries, and the features of one's biblio/biography, seeing through them, through oneself. Then one might state more systematically what one has learned, the meaning of one's acts of inclusion, for the sake of those who could neither have seen nor heard in the same way.

For now, practice still makes perfect, and we do well simply to end just where we began, completing this particular *antāti*, ending, once again, in the middle of things:

She worships lofty Tirutolaivillimaṅkalam
with its great houses, flawless jewels,
so leave her alone, women, have no hopes regarding her;
she cries, "the white, radiant conch and discus,"
she cries, "the wide lotus eyes,"
she keeps standing there
tears welling in her flower eyes
radiant kuvaḷai flowers
she bursts

Notes

Chapter One. Taking A First Look

1. Here, and throughout, all translations of the songs are my own, although as acknowledged in the preface, I readily acknowledge my debt to A.K. Ramanujan, Vasudha Narayanan, and John Carman.

2. Here, and throughout, all translations from the commentaries are my own. Since the comments occur in the elucidation of specific words, verses and songs, only in the case of very long passages will I specify a page number for a quoted text.

3. Or, if you will, *his* disciple, Vaṭakkutiruvītippiḷḷai, who is said to have faithfully written down Naṃpiḷḷai's expositions of *Tiruvāymoḻi*. Following the tradition, I refer throughout to the *Īṭu* as Naṃpiḷḷai's teachings.

4. *Tiruviruttam* was Śaṭakōpaṉ's first work.

5. II.7 has two extra verses because it dedicates a verse to each of the twelve names of Viṣṇu.

6. For examples, see Hardy 1983 and Cutler 1987.

7. Thus, for instance, important work has been done on the *akam* literature, and even on its transformation in the *āḻvār* poetry, particularly Śaṭakōpaṉ's work. From the work of Ramanujan, Cutler, Hardy and others, we know a great deal now about older poetry 1) in praise of the king—by analogy, Śaṭakōpaṉ's Lord, and 2) in the voice of a girl distressed over the absence of a lover—by analogy, the devotee waiting anxiously for God's return. See for instance the preliminary work done by A.K. Ramanujan and Norman Cutler in their "From Classicism to Bhakti," in Bardwell Smith 1983; see also Cutler, Hardy 1983, and Peterson.

8. See Clooney 1992.

9. Narayanan 1994, which provides rich insights into the ritual and social reception of *Tiruvāymoḻi* today, is a particularly apt and highly recommended complement to the textual study undertaken here.

10. See Hardy 1979 and his bibliography; Hardy 1983 makes some of the same points. See also Damodaran, pp. 21–29. The source of most of this rather scanty information are the 11th verses which end each unit of ten verses in each song. Each 11th verse tells us something about Śaṭakōpaṉ: who he is, the excellence of his skill, that he is from Kurukūr, and the devotion which infuses his work. There are a few references with historical value, to his home in Kurukūr, to the rich Vaḻuti land, of which he is the ruler by the Porunal River, to some rather remote hill shrines (of which he alone among the *āḻvārs* sings).

11. For the reasons for this date, see Damodaran. Hardy places Śaṭakōpaṉ earlier, in the 7th or early 8th centuries; pp. 266–267.

12. Māṟaṉ (possibly in honor of a Pāṇḍyan king), Kāri Māṟaṉ ("Māṟaṉ, son of Kāri"), Śaṭakōpaṉ (destroyer [*kopa*] of *satam*, an "air" supposed to bind newborn infants). "Śaṭakōpaṉ" is subject to various interpretations, pointing to his "antagonism" (*kōpa*; Sanskrit, *kopa*) to *śaṭha* (perhaps, wickedness, evil humor); see Hardy 1983, p. 253, n. 26. Hardy's reconstruction of the historical data is interesting: sometime during the 7th century AD or so, in a provincial part of the old Pāṇḍya kingdom, in the town Kurukūr which had, we may assume, only recently acquired a Viṣṇu temple, a local chieftain or dignitary who was still familiar with the old literary tradition of the Tamil literary community (the *caṅkam*) joined the Vaiṣṇava movement and composed numerous poems and songs in Tamil which praise Viṣṇu and promulgate his cult. (41)

13. Despite their secondary and referential role, and their constant reference to Śaṭakōpaṉ of Kurukūr, we cannot definitively dispute the authorship of Śaṭakōpaṉ himself, there are numerous examples of such signature verses in oral poetry in India. See the essays on this point: Kitambi Anantan, "4000 Pirapantaṅkaḷiṉcāṟruppākkaḷ," (*Centamiḻ*, vol. 21 [1922–23], pp. 333–340) who raises some doubts about the attribution of the 11th verses to Śaṭakōpaṉ, and A. Arangaramanujappillai, "Nālāyirappirapantac Cāṟruppākkaḷiṉ ārāycci," (*Centamiḻ*, vol. 21 [1922–23], pp. 429–442) who defends their authenticity. Damodaran refers to the debate, pp. 227–230, somewhat favoring authenticity. The best position is this minimal one: they are distinctive, they are used to fix their preceding songs in order, they neither claim to be by Śaṭakōpaṉ, nor give direct evidence of not being by him; they are "the first commentary on *Tiruvāymoḻi*"—and all of this, even if by Śaṭakōpaṉ himself.

14. In this list we begin to see the variety of names which will be with us throughout this book: Viṣṇu is Kṛṣṇa—Kaṇṇaṉ in Tamil—is Māl, Nārāyaṇa, Keśava, Mātava, etc. The well-known god Brahmā is (in Tamil) either Ayaṉ or the "Four-Faced" one, and Śiva is Araṉ.

15. From his general introduction to *Tiruvāymoḻi*.

16. See also Hardy 1979, 32–3.

17. Or later. There is a continuing dispute over the date and authorship of the *Divyasūricaritam*. In his *History of Sri Vaishnavism in the Tamil Country (Post-Ramanuja)*, pp. 76–81, N. Jagadeesan surveys the arguments for and against attributing the text to a contemporary of Rāmānuja. Admitting that there are serious arguments in favor of a (much) later date for the text, nevertheless he prudently concludes that these arguments are not sufficiently strong to warrant a rejection of the traditional view.

18. For the following summary of the relevant section from the lives of Śaṭakōpaṉ and Maturakavi, I have referred to the edition of the *Prabhāvam* published by Krishnaswami Ayyangar (Trichi, n.d.), pp. 87–101; though there is no translation of the *Prabhāvam*, there are many summaries of it. See Damodaran 21–26, and Narayanan and Carman, 17–18. But Hardy's "The Tamil Veda" is the most useful and important survey of the early accounts of Śaṭakōpaṉ (35–41).

19. *Divyasūricaritam* 45; Hardy's translation, slightly adapted.

20. The *Guruparamparāprabhāvam* gives Maturakavi a more active role. After being taught by Viṣvaksena, Śaṭakōpaṉ remains silent, since he sees no one capable of appreciating his teaching. Things change only when Maturakavi reaches Kurukūr. He finds the boy in meditation; to find out if he is conscious, he throws a pebble in front of him, and Śaṭakōpaṉ opens his eyes. He then wonders if the boy can talk, and asks a riddle: "If a small thing is born in the stomach of a dead thing, what does it eat and where does it lie?" Śaṭakōpaṉ responded laconically, "It eats that, it lies there," but this answer so impressed Maturakavi that he was completely won over by Śaṭakōpaṉ and reverenced him as his teacher.

21. The commentaries are usually denoted by their length as measured in units of 32 syllables known as *paṭis*.

22. Given this factor, throughout I refer to the *Īṭu* as "Nampiḷḷai's commentary," and not as "Vaṭakkutiruvītippiḷḷai's commentary."

23. The Advaita (Nondualist) Vedāntin Śaṅkara (8th century) is probably still the most well-known Vedāntin; his interpretation of the ultimate unity of the

individual self and the cosmic self had to be taken into account by all later Vedāntins, and has been identified as the definitive *Vedānta* position by many modern readers. Yet Śaṅkara is less representative of the wider *Vedānta* consensus than was Rāmānuja (who is often identified as a Viśiṣṭādvaitin, whose Nondualism is "qualified"). Rāmānuja brought to the fore the theistic and devotional elements of *Vedānta,* insisting that the profound unity of self and the highest reality (*brahman,* Lord, God, Viṣṇu) does not preclude the persistence of a real distinction between the divine and the human. Humans exist in and for God, but are not God. Rāmānuja read the Vedānta texts as oriented to the fostering of an overall understanding of the divine-human relationship and of the devotion appropriate to a recognition of the human condition and the need for God.

24. See Annangarachariar 1954 and Narayanan 1987.

25. With adaptation, from Swami Adidevananda's translation of the *Stotraratna* (1979).

26. By way of clarification we can notice how all of this is strikingly different from the tradition of *Vedānta* commentaries on Bādarāyaṇa's *Uttara Mīmāṃsā Sūtras* (including Rāmānuja's) where, in spite of the many commentaries and great reverence for teachers, there is much less repetition, much less irenic and reverential repetition of the masters' words. For the most part the Śrīvaiṣṇava commentaries do not proceed by position and counterposition and by argument—either real or as a pedagogical device—in the way that is common in the *Mīmāṃsā* and *Vedānta* commentaries. Nor are they composed out of the need to defend the text against misinterpretation, nor directly as part of an effort to simplify and organize a large and confusing body of materials, as are the *sūtras* of Jaimini and Bādarāyaṇa in regard to the *Vedas* and *Upaniṣads* respectively. Unlike *Vedānta, Tiruvāymoḻi* did not generate differing schools of commentary until much later—when for instance, Āḻvār Emperumāṉār Cīyar wrote a "northern" (*vaṭakalai*) more Sanskritic commentary on Piḷḷāṉ's first commentary.

27. See Clooney 1993d.

28. For some pertinent remarks on seeing and hearing in the Christian tradition, see Chidester; for a closer analogue that involves yet another tradition, see Elliot Wolfson's brilliant *Through a Speculum that Shines: Vision and Imagination in Medieval Jewish Mysticism.*

29. On these verses see Clooney, 1983.

30. I have not been able to ascertain an explanatory reference for a "Viśvāmitra creation," though the point seems to be that it is an additional, unwanted creation on the part of the great sage Viśvāmitra.

31. Āttāṉcīyar explains that whereas for Rāmānuja, it is the lord's beauty which overwhelms the *āḻvār*, for Bhaṭṭar it is the union with the *āḻvār* which makes the lord beautiful; Ālavantār had made an explicit connection with the previous verse, as this one specifies more about the lord who had been mentioned there; and this is the view that Āṇṭāṉ thought was quite sufficient.

Chapter Two. Getting Inside Tiruvāymoḻi

1. Though, as we shall see in chapter 3, the ācāryas do discover a single narrative unfolding throughout the whole text.

2. For more detail on the literary aspects of the songs, see Cutler, and Damodaran, especially c. 7.

3. In other translations in this volume I have generally not attempted this initial rhyme.

4. I.e., *viṭṭu*, the "pervading," Viṣṇu

5. One might also take a geographical approach, spending time visiting the various holy places mentioned in the songs. Even today Śrīvaiṣṇavas do this, with a vivid sense of the importance of visiting such places, and books and maps are published to facilitate such pious travel. To walk to a temple town, to enjoy the (albeit changed) environs, the shrine, the crowds, to see the lord enshrined in the inner sanctum, to be dazzled by the divine beauty and in turn to be seen: these are holy practices, by which members of the community can enter upon the world of *Tiruvāymoḻi* and the other *āḻvār* works with a certain immediacy—the reality expressed in the songs is for the Śrīvaiṣṇava still real today. Like other holy practices, too, the more one undertakes such visits, the more one's map of the world is recomposed, marked according to the texts: one finds oneself reoriented, placed differently in the world. The range of practices connected with the memorization, recitation and ritualization of *Tiruvāymoḻi* have been described in Narayanan, *The Vernacular Veda*.

6. See also VI.2, IX.9 and X.3, which are in the genre of the dialogue of the cowherd girl with Kaṇṇaṉ.

7. For instance, the few verses we have on the boar (*varāha*)*avatāra*. Some verses merely mention it in a list (I.8.8, I.9.2, V.1.10), or as an epithet of praise

(II.3.5, V.9.6, VI.6.5), occasionally with special emphasis on the *avatāra's* special rescue of the earth goddess (II.8.7, IV.2.6, VII.5.5, X.10.7). One cannot reconstruct the myth from the verses, and in fact very little is told about it in the 10 references to it.

8. All of III.3 and VI.10 are dedicated to Tiruveṅkaṭam; when a few other verses are noted as well, we can note that it is this temple that is praised most by Śaṭakōpan̲.

9. The Śrīvaiṣṇava tradition identifies a total of 10 songs, one in each set of ten songs, as aimed at the instruction of the wider audience.

10. Rewards include: freedom from affliction (I.5.11); abundant learning (I.10.11); good life and prosperity, fame (III.3.11; VI.2.11); lordship (III.10.11, IV.3.11, VI.7.11); ending of troubles (IV.1.11) to be like those whom doe-eyed women love (V.8.11); becoming lovers of lightning-waisted women (VI.1.11); heavenly pleasures (VI.6.11); to be fanned by women (VII.6.11); life on their own land, with good name, their own wives and children (VIII.10.11); to diffuse the fragrance of mallikai flowers (IX.8.11); to reach the bamboo shoulders of the woman (X.2.11) Several songs suggest how the reciters will be pleasing to the gods: IV.2.11, V.7.11. *The ending of deeds*: III.5.11, IV.5.11, VII.1.11, IX.10.11. *The ending of births*: I.3.11, I.6.11, III.1.11, III.7.11, III.9.11, VIII.3.11, VIII.4.11, VIII.7.11, IX.6.11. *Release*: I.1.11, II.9.11, II.8.11, III.2.11. *Vaikuṇṭa*: II.1.11, II.5.11, IV.7.11, IV.8.11, IV.10.11, V.3.11, V.4.11, V.5.11, V.10.11, VIII.6.11, IX.3.11. *Becoming the lord's people*: II.6.11, III.6.11, V.6.11, VI.5.11, VI.9.11, VII.2.11, VII.3.11, VII.8.11, VIII.9.11, IX.1.11, IX.2.11, X.8.11. *Dwelling at the lord's feet*: I.9.11, II.4.11, II.7.13, II.10.11, IV.9.11, V.1.11, VIII.8.11, X.4.11.

11. I.e., Śiva and Brahmā.

12. "Liṅga texts" are those connected with Śiva; the Śākyas are Buddhists.

13. See Narayanan 1994, 127–8, on the ritualized return of Śaṭakōpan̲ to earth at the end of *Tiruvāymoḻi*. On the general literary issues involved, McHale (109–10) has some interesting comments on the postmodern equivalent of *antāti*, whereby some authors have sought to subvert the ending of texts by making these endings the beginnings. Caws (8) has interesting comments on the idea of literary hinges.

14. *Tiruvāymoḻi* is: excellently composed, woven together (I.1.11, I.2.11; I.4.11; I.5.11, IV.1.11), a work of well wrought recitation (VII.4.11), a garland of melodic, unblemished verses (III.2.11, IV.8.11); flawlessly, skillfully uttered, without fault in attention (I.6.11, II.3.11, II.6.11); finely woven (I.7.11); sung with the foremost melody (II.8.11), to bring about understanding (II.10.11); sung intelligently (VI.9.11), more beautifully than the flute (V.8.11).

15. The 11th verses tend to privilege Kaṇṇaṉ as the focus of various songs, even when this is not expected based on the content of the songs. Thus, in I.10, there are several references to Vāmana (vss. 1, 5), and to the Lord at Kuruṅkuṭi, but the 11th verse favors Kaṇṇaṉ: "Kaṇṇaṉ the jewel, Kaṇṇaṉ of the heaven-dwellers, adorning even Himself;" II.6 refers to Rāma (vs. 9) and *narasiṃha* (vs. 6) and to the Lord "before" *avatāra* (on his snake bed, vs. 5), but the 11th verse praises Kaṇṇaṉ; II.7 gives the 12 names of the Lord, but in the 13th verse these names are described as "12 names in these twelve of the thousand about the tall Lord, Kaṇṇaṉ." In VII.4 and VII.5 are particularly striking, several *avatāras* are mentioned before preference is given to Kaṇṇaṉ. In VII.4, references to *varāha* (3), Kaṇṇaṉ (5), Rāma (7) and Kaṇṇaṉ (5,8,10) are summarized by a single reference to Kaṇṇaṉ: "Śaṭakōpaṉ who lives as one with the devotees of the Lord who lifted the mountain." VII.5 refers to Rāma (1), *varāha* (5), *vāmana* (6), *narasiṃha* (8), as well as Kaṇṇaṉ (3,7,9), but the 11th verse focuses on Kaṇṇaṉ: "this ten from the thousand . . . about Kaṇṇaṉ . . ." But here, verse 6 gives the model, in referring to Keśava who "danced marvelously as Vāmana . . ." See also these 11th verses where Kaṇṇāṉ is singled out for special mention: I.4.11, I.10.11, II.2.11, II.6.11, II.7.13, III.7.11, III.9.11, IV.3.11, IV.8.11, V.3.11. Some of the other references to forms of Viṣṇu are apparently unwarranted by the verses, and it is hard to see the reason why they are introduced: e.g., "the lord who leapt the earth," [III.3.11]; "the lord of Tiruveṅkaṭam . . .," [IV.5.11]; "the lord who took three strides . . .," [V.7.11]; "the dwarf who wore the lightning thread . . .," [VI.1.11]; "the lord of good Tiruveṅkaṭam," [VI.6.11]; "the great father, Brahmā the father, Rudra the father, father right for the sages, father of the immortals, the unique, peerless father of the world," [VIII.1.11]; "holy Māl, who is Brahmā, and Śiva and the Lord," [VIII.8.11]. Here too, the point is not that the references are inappropriate or merely extrinsic—for once one begins to look for significance, one may find it, and find that it is indeed there—but that there is no prima facie continuity with the song in theme or style, and that the verses must be considered "later," at least as a second level of reflection.

16. For a fuller analysis of this song, see Clooney forthcoming b.

17. It is not possible here to elaborate a theory of reading, and the pertinent literature on this topic is already abundant. See for instance Iser 1978.

18. Cf. I.5.10, IV.4.4, IV.4.7, IV.8.3, V.8.1, VI.5.10, VI.6.7, VI.9.8, VI.10.1, VIII.9.11, VIII.10.1, IX.8.2, X.5.10, 11.

19. II.7.13, VI.1.4,9, VII.10.7, VIII.2.3.

20. They are all the more frequent if we include references imbedded in terms such as "devotee:" "I-who-am-at-your-feet (*aṭiyeṉ*).

21. See pp. 75–7 above.

22. Pertinent here are Iser's comments on the notion of textual ecstasy and the escape from self which occurs through the fictive shifts that occur in reading. See Iser 1993, pp. 77–8, 303.

23. Thus also Hardy 1983. In both my explanation and his, however, it is important to admit the constructive nature of our judgments about what is central to this text which is never committed to any such position.

Chapter Three. Tiruvāymoḻi *as Meditation, Narrative and Drama: Reading with the* Ācāryas

1. Throughout, I refer to the introductory comments of an *ācārya* on a song—before a first verse is cited—with the "0"; thus, "*Īṭu* I.4.0" refers to Naṃpiḷḷai's introductory comment on song I.4.

2. A comprehensive, diachronic study of the commentaries would provide us with a great deal of evidence regarding the development of this interpretive framework although, even with the recording of memories of earlier oral commentaries in the *Īṭu* (see below, chapter 4), the earlier stages of interpretation will receive only the most fragmentary documentation.

3. See Venkatachari 1978.

4. At I.3.2 Naṃpiḷḷai reviews the end of I.3.1, where the *āḻvār* cried in amazement, "He is accessible to those who love him—what is this!" Naṃpiḷḷai says: "It is well known that after saying 'What is this!' (I.3.1) the *āḻvār* was in a trance for six months. Maturakavi and the rest of his people were there surrounding him, like birds on a fruit-laden tree. It was just like when Lord Guha was dumbstruck at seeing the place where the Lord and Lady [Rāma and Sītā] rested; as it says, 'The good people in Kurukūr' (*Tiruviruttam* 100). They lay there surrounding him like birds gathered on a fruit-laden tree. When he returned to consciousness, he immediately asked, 'What was I saying?' They replied, 'You were explaining "he is accessible to those who love him;" and you cried "what is this!" and went into a trance.' The *āḻvār* thought, 'We were mistaken, we must speak more cryptically'—and this he does in the [toned down] second verse (I.3.2). What's all this about? In the first verse he had his own experience before teaching others; but from the second verse on he simply teaches others." The second episode has already been cited in chapter 1: words in I.10.8—"When I hear someone say, 'Nārāyaṇa our Treasure,' tears

well up, I search for him . . ."—prompts Naṃpiḷḷai to recall how the *āḻvār* sought to find a place where God's name was not invoked.

5. For example, Viṣṇu along with Śiva and Brahmā.

6. This portrayal of the *āḻvār's* anguish (*ārti*) occasions the later designation of Śaṭakōpaṉ as one of the two kinds of persons who surrender completely to God. In his *Prapanna Pārijāta*, Naṭātūr Āmmāḷ puts it this way. Śaṭakōpaṉ, wracked by his *ārti*, would not be a *dṛpta*, "whose misery is in taking another body . . . the *dṛpta*'s contentment arises not out of any physical happiness, which he discards, but out of realizing the working of His will in everything; so a *dṛpta* is not dissatisfied with this body because it is given by God, and is ever ready to do the duties of this life, but longs for the union with God after death." (2.26). Rather, he belongs in the second category; he is an *ārta*; he "grieves even at this body, which is the result of his past Karmas . . . An *ārta*'s misery is not out of any physical suffering which is nothing to him. He feels miserable even at a moment's separation from God; and consequently grieves at this body which keeps him away from the divine union." [ibid.] This misery at one's present experience of the body is precisely what Śaṭakōpaṉ experiences. See also Venkatachari, 131–2.

7. The first introduction to the whole of *Tiruvāymoḻi*, for Piḷḷāṉ wrote none. For fuller expositions of Nañcīyar's introduction, see Hardy 1979, Thiruvengadathan, and Clooney 1992.

8. Lakṣmaṇa, the younger brother of Rāma in the epic *Rāmāyaṇa*, was totally devoted to his brother. See section IV of chapter IV.

9. Prahlāda is the quintessential devotee in the purāṇic Vaiṣṇava tradition.

10. Pp. 57–9.

11. Ibid., 59.

12. Ibid. The account has it that Vālmīki, who had not been a poet, was so distressed at the sight of a hunter killing one of a pair of love birds, that he spontaneously burst into fine verse in order to scold the hunter.

13. Like Arjuna in chapter XI of the *Bhagavad Gītā*, Śaṭakōpaṉ is given the gift of special insight; so too, the Buddha had "a divine eye."

14. Pp. 60–1.

15. The apparent simultaneity of voices is rationalized and distinguished in the *Ācārya Hṛdayam*, which holds that the *āḻvār* speaks in two voices: as the woman, he speaks of love, as a man, he speaks of knowledge.

16. Thibaut 162. Throughout, all excerpts from the *Śrībhāṣya* are from Thibaut's translation, with some slight modifications.

17. There is an interesting parallel discussion in Vedānta Deśika's interpretation of the constraints on perception, in his *Seśvara Mīmāṃsā,* at *Pūrva Mīmāṃsā Sūtra* I.1.4.

18. On this debate, see Clooney, "Hearing and Seeing in Early Vedānta." On the general Advaita position on texts, knowledge and truth, see Clooney 1993, Chapter 3.

19. Thibaut 14.

20. The answer seems to lie in the commentaries on *Tiruvāymoḻi;* see the section on *uruveḷippāṭu* ("visualization") below. In general, see Lester, Chapter 1.

21. We think here of the famous chapter VI.7 of the *Viṣṇu Purāṇa,* which describes in great detail meditation on the imperceptible forms of Viṣṇu and on his visible form. See also Clooney 1988.

22. Thibaut 15.

23. Thibaut 15.

24. Thibaut 15–16.

25. In I.1.4 Rāmānuja restates the basic point: *meditation, informed by a knowledge of the scriptural texts* [i.e., neither mere meditation nor mere textual knowledge], gives the required knowledge of Brahman: "Meditation which consists of uninterrupted remembrance of a thing cognized, the cognition of the sense of texts, moreover, forms an indispensible prerequisite; for knowledge of Brahman—the object of meditation—cannot originate from any other source . . . Through the injunction of meditation the mind is cleared, and a clear mind gives rise to direct knowledge of Brahman . . ." [Thibaut 185, 188] In response to Mīmāṃsā skepticism regarding this meditation as textually based, Rāmānuja reaffirms that meditation on the text is the basis for a knowledge of *Brahman* that is not ultimately dualistic. These themes recur without much variation at several later points in the text: I.2.23, III.4.26, IV.1.3, 7–8. Except for insisting on the steps recounted in the *Bṛhadāraṇyaka* text—hearing, reflection, meditation and, finally vision—and except for some references to the yogic process, Rāmānuja does not specify the steps of meditation in the *Śrībhāṣya.*

26. As amplified slightly by the later commentator Rāmānujacīyar.

27. By messengers, by the literary and romantic conceit of addressing various birds and asking them to intervene with the distant Lord.

28. Śiṣupāla was an enemy of Kṛṣṇa; he was near to Kṛṣṇa in time and space but could not recognize who Kṛṣṇa really was.

29. On visualization, see below, pp. 138–41.

30. At IV.4.10, VIII.1.1; at the introduction to III.6, and more generally in regard to V.5 and VII.7.

31. Āttāṉcīyar notes that *uruveḷippāṭu* can be motivated by fear, as in *Āraṇya Kāṇḍa* 39.15 (where Maricha imagines Rāma, his enemy, in every tree in the forest), or (as here) out of mixed feelings of joy and sorrow, or (as at VII.7) out of pain.

32. Throughout this book, all translations from the *Rāmāyaṇa* are from *Śrīmad Vālmīki-Rāmāyaṇa* (Gorakhpur: Gita Press, 1992).

33. Two other commentators make notable observations in introducing the song. In his general introduction to VII.7, Periyavāccāṉpiḷḷai adds this to our understanding of the term: "When one desires more clarity without disturbing previous clarity—that is visualization." Vātikesari Aḻakiya Maṇavāḷa Cīyar vividly contextualizes visualization in this way: "[Though the *āḻvār* meditates on the Lord's beauty in its many details] this does not culminate in union, and he is very much afflicted. He demonstrates what he is experiencing to his friends and relatives who are themselves depressed when they see his affliction; he does this by means of these verses in which the young woman expresses her suffering to her friend and to her mother, when she is distressed because she cannot get to experience close-up what she has experienced of the features of her beloved Kṛṣṇa as these appear in visualization during her separation from him."

34. See also III.6.1, IV.4.10, VIII.1.1, and Clooney forthcoming a.

35. For the distinction between *bhakti* and *prapatti*, see Chapter 4.

36. See also the *Ītu* on II.3.7 and II.9.2.

37. Pp. 65–6.

38. Naṃpiḷḷai too observes how the *āḻvār* thinks the Lord is laughing at him: "'The fact that his people [in heaven] are now watching must be the cause for his banishing us; and that noise in heaven—that's the people there laughing at our suffering. His glorious place of play—this is our prison.' Deciding that the

Lord has done this to make us suffer like those who are not subject to his grace—'who graciously gives the good of mind which removes confusion' (I.1.1)—the *āḻvār* puts his head at the Lord's feet, and lies there, crying out in such a way that those who hear, melt." (VII.1.0)

39. See VIII.4.6, "I have seen Him at the holy stream of Ceṅkuṉṟūr, with its mighty, solid houses, with 3000 residents of captivating excellence."

40. See Clooney 1983.

41. See chapter 4 for further comment on the importance of this citation.

Chapter Four. Five Ways to Think about Tiruvāymoḻi*: Following the Ācāryas' Practical Response*

1. In examining these strategies, I again limit myself to primary features of what we can learn from the commentaries themselves; I am leaving aside several very important practical uses of the text, including recitation and pilgrimage. Recitation has been amply described by Narayanan in *The Vernacular Veda,* and nothing need be added here. As for pilgrimage, I repeat the observation made at the beginning of chapter 3, that even today Śrīvaiṣṇavas have a vivid sense of the importance of visiting the holy places (*divya deśa*) praised in the works of the *āḻvārs.* One puts into practice what one hears by going here and there: to walk to a temple, to enjoy the town, the shrine, the crowds, to see the Lord enshrined in the inner sanctum, to be dazzled by the divine beauty and in turn to be seen. That is, of course, the point of the song with which we began this book, VI.5, which regarded what occurred at Tirutolaivillimaṅkaḷam.

2. Throughout this chapter I use the form "*Aum*" instead of the more familiar "*Om*," since the *ācāryas* frequently gloss three letters a, u, m, individually.

3. On the mantras in general, see the introduction to Mumme's 1987 translation of the *Mumukṣuppati,* and also Reddiar. It is clear from both Mumme and Reddiar that we do not have much evidence about these mantras from the period before the *Īṭu,* excepting Bhaṭṭar's *Aṣṭaślokī,* which Mumme rightly observes to be "very cryptic," and "impossible to translate without a knowledge of the *rahasya* commentatorial tradition"—from the generations after Naṃpiḷḷai. (12) Among such helpful works, the general reader can look most helpfully at the translations, by Mumme and Rajagopala Ayyangar respectively, of the *Mumukṣuppati* and of the *Śrīmadrahasyatrayasāra* (especially chapter 27). Closer at hand, we find in the *Īṭu* anecdotes which testify to the

esteem in which the mantras were held as expressions of the very essence of vital Vaiṣṇava faith. For example, learning the mantras was a privileged moment, available selectively, and only to those who were thought ready for it. We learn how Bhaṭṭar and Śrīrāmapiḷḷai came to learn the Tirumantra: "*The good that grows beyond reckoning, the radiant, the unceasing shining praise, Nārāyaṇa: attach yourself to his steadfast feet.* (I.2.10) By this verse the *āḻvār* expresses the [Tiru]mantra and its meaning. When Āḻvāṉ got to teaching this verse, he said, 'Let each of you hear it from his own teacher . . .' But when Bhaṭṭar and Śrīrāmapiḷḷai got up to go, he called them back, saying, 'We do not know who will live and who will die; stay, hear [the mantra here and now.]' He taught them the mantra, explaining it, saying, 'This verse gives the meaning of the mantra.' " (I.2.10) A generation later, when Bhaṭṭar had become the teacher, he was the one to decide with whom he would or would not share the Dvaya: "One day, Bhaṭṭar graciously decided to teach the Dvaya to Piḷḷai Aḻakiyamaṇavāḷa Aṟaiyar, so he announced, 'Let everyone else leave.' Nañcīyar too got up and left, saying angrily, 'He did not say to me, 'You stay.' ' But Bhaṭṭar then asked, 'Where is Cīyar?' He searched and called for him, and had him brought near; and only then did Bhaṭṭar graciously teach the mantra. Nañcīyar himself recounts this." (VI.10.10) Despite the deep reverence and even secrecy that surrounds the mantras, however, there is a democratizing tendency in the mantra tradition, and the secret is for everyone: "[The *āḻvār* says,] 'Give him the message I composed for you and made you learn:' when the heart is perishing, she teaches things that will help her endure. Just so, in a continuous tradition our predecessors have helped people learn the Dvaya without distinguishing 'Small people, great people.' (VI.8.6)" So too, we recall here the famous anecdote about Rāmānuja: how, on an 18th visit, he finally succeeded in persuading Tirukoṭṭiyūr Nampi to teach him the Tirumantra, and how, after hearing his teacher's solemn warning that he not reveal the mantra to anyone, he went up in the temple gopuram and shouted out the mantra for all to hear. For a brief account of this incident, see John Carman, *Theology of Rāmānuja,* p. 39–40.

4. Although the name "Tirumantra" is not used, it is only with reference to the mantra that the otherwise uncalled-for introduction of the "*Aum*" in Periyavāccāṉpiḷḷai's comment on V.9.1 makes sense: "*this servant at the feet of the king—king* is the meaning of the word *Nārāyaṇa; this servant* is the meaning of *Aum.* The āḻvār's condition of being totally dependent is constant, whether in the state of the girl or his own proper state."

5. See Clooney 1991.

6. As noted in chapter 1, he is the author of the "12,000-unit commentary."

7. See Mumme, 1987.

8. On the uses of creeds in a comparative context, see Christian.

9. For an introduction to the *Ācārya Hṛdayam*, see Damodaran 1976.

10. See Venkatachari: 43–4, 61; his Sanskrit name is Andhrapūrṇa, and he is also author of *Yatirājavaibhava*.

11. See Venkatachari, 129–133 on the *Arthapañcakam*, Piḷḷailōkācārya's later and more developed treatise on these five features of the way to salvation. It is not surprising, of course, that Periyavaṅkippurattunampi's early, pioneering version does not formally present itself as a treatment of the five features.

12. I take the treatment of these themes to be an introductory portion of Periyavaṅkippurattunampi's text (First Introduction, 168–175).

13. *Pakavat Viṣayam*, vol. 1, 1975, pp. 175–6.

14. Ibid., 177.

15. Ibid., 178–9.

16. Ibid., 179–80.

17. Ibid., 180–1.

18. Ibid., 181–2.

19. Ibid., 182–3.

20. Ibid., 184–6.

21. Ibid., 186–8.

22. Ibid., 188–90.

23. Ibid., 190.

24. Ibid., 191.

25. The necessary theological clarifications and refinements which appear in writing only later on are necessarily beyond the scope of our consideration. In the generations after the *Īṭu*, *ācāryas* spell out and refine in great detail the distinction between *bhakti* and *prapatti*, supporting this distinction with many scriptural citations and rational arguments. While we must assume that these systematizations were taking form even while our commentaries were being composed—we have seen reference to the distinction in Periyavaṅkippurattunampi's incipient systematization of the theology of *Tiruvāymoḻi*—

and precisely in relation to them, it is also quite clear that there is no systematic presentation of *bhakti* and *prapatti* in the commentaries, where theology still stands at the service of exegesis. Nevertheless, in the course of explicating the meaning of the songs the *ācāryas* refer to *bhakti* and *prapatti* frequently.

26. The *Tiruvāymoḻivācakamālai* of Tirukkōneri Dāsyai is a commentary, probably from several generations after the *Īṭu,* which has as its operative rule the task of showing how each song of *Tiruvāymoḻi* is in some way illustrative of the first verse.

27. See below, in section five, the multiple interpretations of this verse.

28. Naṃpiḷḷai observes that it must be certain for the *ācāryas* that the *āḻvār* himself opts for *prapatti;* reliance on the lord makes very swift and very easy an otherwise arduous process: "Already in I.1 the *āḻvār's* acquisition was knowledge in the form of devotion; but he could not simply present his acquisition to others all at once, so he proceeds slowly [gradually unfolding this distinction]: superior devotion originates gradually in the inner mind purified by ritual action and meditative knowledge . . . But when the Lord's grace takes the place of that knowledge and action, superior devotion grows up at once." To the related question of whether or not Śaṭakōpaṉ's *bhakti* could be that orthodox devotion which is arduous, based on ritual action and meditative knowledge, requiring years of preparation, etc., Naṃpiḷḷai responds in the negative. He says that the *āḻvār's* own *bhakti* is due only to the lord's grace; for were it orthodox *bhakti,* it would be the kind available only to those males in the three highest classes who are able to undertake the requisite ritual action and meditative knowledge—and hence would be unavailable to Śaṭakōpaṉ, who is of the fourth class.

29. The reason for the inclusion of devotion among the things the *āḻvār* does not have—even though V.7.1 does not mention devotion—is perhaps best understood by way of attention to a citation. Naṃpiḷḷai explains the inadequacy of "ascetic deeds" and "subtle knowledge" with the help of verse 22 from the *Stotraratna* by Āḷavantār, one of Rāmānuja's greatest predecessors; the second line is a kind of extension of Śaṭakōpaṉ's line just cited: "I am not established in dharma, nor do I know the Self, nor do I have devotion for your lotus feet; without anything, with nowhere else to go, my refuge, I take refuge at your feet." (*Stotraratna* 22) What is most striking is that, seemingly with Āḷavantār's verse in mind—which evidently echoes VI.10.10 too—the *ācāryas* see V.7.1 as ruling out orthodox *bhakti*—"devotion for your lotus feet"—though it mentions only "ascetic deeds" and "subtle knowledge." Theological and exegetical expectations take the lead in finding a right meaning for the

verse; Āḷavantār's words—"nor do I have devotion for your lotus feet"—are understood as implied by the *āḻvār:* if there is neither ritual action nor knowledge, how then could there be that devotion which follows upon them? In making these points, though, Naṃpiḷḷai also admits one obvious objection: isn't it quite clear that the *āḻvār does* have devotion, *bhakti*? He responds that in the *āḻvār's* case his evident devotion is a gift of grace alone and not the religiously and culturally determined devotion that *bhakti* had come to signify: "Yes, he has 'devotion as meditation on something, preceded by love.' Isn't that a means then? No. That superior devotion which arises in an inner self prepared by ritual action and meditative knowledge is talked about in the scriptures as a means—and [the *āḻvār's*] devotion cannot be of that sort. For his devotion (*prapatti*) comes about solely by the Lord's favor, and it constitutes his very nature. The other devotion (*bhakti*) is the kind talked about in the ancient *Purāṇas*, where actions and knowledge are discussed as means; but that is different from his devotion."

30. Pp. 432–3.

31. P. 483.

32. P. 485.

33. P. 486–7. The quotation, cited also at X.4, is unidentified.

34. The postlude after the third explanation of VI.10.10 offers of vivid parallel which highlights the necessity and value of surrender. Naṃpiḷḷai recounts the conversation that ensued between Sītā and and the monkey Hanumān, when the latter offered to tear apart the demonesses who have been guarding and tormenting her. Naṃpiḷḷai recalls how Sītā argued for compassion, rebuked Hanumān for acting like a brute monkey, and pointed out that everyone is is need of forgiveness, herself and Rāma included. It may strike us as odd to have the commentary on VI.10.10 come to an end with this exchange, but this sense of human imperfection and divine mercy can be recognized as the most precious fruit of the *ācāryas'* reading of the song: life is misery; all are guilty; surrender is necessary; mercy is certain; Śrī Lakṣmī stands with those who surrender. By recounting this dialogue, Naṃpiḷḷai constructs a vivid and accessible counterpart for Śaṭakōpaṉ's verse VI.10.10, a place next to the verse where the audience can imagine itself—if not like the *āḻvār*—at least as sinners who can become part of this drama and receive forgiveness.

35. According to the Sanskrit *Rāmāyaṇa* of Vālmīki, which the *ācāryas* use.

36. This narrative is, of course, open to many developments in many contexts, and the *Rāmāyaṇa* has flourished richly in almost every part of the wider India. See *Many Rāmāyaṇas*.

37. In the tradition, most important is Periyavāccāṉpiḷḷai's *Taniślōkam* and the modern work, the *Rāmāyaṇasaurabham*. For the *ācāryas*, the *Rāmāyaṇa* was particularly communicative of "the power and salvific importance" of Śrī [Sītā] as mediator; the text perfectly exemplified their teachings on surrender to the lord—and thus finely calibrated the proper behavior of the members of the community in the various situations in which she or he might stand in relation to the Lord. In her essay "*Rāmāyaṇa* Exegesis in Teṉkalai Śrīvaiṣṇavism," [in Richman, pp. 202–216), Patricia Mumme has helped us to understand the use of the *Rāmāyaṇa* in the post-commentarial works of generations just after those we have been considering, and particularly the refined usage in those subsequent generations of the image of Sītā to illuminate the role of Śrī: "Sītā, who is the incarnation of the Goddess Śrī, has a dual importance for the Teṉkalai school. First, as the Lord's beloved wife and mother of all souls, she is the merciful mediator (*puruṣakāra*) between the soul in need of salvation and the omnipotent Lord . . . Sītā is also a separate soul (*cetana* or *jīva*) like us, dependent and perfectly submissive to the Lord, who is her master and protector. As such, Sītā in the *Rāmāyaṇa* exemplifies the ideal relationship between the soul and the Lord, and Rāma's rescue of Sītā from Laṅkā can be seen as an allegory for the process of salvation. Just as Rāma rescued Sītā from Laṅkā and brought her back to Ayodhyā to attend him, the Lord rescues the soul from the throes of *saṃsāra* and takes it after death to Vaikuṇṭha, Viṣṇu's heavenly abode, where the soul can fully realize its subservient nature by serving the Lord directly." (205) More briefly, Mumme also explores how other incidents from the *Rāmāyaṇa* are used, again for the sake of calibrating various qualities of more or less total surrender.

38. Verses 1–6 are quoted in chapter 2, p. 65.

39. *Sundara Kāṇḍa* 14.28.

40. *Ayodhyā Kāṇḍa* 53.4.

41. *Yuddha Kāṇḍa* 5.10, 6.

42. *Sundara Kāṇḍa* 34.16.

43. *Bāla Kāṇḍa* 4.7.

44. *The Saṃṣkepa* ["Summary"] *Rāmāyaṇa* 31.

45. *Sundara Kāṇḍa* 15.52.

46. *Sundara Kāṇḍa* 40.13.

47. *Kiṣkindhā Kāṇḍa*.

48. In light of the extended citation given above, it makes sense to think of Rāma as the one isolated and cut off from the one he seeks; of course, the

same dynamic could be expressed by showing how Sītā suffers in separation from Rāma.

49. See also IX.1.0, and references to VIII.10.

50. This is my impression based on my record of *Rāmāyaṇa* citations in the *Īṭu.*

51. Nañcīyar's introduction, p. 57.

52. Ibid.

53. P. 135.

54. Pp. 136, 138.

55. Nañcīyar occasionally praises the *ālvār* in even bolder words (so boldly, in the first case, that it is one of the few passages in Nañcīyar's commentary that is not repeated in the first Introduction to the *Īṭu*): "He possessed so great a glory that no equal could ever be seen to his total service of the Lord: neither the Lady [Sītā] nor Lakṣmaṇa nor Bharata were even close to him in this." [57–58] At II.1, Nañcīyar again gives the *ālvār* clear precedence over Lakṣmaṇa, due to the wideness of the *ālvār's* sadness and compassion: "Unlike Sītā and Lakṣmaṇa who in the time of their separation from Rāma [at *Ayodhyā Kāṇḍa* 103] speak of how they cannot bear it and use the example of the fish separated from water, instead she [the girl, Śaṭakōpaṉ] realizes how all beings in the whole world, though they are intent on other things, are in fact like herself, grieving in separation from the Lord; by reflection on their grief she grieves doubly."

56. Only the words, "Tightly pressing the feet of Rāma his brother" are actually cited. Or, as Periyavāccāṉpiḷḷai puts it in his *Taṉiclōkam,* " When Rāma graciously tells Lakṣmaṇa, 'Stay here, be a support to Bharata,' still Lakṣmaṇa has a desire to serve, even going with [Rāma] into the woods; so Rāma's words are unbearable. So Lakṣmaṇa enters refuge at the Lord's feet in front of the Lady [Sītā], saying, 'I must go with you.' "

57. Other texts too are likewise cited repeatedly: e.g., the protestations of Rāma and Sītā as to their inability to survive without one another; the several ways in which Bharata and Śatrughan too serve the lord; the surrender of Vibhīṣaṇa as a former enemy become devotee; as we have seen, the salvation of Kāka and the destruction of Rāvana because the former takes refuge at the lord's feet while the latter does not; the sentiments of the sages in the forest.

58. I.2.6, II.3.3, II.9.9, III.3.0, IV.7.8, IV.8.2, IV.9.10, V.8.7, VIII.2.11, VIII.3.7, IX.6.9, IX.8.2, X.2.3, X.6.1.

59. See also III.3.8; cf. IV.3.7 and IV.8.2.

60. The best available analysis of the role of audience in relation to *Tiruvāymoḻi* and other *bhakti* texts can be found in Cutler, pp.19–77.

61. I am indebted here to Satyamurthi Ayyangar's gloss, which clearly distinguishes the three interpretations.

62. At the same verse, Śrīrāmappiḷḷai is remembered as reminiscing with Bhaṭṭar about how the two of them were filled with joy when they heard Empār explain the words "her inner life has been chilled."

63. At V.7.7 Bhaṭṭar is cited as using the same analogy with more or less the same point.

64. Other anecdotes too stress equality; see III.7.10 and IV.8.2 regarding class, and, as mentioned above, see VI.8.6 regarding the "great" and "small" in society.

65. Yearley's observations (Yearley, c. 1) on practical reason and its role in understanding virtue are pertinent.

Chapter Five. Seeing through Texts: Some Marginal Insights Presented in Reflections

1. I have touched on relevant background issues in *Theology after Vedānta*. Without introducing that analysis here, I repeat the major point: when we read, we bring our prior reading, what we have read and how it has taught us to read, to what we read now; and we learn to anticipate differently too. I read *Tiruvāymoḻi* according to everything I have read previously. Likewise, what we have been reading lately reshapes our way of reading even when we return to our home tradition after studying someone else's texts: because I have read *Tiruvāymoḻi*, my reading of the Biblical and Christian traditions has changed. The dynamics of mutual influence are operative either in an explicit fashion, replete with footnotes and bibliography or simply through an implicit refining of one's expectations, a subtle shift in one's tastes.

2. On "collage" as a strategy in comparative theology, see Clooney, 1993d, 173–4.

3. Iser, 233–4.

4. Iser, pp. 227–8.

5. Translations from the *Song* are those of Pope.

6. See Murphy, Pope.

7. For a useful and vivid survey of a range of medieval uses of the *Song*, see Astell.

8. Smith, 30–1.

9. See Mariaselvam 1988.

10. The Bellarmine Lecture at Fairfield University, October 23, 1991.

11. *The Journey of the Mind to God*, translation by Philotheus Boehner, OFM; ed. by Stephen F. Brown (Hackett Publishing Company, Indianapolis, 1993): pp.1–2.

12. These quoted subtitles are according to the Boehner/Brown translation.

13. Ibid. 37.

14. Ibid. 37–8.

15. Ibid. 39.

16. Ibid. 38–9.

17. Ibid. 38.

18. These *Spiritual Exercises* also has played a role in my own background, since it is the basic text of the Society of Jesus, and the text which all Jesuits use on innumerable occasions—to read, to study, and most importantly to have on hand as one practices meditation and helps others to meditate. On the *Exercises* and their role in the early Society of Jesus, see O'Malley, especially 37–50. Translations from the *Exercises* are those of Puhl.

19. See Begheyn.

20. But for a rather strong (if brief) critique of Barthes' reading (and Barthes' interest in writing), see de Nicolas, 65–6.

21. Barthes, 60–1

22. Barthes 62–3.

23. Ibid., 68.

24. O'Donnell, 8. See also Oakes 1994.

25. *Prayer* 93–4.

26. Ibid., 251–2.

27. Ibid., 17–18.

28. *Prayer* 267.

29. The *Mīmāṃsā* text is the comment of Śabara at *Pūrva Mīmāṃsā Sūtras* I.1.30. I have used the translation by Jha (1973).

30. See Clooney 1985 on the original and positive view of authorship proposed by the Śrīvaiṣṇava *ācāryas*.

31. As translated by Deussen, p. 205.

32. And, as noted in chapter 1, Wolfson's *Through a Speculum that Shrines* suggests quite striking parallels with the Jewish mystical tradition.

33. On the issues connected to the formation of community from the comparative context, see Clooney 1992.

34. Gilman argues in favor of the power of narratives to draw in listeners, to make a tradition intelligible, yet without sacrificing concreteness: "Insofar as these narratives interpret human experiences, they interpret emotional judgments (how the world is) and projects (how the world ought to be) of a community." (228)

35. For a nuanced set of presentations of pluralism, see Hick and Knitter; for critiques of the same, see D'Costa.

36. See Clooney 1992.

37. See chapter 2, pp. 74–5.

38. See Iser 77–8, 303.

Selected Bibliography

Editions of Tiruvāymoḻi *with Its Commentaries (Pagavat Viṣayam)*

S. Krishnamachariyar, ed. 1924–30. *Pakavat Viṣayam.* 10 vols. Madras: Nobel Press.

Krishnaswami Ayyangar, ed. 1975. *Pakavat Viṣayam,* vol. 1 [*Tiruvāymoḻi* I.1–2]. Trichi: Books Propagation Society.

Krishnaswami Ayyangar, ed. 1977–87. *Pakavat Viṣayam,* vols 2–4 [*Tiruvāymoḻi* I.3–III]. Trichi: Srinivasam Press.

Purushottama Naidu, B.R. 1951–59. *Tiruvāymoḻi Īṭiṉ Tamiḻ Ākkam.* 10 vols. Madras: University of Madras.

Translations of Tiruvāymoḻi

Clooney, Francis X., tr. 1992. *Tiruvāymoḻi.* Manuscript.

Ramanujan, A.K. 1983. *Hymns for the Drowning.* Princeton: Princeton University Press.

Satyamurthi Ayyangar. 1981. *Tiruvāymoḻi.* English Glossary. Bombay: Ananthacharya Indological Research Institute. 3 volumes.

Srirama Bharati and Sowbhagya Lakshmi. 1987. *The Tiruvāymoḻi of Nammāḻvār rendered in English.* Melcote: Tyaga Bharati Music Education Mission.

Other Primary Texts and Translations

Āḷavantar. 1979. *Stotraratna*: Tr. Swami Adidevananda. Madras: Sri Ramakrishna Math.

Deussen, Paul. 1987. *Sixty Upanisads of the Veda*. Translated by V. M. Bedekar and G.B. Pasule. New Delhi: Motilal Banarsidass.

Jha, Ganganatha, tr. 1973. *Śābara-Bhāṣya*. 3 volumes. Baroda: Oriental Institute.

Garuḍa Vāhana Paṇḍita. 1978. *Divyasūricaritam*. Ed. by T.A. Sampath Kumaracharya and K.K.A. Venkatachari. Bombay: Ananthacharya Reseach Institute.

Mumme, Patricia, tr. 1987. *The Mumukṣuppaṭi of Piḷḷai Lokācārya with Maṇavāḷamāmuni's Commentary*. Bombay: Ananthacharya Indological Research Institute.

Naṭātūr Āmmāḷ. 1971. *Prapanna Pārijāta*. English translation. Madras: Visistadvaita Pracharini Sabha.

Piṉpaḻakīya Perumāḷ Jīyar. 1975. *Guruparaṃparāprabhāvam*. Krishnaswami Ayyangar, ed. Trichi: Puttur Agraharam.

Rāmānuja. 1970. *Saranaagati Gadya with English translation of the text and its commentary by Srutaprakaasika Acharya*. Tr. K. Bhasyam. Madras: Visishtadvaita Pracharini Sabha.

_____. 1976. *The Vedānta Sūtras with the Commentary of Rāmānuja*. Tr. Thibaut, G. The Sacred Books of the East, vol. 48. Delhi: Motilal Banarsidass.

Vālmīki. 1992. *Śrīmad Vālmīki-Rāmāyaṇa*. Text and translation. Gorakhpur: Gita Press.

Vedānta Deśika. N.d. *Śrīmadrahasyatrayasāra*. Tr. M.R. Rajagopala Ayyangar. Kumbakonam.

Other Primary Sources

The Holy Bible, Revised Standard Version, 1973. New York: World Bible Publishers.

Bonaventure. 1993. *The Journey of the Mind to God*, tr. Philotheus Boehner, OFM; ed. by Stephen F. Brown. Indianapolis: Hackett Publishing Company.

Loyola, Ignatius. 1957. *The Spiritual Exercises.* Tr. by Louis J. Puhl, S.J. Westminster, MD: The Newman Press.

Pope, Marvin. 1977. *The Song of Songs: a new translation with introduction and commentary.* Anchor Bible Series. Garden City: Doubleday.

von Balthasar, Hans Urs. 1986. *Prayer.* San Francisco: Ignatius Press.

Secondary Sources Related to Tiruvāymoḻi *and Its Commentaries*

Annangachariar, P. B. 1954. *Tramiṭōpaniṣatprapāvasarvasvam.* Kumbakonam: Sri Ramanuja Press.

Anantan, Kitambi. "4000 Pirapantaṅkaḷiṉcāṟṟuppākkaḷ," *Centamiḻ*, vol. 21 [1922–23], pp. 333–340.

Arangaramanujappillai, A. "Nālāyirappirapantac Cāṟṟuppākkaḷiṉ ārāycci," *Centamiḻ*, vol. 21 [1922–23], pp. 429–442.

Carman, John B., and Narayanan, Vasudha. 1989. *The Tamil Veda: Piḷḷāṉ's Interpretation of the Tiruvāymoḻi.* Chicago: University of Chicago Press.

Clooney, Francis X. 1983. "Unity in Enjoyment: An Exploration into Nammāḻvār's Tamil Veda and its Commentaries," *Sriramanujavani* [Madras]. Vol. 6: 34–61.

_____. 1985. "Divine Word, Human Word in Nammāḻvār," *In Spirit and In Truth.* Madras: Aikiya Alayam.

_____. 1988. "I Created Land and Sea: A Tamil Case of God-Consciousness and its Śrīvaiṣṇava Interpretation," *Numen* 35: 138–159.

_____. 1988. "In Joyful Recognition: A Hindu Formulation of the Relationship between God and the Community, and its Significance for Christian Theology," *Journal of Ecumenical Studies* 25/3: 358–369.

_____. 1991. "Nammāḻvār's Glorious Tiruvallavāḻ: an exploration in the methods and goals of Śrīvaiṣṇava commentary," *Journal of the American Oriental Society* 111: 260–76.

_____. 1992. "Extending the Canon: Some Implications of a Hindu Argument about Scripture," *Harvard Theological Review* 85:2: 197–215.

_____. 1993a. "In Search of Nammāḻvār," *Journal of Vaisnava Studies* 1.2: 8–26.

_____. 1993b. "Living for God: Nammāḻvār and the Srivaisnavas of South India," *Bulletin of the Ramakrishna Mission Institute of Culture* XLIV.10: 315–323.

_____. 1993c. "Śrīvaiṣṇava Studies Today: Writings in a yet Richer Language," *Journal of Vaisnava Studies* II.1:171–181.

_____. 1994. *The Art and Theology of Śrīvaiṣṇava Thinkers,* T.R. Publications for Satya Nilayam Publications, Madras.

_____. Forthcoming a. "*Uruveḷippāṭu*: notes on a Tamil practice of visualization and its larger significance," Proceedings of 8th International Tamil Conference, Tanjore, India.

_____. Forthcoming b. "*Upāsanā* and The Loving Reading of Texts: reflections on the development of Rāmānuja's understanding of *upāsanā* in the commentaries on *Tiruvāymoḻi,*" The Proceedings of the 1992 International Conference on *Upāsanā*, Bombay, India.

_____. Forthcoming c. "When Meditation Overflows: *Tiruvāymoḻi* as the Fruit of Meditation," for the *Proceedings of the 1989 International Conference of Scholars Engaged in the Study of Śrīvaiṣṇavism and South Indian Religions.*

Cutler, Norman. *Songs of Experience: The Poetics of Tamil Devotion.* 1987. Bloomington Indiana: Indiana University Press.

Damodaran, G. 1976. *Ācārya Hṛdayam*: a critical study. Tirupati: Tirumala Tirupati Devasthanams.

_____. 1978. *The Literary Value of Tiruvāymoḻi*. Tirupati: Sri Venkateswara University.

Hardy, Friedhelm. 1979. "The Tamil Veda of a Śūdra Saint," in Gopal Krishna (ed.), *Contributions to South Asian Studies*, New Delhi: Oxford University Press: 42–114.

____. 1983. *Viraha Bhakti: The Early History of Kṛṣṇa Devotion in South India*. Oxford: Oxford University Press.

Jagadeesan, N. 1977. *History of Sri Vaishnavism in the Tamil Country* (*Post-Ramanuja*). Madurai: Koodal Publishers.

Jnanasundaram, T. 1989. *Vaiṇava Uraivaḷam*. Madras: Tayammai Publishers.

Mumme, Patricia. 1988. *Śrīvaiṣṇava Theological Dispute: Maṇavāḷamāmuni and Vedānta Deśika*. Madras, New Era Publications.

Narayanan, Vasudha. 1994. *The Vernacular Veda*, University of South Carolina Press.

______. 1987. *The Way and the Goal*. Cambridge: Center for the Study of World Religions, Washington, D.C.: Institute for Vaishnava Studies.

Rangarajan, R. 1986. *Nampiḷḷai Uraittiraṉ*. Madras: Amutha Nilaiyam Limited.

Reddiar, N. Subbu. 1977. *Religion and Philosophy of Nālāyiram with Special Reference to Nammāḻvār*. Tirupati: Sri Venkateswara University.

Smith, Bardwell L. ed. 1983. *Essays in Gupta Culture*. Delhi: Motilal Banarsidass.

Tathacharya, Agnihotram Ramanuja. 1973. *Varalāṟṟil piṟanta vaiṇavam*. Kumbakonam: Sri Cārṅkapāṇi Cuvāmi Tēvastāṉam.

Thiruvengadathan, A. 1985. "The Tamil Movement in Śrī-vaiṣṇavism." In Mm. Professor Kuppuswami Sastri Birth

Centenary Commemoration Volume. Part 2, pp. 119–130. Ed. by S.S. Janaki. Madras: The Kuppuswami Sastri Research Institute.

Varadarajan, M. 1989. *Pannīrāyirappaṭi: Ōr āyvu.* Tirupati.

Venkatachari, K.K.A. 1978. *The Maṇipravāḷa Literature of the Śrīvaiṣṇava Ācāryas.* Bombay: Ananthacharya Indological Research Institute.

Other Secondary Sources

Astell, Ann. 1990. *The Song of Songs in the Middle Ages.* Cornell University Press.

Barthes, Roland. *Sade, Fourier, Loyola.* 1971. Paris: Éditions du Sueil.

Baxandall, Michael. 1985. *Patterns of Intention: on the historical interpretation of pictures.* New Haven: Yale University Press.

Begheyn, Paul, ed. 1981. *A Bibliography on St. Ignatius's* Spiritual Exercises. Studies in the Spirituality of Jesuits 23.3. St. Louis: Institute for Jesuit Sources.

Carman, John B. 1994. *Majesty and Meekness: A Comparative Study of Contrast and Harmony in the Concept of God.* Grand Rapids: William B. Eerdmans Publishing Company.

_____. 1974. *The Theology of Rāmānuja.* New Haven: Yale University Press.

Caws, Maryanne. 1981. *Metapoetics of the Passage: architextures in surrealism and after.* Hanover: University Press of New England.

Chidester, David. 1992. *Word and Light: Seeing, hearing and religious discourse.* Urbana: University of Illinois Press.

Clooney, Francis X. 1986–92. "Hearing and Seeing in Early Vedānta: An exegetical debate and its implications for the study of religion," *Journal of Oriental Research* (Madras) LVI–LXII: 213–226.

______. 1988. "Why the Veda has No Author: Some Contributions of the Early Mīmāṃsā to Religious and Ritual Studies," *Journal of the American Academy of Religion* 55: 659–684

______. 1993d. *Theology after Vedānta: an exercise in comparative theology*. In the series Toward a Comparative Philosophy of Religion, State University of New York Press.

D'Costa, Gavin. 1990. *Christian Uniqueness Reconsidered: The Myth of a Pluralistic Theology of Religions*. Maryknoll: Orbis.

de Nicolas, Antonio T. 1986. *Powers of Imagining: Ignatius de Loyola*. Albany: State University of New York.

Frank, Joseph. 1991. *The Idea of Spatial Form: essays on twentieth-century culture*. New Brunswick: Rutgers University Press.

Gilman, James E. 1994. "Reenfranchising the Heart: Narrative Emotions and Contemporary Theology," *Journal of Religion* 74:218–239.

Halbfass, Wilhelm. 1991. *Tradition and Reflection: Explorations in Indian Thought*. Albany, New York: State University of New York Press.

Hick, John, and Knitter, Paul. 1987. *The Myth of Christian Uniqueness: Toward a Pluralistic Theology of Religions*. Maryknoll: Orbis.

Iser, Wolfgang. 1978. *The Act of Reading: A Theory of Aesthetic Response*. Baltimore: Johns Hopkins University Press.

______. 1993. *The Fictive and the Imaginary*. Baltimore: Johns Hopkins University Press.

Lester, Robert. 1976. *Rāmānuja on the Yoga*. Madras: The Adyar Library and Research Centre.

Levering, Miriam. ed. 1989. *Rethinking Scripture: Essays from a Comparative Perspective*. Albany: State University of New York.

Mariaselvam, Abraham. 1988. *The Song of Songs and Tamil Love Poems: Poetry and Symbolism.* Rome: Biblical Institute.

McHale, Brian. 1987. *Postmodernist Fiction.* London: Routledge.

Murphy, Roland. 1990. *The Song of Songs: A Commentary on the Book of Canticles, or the Song of Songs.* Hermeneia Series. Minneapolis: Fortress Press.

Oakes, Edward T. 1994. *Patterns of Redemption: The Theology of Hans Urs von Balthasar.* New York: Continuum.

O'Donnell, John. 1992. *Hans Urs von Balthasar.* Collegeville, MN: The Liturgical Press.

O'Malley, John. 1993. *The First Jesuits.* Cambridge: Harvard University Press.

Peterson, Indira. 1989. *Poems to Śiva.* Princeton: Princeton University Press.

Richman, Paula, ed. 1991. *Many Rāmāyaṇas: The Diversity of a Narrative Tradition in South Asia.* Berkeley: University of California Press.

Smith, Brian K. 1994. *Classifying the Universe.* New York: Oxford University Press.

Timm, Jeffrey. Ed. 1992. *Texts in Context: Traditional Hermeneutics in South Asia.* Albany: State University of New York.

Wolfson, Eliott R. *Through a Speculum that Shines: Vision and Imagination in Medieval Jewish Mysticism.* Princeton: Princeton University Press, 1994.

Yearley, Lee H. 1990. *Mencius and Aquinas: Theories of Virtue and Conceptions of Courage.* Albany: State University of New York.

Index of Full Verses Cited from *Tiruvāymoḻi*

Index of Names and Subjects

✓ J
✓ Nancy
Tim
Brian
✓ Tibor
✓ Kathy
Kathern

- Peter won't see more of Ellie or work w her
  He will support my time w Ellie.
- Michaela will make her choice as to what she
  can handle

- I will be the main person w Ellie, but I will
  make sure she knows she won't be living @ home.